The Profound Reality of Interdependence

The Profound Reality of Interdependence

An Overview of the Wisdom Chapter of the Way of the Bodhisattva

KÜNZANG SÖNAM

Introduced and Translated by
DOUGLAS S. DUCKWORTH

OXFORD
UNIVERSITY PRESS

OXFORD
UNIVERSITY PRESS

Oxford University Press is a department of the University of Oxford. It furthers the University's objective of excellence in research, scholarship, and education by publishing worldwide. Oxford is a registered trade mark of Oxford University Press in the UK and certain other countries.

Published in the United States of America by Oxford University Press
198 Madison Avenue, New York, NY 10016, United States of America.

CIP data is on file at the Library of Congress
ISBN 978-0-19-091191-1

1 3 5 7 9 8 6 4 2

Printed by Sheridan Books, Inc., United States of America

For the future of an illusion—may the precious spirit of awakening rise

Contents

Acknowledgments

AS THE WORDS of this translated text show, everything in the world is indeed dependent on conditions. I thus would like to first thank all my teachers and acknowledge some of the people who contributed to this project: Adam Pearcy, Anyen Rinpoché, Geshe Yeshe Thabkhe, David Carpenter, Jeffrey Hopkins, John Dunne, Geshe Yarpel, Sonam Thakchoe, Jay Garfield, Jonathan Gold, Charles Goodman, Jessica Sitek, Barom Chon, Karin Meyers, Matthieu Ricard, Tokpa Tulku, Andrew Nicholson, and Khenpo Tsöndrü Zangpo. Paul Hackett's Buddhist Canon's Research Database was also indispensable for tracking down Künzang Sönam's many citations. A sabbatical leave and summer research award from Temple University supported the research for this project. The Rangjung Yeshe Institute in Nepal and Dharma Drum Mountain in Taiwan provided supportive environments to engage this work. A section of this translation appeared in an appendix of my book, *Tibetan Buddhist Philosophy of Mind and Nature,* which was also published this year by Oxford University Press. I want to thank the press and editors for helping to bring these books into existence. Last but not least, thanks to my wife, Jasmine, for her love and support. Thanks to all, and homage to the bodhisattvas!

Translator's Introduction

The Way of the Bodhisattva

The *Way of the Bodhisattva* (*Bodhicaryāvatāra*), composed by Śāntideva in eighth-century India, is a Buddhist treatise in verse that beautifully and succinctly lays out the theory and practice of the Mahāyāna path of a bodhisattva. Over one thousand years after Śāntideva's composition, Künzang Sönam (1823–1905), a student of the famed Paltrül Rinpoché (1808–1887), in eastern Tibet, composed the most extensive commentary on the *Way of the Bodhisattva* ever written. Paltrül Rinpoché is said to have requested him to write a commentary on the *Way of the Bodhisattva* in accordance with the interpretation of the "new schools" (*gsar phyogs*).[1] He did so in nearly one thousand pages.

There are several commentaries on the *Way of the Bodhisattva* from India, but only one has survived in Sanskrit, a lucid commentary from the eleventh century by Prajñākaramati. There are many Tibetan commentaries on the *Way of the Bodhisattva* as well, including important commentaries composed between the twelfth and sixteenth centuries by Sönam Tsemo (1142–1182), Gyelsé Tokmé (1295–1369), Sazang Mati Paṇchen (1294–1376), Butön Rinchendrup (1290–1364), Tsongkhapa (1357–1419), Gyeltsapjé (1364–1432), and Pawo Tsuklak Trengwa (1504–1566).

The nineteenth century witnessed a revival of the study and practice of the *Way of the Bodhisattva*, spearheaded by Paltrül Rinpoché.[2] Paltrül Rinpoché is said to have explained the *Way of the Bodhisattva* in accordance with the distinctive traditions of commentary in Tibet: the Sakya (*sa skya*) tradition in accord with Sönam Tsemo's commentary, the Kagyü (*bka' brgyud*) tradition in accord with Pawo Tsuklak Trengwa's commentary, the Geluk (*dge lugs*) in accord with Gyeltsapjé's commentary, and the Nyingma (*rnying ma*) in accord with Prajñākaramati's and Gyelsé Tokmé's commentaries. In this way, he fostered a teaching style that discouraged sectarian disputes and harmonized Buddhist traditions without compromising their distinctive interpretative styles of commentary.[3]

Paltrül Rinpoché was part of what the late Gene Smith called "the Gemang (*dge mang*) movement,"[4] which was characterized by a rise in Nyingma monastic scholarship fused with an ethos of the Great Perfection (*rdzogs chen*). Evidence for this movement can be seen to stem from the activity of Gyelsé Shenpen Tayé (1800–1855?), who established the first Nyingma monastic college of Śrī Siṃha at Dzokchen monastery. Paltrül Rinpoché and his disciples took up this vision for Buddhist scholarship and practice at the Gemang retreat affiliated with Dzokchen monastery in Dzachuka (*rdza chu kha*), near the source of the Mekong River.

Paltrül Rinpoché embodies this spirit of fusion of study and practice, as seen in his life and works. In particular, we see this exemplified in a popular text he composed on the stages of the path as a preliminary to the Great Perfection, which has been rendered in English as the *Words of My Perfect Teacher.*[5] Shabkar Tsokdruk Rangdröl (1781–1851), a kindred spirit with Paltrül Rinpoché, also flourished in this region of eastern Tibet, and his works similarly combined mind-training (*blo sbyong*) and the stages of the path (*lam rim*) with the Great Perfection in an ecumenical way. In contrast to a divisive approach that is sometimes found to fly under the banner of a "nonsectarian movement" (*ris med*)—where "nonsectarian" excludes the Geluk tradition—"the Gemang movement" brings together the best aspects of both the Nyingma and Geluk traditions, which harkens back to Gampopa's twelfth-century synthesis of the lineages of Mahāmudrā and Kadampa.

Paltrül Rinpoché taught the *Way of the Bodhisattva* in Sakya, Geluk, Nyingma, and Kagyü monasteries. The tradition of its annual teaching that he instituted has continued at many monasteries in Dzachuka, such as Gegong (*dge gong*) and Sershül (*ser shul*).[6] His commentarial style was tied to a practical orientation, and he outlined the ten chapters of the text into four sections around a prayer for the cultivation of *bodhicitta*, "the spirit of awakening":

May the precious spirit of awakening
Arise where it has not arisen,
Where it has arisen, may it not dissipate,
But further and further increase.

The first three chapters are explained to bring about the spirit of awakening where it has not arisen; the second set of three chapters make it not dissipate where it has arisen; and the next three chapters bring it to further and further increase. The culmination of the ultimate spirit of awakening, the purview of wisdom (*shes rab*), is the ninth chapter, after which the text closes with a dedication for others in the tenth and final chapter.[7]

Künzang Sönam composed two works on the famous ninth chapter of the text, one that consists of a commentary on the verses of the text and an "overview" (*spyi don*), which is translated in this volume. At the end of his text, he mentions a tradition that says some excellent things come from the *Way of the Bodhisattva* when it is understood in accord with the way it is explained in Gyeltsapjé's commentary, which he emulates in his own commentary. Other commentaries composed by Paltrül Rinpoché's students include an influential one by Khenpo Künpel (1870/2–1943), which has been translated into English as *The Nectar of Manjushri's Speech*.[8] Khenpo Künpel was also a student of Mipam Rinpoché (1846–1912), who was himself a student of Paltrül Rinpoché and received teachings from him on the *Way of the Bodhisattva* as well. In contrast to Künzang Sönam's commentary, which relies on Gyelstapjé, Khenpo Künpel's commentary on the ninth chapter closely follows Mipam's commentary on that chapter, the *Ketaka Jewel*. Mipam's text famously sparked controversy and conversation from within Geluk scholarly circles. Mipam's commentary on this chapter, along with one of the criticisms it invoked and his response to that critic, have recently been translated into English in *The Wisdom Chapter*.[9]

Khenpo Künpel was reported to teach the *Way of the Bodhisattva* to Khunu Lama (1895–1977),[10] who taught it to the Fourteenth Dalai Lama. The Dalai Lama has said, "If I have any understanding of compassion and the bodhisattva path, it is entirely on the basis of this text that I possess it."[11] The Dalai Lama often teaches this text, and in 1993, he presented an oral commentary on it in France that was published in a volume entitled *Practicing Wisdom*.[12] In it, the Dalai Lama draws primarily from the commentaries of Khenpo Künpel and Künzang Sönam, and he points out areas of compatibility and contrast between them. When the Dalai Lama taught the first eight chapters and tenth chapter of the *Way of the Bodhisattva* in France in 1991, he requested that the two commentaries on the ninth chapter be translated into English before he completed the teaching on this chapter two years later; this sparked a volume of these two translations in *Wisdom: Two Buddhist Commentaries*.[13] Therein, we find Künzang Sönam's "word-commentary" (*gzhung 'grel*) on the stanzas of the ninth chapter, and here in this volume a translation of his other commentary on the ninth chapter in the form of an "overview" (*spyi don*).

As mentioned, Künzang Sönam's word-commentary on the *Way of the Bodhisattva* closely follows the commentary by Tsongkhapa's student Gyeltsapjé. Künzang Sönam's overview of the chapter is also framed by Tsongkhapa's interpretation of Madhyamaka, and it, too, integrates many passages from Śāntideva's other extant text, the *Anthology of Training* (*Śikṣāsamuccaya*), in addition to citing passages from over one hundred different sūtras and treatises. Künzang Sönam's overview, in particular, integrates Candrakīrti with Śāntideva as representing a single voice of Prāsaṅgika-Madhyamaka, framed in terms of the unique features of Tsongkhapa's Prāsaṅgika view.

Tsongkhapa's unique presentation of Prāsaṅgika comes up across Künzang Sönam's overview, and stems from Tsongkhapa's influential commentary on Candrakīrti's *Introduction to the Middle Way* (*Madhyamakāvatāra*), in which he identifies eight unique features of Prāsaṅgika: the unique ways of (1) denying the reality of a basic consciousness (*kun gzhi rnam shes*) that is distinct from the six sensory consciousnesses and (2) denying self-awareness; (3) not asserting that autonomous arguments (*rang rgyud kyi sbyor ba, svatantraprayoga*) generate the view of reality in the continuum of an opponent, (4) the necessity of maintaining the reality of external objects in the same sense that the one maintains the reality of cognitions, (5) asserting that both Disciples (*nyan thos*) and Self-Realized Ones realize the selflessness of phenomena, (6) asserting that apprehending the self of phenomena is an afflictive obscuration, (7) asserting that disintegration is an entity, and (8) the consequent unique presentation of the three times.[14] These features are all woven into Künzang Sönam's interpretation of the ninth chapter of Śāntideva's *Way of the Bodhisattva*. They are undergirded by his claim that nothing exists on its own, even conventionally, which is used to support the Madhyamaka view of the unity of the two truths of appearance and emptiness. Before we further explore the contents of his text, I will first introduce the author.

Life of Künzang Sönam

Künzang Sönam, who is also known as Minyak Künsö or Tupten Chökyi Drakpa, was born in Minyak (*mi nyag*) in Dokham.[15] He studied old and new schools of Buddhism in Tibet ecumenically, at places like Sershül, Sera, and Drepung (*se 'bras*).[16] He was said to take up sūtra in accord with the new schools and tantra in accord with Nyingma.[17] Along with his associations with Geluk monasteries, in his biographies he has been identified as a Sakya[18] and a Nyingma,[19] and he also reportedly self-identified as a monk from a Kagyü monastery.[20] Indeed, he was a real nonsectarian!

Not a lot is known about Künzang Sönam's life, likely because he was not recognized as an incarnate lama (*sprul sku*), with a monastery or administrative duties. Künzang Sönam was certainly a great scholar, and he studied with some of the extraordinary teachers of his day, such as Jamyang Khyentsé Wangpo (1820–1892) and Paltrül Rinpoché, in particular.[21] With Paltrül Rinpoché he studied Indian and Tibetan treatises in general; the *Guhyagarbhatantra;* and profound practices, including the experiential instructions of the Great Perfection from the great Heart Essence (*rdzogs chen snying thig chen mo'i myong khrid*).[22] He also studied essential points of practical instructions and the *Way of the Bodhisattva* with Paltrül Rinpoché, who heaped praise on Künzang Sönam as being even more learned than himself regarding the text.[23] Künzang Sönam is reported to have received teachings on this text from Paltrül Rinpoché nearly eighty times.[24]

There is a story of Künzang Sönam arriving with his entourage to visit a wealthy nomad tent, where Paltrül Rinpoché had been staying incognito as a shabbily dressed nomad. When Künzang Sönam saw his teacher there among the crowd that had gathered to receive him, Künzang Sönam dismounted his horse and prostrated himself before his teacher. The crowd then knew that the nomad was the famed teacher Paltrül Rinpoché. Paltrül Rinpoché scolded Künzang Sönam for exposing his cover, and thereafter, Künzang Sönam was said to vow to never again ride a horse but to walk on foot and live a hermit's life.[25]

Another story conveys Paltrül Rinpoché saying to some visitors who came to see him, "There is no one to meet here. The little discipline I had has been taken by Minyak Künsö [Künzang Sönam]. The little intellect I had has been taken by Mipam. The little realization I had has been taken by Nyoshül Lungtok (1829–1901)."[26] Among Paltrül Rinpoché's four main students, Künzang Sönam was said to exceed Paltrül Rinpoché in conduct.[27]

Künzang Sönam met Mipam Rinpoché during the seven years he spent studying with Jamyang Khyentsé Wangpo. During this time, Mipam requested teachings on the *Ornament of Manifest Realization* (*Abhisamayālaṃkāra*) from Künzang Sönam, after which Mipam composed a commentary on it.[28]

It is said that when Künzang Sönam was in central Tibet, he had a vision of a dharma protector, who said to him, "If you stay here, you will become the throne holder of Ganden (*dga' ldan khri*), but there is more benefit if you return to your homeland," which he did.[29] At one point, he was preparing to become a wandering mendicant, but Paltrül Rinpoché told him and Nyoshül Lungtok that there was no need to go wandering. He said that, instead, they would benefit the teachings and beings if they both stayed in a hermitage in their own homelands. He then gave Künzang Sönam a brick of tea and a copy of the *Way of the Bodhisattva*.

Künzang Sönam then returned to Minyak and stayed in solitary places such as Bazhap Drakkar (*sba zhabs brag dkar*) and the hermitage of Belo (*be lo ri khrod*), giving teachings. He would think of the kindness of his teacher whenever he saw the tea Paltrül Rinpoché had given him, folding his hands together. He would brew a bit of it on the occasion of the New Year and invite his disciplines to drink, saying with faith and reverence, "This is nectar with the blessings of the spirit of awakening given by Paltrül Rinpoche!"[30]

Besides his two main teachers, Paltrül Rinpoché and Jamyang Khyentsé Wangpo, Künzang Sönam studied with Orgyen Tenzin Norbu (c. 1841–1900);[31] Dzokchen Pema Damchö Özer (a.k.a. Khenpo Pema Vajra, c. 1807–1884); Gyelsé Zhenpen Tayé; Kongtrül Lodrö Tayé (1813–1899); and the Fourth Dzokchen Rinpoché, Mingyur Namkhé Dorjé (1793–1870).[32] He was given his monastic name, Tupten Chökyi Drakpa, by Lingtrül Rinchen Tupten Gyeltsen,[33] the seventh abbot of Śrī Siṃha monastic college at Dzokchen monastery.

Künzang Sönam's collected works were published in three volumes by the Degé printing house after he died, an effort facilitated by his students Loter Wangpo (1847–1914) and Apel.[34] Loter Wangpo was an important Sakya scholar and the main student of Künzang Sönam;[35] Apel, his other principal student, was invited to teach at the Nyingma monastic college of Śrī Siṃha by the Fifth Dzokchen Rinpoché.[36] Another volume of Künzang Sönam's works, which includes commentaries on the Wisdom Chapter of the *Way of the Bodhisattva* that were not included in his three-volume collected works, was published in a separate volume.

Künzang Sönam's writings include a commentary on the Vinaya; a lucid commentary on the *Thirty-Seven Practices of the Bodhisattva,* translated into English as *Uniting Wisdom and Compassion*;[37] practices of mind-training; and practices of life release (*tshe thar*) and severance (*gcod*), among others. By far his most extensive work is his elaborate treatment of the *Way of the Bodhisattva.* His three-part commentary (a massive commentary on the first eight chapters, and two commentaries on the ninth chapter) provides us with the longest commentary on this text ever written in any language.[38] Künzang Sönam's ecumenical spirit, and the tradition of scholarship and practice that he received from his teachers, lives on to the present day in the legacy of his students and the influence of his writings.

Wisdom: The Ninth Chapter

The ninth chapter of the *Way of the Bodhisattva,* the Wisdom Chapter, is notoriously difficult, given that it is often cryptic and truncated, and it presumes knowledge of many Buddhist and non-Buddhist systems. It also propounds the view of emptiness and describes emptiness and interdependence as the metaphysical basis of ethics. The ninth chapter is also where we see pronounced differences in the interpretation of the text, as different commentaries on the other chapters for the most part accord with one another. Künzang Sönam's interpretation of the ninth chapter bears the mark of Tsongkhapa's Prāsaṅgika-Madhyamaka, and he consistently emphasizes the unity of emptiness and interdependence, and the integration of an understanding of emptiness and ethics.

For the most part, Künzang Sönam's overview follows the order of the verses in the chapter, but he highlights particular verses, and skips others, as he puts the chapter into his own structure. The beauty of an "overview" (*spyi don*) style of commentary is that the author is not bound to follow a text word for word, but can elucidate the text's meaning more freely, in a way that is most appropriate to convey a clear message.

The first verse of chapter nine begins, "All these aspects were taught by the Sage for the purpose of wisdom."[39] Künzang Sönam shows that all the aspects of method taught in the previous eight chapters, which bring happiness, are taught for the purpose of wisdom, which brings liberation. The second stanza goes straight into the two truths, where Śāntideva states that the conventional is within the domain of mind and that the ultimate is beyond that domain. On this topic Künzang Sönam gives an extensive, nine-part discussion of the two truths. Therein, he states that the basis of division of the two truths is objects of knowledge (*shes bya*), after showing that the two truths are defined in various ways by different Buddhist philosophical systems. He says that what distinguishes Buddhist philosophy is that it is "free from extremes" and that, though many different philosophies claim to be free from extremes, only the Prāsaṅgika-Madhyamaka lives up to that claim.

In his presentation of Madhyamaka, Künzang Sönam says that the relationship between the two truths is such that they are "essentially the same yet conceptually distinct" (*ngo bo gcig la ldog pa tha dad*). In other words, the conventional and ultimate truths are essentially the same, for one cannot exist without the other, yet they are distinct from the standpoint of their conceived aspects. While "conventional truth" has several meanings, he says that in the context of the *Way of the Bodhisattva* the "conventional" means what is obscuring or concealing, and he describes it as "everything that is understood to be truly existent by a conventional mind, like pots and so forth."[40] Notably, he says that a conventional *truth*, in contrast to what is merely conventional, is necessarily realized *after* the ultimate truth. This is because to understand anything to be *merely* conventional, and hence to understand it as it *truly* is, one must first understand that it is unreal, lacking true existence.[41]

Following the tradition of Tsongkhapa, he highlights an important distinction between conventional *truth* and conventional *existence*,[42] showing that everything that *exists* (including emptiness) does so only conventionally, whereas a *truth* that is conventional is just one of two truths (the other being the ultimate truth of emptiness). Likewise, there is a distinction to be made between that which is the *ultimate truth*, which is the lack of true existence, and that which is *ultimately existent*, which is a false conception that does not exist at all.

While making these distinctions, he points to another central topic in Tsongkhapa's presentation of Madhyamaka: identifying the object of negation. In doing so, he draws another important distinction between *misconceptions* (e.g., apprehending a truly existent self) and the *objects* of those misconceptions (e.g., a truly existent self). Similar to the distinction between (an existent) "belief in God" and a (nonexistent) "God," the latter (e.g., truly existent self) does not exist, whereas only the former (e.g., apprehension of a truly existent self) does.[43]

The third stanza of the ninth chapter continues by outlining the world in terms of the perspectives of ordinary beings on the one hand, and of yogis on the other. Künzang Sönam here describes the primary meaning of "ordinary beings" as those who have not been influenced by philosophical systems, in contrast to yogis, who have either directly realized emptiness or who understand it through study and contemplation. He explains that there are ascending levels of yogis, culminating with Prāsaṅgika-Mādhyamikas, those who are free from the two extremes of existence and nonexistence.

Künzang Sönam's overview does a lot to clarify the distinction between Svātantrika and Prāsaṅgika, the two interpretations of Madhyamaka first distinguished as distinct schools in Tibet. He says that Svātantrikas maintain a basis of conventional truth that can be found upon analysis, whereas Prāsaṅgikas deny this and also deny that anything exists on its own (*rang mtshan gyis grub pa*), even conventionally. In describing a Svātantrika, "a proponent of autonomous probative arguments," he states that "autonomous" (*rang rgyud*), "independent" (*rang dbang*), and "objective" (*rang ngos nas grub pa*) have the same meaning.[44] In contrast, he characterizes a Prāsaṅgika as a Mādhyamika who does not accept that anything exists on its own, even conventionally, and as "one who accepts that the inferential understanding to be established in the continuum of an opponent arises only by means of a *reductio*."[45]

A central element in this interpretation is the denial, even conventionally, of anything that exists on its own, a technical phrase that some translators have rendered as "established in virtue of its own characteristics," but I have translated here as "exists on its own" for clarity. One should keep in mind that the key term in this technical phrase, *svalakṣaṇa* (*rang mtshan*), takes on different shades of meaning in different contexts of Buddhist philosophy: in Abhidharma, it refers to a thing's specific characteristic in contrast to its shared properties; in the epistemological tradition of Dharmakīrti, it refers to an ineffable and efficacious particular in contrast to a concept or universal; and in the context of this interpretation of Madhyamaka, it demarcates the subtle object of negation that is only realized in Prāsaṅgika.[46] It is the meaning in this last context that is important for understanding Künzang Sönam's reading of Śāntideva's text as Prāsaṅgika-Madhyamaka.

In contrast to Prāsaṅgika-Madhyamaka, Künzang Sönam says that the system of Svātantrika-Madhyamaka maintains a distinction between correct and incorrect conventional truths. Prāsaṅgikas, however, do not accept this division because in this system, "Whatever is conventional necessarily does not exist the way it appears."[47] The reason Svātantrikas assert a distinction between correct and incorrect conventional truths, he says, is because they accept conventional truth to exist on its own; Prāsaṅgikas do not accept this, and so they need not make a distinction between correct or incorrect conventional truths. In this context, he adds that "correct" (*yang dag pa*) effectively means "on its own" (*rang gi mtshan nyid kyis grub pa*).[48]

Künzang Sönam claims that accepting the difference between the respective existence and nonexistence of a real body and an illusory one does not conflict with Prāsaṅgikas not accepting correct or incorrect conventional truths.[49] For a Prāsaṅgika, the difference between a conventional illusion (e.g., a rope-snake) and a conventional reality (e.g., a rope) can be and is drawn, but it is not a difference that is drawn *objectively* (*yul de'i rang ngos nas*).[50] The essential point of the Prāsaṅgika view is that distinctions within the conventional—between truth and falsity, existence and nonexistence, real and unreal—are not objective; that is, they are not determined from the objects themselves.

Conventional distinctions between what is real and unreal are for Prāsaṅgikas made *in terms of mundane conventions*. These distinctions are not made based on any real differences in objects themselves; rather, what constitutes what is real and unreal is determined *intersubjectively*. Significantly, what is intersubjective necessarily incorporates a subjective dimension.

One might think that if a Prāsaṅgika does not accept objective distinctions, then this position would not be different from the subjective idealism of the Mind-Only school. Rather than claim that the mind is independently real in contrast to unreal external objects, as a subjective idealist does, Śāntideva explicitly affirms the interdependency of minds and objects.[51] Following this, Künzang Sönam describes how minds and external objects are equally existent in mundane convention (and in Abhidharma) and equally nonexistent when their nature is sought in analysis (and in a sublime being's meditative equipoise). He argues that Prāsaṅgikas accept external objects conventionally because the coextensive presence or absence of objects and cognitions undermines the claim that even conventionally, there are no external objects. He reiterates this point by saying that not only does no *conventional* analysis negate external objects, but that conventional analysis undermines the absence of externality.[52]

Elaborating on the difference between Madhyamaka and Mind-Only, Künzang Sönam says that "the distinction of whether or not external objects are accepted conventionally also comes down to whether or not one accepts something to exist on its own (*rang mtshan gyis grub pa*)."[53] Once again, this is the main issue for his Prāsaṅgika interpretation. He argues that proponents of Mind-Only are not satisfied with assenting to the reality of the external world as it is accepted by ordinary people; they think that if there were external objects, they would have to be the types of things that would be findable upon analysis and that would exist separately from cognition.[54] Yet since there are no such things, they deny them. Prāsaṅgikas, in contrast, assert the existence of external objects without appealing to these criteria, that is, without requiring any objective basis of designation for these claims. Thus, Prāsaṅgikas simply assent to external objects in accord with the ways of the world, and this is, once again, because of the fact that nothing is accepted to exist on its own, neither an external nor an internal world, even conventionally.[55]

Künzang Sönam clarifies the Prāsaṅgika's acceptance of the empirical reality of external objects by arguing that it is not at all like the claims of those who posit the reality of external objects based on analysis, such as the Vaibhāṣikas and the Sautrāntikas. This is because Prāsaṅgikas reject the kind of realism that is implicated in accepting an analytically determined external world. Rather, Prāsaṅgikas simply accept external objects (conventionally) in accord with the ways of the world, without (ontological) analysis.[56] There is a subtle distinction to be made here that can easily be overlooked. That is, Prāsaṅgikas are not external realists, despite claiming the reality of an external world, because they acknowledge that the external world does not stand on its own, even conventionally; like minds and objects, an external world rises and falls together with an internal world.

As Śāntideva states in chapter five of the *Way of the Bodhisattva*, the instruments of torture in hell and hell itself are products of an evil mind.[57] Thus, neither hell realms nor human worlds are external, but that does not necessarily mean that they are "all in your head," either. It is important to see that a Prāsaṅgika's affirmation of an external world is not an assertion from her own perspective that there is an external world in reality; it is only an assent to intersubjective agreement determined by mundane convention. Ultimately, there is no external world (or an internal world) for Prāsaṅgikas, so though Prāsaṅgikas may not be idealists, they are certainly not external realists either. In any case, the reason Künzang Sönam understands Śāntideva's Prāsaṅgika to deny objective foundations such as self-awareness (*rang rig*),[58] the dependent nature (*gzhan dbang*), and the basic consciousness (*kun gzhi*) comes down again to the same issue: there is nothing that exists on its own even conventionally.[59]

Tibetan interpreters of Śāntideva like Künzang Sönam clearly see the *Way of the Bodhisattva* as a Prāsaṅgika text. The key to the placement in this category is that, for Künzang Sönam, Śāntideva supports the idea that nothing exists on its own even conventionally. Śāntideva therefore has no need to ground conventions in any deeper foundation. Without the need for conventional foundations, such as a dependent nature or a basic consciousness, he needs no ultimate foundations either, as if a *real* ultimate were needed to ground *unreal* conventions. As Śāntideva says, an illusory buddha works just as well as a truly existent one.[60] When there are nothing but groundless conventions—all the way up and all the way down—the ultimate and the conventional are no longer separate; the two truths are none other than two aspects of the same thing. For this reason, the two truths are not only noncontradictory; they are mutually entailing. This is a key to Künzang Sönam's interpretation of Śāntideva's *Way of the Bodhisattva* as representing Prāsaṅgika-Madhyamaka.

After presenting a section in which he outlines the position of the proponents of Mind-Only, their critique, and a response to this critique,

Künzang Sönam then expands on self-awareness and its refutation. Here he elaborates further distinctions of a Prāsaṅgika-Madhyamaka interpretation of Śāntideva's text. He argues that self-awareness is a reification and that it does not provide an adequate account of knowledge or memory. Following Śāntideva's verses in the *Way of the Bodhisattva,* he also says that it is a contradiction for the mind to act on itself; as a knife cannot cut itself, a mind cannot know itself, either.[61] He says that self-awareness is simply a subjective representation of mind that proponents of Mind-Only want to maintain as something that acts as both a subject and a nondual awareness, which is a contradiction. Further, he says that there is no source of knowledge (*tshad ma, pramāṇa*) that can lay claim to a nondual mind, such as a pure dependent nature or self-awareness, so it is nothing but a theoretical posit, and one that should be relinquished, even conventionally, because if something like it were to exist, it would exist on its own, and Prāsaṅgikas concede nothing to exist this way, even conventionally.

Künzang Sönam does not only say that theoretical accounts of self-awareness are misconceived; he also argues against an alternative account of awareness, other object-awareness (*gzhan rig*). He says that a model of knowledge that takes the mind to stand apart from, yet know, what is other is also not a coherent account of the process of knowledge; nor is it a model that adequately accounts for the relationship between mind and world. In fact, he argues that all analytically determined accounts of knowledge, including self-awareness and other object-awareness, are misconceived. This is because any time a rich analysis of the conventional world is engaged, one is necessarily committed to the ultimate status of what is found. Moreover, it is because anything that is found in its basis of designation, even in the case of a conventional analysis, is by implication an ultimate entity, which Prāsaṅgikas unequivocally deny.

In his depiction of Prāsaṅgika, there is no way to find any basis of designation, behind or beyond designation, other than emptiness. So what we are left with to account for the conventional world is simply the consensus of mundane conventions—"I see blue," "I remember her," etc.—period. Other than mundane convention, there is no deeper structure or rich account that gets us any closer to the way things are; and furthermore, when we seek anything more than this and find something other than emptiness, we are deceived.

Despite being established by consensus, the world as it is understood by ordinary beings is always wrong in a fundamental way, as Śāntideva says:

Even the objects of perception, such as visible forms,
Are established by consensus, not by sources of knowledge.
That consensus is wrong,
Like the popular view that impure things are pure.[62]

Following Tsongkhapa, Künzang Sönam explicitly says that for Prāsaṅgikas, being a distorted cognition (*'khrul shes*) does not contradict being a source of knowledge (*tshad ma*).[63] In this way, sources of knowledge for conventional truths can be held to be right or wrong pragmatically (or intersubjectively) and at the same time be mistaken in terms of the ontological status of these truths when they appear as if they are truly existent. For this reason, an ordinary being's understanding of the conventional world is superseded by a perspective of higher knowledge, for which the way things appear does not conflict with the way things are—namely, when things are seen as illusion-like and empty of true existence. Künzang Sönam's description of epistemology (*tshad ma*) in his overview closely follows that laid out by Tsongkhapa's student, Khedrupjé (1385–1438), in his *Great Exposition*, which has been translated into English by José Cabezón in *A Dose of Emptiness*.[64]

That conventional truth is intersubjective, that it "accords with the world," should not be confused with a view of relativism: the fact that things are empty and that the process of causality (karma) is incontrovertible are nonnegotiable in this interpretation of Prāsaṅgika. Indeed, Künzang Sönam argues that causality proceeds while things are merely nominally existent or while they are empty. Yet in his interpretation of Prāsaṅgika, a tension remains between what is represented as a correct truth *for the world*, as an intersubjective truth, and what is held to be the correct truth for anyone, as an objective truth—namely, emptiness (as a nonnegotiable ultimate truth) and the undeviating causal process (as a nonnegotiable conventional truth).[65] For the Geluk tradition in general, epistemic warrants come into play to keep the radical dialectic of Prāsaṅgika within the boundaries of Buddhist doctrine and in service of defending Buddhist claims of emptiness and the causal process.

Despite an ordinary being's conventional sources of knowledge always being wrong about the way things are, they are seen to deliver objects that to some degree correspond to objects in the world; thus, they are necessary, at least as long as the conditions for their existence (i.e., ignorance) are present. In other words, partially warranted and partially distorted conventional sources of knowledge continue to function until the ultimate is realized, just as an illusion continues as long as the conditions for its appearance remain, as Śāntideva said:

> *For as long as the conditions are assembled,*
> *For that long illusions, too, will persist.*[66]

Thus, as long as the conventions of the world continue to function and are not undermined by another conventional source of knowledge, they work (for the time being).

Künzang Sönam further defends an interpretation of the *Way of the Bodhisattva* that is in tune with Tsongkhapa's interpretation of Prāsaṅgika-Madhyamaka when he argues that everyone, including Disciples and Self-Realized Ones, must completely realize emptiness in order to achieve nirvana. He argues that there is really only one kind of emptiness, the lack of any findable reality, which has many different substrates, such as persons or phenomena. His interpretation of Prāsaṅgika thus claims that to apprehend true existence is an afflictive obscuration, not a cognitive obscuration, because there is no hard distinction between the self of persons and phenomena (other than simply being a different substrate).[67] Therefore, he says that it is necessary to realize emptiness fully, the lack of intrinsic existence in phenomena, in order to achieve just liberation. In doing so, the way he distinguishes between Buddhist vehicles (i.e., Disciple, Self-Realized Ones, Bodhisattva) is explicitly based on a distinction with regard to *method,* not a distinction in terms of *view,*[68] because he holds that all Buddhist paths to liberation necessarily entail the realization of emptiness as it is expressed in Prāsaṅgika-Madhyamaka.

After an extended discussion in which he establishes the validity of the Mahāyāna against dissenters and outlines the meaning of obscurations and the stages upon which they are eliminated, Künzang Sönam continues with a presentation and refutation of non-Buddhist positions that Śāntideva addresses in his text. He first treats the Sāṃkhya and then the Nyāya-Vaiśeṣika, before returning to a further defense of the unique features of Prāsaṅgika-Madhyamaka. As he mentions in the context of his presentation of the philosophical system of Mind-Only, it is important to identify a position in order to understand how and why it is refuted. Without understanding the position of another, one will not understand one's own system, nor will one understand the *Way of the Bodhisattva* when it references those views.

Later in his overview he comes back to refute the theistic views of those who claim a singular, permanent, and independent creator God, like Īśvara. He also critiques the position of the Jains (a.k.a. Nigranthas) in the context of refuting a view of causality that accepts arising from both self and other. Künzang Sönam's explanation of non-Buddhist philosophical systems relies closely on Jamyang Shepa's *Great Exposition of Philosophical Systems,* which has been translated into English by Jeffrey Hopkins in *Maps of the Profound.*[69]

In between Künzang Sönam's refutations of different non-Buddhist views, he returns to a defense of Tsongkhapa's unique features of Prāsaṅgika. In presenting a Prāsaṅgika account of causality without substances, he describes the "entity of disintegration" (*zhig pa'i dngos po*) and the unique presentation of the three times that follows from this distinctive interpretation of causality.

After defending these last two features that Tsongkhapa had claimed were distinctive to Prāsaṅgika-Madhyamaka, Künzang Sönam recapitulates the arguments against a self framed in terms of a relationship between the self and the aggregates. He elaborates first on a fivefold reasoning from Nāgārjuna's *Fundamental Verses of the Middle Way* (*Mūlamadhyamakakārikā*) and then on a sevenfold reasoning from Candrakīrti's *Introduction to the Middle Way* to show that a self is unfindable upon analysis when sought for as either identical with or different from the aggregates. He argues that the self is simply a nominal convention, designated in dependence upon the aggregates, just as a chariot is designated in dependence upon its parts. Any other self or chariot beyond mere designation cannot be found, nor is anything found in its basis of designation in Prāsaṅgika-Madhyamaka, even conventionally.

The fact that nothing is found in its basis of designation, even conventionally, is an important feature of Künzang Sönam's nominalist interpretation of Prāsaṅgika-Madhyamaka and a reason he does not accept any rich theory of causality—because such theories imply realism. That is, rich accounts of causality are those that are sought out in terms of a relationship between discrete things that are found upon analysis (e.g., to be the same or different); therefore, they are based on realist presumptions (e.g., identity and difference). In contrast, Künzang Sönam shows the way that causality can function while being merely asserted conventionally, based on named regularities in the world rather than based in any substructure or rich theoretical story beyond conventional designation.

Despite his claims, and his valiant effort to present a nominalist theory of causality, Künzang Sönam may be guilty of going against his own nominalist strand of Prāsaṅgika in his defense of the "entity of disintegration." The impetus for the theory of the entity of disintegration, or so it seems, is to provide an account of causality in the absence of foundations. That is, disintegration is said to function as other entities do in the absence of *real* entities. With no real entities, an entity's disintegration—which is typically held within Buddhist philosophical systems to be a non-entity—is thus attributed with the same status as an efficacious entity (nominal). That is, both an entity and its disintegration are nothing more than nominal designations. Although attributing causal power to disintegration is an attempt to preserve a nominalist theory of causality, this theory invites other problems such as the reification of absence (i.e., treating emptiness as a "thing"), which has been a frequent target for critics of the Geluk tradition. Others have argued that the notion of an entity of disintegration goes against the Prāsaṅgika commitment to accord with mundane convention renowned in the world.[70] In any case, I leave the relative merits and demerits of this system of Prāsaṅgika for readers to evaluate for themselves, and I will continue to outline this interpretation to set the stage for the translation of his overview of the Wisdom Chapter below.

In the next section, Künzang Sönam presents the fourfold "application of mindfulness"—of body, feeling, mind, and phenomena—before turning to the practices of calm abiding (*zhi gnas*) and special insight (*lhag mthong*). For calm abiding, he reiterates the nine stages of mental abiding that lead to a genuine calm abiding, drawing from the *Stages of Meditation* (*Bhāvanākrama*), *Distinguishing the Middle and the Extremes* (*Madhyāntavibhāga*), and the *Ornament of the Mahāyāna Sūtras* (*Mahāyānasūtrālaṃkāra*). He then describes two kinds of special insight: mundane and transcendent. Only the latter special insight into selflessness leads to liberation. He again mentions that it is necessary to realize selflessness completely for liberation, and that this is to understand that nothing exists on its own, even conventionally. For him, this is the province of Prāsaṅgika-Madhyamaka and the root of all its distinctions from realist views.

Künzang Sönam next connects Śāntideva's verses to a presentation of three arguments that establish the selflessness of phenomena. Drawing heavily from Candrakīrti's *Introduction to the Middle Way*, he first lays out "the argument of the diamond shards," which is a refutation of four positions that, respectively, assert that causality is a process of arising from self, other, both, or without cause. He pins the position of causeless arising on the materialist Cārvāka school, and the position that there is self-arising on the Sāṃkhyas. The claim to arising from both self and other he attributes to the Jains and says that arising from other is a position found in realist Buddhist schools, from the Svātantrika on down.

In his presentation of a second argument for selflessness, that of interdependence, Künzang Sönam explains three meanings of dependent arising as "meeting" (*phrad*) "relying" (*ltos*), and "depending" (*brten*). The first, "meeting," connotes the dependent arising that is part of the general grammar of Buddhism. Dependent arising here is a feature of causal processes, the way there are regularities without substances: "When this is present, that arises; when this ceases, that ceases." Indeed, Śāntideva consistently links his *Way of the Bodhisattva* with this central feature of Buddhist doctrine.

The notion of dependent arising also extends from causal processes, or chains of events, to spatial relationships as well. This is where we find a second meaning of dependent arising, "relying," that Künzang Sönam mentions. Here, dependent arising is interpreted to connote the interdependent relationship between parts and wholes. The meaning of dependent arising here also has a major role to play in Buddhist thought in general, where singular persons or selves, like chariots, are critiqued as lacking singular, autonomous existence. "Teeth, hair, and nails, are not the self . . . "[71] Śāntideva takes up this kind of analysis in the eighth and ninth chapters, when he deconstructs the notion of self and phenomena with analyses of the body, feelings, mind, and phenomena.

The last and subtlest view of dependent arising is found in the third of the three connotations of dependent arising, "depend." That all things exist in dependence upon linguistic and conceptual designation is a feature of a Madhyamaka view. Yet the fact that things do not exist otherwise, *even conventionally*, is a unique feature of Prāsaṅgika-Madhyamaka for Künzang Sönam—where all things without exception are conceptually or linguistically designated.

He calls the argument of interdependence "the king of reasoning" because it is the one through which the extreme of existence can be overcome through appearance (merely conventionally existing) and the extreme of nonexistence can be overcome through emptiness (merely the lack of intrinsic existence of appearances). This is a special argument, he says, because "there are no other arguments that formulate evidence from the side of emptiness that can simultaneously elicit certainty in both appearance and emptiness."[72] The last of the three arguments he presents to establish selflessness is the argument that negates the production of an existent or nonexistent thing.

After presenting these three arguments, Künzang Sönam concludes his overview where Śāntideva concludes his chapter, with the benefits of realizing emptiness. He says that the function of realizing emptiness, the accumulation of gnosis, is the accumulation of merit, which manifests through an enacted understanding of the causal process. Thus, he links the logic of the end of the chapter with the logic with which it began, where "All these aspects are taught by the Sage for the purpose of wisdom." That is, he shows how the two accumulations of merit and gnosis comprise the six transcendent perfections, and how emptiness is integrated with compassion. He thus shows how emptiness serves as both the culmination and the basis for ethics in Mahāyāna Buddhism. What is distinctive about this interpretation, and Madhyamaka, is that it seamlessly integrates the Buddhist view (interdependence/emptiness) with Buddhist conduct (nonviolence and altruism), without promoting one at the expense of the other (either by making ethics merely instrumental to realizing the view of emptiness or by claiming that ethical conduct is a natural or magical product of realizing a view of emptiness that is disconnected from ethics).

Künzang Sönam largely follows the order of the verses in his overview, but he organizes the chapter into his own structural outline, which allows him to jump to important verses that highlight the points he wants to draw out to get his message across. To make it easier for readers to identify the verses around which he frames his overview, in the translation I have used boldface font for quotations that are drawn directly from the *Way of the Bodhisattva*. The page numbers in hard brackets are from the second edition of the text, published in Beijing in 2007. Citations of Tibetan canonical texts in endnotes follow the pagination of the Lhasa editions of the translated Word and translated treatises.

Outline of the Text

The Translation

A LAMP COMPLETELY ILLUMINATING THE PROFOUND REALITY OF INTERDEPENDENCE: AN OVERVIEW OF THE WISDOM CHAPTER OF THE "WAY OF THE BODHISATTVA"
BY KÜNZANG SÖNAM

oṃ svastisiddhi (May all be well!)

I praise the peerless protector, the Lion of the Śākyas!
You understood the middle way of interdependence, profound, peaceful, and free from constructs,
Without obstruction and thereby became realized;
You then taught it to others with non-referential compassion.

I bow down to the lord of speech, Mañjughoṣa!
You are unrivalled in the midst of a great assembly
Of countless bodhisattvas and Victorious Ones,
Speaking profound words of perfect emptiness.

I bow down in respect to the glorious Nāgārjuna and his son,
The supreme Āryadeva!
By proclaiming the three great soundings of the dharma, profound and vast,
You ornament the world as a magnificent chariot.

I respectfully praise the scholar and accomplished one, Buddhapālita, who first explained
The consummate, sublime view as Prāsaṅgika, and
To Candrakīrti as well, who expanded upon
The unexcelled way of this great tradition!

I bow to Śāntideva, who made great waves of accomplishment
Benefiting the teachings and beings through seven miraculous activities;
And to my teacher, the gentle protector and Sun of Speech,
My friend who clarified the good path of the wondrous middle way!

I respectfully pay homage to all the supreme beings, the upholders of the teachings of the Sage in general,
And the tradition of Madhyamaka in particular;
And to my teachers, who bestow the essential nectar
Of the practical instructions, sustaining me with a loving heart!

Among all the teachings displayed by the supreme teacher
In accord with the minds of countless disciples,
The most excellent, exalted speech,
Is the precious canon of the supreme Transcendent Perfection of Wisdom (sher phyin, prajñāpāramitā).

The essence of its subject matter is immensely profound,
Subtle, and difficult to understand—it is the middle path;
This itself is the path of the Victorious Ones of the three times,
And the gateway for those seeking liberation is only this.

Therefore, it is reasonable for discerning fortunate ones
To earnestly pursue this profound topic,
And to cherish the followers, the great chariots,
Since it is difficult to realize the profound viewpoint of the Victorious Ones.

Thus, the sublime Nāgārjuna explained well the meaning of the Mother *as it is,*
And was acclaimed in prophesy;
The consummate essential point of his profound viewpoint
Is proclaimed with the great roar of Prāsaṅgika reasoning.

Since the three masters share a single voice on the view,
Here is a witness to what they brought forth
By the stainless path of reason –
Their scriptural tradition of Madhyamaka in general,

And specifically, what principally presents emptiness: the Introduction to the Middle Way*'s*
Root text and commentary [648] on the Wisdom Chapter.
In accord with this, I will progressively elaborate an overview of the Way of the Bodhisattva*'s Wisdom Chapter,*
Which principally presents the spirit of awakening.

The elegant speech herein is a precious lamp:
This discussion will disclose the reality of profound interdependence
To clear away the darkness of confusion;
It will illuminate again the good path of the middle way.

The Actual Text

This section has two parts: (1) a general explanation of the history and (2) a specific explanation of the meaning of the text.

1. General Explanation of the History

Our teacher, who embodies limitless compassion, is extolled as a white lotus among the thousand buddhas of this good eon. He is the unexcelled king of dharma in the three realms, who enacts the benefit of disciples through manifesting great non-referential compassion without conceptualization. Since sentient beings have various constituents, abilities, and inclinations, he knows that they cannot be trained simply by demonstrating a single activity of body, speech, or mind. So through an inconceivable and infinite display of the three mysteries, he directly and indirectly guides disciples to progressively achieve the state of their own attainment. As for the main method of training disciples, it is stated in the *Jewel Lamp* (*Ratnolkādhāraṇīsūtra*):

> *As many ways as beings act,*
> *That many gateways of dharma there are to be entered.*
> *These gates of liberation are all pure;*
> *In accord with their inclinations, he trains beings in the world.*[1]

Displaying forms such as that of a supreme Emanation Body (*mchog kyi sprul sku*), he discloses infinite gateways of dharma that become antidotes to any kinds of activities of attachment and so on that take place in disciples' continua. The supreme among all these is the precious canon of the Transcendent Perfection of Wisdom. The essence of its subject matter is the nectar of emptiness—profound, peaceful, and free from constructs. After actualizing this on his own, the powerful Sage exclaimed the lion's roar of selflessness, overwhelming all the wild beasts that proclaim wrong views, such as non-Buddhist teachers, and so forth. He is unrivaled in speech and his words are unexcelled; thus, there is never an opportunity for any fault to be found in accord with the [649] dharma by any other disputer of his teaching. The *Condensed Perfection of Wisdom* (*Prajñāpāramitā-Sañcayagāthā*) states:

> *As a lion residing on a mountain range with no fear*
> *Frightens many small animals with a loud roar,*
> *The Lion of Men residing in perfect wisdom*
> *Frightens many extremists with the sound of his proclamation in this world.*[2]

This demonstrates that understanding the meaning of profound interdependence is the unexcelled understanding, and teaching it is the unexcelled teaching.

For this reason, Nāgārjuna, the second Buddha, saw this discourse—on the meaning of interdependence as the nature of emptiness—as unexcelled, the sublime doctrine superior to that which was spoken by other teachers. Thus, he praised it with amazement. He said in the *Praise to the Inconceivable* (*Acintyastava*):

> *I pay homage to the one who taught that*
> *Interdependent entities are essenceless,*
> *Whose unequaled gnosis is inconceivable,*
> *You are incomparable!*[3]

And,

> *You destroy the fear of apprehending real entites and*
> *Frighten the non-Buddhist beasts*
> *With the lion's roar of selflessness –*
> *This is your wonderful speech.*
> *You beat the great drum of the most profound*
> *Doctrine of emptiness;*
> *You blow the conch of the doctrine*

With the great sound of essencelessness.
Your speech is the substance of truth –
The nectar of the Buddha's teaching.[4]

The *Fundamental Verses of the Middle Way* states:

The one who taught dependent arising . . .[5]

Also, *Reason in Sixty Verses* (*Yuktiṣaṣṭikā*) states:

I pay homage to the powerful sage,
The one who taught
Dependent arising,
The means by which arising and ceasing are relinquished.[6]

Dispelling Disputes (*Vigrahavyāvartanī*) says:

I pay homage to the Buddha,
The one who taught that emptiness and dependent arising
Have the same meaning in the path of the middle way –
Your supreme speech is unparalleled.[7]

Thus, the teacher is praised in the "Collection of Praises" and the "Collection of Reasonings" with such terms as "inconceivable," "unexcelled," "the best of speakers," "unparalleled," and "incomparable."

The main Transcendent Perfection of Wisdom Sūtras that teach the subject matter of this profound interdependence are the triad of the extensive, middling, and condensed *Mother*. There are several treaties that are commentaries on their viewpoint. The main ones are (1) the *Ornament of Manifest Realization* treatise by the Victorious One's regent, "the undefeated" [Maitreya], and (2) the sixfold Madhyamaka "Collection of Reasonings" by Nāgārjuna. The former explains the hidden meaning—the stages of manifest realization (*sbas don mngon rtogs kyi rim pa*)—by correlating the stages of the practice of the path and bringing together the body of the *Mother Sūtras* in eight subjects (*dngos brgyad*) and seventy topics. The latter explains the explicit teaching—the structure of emptiness (*dngos bstan stong nyid kyi rim pa*)—correlating the stages of practicing the profound path.

[650] These are two different ways of explaining the viewpoint of the *Mother Sūtras*; they are not the two chariot traditions of Madhyamaka. This

is because the two chariot traditions of Madhyamaka and Mind-Only are determined to be the authentic chariot traditions that are commentaries on the viewpoint of the Word. This is so because the tradition of Madhyamaka set forth by Nāgārjuna, relying on the quintessential instructions of Mañjughoṣa, follows the *Akṣayamati Sūtra*. The tradition of Mind-Only set forth by the Noble Asaṅga, relying on the quintessential instructions of Lord Maitreya, follows the *Sūtra Explaining the Intent* (*Saṃdhinirmocanasūtra*). Thus, relying on the Mahāyāna Sūtras, these two masters ascertained the ways of distinguishing what is provisional and definitive in meaning (*drang nges*) with numerous scriptures and reasonings; thereby, they initiated the distinct traditions of Madhyamaka and Mind-Only. Secondarily, they explained the respective positions of Madhyamaka and Mind-Only regarding the viewpoint of the Hīnayāna Sūtras as well. They also clearly and completely laid out the stages of practice of the profound and vast Mahāyāna path. Before then, the Disciple schools were thriving, while the view and training of Mahāyāna was faltering. Afterward, the Mahāyāna teachings swelled like water in a summer lake. Thus, the immense kindness they showed the teaching is pervasive, like that of our teacher himself.

As for Nāgārjuna, he was born four hundred years after our teacher died and lived for 600 years, according to the *Root Tantra of Mañjuśrī* (*Mañjuśrīmūlatantra*).[8] His opening of the tradition of Madhyamaka free from the two extremes of existence and nonexistence was also spoken of in the *Descent to Laṅka Sūtra* (*Laṅkāvatārasūtra*).[9] Further, he was prophesied in other sūtras like the *Twelve Thousand Great Clouds* (*Mahāmegha*) and the *Great Drum* (*Mahābheri*).[10] There are different accounts in these sūtras, such as his achieving the first bodhisattva ground in this life and then going on to the Land of Bliss (Sukhāvatī), his being a seventh-ground bodhisattva, and his becoming a buddha named Jñānakāraprabhā in the future. This does not conflict with Candrakīrti's *Commentary on the "Illuminating Lamp"* (*Pradīpoddyotanaṭikā*) that says that he achieved the state of Vajradhāra in this life because there is a difference between how things are and how things appear for trainees, and also, because it is stated these ways based on the respective perspectives of the ordinary and extraordinary vehicles.[11]

Since this master also disclosed the Mahāyāna in general, he composed many treatises on sūtra and tantra. In particular, he brought out the *Mother Sūtras* from the *nāga* realm and composed treatises that were commentaries on their viewpoint. Among those, the "Sixfold Collection of Reasonings" establishes the consummate profound meaning through reasoning. He also composed the *Anthology of Sūtras* (*Sūtrasamuccaya*), which establishes this with scriptures that are definitive in meaning. It is also widely known that there is a "Fivefold Collection of Reasonings," and when six are included, there are different ways of identifying them. Here, the five are the *Fundamental Verses of the Middle Way, Emptiness in Seventy Verses* (*Śūnyatāsaptati*), *Dispelling Disputes, Reason in Sixty Verses,* and [651] the *Finely Woven* (*Vaidalyasūtra*); in addition to these, it has been said that it makes sense to put the *Precious Garland* (*Ratnāvalī*) as the sixth because of the way it teaches its subject matter.

The *Fundamental Verses of the Middle Way* is like the root of all Madhyamaka texts. It is widely held that there were eight commentaries on it in India. Four made it to Tibet. Among these, the three main ones are the commentaries by Buddhapālita, Bhāviveka, and Candrakīrti. *Emptiness in Seventy Verses* and *Dispelling Disputes* are offshoots of the *Fundamental Verses of the Middle Way;* these two, along with the *Finely Woven*, have autocommentaries.

As for Asaṅga, he was born about 900 years after our teacher died. He distinguished the sūtras that are definitive and provisional in meaning and lived for 150 years, as stated in the great commentary on the viewpoint cited in the *Root Tantra of Mañjuśrī.*[12] Even though he was a third-ground bodhisattva, he taught Mind-Only for a while to train Vasubandhu, as was stated by Dharmamitra in his explanation in *Clarifying Words* (*Prasphuṭapadā*).[13] Thus, he disclosed the tradition of Mind-Only in order to take care of those with the Mind-Only heritage. Nevertheless, his consummate viewpoint lies in Prāsaṅgika, as is very clear in the commentary he composed on the *Sublime Continuum* (*Uttaratantra*).

The main commentator on the viewpoint of Nāgārjuna is Āryadeva, his foremost son. He composed many treatises on sūtra and tantra, such as the *Four Hundred Verses* (*Catuḥśataka*). Followers regard him to be genuinely like Nāgārjuna, so early scholars called these two "Mādhyamikas of the source texts" (*gzhung phyi mo'i dbu ma pa*), while referring to the others as "partisan Mādhyamikas" (*phyogs 'dzin pa'i dbu ma pa*). The reason for this is that they did not take a side upon dividing Madhyamaka into Prāsaṅgika and Svātantrika. Since they are engaged with both Prāsaṅgika and Svātantrika in general, they are "Mādhyamikas of the source." Partisan Mādhyamikas clearly distinguish the positions of Prāsaṅgika or Svātantrika based on scripture and reasoning. Like Buddhapālita and Bhāviveka, they take exclusively one side of Madhyamaka.

The commentary on the *Fundamental Verses of the Middle Way* by Buddhapālita first initiated the tradition of explaining the consummate viewpoint of the text as Prāsaṅgika. Nevertheless, he did not clearly express the way that *reductios* are suitable and autonomous arguments are not. After him, master Bhāviveka wrote his commentary on the *Fundamental Verses of the Middle Way*, the *Lamp of Wisdom* (*Prajñāpradīpa*), where he voiced several problems in each of the *reductios* found in Buddhapālita's commentary, in contexts such as those where production from the four extremes is refuted. Bhāviveka expressed many reasons why it is necessary to formulate autonomous arguments, and was the first to initiate the tradition of Svātantrika commentary.

After him, the glorious Candrakīrti composed his commentary on the *Fundamental Verses of the Middle Way, Clear Words* (*Prasannapadā*). [652] There he showed the reasons why the problems of Buddhapālita's commentary voiced by Bhāviveka do not hold. He argued extensively to establish that Mādhyamikas do not accept autonomous arguments and refute their acceptance. Thus, he disclosed the great chariot tradition of commentary on the unique viewpoint of Nāgārjuna as Prāsaṅgika. Moreover, he wrote commentaries on *Reason in Sixty Verses, Emptiness in Seventy Verses,* and the *Four Hundred Verses.* Furthermore, he composed independent compositions such as the root text and autocommentary of the *Introduction to the Middle Way.* This master's oeuvre is widely acclaimed.

Bhāviveka's follower, master Jñānagarbha, wrote *Distinguishing the Two Truths* (*Satyadvaya*) along with its autocommentary. These two, father and son, are referred to as "Sautrāntika-Svātantrika-Mādhyamikas" because they maintain that external objects exist conventionally and do not accept self-awareness. Master Śāntarakṣita composed the *Ornament of the Middle Way* (*Madhyamakālaṃkāra*) together with an autocommentary. Since he maintains that external objects do not exist conventionally and affirms self-awareness, he initiated the tradition renowned as "Yogācāra-Svātantrika-Madhyamaka." His student, Kamalaśīla, composed an excellent Svātantrika text, the *Light of the Middle Way* (*Madhyamakāloka*), and also such texts as the *Stages of Meditation* (*Bhāvanākrama*). These two, father and son, are said to have been tremendously kind to us in the Land of Snows. Before Śāntarakṣita, there was Vimuktisena. Although he was a Yogācāra-Svātantrika-Mādhyamika, he is not attributed to be the initiator of this tradition. There are others like this. Haribhadra, a student of Śāntarakṣita, is also classified as a Yogācāra-Svātantrika-Mādhyamika.

Another twofold division is drawn among these scholars based on the way they assert the conventional—whether they accept external objects or not. Those who accept them include Bhāviveka, Candrakīrti, and their followers; those who do not accept them include Śāntarakṣita, father and son [Kamalaśīla], and their followers. There is another twofold distinction based on the way the view is generated in the continuum: that between Svātantrika and Prāsaṅgika. Among the Svātantrikas, there are Sautrāntika-Svātantrika-Mādhyamikas and Yogācāra-Svātantrika-Mādhyamikas. The former includes such figures as Bhāviveka and Jñānagarbha. The latter includes such figures as Śāntarakṣita, father and son [Kamalaśīla], the pair of Vimuktisena and Haribhadra, and so on. As for the Prāsaṅgikas, there are such figures as Āryaśūra, Nāgabodhi, Buddhapālita, Candrakīrti, and the Victor's child, Śāntideva.

All the Svātantrika and Prāsaṅgika masters are exclusively followers of the sublime Nāgārjuna and comment on his viewpoint. There are many different reasons why they are included as initiators of a particular tradition or not, whether they are partisans or not, and even whether or not [653] they maintain a view. This has only been a partial introduction that should be known in detail elsewhere.

2. Specific Explanation of the Meaning of the Text

The text to be explained here specifically is the Wisdom Chapter of the *Way of the Bodhisattva*. Its author is the Victor's child, Śāntideva, the great upholder of the chariot tradition of the sublime way. He lived shortly after the glorious Candrakīrti, and the qualities of his magnificent body bore the mark of being sustained by Mañjuśrī for several generations. In this life, he renounced his kingdom and took ordination from the preceptor of Nālandā, Jayadeva. He understood the entirety of the corpus of scriptures by hearing them from Mañjughoṣa and the preceptor himself. His life story is famously recounted in seven miraculous episodes:

I prostrate to the sevenfold wonder,
Who relinquished his kingdom, became accomplished,
Mastered two bodies of knowledge, became a monk,
Saw the truth, and performed miracles!

In some of the commentaries on the *Way of the Bodhisattva* there is an abbreviated account of the progression of activities in his life story. Also, in Butön's history there is a concise biography that accords with this sequence:

> *He discovered his exalted deity and*
> *Made wonderful arrangements at Nālandā.*
> *He dispelled objections, and tamed a heretic, beggars,*
> *A king, and a non-Buddhist.*[14]

In addition to these, there are several other different accounts. Master Jetāri said: "The emanation of Mañjughoṣa, Śāntideva." The master himself displayed the way of conduct of a *bhusuku*[15] merely in the perspective of others, claiming to be an ordinary being. Yet master Prajñākaramati referred to him as a sublime being (*'phags pa, ārya*), saying, "the sublime Śāntideva."[16] Also, Vibhūticandra said:

> *There have been many beings with the*
> *Greatness of the Victorious One's teaching,*
> *But none are found with experience and realization*
> *Like that of Śāntideva.*[17]

The Indian masters who wrote commentaries on the *Way of the Bodhisattva* thus praised his extraordinary activities. The master himself wrote three texts that explain the viewpoint of Nāgārjuna as Prāsaṅgika: the *Anthology of Training,* the *Anthology of Sūtras,* and the *Way of the Bodhisattva.* These were also renowned in the Noble Land of India to be exceptionally authentic texts.

Butön said, "There were one hundred commentaries on the *Way of the Bodhisattva* renowned in India, but eight were translated into Tibetan."[18] [654] Counting the commentaries on the Wisdom Chapter and summaries, I think now there are eleven. As for commentaries and summaries of the text composed by Tibetan teachers, there are about sixty titled texts, and many untitled that are available.

To summarize, it says in the Kadam History that Geshé Sharwa took the Indian text from Ratreng (*ra sgreng*) and that it was translated by Patsap Nyimadrak (*pa tshab nyi ma grags*), yet this does not appear in the present Tengyur (canon of translated treatises). The triad of the great Victor's child [Śāntideva] himself, Buddhapālita, and Candrakīrti are said to have the same viewpoint in their commentaries on the complete and consummate viewpoint of sublime beings. Tsongkhapa's explanation of the *Introduction to the Middle Way*[19] states:

The philosophical system of Nāgārjuna and Āryadeva
Was explained by the three great chariots.
The complete and unique essential meaning
Is seen well by the stainless eye of intelligence.[20]

And,

The ones who explained perfectly –
The tradition of the glorious Buddhapālita, Candrakīrti, and Śāntideva –
The claims of these three lords of accomplishment,
Integrated as one . . .[21]

Specifically, he said that Candrakīrti and Śāntideva have the same viewpoint and the same voice.[22] Below there will be several reasons for this. In Gyeltsapjé's commentary on the *Way of the Bodhisattva*, the *Gateway to the Bodhisattvas*, it says:

The meaning of Madhyamaka, dependent arising free from extremes,
Claimed by the protector, Nāgārjuna,
Is clearly explained, as it is, in one viewpoint by
Buddhapālita, Candrakīrti, and Śāntideva.[23]

Also, in the great commentary of the Wisdom Chapter by Prajñākaramati, this is established through his many citations of passages from the *Introduction to the Middle Way* in the contexts of the two truths, and so on. Therefore, in accord with the general scriptures of Madhyamaka—the teachings of Nāgārjuna, father and son [Āryadeva]—and in particular, the root text and autocommentary of the *Introduction to the Middle Way* and the *Anthology of Training*, the explanation of the Wisdom Chapter here has three parts: (1) a brief description, (2) an extensive explanation, and (3) a summary.

1. Brief Description

[IX.1] ***All these aspects were taught by the Sage for the purpose of wisdom.***
So those wishing to alleviate suffering should cultivate wisdom.

This encompasses the essential points of the scriptures in general. There are many kinds of condensed presentations of the stages of the path. To touch upon this in this context here, our text here shows the stages of the profound and vast path following the master Nāgārjuna. Among his compositions, there are three texts that show the complete body of the path of both the vast and profound. [655] The first among these, the *Precious Garland*, shows how all the teachings are subsumed within the twofold methods for accomplishing higher states (*mngon mtho*) and definite goodness (*nges legs*). The *Precious Garland* says:

> *First is the doctrine for higher states*
> *Then comes definite goodness.*
> *Since by achieving higher states*
> *One gradually comes to definite goodness.*[24]

This means that one should train in the sequence of the path: first in the path to attain higher states and then in the path to definite goodness. This is because one must accomplish definite goodness gradually based on achieving a continuity of higher states; one cannot accomplish this based in lower realms. Also:

> *If you wish for the happiness of higher states, and*
> *Liberation that is definite goodness,*
> *Their accomplishment, in brief,*
> *Is comprised within faith and wisdom.*[25]

It concisely shows that faith and wisdom are the main causes that comprise the methods for accomplishing both the happiness of gods and humans, which are the higher states, and liberation, which is definite goodness. Also:

> *The faithful rely on the doctrine;*
> *The wise on correct understanding.*
> *Wisdom is the main one of these two;*
> *It is preceded by faith.*[26]

This shows that those who are faithful rely on practices like the ten virtues to achieve higher states. Those with the wisdom that realizes selflessness understand the correct meaning of reality; based on this, they achieve liberation, which is definite goodness. Thus, wisdom is the main one of these two, and its preliminary is such things as faith that believes in karmic causality. The importance of both faith and wisdom will be explained a bit below.

Specifically, the path to attain the supreme, definite goodness is shown to consist of three main causes:

Its root is the spirit of awakening,
Stable like the powerful king of mountains,
Compassion that is all-encompassing,
And gnosis that does not rely on duality.[27]

Also,

In the Mahāyāna
All activities are preceded by compassion.[28]

And,

The qualities of a bodhisattva
Are taught, in brief, to be:
Generosity, discipline, patience, diligence,
Meditative concentration, wisdom, compassion, and so on . . .
Attaining the protector of the world.[29]

Based on great compassion, the spirit of awakening, and the practices of the six transcendent perfections, it shows the path to becoming a buddha through the stages of the ten grounds. *Praise to the Basic Field of Reality* (*Dharmadhātustotra*) teaches going for refuge, the spirit of awakening, the ten transcendent perfections, and the ten grounds as the concise body of the path. The meaning of this is elaborated in the *Anthology of Sūtras.* It establishes this through citing many passages from sūtras that show the difficulty of finding the freedoms and advantages, faith, the spirit of awakening, and compassion. Also, [656] it shows how it is difficult to relinquish things like karmic obscurations that wound or disparage the spirit of awakening, demonic actions, and actions of rejecting the dharma. The *Four Hundred Verses* also taught the body of the path as the complete twofold vast and profound. Aśvaghoṣa taught the cultivation of the conventional spirit of awakening, which includes:

Nonviolence and truth,
Taking what is given, pure conduct, and
Relinquishing all clinging –

These are activities for the realms of happiness.
Having seen fully the suffering of cyclic existence,
To relinquish it—cultivating the true path
And rejecting the two kinds of misdeed –
These are activities for peace.
All these are to be adopted;
They are aspects of the path of definite emergence.
By realizing the emptiness of all phenomena,
A continuous stream of compassion springs forth for beings;
Limitless actions of skillful means
Is the activity of supreme, definite emergence.[30]

He shows the progressive path of three types of beings through three kinds of activities: the activities for the realms of happiness, the activities for peace, and the activities for supreme, definite emergence. In the context of great beings, the two lines beginning with "All these . . ." indicate the path in common with that of lesser and middling beings. The last stanza shows the actual path of supreme beings—the spirit of awakening (which is emptiness with the essential nature of compassion) together with its activity (which is the practice of the six transcendent perfections).

The *Introduction to the Middle Way* teaches the spirit of awakening for ordinary beings in a threefold practice. Among these, it shows that its root is great compassion,[31] which is important for the accomplishment of buddhahood in the beginning, middle, and end. Then, it teaches the stages of the path in the ten grounds of the sublime bodhisattvas all the way to the stage of a buddha, while specifically expanding upon the way to ascertain the unique view.

The great Victor's child [Śāntideva] composed the *Anthology of Training*, which is a meaning-commentary on Nāgārjuna's *Anthology of Sūtras*, so it elucidates and expands upon its meaning. It first describes contemplations on the importance of the freedoms and advantages, and their being difficult to find, which generates the wish to extract the essence of this life. Then, based on a general faith, and mainly, a stable faith that sees the qualities of the Mahāyāna, it teaches the cultivation of the aspirational spirit of awakening (*smon sems*) and upholding the commitment to engage it. Next, it teaches all the trainings of the spirit of awakening, consisting of the six transcendent perfections, and shows the way it is practiced through a twelvefold: giving, protecting, purifying, and developing one's threefold body, enjoyments, and roots of vitue. It states this extensively with many citations from sūtras.

Among these, faith is important here as the root of all positive qualities. The *Anthology of Training* states:

> *Those who want to be free from suffering, and*
> *Those who want to reach the extent of happiness*
> *Should make the roots of faith sturdy.*[32]

The reason for this is stated in the *Jewel Lamp*:

> *With faith in the Victorious Ones and the Victorious Ones' teaching,*
> *One will have faith in the activities of the buddha's heirs.*
> *Thereby, one will have faith in unexcelled awakening*
> *And give birth to the spirit of awakening of great beings.*
> *Faith is a prerequisite; like a mother, it is generative.*
> *It guards all good qualities [657] and develops them.*
> *It dispels doubts and frees from the rivers;*
> *Faith is what illustrates the city of goodness and happiness.*
> *Faith lacks impurity; give rise to faith in mind.*
> *It delivers from pride and is the root of reverence.*
> *Faith is wealth, a treasure, and supreme legs;*
> *Like hands, it gathers the roots of virtue.*[33]

It states many good qualities of faith. Furthermore, through citing the *Tenfold Qualities* (*Daśadharmaka*), the *Vast Display* (*Lalitavistara*), and the *Lion's Inquiry* (*Siṃhaparipṛcchā*), it establishes the importance of faith in general, and specifically, of faith in the Mahāyāna. Then it says, "Make the mind stable in awakening as well,"[34] explaining progressively from the cultivation of the spirit of awakening.

Our text here teaches the stages of the path of both the vast and profound in general, and specifically, elaborates upon the cultivation of the spirit of awakening and the ways to practice its activities. It teaches the Mahāyāna heritage (*rigs*) endowed with the freedoms and advantages, which is the distinctive bodily support, and the intention to relinquish evil and practice virtue, and so on, which is the mental support. Through this, its main explicit teaching is the mental training of great beings, and as an ancilliary, the mental trainings common to lesser and middling beings. Preceded by this, it first teaches a contemplation of the benefits of the spirit of awakening, generating enthusiasm. Then, it teaches the confession of evil, those conditions opposed to the development of a mind with beneficial qualities. Through to the third chapter, it also teaches the ways of upholding the precious spirit of awakening in one's continuum through the force of great love and compassion, the distinctive mental support based on gathering the accumulations of conducive conditions.

Next, for how to train in the activities, the fourth chapter teaches how to rely on viligance as a method to prevent the decline of the training in the practices of the six transcendent perfections. The tenth chapter mainly teaches the distinctive practice of dedication, the generosity of giving to others one's body, enjoyments, and roots of virtue. The fifth chapter teaches how to train in discipline through mindfulness and meta-awareness. Then, the next three chapters respectively teach how to train in patience, diligence, and meditative concentration. After that, the ninth chapter teaches the practice of the transcendent perfection of wisdom, showing with the interlude that from the initial generation of the spirit of awakening up to meditative concentration, that:

> [IX.1a] ***All these aspects were taught by the Sage for the purpose of wisdom.***

The meaning of *these aspects* was described by the precious lord of doctrine, Gyelsé Tokmé, in his commentary as follows: "The aspects from the generation of the spirit of awakening to meditative concentration—this whole collection of causes for wisdom—are said by the Sage to be for the purpose of generating wisdom."[35]

To say a bit here about the importance of wisdom, in general, wisdom is that which completely discerns phenomena; it is the root of all good qualities in this life and in the future. Nāgārjuna said:

> *All qualities, both seen and unseen,*
> *Are rooted in wisdom.*
> *Since it accomplishes the benefit of both,*
> *Completely uphold wisdom.*
> *Awareness is the great source of*
> *Things desired and liberation.*
> *Thus, first uphold [658] with respect*
> *The great mother, wisdom.*[36]

He extensively praised wisdom. Also, Āryaśūra said:

> *Wisdom is like a mother loving her child;*
> *It is no suprise that such abundance comes from this.*

The perfect strength of the ten powers of the buddha,
All that is unparalleled and supreme, and
Every other assemblage of qualities without exception
Are dependently arisen from the cause of such wisdom.[37]

He spoke a lot of praise for wisdom. Also, he said:

Attend and serve a teacher worthy to be relied upon, and
Seek out study in order to gain wisdom.[38]

And,

With little study one is blind, not knowing how to meditate.
Lacking this, what is it that is contemplated?
Therefore, from the cause of perseverance in study
Comes an expansive wisdom from meditation with contemplation.[39]

Since all good qualities come from wisdom, if you rely on the wise and study, wisdom from study, contemplation, and meditation will progressively unfold. It is said that this will not happen if you have not studied.

In particular, what is taught here is the wisdom that realizes the subtle selflessness. This is extremely important because without it, there is no path that eliminates the two obscurations otherwise. Thus, the *Sublime Continuum* says:

Other than wisdom, there is nothing other
That is a cause for eliminating these.
Thus, wisdom is supreme; since it is based in study,
Study is supreme.[40]

Also, a sūtra says: "Noble child, wisdom will emerge if you have studied. Afflictions will be completely pacified if you have wisdom. Without afflictions, demons will have no opportunities."[41]

To explain in accordance with our text, whatever enumerations of doctrines there are, like generosity, all that was taught by the Sage was exclusively done so, explicitly or implicity, as a method—a method for disciples to give rise in their continua to the wisdom that realizes reality, to sustain it where it has already arisen, and to further and further develop it. Why is this? It is because it is difficult to realize reality that is the mode of existence of all phenomena, and one will not be freed from cyclic existence without realizing this. Yet if it is realized, this is the special method for liberation from cyclic existence. Seeing this, our compassionate teacher brought disciples to understand reality through many methods and forms of reasoning. Furthermore, the *Inquiry of Rāṣṭrapāla* (*Rāṣṭrapālaparipṛcchā*) says:

> *Beings wander without knowing*
> *The way of emptiness, peace, and the unborn;*
> *The Compassionate One took them in*
> *Through methods and hundredfold reasonings.*[42]

Also, the middle *Stages of Meditation* says: "All the words of the Blessed One are well spoken. Directly or indirectly they elucidate reality; they engage reality."[43] He says that all the scriptures engage [659] reality; they singly come down to reality.

In particular, according to the assertions of the three masters—Buddhapālita, Candrakīrti, and Śāntideva—even those who wish to pursue the mere awakening of a Disciple or Self-Realized One, which is the pacification of the sufferings of existence, must generate in their continua the wisdom that realizes emptiness—so needless to mention it is necessary for omniscience. This is held to be the viewpoint of the Perfection of Wisdom Sūtras and the scriptures of sublime beings; this will be explained a bit below.

Specifically, both *Reason in Sixty Verses* and the *Precious Garland* mainly establish that it is necessary to realize the subtle emptiness in order to be liberated from cyclic existence. *Reason in Sixty Verses* states:

> *One is not freed through existence,*
> *Nor is there freedom from cyclic existence through nonexistence;*
> *By completely knowing entities and non-entities,*
> *Great beings are liberated.*[44]

It shows that there is no opportunity for liberation from cyclic existence when falling to the extremes of existence and nonexistence, and that there is liberation through knowing reality that is free from the two extremes of entities and non-entities. Also, the *Precious Garland* says:

> *The mirage-like world*
> *Is said to exist and not to exist.*
> *Holding onto this is confusion;*
> *When there is confusion, there is no liberation.*

Those who hold onto existence go to the realms of happiness;
Those who hold onto nonexistence go to the lower realms.
Due to correctly knowing the way it is,
Those who do not rely on duality are liberated.[45]

It says that to be liberated from cyclic existence one should avoid both the view of existence, which apprehends phenomena to intrinsically exist, and the view of nonexistence in which even conventionally there is no karmic causality and so on. Also, Prajñākaramati's commentary says that one needs to realize reality to attain even a mere liberation that is free from birth and aging, and so on.

Here it teaches that the aspects of method, like generosity, need to precede the wisdom that realizes emptiness. It shows that in order to eliminate the cognitive obscurations (*shes sgrib*) that obstruct the attainment of omniscience, the wisdom that realizes emptiness needs to be connected to a great cause, which is the aspect of method. It does not say that a mere realization of emptiness needs to be definitely preceded by a great cause, the aspect of method. Therefore, the distinction as to whether or not wisdom that realizes emptiness becomes an antidote for cognitive obscurations, and the differences between the Mahāyāna and Hīnayāna as well, are distinguished in this Prāsaṅgika system based on method, not based on view. This is because it is claimed that there are no distinctions between higher or lower in terms of the view that is the object of meditation for persons in any of the three vehicles.

Thus, in the way that a father is the cause for delineating the heritage of his children, the aspects of method—like great compassion and [660] the spirit of awakening—are the unique causes for delineating the Mahāyāna and Hīnayāna heritages. In the way that a mother is a shared cause for her children, the wisdom that realizes emptiness is a cause shared among the four children. The *Sublime Continuum* says:

Interest in the supreme vehicle is the seed, and
Wisdom is the mother that generates the qualities of a buddha.[46]

It says that the spirit of awakening is like a father's seed, and that the wisdom that realizes emptiness is like a mother. The *Densely Arrayed* (*Gaṇḍavyūha*) says: "The spirit of awakening is like a seed that produces all the qualities of a buddha."[47] Also, the *Ornament of Manifest Realization* says that the transcendent perfection of wisdom is the mother of all four sublime beings.

Therefore, wisdom that realizes the emptiness that eliminates the extreme of existence is also in the Hīnayāna, but they do not have the great compassion that eliminates the extreme of peace. For this reason, the paths of the Disciples and Self-Realized Ones can eliminate the extreme of existence, but cannot eliminate the extreme of peace.

The paths of liberation for both Disciples and Self-Realized Ones have aspects of both wisdom and method. As for wisdom, they must realize the subtle selflessness that is the lack of intrinsic nature in both persons and phenomena like aggregates. As for the aspect of method, for the purpose of only their own peace, they claim that it is necessary to cultivate the practices of discipline, meditative equipoise, the four truths, the twelve links of dependent arising, and the four *brahma* abodes (*brahmavihāra*). They have the immeasurables of love and compassion, but they lack *great* compassion. Alternatively, it is also said that they have great compassion, but lack the great compassion that can induce the superior intention to bear the burden of benefiting others. Yet we follow the first one.

2. *Extensive Explanation*

This section has three parts: (1) explaining the structure of the two truths, (2) showing the necessity of realizing emptiness even for those wishing for only liberation, and (3) an extensive presentation of the arguments that establish emptiness.

1. Explaining the Structure of the Two Truths

This section has three parts: (1) the definitions and divisions of the two truths, (2) individuals who ascertain the two truths, and (3) resolving disputes regarding the way the two truths are presented.

1. The Definitions and Divisions of the Two Truths

[IX.2] ***The conventional and the ultimate . . .***

[661] In the way of presenting the two truths according to the Vaibhāṣika's system, a conventional truth is a phenomenon, apprehended by cognition, that can be eliminated through separating it into parts, either by demolishing it physically or analyzing it mentally. For instance, a pot is demolished by a hammer, and water can be analyzed into its color, scent, taste, and so on, such

that the mind does not engage it. In contrast, an ultimate truth is a phenomenon that cannot be eliminated by a cognition apprehending it, either by physical demolition or mental analysis. For instance, an ultimate truth is like a partless minute particle or a partless moment of cognition. In this way, the *Treasury of Metaphysics* (*Abhidharmakośa*) says:

> *That which is not engaged by cognition when demolished or mentally analyzed*
> *Is conventionally existent, like a pot and water; what is ultimately existent is otherwise.*[48]

The Sautrāntikas following scripture also accept this.

In the system of Sautrāntikas following reasoning, the essence of ultimate truth is that which objectively withstands analysis by reasoning and is not dependent on linguistic or conceptual designation. Here, "ultimate truth" (*don dam bden pa*), "entity" (*dngos po*), "particular" (*rang mtshan*), "efficacious phenomenon" (*don byed nus pa'i chos*), etc., have the same meaning. The essence of conventional truth is a phenomenon that exists merely as a linguistic or conceptual posit. Here, "conventional truth" (*kun rdzob bden pa*), "non-entity" (*dngos med*), "universal" (*spyi don*), "unefficacious phenomenon" (*don byed mi nus pa'i chos*), etc., have the same meaning. As it is said in the *Commentary on Epistemology* (*Pramāṇavārttika*):

> *That which performs an ultimate function here is an ultimate existent.*
> *The others exist as conventional; these are said to be particulars and universals.*[49]

At this point of explaining the two truths in the Madhyamaka system, I will elaborate a bit on the general structure of the two truths in nine subsections: (1) the basis of division of the two truths, (2) the definite number of two truths, (3) the definite sequence of the two truths, (4) the way the two truths are essentially the same, and how they are different, (5) the definitions of the two truths, (6) the divisions of the two truths, (7) an etymology of the two truths, (8) the problems with not knowing the reality of the two truths, and (9) the benefits of knowing the reality of the two truths.

1. Basis of Division of the Two Truths

The basis of the division of the two truths has been posited as mere appearance, truth, the interdependent manifold, the domain without superimposition, and so forth; nevertheless, here the basis necessarily is just objects of knowledge (*shes bya*). It says in the *Meeting of the Father and Son Sūtra* (*Pitāputrasamāgamasūtra*), cited in the *Anthology of Training*:

> Thus, the Tathāgatas realize the two truths, the conventional and the ultimate, the objects of knowledge. The conventional and the ultimate truths are all there is. Moreover, since the Blessed Ones see emptiness, fully know it, and actualize it, they are called "omniscient."[50]

The words of this sūtra, "objects of knowledge," show the basis of division. "All there is" shows the definite number of *two* truths. "The Tathāgatas realize the two truths" shows that omniscience sees and discerns the two truths; this repudiates claims that the ultimate truth cannot be understood by any mind or that it is not an object of knowledge.

2. Definite Number of Two Truths

The two truths are definitely two because there is a twofold division within objects of knowledge. There is no need for more to be enumerated, and no fewer can encompass them. [662] The way this definite number is established by reason is as follows: If the basis of division is objects of knowledge, then anything must be either one of the two truths. It is impossible for there to be something that is a third category—both or neither—that is neither of the two truths. This is because the two truths are mutually exclusive; they are in direct contradiction. This is the case because anything that has been conclusively determined (*yongs gcod*) by cognition to be a conventional truth is necessarily precluded (*rnam bcad*) from being an ultimate truth. And contrarily, anything that has been conclusively determined by cognition to be an ultimate truth is necessarily precluded from being a conventional truth, as was stated in the *Light of the Middle Way*.[51]

The definite number is established in this way by scripture as well, as has been cited in the *Meeting of the Father and Son Sūtra*. Furthermore, this sūtra says:

> *The knower of the world taught just two truths;*
> *Do not listen to another.*
> *There is the conventional and likewise, the ultimate;*
> *There is no other third truth.*[52]

Also, it says in the *Fundamental Verses of the Middle Way*: "The Buddhas taught the dharma . . ."[53] How the four truths are subsumed within the two truths here is that the truth of cessation is the ultimate truth and the other three are conventional truths. The autocommentary on the *Introduction to the Middle Way* shows the definite number and the way of subsuming the four truths in this way.

3. Definite Sequence of the Two Truths

As for the way of ascertaining the two truths here, to ascertain a conventional truth (such as a pillar or a pot) with a source of knowledge, one must have ascertained the ultimate truth with a source of knowledge. This is because it is impossible for someone who has not correctly ascertained the ultimate truth to have correctly ascertained the conventional truth. This is because to cognize something like a pot or pillar as an object that is a conventional truth, it must be established to be unreal, and to establish that depends on the negation of true existence by a source of knowledge.

Just cognizing something like a pillar or pot that is unreal or a conventional truth is not sufficient for having arrived at the view of Madhyamaka, because the minds of unreflective (*rang dga' ba*) people also see and cognize them. That is, while unreal things like pillars and pots are seen by unreflective people, they are not necessarily established to be unreal because it is like when the illusion of a horse or bull is seen in a magic show, the audience has not necessarily established that those appearances are unreal while seeing them. This is stated in Tsongkhapa's explanation of the *Introduction to the Middle Way*. It is said as follows in the *Fundamental Verses of the Middle Way*:

> *Without relying on the conventional*
> *The ultimate cannot be realized.*[54]

And the *Introduction to the Middle Way* says:

> *The conventional truth is the method and*
> *The ultimate truth is what arises from the method.*[55]

These statements do not contradict what was said previously, for it is necessary to realize the ultimate by relying on the unmistaken framework of the customs of conventional truth, as when using a vessel when you want water.

4. Way the Two Truths Are Essentially the Same, and How They Are Different
[663] The *Introduction to the Middle Way* states:

> *[The Buddha] said that all entities found by veridical and deceptive perceptions*
> *Are apprehended as two natures.*[56]

Conventionally, each phenomenon is said to be apprehended with two natures, so all phenomena have natures. If they have these natures, they need to be either the same or different. The necessity for existent things to be either the same or different is established by reason. Therefore, here the two truths are essentially the same yet conceptually distinct (*ngo bo gcig la ldog pa tha dad*). They have a relationship of essential identity for which without one there is not the other. This relationship is held to be like that of a product and an impermanent phenomenon, or like a conch and the white of the conch, as it is stated in the *Commentary on the Spirit of Awakening* (*Bodhicittavivaraṇa*):

> *Apart from the conventional*
> *The ultimate (de nyid) is not observed;*
> *The conventional is said to be emptiness.*
> *Emptiness itself is the conventional because*
> *Without one there is certainly not the other—*
> *Like a product and an impermanent phenomenon.*[57]

Therefore, if phenomena (*chos can*) were essentially distinct from their basic nature (*chos nyid*)—their emptiness of true existence—they would be truly existent. For this reason, (1) lacking true existence and (2) being conventionally existent are essentially the same yet conceptually distinct. Furthermore, that which conventionally exists is essentially the same as that which is empty of true existence, and that which exists while empty of true existence itself is essentially the same as that which conventionally exists. This is because that which is empty of true existence is not essentially other than that which conventionally exists, and that which conventionally exists is not essentially other than that which is empty of true existence. All phenomena, illustrated by form, can be known in this way, as the *Heart Sūtra* states: "Form is empty; emptiness is form. Emptiness is not other than form; form is also not other than emptiness."[58] These four lines show the meaning of the four stated previously, and feeling, etc., can be applied here as well.

Moreover, the *Sūtra Explaining the Intent* says that if the two truths were the same, and not even conceptually distinct, then there would be four problems; and that if they were essentially the same, there would be four problems as well.[59] Its viewpoint is explained this way by proponents of Mind-Only; and here, too, Mādhyamikas accept that the two truths are essentially the same yet conceptually distinct.

This is how four problems result if the two truths were the same, and not divisible even conceptually. To illustrate this with something like a pot, if a pot and the pot's emptiness of true existence were conceptually the same, there would be four problems. It would absurdly follow that (1) the aspect of ultimate truth, the pot's emptiness of true existence, would be an object perceived by ordinary beings; (2) afflictions like attachment would arise when perceiving the emptiness of the true existence of a pot; (3) it would not be necessary for yogis to strive to ascertain the emptiness of the true existence of a pot that is different from a perception of a pot; and (4) the emptiness of the true existence of a pot would also have phenomenal features like shape and color.

[664] If a pot and the pot's emptiness of true existence were essentially different, then there would be four problems. It would absurdly follow that (1) the source of knowledge that apprehends a pot and the pot's emptiness of true existence would not eliminate the superimposition that apprehends the pot as truly existent; (2) the emptiness of the pot's true existence would not be the pot's basic nature; (3) the emptiness of the pot's true existence would not be the basis of negation for the pot's true existence; and (4) the continuum of a sublime buddha would simultaneously have the apprehension of the pot as truly existent and the wisdom that realizes the pot as lacking true existence.

One might wonder, "But the *Sūtra Explaining the Intent* states:

> *The character of the conditioned realm and the ultimate*
> *Is a character free from being the same or different;*
> *Thus, those who conceive them as the same or different*
> *Have entered into an improper view.*[60]

This says that the two truths are neither the same nor different. How is this to be understood?"

This refers to being the same without any conceptual distinction, or being different without also being just essentially the same. The aforementioned problems result if they are understood in these ways, so they are explained to be improper. Therefore, this sūtra, too, teaches the two truths to be essentially the same yet conceptually distinct. There is another way to explain this as well, as in "Neither different nor the same,"[61] that is, neither *truly established* as different nor *truly established* as the same.

5. The Definitions of the Two Truths

The *Introduction to the Middle Way* states:

> *The object of veridical perception is reality (de nyid);*
> *Deceptive perception is conventional truth.*[62]

The definition of the conventional truth is an object of deceptive perception that is found by a source of knowledge investigating the conventional, and the definition of the ultimate truth is an object of veridical perception that is found by a source of knowledge investigating the consummate reality. This is just the general way to understand these definitions; it encompasses all the objects observed by beings who have not reached the end of the continuum (*rgyun mtha'*)—those who have not integrated meditative equipoise and postmeditation. Yet it does not include the way of knowing for a sublime buddha, for whom each gnosis—the gnosis that knows what is and the gnosis that knows whatever there is (*ji lta ji snyed mkhyen pa'i ye shes*)—perceives both truths simultaneously.

Therefore, to present them to encompass the buddhas as well, the definition of the conventional truth is an object found by a source of knowledge investigating the conventional with respect to one's own source of knowledge investigating the conventional, and the definition of the ultimate truth is an object found by a source of knowledge investigating the consummate reality with respect to one's own source of knowledge investigating the consummate reality.

An illustration (*mtshan gzhi*) of a conventional truth is a conventional object of knowledge like a pot, a conventional cognition like a conceptual apprehension of a pot, and a conventional means of expression like the name "pot." The following have the same meaning: "conventional truth" (*kun rdzob bden pa*), "customary truth" (*tha snyad bden pa*), "the conventional" (*kun rdzob pa*), "deceptive phenomena" (*slu ba'i chos*), and "phenomena whose mode of appearance and mode or reality are different" (*snang tshul dang gnas tshul mi mthun pa'i chos*). An illustration of an ultimate truth is, for instance, a pot's emptiness of intrinsic nature. The following have the same meaning: "ultimate truth" (*don dam bden pa*), "consummate reality" (*gnas lugs mthar thug*), [665] "emptiness" (*stong nyid*), "non-deceptive phenomena" (*mi slu ba'i chos*), and "phenomena that appear in accord with the way they are" (*snang tshul dang gnas tshul mthun pa'i chos*).

6. Divisions of the Two Truths

This section has two parts: (1) divisions of conventional truth and (2) divisions of ultimate truth.

1. Divisions of Conventional Truth

Svātantrikas accept that an appearance of cognition existing on its own (*rang gi mtshan nyid kyis grub pa*) exists the way it appears, so a cognition is necessarily a correct conventional truth. Thus, they do not divide subjects into correct and incorrect. Yet they divide objects into correct and incorrect based on whether their appearance to cognition performs a function in accord with the way it appears. *Distinguishing the Two Truths* says:

> *While appearing similarly,*
> *Since one is efficacious and the other is not,*
> *There is a division of the conventional*
> *Into correct and incorrect.*[63]

In the Prāsaṅgika system, conventional truth is divided as follows: The *Introduction to the Middle Way* states:

> *There are two types of deceptive perceptions:*
> *Those with clear faculties and those with impaired faculties.*
> *The cognitions of those with impaired faculties*
> *Are held to be incorrect in relation to those with good faculties.*
> *What is apprehended by the six unimpaired faculties*
> *Is understood by the world;*
> *It is truth for the world only.*
> *The rest is regarded as incorrect by the world only.*[64]

The first stanza presents the division between correct and incorrect in terms of subjects, and the latter stanza presents the division between correct and incorrect in terms of objects. Moreover, the correct and incorrect are distinguished based on the perspective of the world. Since there is no correct conventional truth in the Prāsaṅgika's system, there is no division of the conventional into correct and incorrect.

The reason for this is that it is does not make sense to divide the conventional into that which does and does not exist the way it appears because whatever is conventional necessarily does not exist the way it appears. Therefore, conventional phenomena are unreal appearances whose mode of appearance is different from their mode of reality, even conventionally. Further, since the sensory consciousnesses are necessarily mistaken with regard to their perceived objects, there is no distinction made between correct and incorrect in terms of objects or subjects.

One might wonder, "If the sense faculties are mistaken, even conventionally, then it is not reasonable to posit sources of knowledge that warrant conventional phenomena like forms."

If you understand real things to be warranted, then you would need an unmistaken means of evaluating them, but if you understand unreal things to be warranted, it is completely reasonable to posit a mistaken means of evaluating them. In the Svātantrika tradition and below, it is asserted that a reliable source of knowledge is necessarily not mistaken regarding its warranted object. Nevertheless, here in Prāsaṅgika, for a source of knowledge in the continuum of an ordinary being, and for a conventional source of knowledge in the continuum of a sublime being who is impaired by predispositions for the distortions of dualistic appearance, whatever is an epistemically warranted object is held to be necessarily a distorted cognition. Thus, a distorted cognition and a source of knowledge are held to be non-contradictory.

Svātantrikas accept a correct conventional truth; this is a product of their accepting [666] something that conventionally exists on its own (*rang gi mtshan nyid kyis grub pa*). Prāsaṅgikas, however, maintain that objects are unreal even conventionally and do not accept a correct conventional truth. This also is a product of the essential point here: not accepting anything to exist on its own, even conventionally.

One might wonder what then is the difference between the correct and incorrect in relation to the perspective of the world. Simply in general, a cognition that is not impaired by a temporary distorting cause, together with its object, is said to be correct in relation to the world. A cognition that is impaired by a temporary distorting cause, together with its object, is said to be an incorrect conventional truth in relation to the world.

Moreover, among temporary distorting causes, there are internal causes of distortion—like defects in the physical faculties, eye disorders, jaundice, ingested psychoactive herbs, etc.; external causes of distortion—like mirrors, mirages, sounds in empty caves, etc.; and causes that impair the mental faculty—like bad philosophies, bogus arguments, and dreams. As for the way that these produce mistaken cognitions, eye disorders cause the mistaken sensory cognition of falling hairs, and jaundice causes the mistaken sensory cognition of a white conch to appear as yellow.

The difference between these two in detail is this: An accurate subject is a subjective cognition that, from the perspective of the world, cannot be understood to be a mistaken cognition by a conventional source of knowledge in the continuum of someone who has not realized emptiness. An inaccurate subject is a subjective cognition that, from the perspective of the world, can be understood to be a mistaken cognition by a conventional source of knowledge in the continuum of someone who has not realized emptiness. Illustrations of these are, respectively, a visual cognition apprehending a visible form and a visual cognition apprehending a reflection. A correct object is that which, from the perspective of the world, cannot be understood not to exist the way it appears by a conventional source of knowledge in the continuum of someone who has not realized emptiness. An incorrect object is that which, from the perspective of the world, can be understood not to exist the way it appears by a conventional source of knowledge in the continuum of someone who has not realized emptiness. Illustrations of these are, respectively, a visible form and a reflection.

To summarize the meaning here, what is incorrect from the perspective of the world is all the subjects and objects that can be understood as incorrect by a conventional source of knowledge of a mind not oriented toward reality. What is correct from the perspective of the world is all the subjects and objects that cannot be understood to be incorrect by this kind of source of knowledge. Therefore, "cognition from the perspective of the world" does not refer to just any conventional source of knowledge; rather, it refers to an unreflective (*rang dga' ba*) mundane cognition that is not oriented to reality, and a conventional source of knowledge in relation to that. Thus, being correct from the perspective of the world does not entail being correct and true. Even though it is said to be a correct conventional truth in relation to the perspective of the world, [667] it is in relation to that perspective that it is correct and, in general, conventional. Nevertheless, this does not mean that there is a common basis for what is correct and what is conventional from this mundane perspective.

Here the sense of "correct" in "the Prāsaṅgika system does not accept the *correct*, even conventionally" necessarily refers to something that exists on its own. This is because what is meant by "the Madhyamaka system" in this context is similar to "what is based on an intelligent cognition (*rigs shes*)" or "what is based on the perspective of a sublime being's vision," as is stated in Tsongkhapa's explanation of the *Introduction to the Middle Way*. Based on this, to posit something like a pillar or pot as correct is nothing less than to posit it as existing on its own. It is said that "asserting the difference between correct and incorrect in relation to the perspective of the world" must be interpreted as being merely true based on mundane conventions for what is correct. Thus, when a substance is stolen, it is said to be true that it is stolen, and when the body of the god Īśvara is painted, it is held to be the body of Īśvara; one must posit truth and correctness from an unreflective perspective, a conventional source of knowledge. Otherwise, when a substance is stolen, to say "it was not stolen," or to maintain that a painting of the body of the god Īśvara is the body of Viṣṇu is to be incorrect and wrong according to mundane conventions.

2. Divisions of Ultimate Truth

There is a twofold division of the ultimate in terms of the basis of emptiness or in terms of essence: the emptiness that is the emptiness of a personal self and the emptiness that is the emptiness of a self of phenomena. Within these, there is a fourfold division of emptiness: the emptiness of entities, the emptiness of nonentities, the emptiness of intrinsic nature, and the emptiness of extrinsic nature. There are further divisions, including divisions into sixteen emptinesses, eighteen, twenty, and so on.

As for a division of the ultimate in terms of its mode of expression (*sgra brjod rigs*), *Distinguishing the Two Truths* states:

> *Since the negation of arising and so on*
> *Concords with what is correct*
> *We assert it to be ultimate.*[65]

As stated in this context, two ultimates are accepted here as well: the actual ultimate (*don dam dngos*) and the concordant ultimate (*mthun pa'i don dam*). These are also divided into the subjective ultimate (*yul can don dam*) and the objective ultimate (*yul don dam*). The subjective ultimate, too, is divided into the actual subjective ultimate and the concordant subjective ultimate; the former, and "the non-figurative subjective ultimate" (*yul can gyi rnam grangs ma yin pa'i don dam*) have the same meaning. An illustration is, for instance, a perceptual source of knowledge that directly realizes emptiness. The latter [concordant subjective ultimate] and "the figurative subjective ultimate" (*yul can gyi rnam grangs pa'i don dam*) have the same meaning. An illustration is, for instance, an inferential source of knowledge that realizes emptiness conceptually (*don spyi'i tshul*).

There is also a twofold division of the objective ultimate: (1) the actual objective ultimate and (2) the concordant objective ultimate. The former and the non-figurative objective ultimate [668] have the same meaning. An illustration is a non-implicative negation, such as a sprout's lack of true existence. The latter [concordant objective ultimate] and the figurative objective ultimate have the same meaning. An illustration is an implicative negation, such as the conjoined meaning of a sprout and its lack of true existence. Thus, there are four subdivisions of subjective, objective, actual, and concordant ultimates. The genuine (*mtshan nyid pa*) ultimate truth is the actual objective ultimate; the other three are nominal (*btags pa ba*) ultimate truths. For this reason, this is said to be a division "in terms of its mode of expression."

7. *Etymology of the Two Truths*

This section has two parts: (1) the etymology of "conventional truth" and (2) the etymology of "ultimate truth."

1. Etymology of "Conventional Truth"

An object like a pot is said to be a conventional truth because it is a truth from the perspective a deluded, conventional mind, or from a perspective that apprehends true existence. Alternatively, to describe the words "conventional" and "truth" individually: a subject that apprehends something as truly existent is said to be conventional because it obscures seeing the reality of the thing. Here, the word for conventional is *saṃvṛti,* which has an etymology that conveys that which is completely obscuring or concealing. This describes the word "conventional" with reference to the apprehension of true existence. Furthermore, what is unreal (*brdzun pa*) is said to be conventional; what is customary (*tha snyad*) is described as conventional, too. *Clear Words* describes a threefold explanation of the term.[66] Nevertheless, the latter two are simply explanations of the word "conventional"; they do not identify the conventional as everything that is understood to be truly existent by a conventional mind, like forms and so forth. The first one does, so this is the principal meaning in the context here.

As for the meaning of "truth," conventional phenomena like forms are only said to be true due to being true from a perspective that apprehends true existence. Among cognitions and objects, they are said to be true in dependence on that kind of cognition; they are not objectively true. It is stated as follows in the *Introduction to the Middle Way*:

> *The Sage said that the conventional truth is*
> *That which is artificial, appearing as if true.*
> *Since delusion conceals the actual nature, it is conventional.*[67]

The autocommentary says, "Conventional truth is posited due to the force of afflictive ignorance."[68] This does not say that apprehending true existence is the reason for something to be posited as conventional; rather, it identifies the reason as being the apprehension of true existence that understands forms and so on as true from the perspective of any conventional mind. Nevertheless, everything that is held to be merely true from a perspective that apprehends true existence is not posited as conventional truth, for instance, like the basic nature and the twofold self. "Conventional" (*kun rdzob*) in the term "conventional truth" refers to the ignorance that apprehends true existence. "Customary" (*tha snyad*) in the term "customary truth" refers to all conventional truths, so there is a difference in extension between them.

Likewise, [669] the "conventional" in "conventional truth" (*kun rdzob bden pa*) and the "conventional" in "conventionally exists" (*kun rdzob tu yod*) are the same word with different meanings. The former refers to the innate apprehension of true existence because all conventional phenomena are said to be "conventional truths" due to being true from the perspective of a conventional mind with an innate apprehension of true existence. The latter refers to a source of knowledge that investigates the conventional because what is found by a source of knowledge investigating the conventional is posited to conventionally exist.

2. Etymology of "Ultimate Truth"

Most Svātantrikas give an etymology of the term "ultimate" with reference to both the subject and object, describing it as the object (*don*) of the gnosis of a sublime being's meditative equipoise that sees the paramount (*dam pa*) way things are. Here in the Prāsaṅgika system, however, it is explained without separating the object and the paramount; an etymology of the term is given with reference to an object comprising their common basis, as is stated in *Clear Words:* "It is an object and it is also paramount, so it is the ultimate (*don dam pa*). That itself is a truth (*bden pa*), so it is the ultimate truth (*don dam bden pa*)."[69] Thus, there is a reason why something like the basic nature (*chos nyid*) of a pot is said to be ultimate: it is so called because it is an object, it is paramount, and it is also a truth.

It is an object because it is an object found by an intelligent cognition (*rigs shes*) investigating the consummate. It is paramount because it is the consummate reality. It is a truth because its appearance and reality incontrovertibly accord. Furthermore, the term "truth" in the sense of being empty of *true* existence, even conventionally, and "truth" in the sense of ultimate *truth* have a different meaning. This is because the former truth refers to a phenomenon that exists in reality, which Prāsaṅgikas do not accept even conventionally. The latter truth refers to what is incontrovertible because phenomena that appear in accord with how they are conventionally exist.

8. Problems with Not Knowing the Reality of the Two Truths

If one does not understand the ultimate truth of emptiness, based on a mistaken, superimposing view that conceives phenomena to truly exist, one is not able to attain liberation and become free from existence. If one does not understand the framework of causality, based on a mistaken, denigrating view that conceives these phenomena to not exist even conventionally, one is not able to attain even the liberation from the sufferings of the lower realms in the higher realms. The *Fundamental Verses of the Middle Way* states:

> *Those who do not know*
> *The division of the two truths*
> *Do not know the profound reality*
> *Of the Buddha's teaching.*[70]

Also, the *Introduction to the Middle Way* says:

> *Those who do not know the division of the two truths*
> *Have entered the mistaken path of distorted conception.*[71]

Furthermore, it is also stated in this way in *Reason in Sixty Verses* and in the *Precious Garland,* cited above.

9. Benefits of Knowing the Reality of the Two Truths

[670] By properly ascertaining the two truths, the two accumulations are gathered; and from this, the two embodiments of buddhahood (*sku*) emerge. It is said in *Distinguishing the Two Truths*:

> *Those who understand the division of the two truths*
> *Are not confused about the words of the Sage.*
> *They all gather the accumulations and*
> *Cross over to perfection.*[72]

2. Individuals Who Ascertain the Two Truths

[IX.3] ***Here two types of world are observed . . .***

This section, by way of a brief overview, has two parts: (1) a general brief demonstration of the sequence of four philosophical systems, and (2) a specific brief explanation identifying Madhyamaka.

1. General Brief Demonstration of the Sequence of Four Philosophical Systems

There are two kinds of individuals who ascertain the two truths: ordinary beings and yogis. Among the ordinary beings, there are also two: the primary ones are the realists (*dngos smra ba*), and the ancillary ones are those who have not been influenced by philosophies. The realists are said to be primary because they have directly engaged in the ascertainment of the two truths by reason. Those who are not influenced by philosophies are ancillary because they need to engage reason in this way. There are also two types of yogis: the sublime beings who have directly realized emptiness, and individuals who understand emptiness through study and contemplation.

The philosophical systems of ordinary realists are undermined by the Mādhyamika yogis' reasoning. Among the realists, the higher ones supersede the lower ones; and among the Mādhyamika yogis as well, the higher ones overcome the lower ones through their distinctive intelligence. It is stated this way in master Kalyāṇadeva's commentary:

> Ordinary beings in the world say that a woman is clean after she has bathed and so on. Yogis undermine this by believing (*mos*) that she is unclean. This, too, is undermined by seeing her body as minute particles, because there is nothing unclean leaking out of what is partless, just like a cognition . . . This, too, is undermined by the reasoning of Mind-Only that minute particles have parts so are not partless, like a vase. This again is undermined by Madhyamaka reasoning that whatever exists is not real, like an illusion.[73]

Also, this is stated extensively in Prajñākaramati's commentary; he cites the *Introduction to the Middle Way* to declare that while ordinary beings do not invalidate yogis, yogis invalidate ordinary beings:

> *Just as the observation by one with an eye disorder [671]*
> *Does not invalidate the cognition by someone without an eye disorder,*
> *Likewise, a mind that has relinquished stainless gnosis*
> *Cannot invalidate a stainless mind.*[74]

This also shows that the reasoning of higher philosophical systems invalidates the objects falsely presumed in the claims of lower ones, but it does not show that the higher systems refute all the assertions of the lower ones. Further, most of the assertions of the lower systems are stepping stones, or methods, for entering the higher ones. In terms of just the way that selflessness is taught here, there are disciples who, for the time being, are not able to realize profound emptiness. In order to guide them progressively to the subtle selflessness, some scriptures teach that there is a self, and others teach that there is no self of persons that is permanent, singular, or independent. From there, it is progressively shown that there is no self of persons—that it is empty of any self-subsisting substance, and so on. It is taught in this way in *Reason in Sixty Verses*:

> *For those seeking reality,*
> *First it is said that all exists.*
> *When these objects are analyzed and there is no attachment,*
> *They are later shown to be absent.*[75]

In the commentary, it is said: "If people who have not trained their intellects are first enjoined to the view of emptiness, they will become extremely confused. Therefore, sublime beings do not teach emptiness in the very beginning."[76] Also, the *Precious Garland* says:

> *Just as a grammarian*
> *First teaches reading letters,*
> *So the Buddha teaches the doctrine*
> *In accord with what disciples can bear.*
> *To some he teaches the doctrine*
> *In order to avert negative actions,*
> *For others in order to accumulate virtue.*
> *To some he teaches based on duality,*
> *To others he teaches based on nonduality.*
> *To some he shows what is profound yet frightening to the anxious –*
> *Emptiness with the heart of compassion –*
> *That which accomplishes awakening.*[77]

Here is what this passage means: The first stanza shows how, like a grammarian first teaches letters before having a student read, the Buddha does not initially teach the profound that is difficult to realize, but teaches the doctrine in accordance with what a disciple's mind can bear. The way this is done is demonstrated in what follows. The next three lines show how abandoning evil actions and accomplishing virtues bring about the higher states. Then one line shows the absence of the self of persons and the presence of the duality of apprehender and apprehended for the two types of realists [Vaibhāṣika and

Sautrāntrika]. Then a line for those of the Mind-Only, Mahāyāna type shows there to be an emptiness of apprehender-apprehended duality that negates external objects. Then the last three lines show the way of accomplishing awakening for those Mahāyāna types with supreme faculties—the path of profound Madhyamaka, emptiness with a heart of compassion—which frightens those with the anxiety of conceiving true existence.

[672] Furthermore, the *Fundamental Verses of the Middle Way* says: "The self, too, is a designation . . . ,"[78] and the *Four Hundred Verses* also expresses this meaning: "Malevolence is averted in the beginning . . ."[79] Even though this is extremely important, for the moment I will leave it at this. The method for engaging the meaning of selflessness proceeds from the earlier stages to the later ones because it is easier to realize the earlier stages than the later ones.

Moreover, among Buddhist philosophers, it is not just Mādhyamikas, but even realists have their own distinctive ways of eliminating the two extremes and asserting the middle way. They each accept their own middle path, and no others. To show this with a brief illustration: the two Disciple schools assert the dependent arising of conditioned phenomena that arise in dependence upon causes and conditions. By this, they claim to eliminate the extremes of permanence and annihilation. Vaibhāṣikas claim that when an effect like a sprout is produced, the seed ceases; so the extreme of permanence is eliminated. Since an effect arises immediately after its cause, they claim to eliminate the extreme of annihilation. Sautrāntikas claim to be free from the extreme of permanence because they accept that conditioned phenomena disintegrate from moment to moment; they claim to be free from the extreme of annihilation because of the uninterrupted continuity of a series of momentary phenomena. The essential point of these two systems is the same.

Proponents of Mind-Only also claim that their system is the path free from the two extremes. They claim to be free from the extreme of existence because the imagined nature (*kun btags*) does not truly exist; they claim to be free from the extreme of annihilation because the other two natures are truly existent. The reason for this is that, according to their reasoning, they believe that the Vaibhāṣikas and Sautrāntikas fall to the extreme of existence while the Svātantrikas and Prāsaṅgikas fall to the extreme of annihilation.

Mādhyamikas claim to be free from the extreme of existence because no phenomenon ultimately exists, and claim to be free from the extreme of annihilation because phenomena conventionally exist. In this way, each of the lower philosophical systems has its own system of avoiding the two extremes in its own perspectives. Nevertheless, when analyzed by the reasoning of

Prāsaṅgika-Madhyamaka, not only are all the Buddhist philosophies from Mind-Only and below not free from the two extremes in various ways, but the Svātantrikas have yet to negate the subtle extreme of existence or permanence. This is because they assert that when positing any phenomenon, one must do so on the grounds of the distinct basis of designation for that phenomenon that has been sought out. If this kind of objective existence (*rang mtshan*) is negated, however, the Svātantrikas believe that one would not be able to posit its conventional existence. Therefore, they accept the conventional existence of this kind of objective existence.

Nonetheless, they are considered Mādhyamikas because [673] they maintain that no phenomenon truly exists; they negate true existence through several arguments. Since they negate the true existence of all phenomena such that the way things are empty is the same meaning as their interdependence, this way of eliminating the two extremes with respect to all phenomena is much subtler than that of the proponents of Mind-Only. For this reason, the proponents of Mind-Only are not called "Mādhyamikas" whereas Svātantrikas are; there are several other reasons for this as well. Nevertheless, it is said that only Prāsaṅgikas realize the meaning of the subtle interdependence that is free from all extremes.

2. *Specific Brief Explanation Identifying Madhyamaka*

Our tradition of Madhyamaka accepts the illusion-like lack of true existence, having completely negated the extreme of existence that holds any phenomenon to truly exist, and the extreme of nonexistence that holds that phenomena do not exist even conventionally. "Mādhyamika" and "proponent of essencelessness" (*ngo bo nyid med par smra ba*) have the same meaning. One might wonder why these terms are used. One is called a "Mādhyamika" because of accepting the middle free from the two extremes; one is called a "proponent of essencelessness" due to not accepting any phenomenon to have even the slightest truly existent essence.

There is a division within Madhyamaka into Prāsaṅgika and Svātantrika, which are respectively identified as follows: A Svātantrika is a Mādhyamika who accepts that things exist on their own (*rang gi mtshan nyid kyis grub pa*) conventionally. Due to negating truly existent entities by relying upon correct reasons with the three modes existing objectively (*rang ngos nas grub pa*), they are called "Svātantrikas." "Autonomous" (*rang rgyud*), "independent" (*rang dbang*), and "objective" (*rang ngos nas grub pa*) are said to have the same meaning. A Mādhyamika who does not accept anything to exist on its own, even conventionally, is a Prāsaṅgika; one who accepts that the inferential understanding to be established in the continuum of an opponent arises by means of only a *reductio* is called a "Prāsaṅgika."

One might wonder, "If a Mādhyamika is so called because of abiding in the middle between the extremes, then what are the extremes? And what is the reality of the path that is free from extremes like?" The *Fundamental Verses of the Middle Way* states:

> *Holding onto "existence" is the extreme of permanence;*
> *"Nonexistence" is the extreme of annihilation.*
> *Therefore, the wise do not abide*
> *In either existence or nonexistence.*[80]

Thus, there are two extremes: existence and nonexistence. Also, "extreme of existence" (*yod mtha'*), "extreme of permanence" (*rtag mtha'*), and "extreme of superimposition" (*sgro 'dogs kyi mtha'*) have the same meaning; and "extreme of nonexistence" (*med mtha'*), "extreme of annihilation" (*chad mtha'*), and "extreme of denigration" (*skur 'debs kyi mtha'*) have the same meaning. Nevertheless, "extreme" and "holding onto an extreme" do not have the same meaning; extremes do not even conventionally exist, while holding onto extremes is something that does conventionally exist. As for the meaning of "extreme," the *Principles of Elucidation* (*Vyākhyāyukti*) says:

> *Extreme means exhaustion, limit,*
> *Close, position, and inferior.*[81]

"Extreme" has many meanings, but in this context it means a place to fall. In this world if you walk in any place and fall into an abyss that brings about your decline, that is an extreme; [674] to fall into it is to "fall to an extreme." Similarly, existence, nonexistence, permanence, and annihilation are called "extremes"; one who holds onto any of these falls into the abyss of a wrong view and is ruined. Thus, the reality of interdependence, which is free from the extremes of permanence and annihilation—which are places of ruin for whoever holds onto them—is the "middle" or "middle way"; it is like the center that relinquishes the two extremes of permanence and annihilation. The *Jewel Heap* (*Ratnakūṭa*) says:

> Kāśyapa, "existence" is one extreme; "nonexistence" is the other extreme. The middle between these two extremes is inscrutable,

> indemonstrable, baseless, without appearance, uncognizable, and unlocated. Kāśyapa, this is the middle way, the discernment of phenomena.[82]

This shows that the extremes of existence and permanence do not abide due to the lack of true existence, and so on, while the extremes of nonexistence and annihilation do not abide either due to all frameworks being suitable as merely conventionally existent. This is the middle way.

Bhāviveka also said: "Since it is like the middle that rejects the two extremes, it is Madhyamaka,"[83] yet the *King of Meditative Stabilizations Sūtra* (*Samādhirājasūtra*) states:

> *"Existence" and "nonexistence" are both extremes;*
> *"Pure" and "impure" are also extremes.*
> *Thus, having rejected the two extremes*
> *The wise do not even abide in the middle.*[84]

One might wonder, "Is this not also negating abiding in the middle between the two rejected extremes?" There is no problem because the meaning here is not to abide in a middle held to be truly existent, having negated partial extremes (like the realists), and merely being free from those. It is not saying that there is no middle that is free from the extremes of existence and nonexistence and so on. Here, the middle path that is free from the extremes is also called interdependence and emptiness. Nāgārjuna said:

> *That which is dependently arisen*
> *Is itself said to be emptiness.*
> *That being a dependent designation*
> *Is called the middle way.*[85]

Also, *Clear Words* says: "The terms emptiness, dependent designation, and middle way are different words for interdependence."[86] Further, "the Madhyamaka view free from extremes" should be a conjunction of (1) no phenomenon having the slightest nature that is truly existent with (2) the certainty of being able to account for all causal processes. Therefore, being free from all constructed extremes is exclusively a Madhyamaka view; it is not found elsewhere. *Clear Words* says: "Thus, for only the Madhyamaka view, it does not follow that it is a view of existence and nonexistence; one should know that this is not the case for other views like those of the proponents of Consciousness."[87] Also the *Precious Garland* states:

Ask those in the world who assert persons and aggregates,
Sāṃkhyas, [675] Vaiśeṣikas, and Jains:
"Do you profess what is beyond existence and nonexistence?"
Thereby, know the Buddha's teaching to be
Profound ambrosia, beyond existence and nonexistence –
This is the distinctive feature of this doctrine.[88]

Here is what this means: Among those who profess the substantial existence of persons and aggregates in our Buddhist schools, and in other schools who profess this as well—like the Sāṃkhyas, Vaiśeṣikas, and Jains—ask them if they profess what is free from the constructed and beyond the extremes of existence and nonexistence. They cannot respond in the least. Therefore, know that the Buddha's teaching of the profound path that bestows the state of immortality's ambrosia—free from constructs—is unique to the Buddha's doctrine; it is its distinguishing feature.

Here, "beyond existence and nonexistence" means that it is beyond both true existence and absolute nonexistence; it does not mean that it is neither existent nor nonexistent because it is impossible for something to be neither existent nor nonexistent. This is stated in the autocommentary on the *Introduction to the Middle Way*: "When both of these are not established, it is impossible for it to be neither existent nor nonexistent."[89] Furthermore, the *Condensed Perfection of Wisdom* says:

When something does not exist, it is said to be nonexistent;
Immature beings impute this, constructing existence and nonexistence.
Existent and nonexistent things are both nonexistent.[90]

Here is what this means: Phenomena are not ultimately existent; therefore, ultimately existent things are said to be nonexistent. Immature beings superimpose phenomena to be ultimately existent and denigrate phenomena as not existent even conventionally. Both of these extremes are nonexistent because phenomena are neither ultimately existent nor conventionally nonexistent. Moreover, Āryadeva said:

Not existent, not nonexistent, not both,
And not neither;

Mādhyamikas know the reality
Free from these four extremes.[91]

Also, the *Introduction to the Middle Way* states: "If it exists, it does not need to be produced, and if it does not exist, what could it do?"[92] And there are other such statements like: "All phenomena are not existent, nor nonexistent, not both, and not neither." The meaning of words like these here in the context of Madhyamaka is that all phenomena are not ultimately existent, and phenomena are not absolutely nonexistent. All phenomena are not both existent and nonexistent. All phenomena are also not neither existent nor nonexistent. This is explained to be the meaning of the autocommentary on the *Introduction to the Middle Way*.

Furthermore, it is said that "there are no entities, and no non-entities, either." This means that there are no truly existent entities and no truly existent non-entities either. When it is said, "Not the same, nor different," it should be explained by qualifying the object of negation in both cases, "not *truly existent* as the same and not *truly existent* as different." Also, "Do not say 'empty'; [676] do not say 'not empty,' either."[93] This means that the emptiness of true existence is not ultimately existent and that the non-emptiness of true existence is not ultimately existent, either. In the contexts of Mind-Only, too, one must explain the different interpretations of these words in accord with the philosophical system at hand. Logicians say this, too; I mentioned this as an aside.

3. Resolving Disputes regarding the Way the Two Truths Are Presented

This section has three parts: (1) refuting the realists like the Sautrāntikas in general, (2) refuting the assertions of Mind-Only in particular, and (3) responding to the objection that the Madhyamaka path is pointless.

1. Refuting the Realists like Sautrāntikas in General

[IX.4c] ***With examples accepted by both . . .***

The context here is a realist disputing the soundness of the Prāsaṅgika-Madhyamaka's claim that all phenomena lack intrinsic nature. Thus, to the extent that intrinsic nature is posited, and to the extent to which a lack of intrinsic nature is claimed, it is necessary here to know the criteria for the object of negation. Therefore, I will explain the identification of the object of negation here in two parts: (1) a brief demonstration of the necessity of identifying the object of negation and enumerating the objects of negation, and (2) an extensive explanation of the ways the objects of negation are respectively identified by Prāsaṅgikas and Svātantrikas.

1. Brief Demonstration of the Necessity of Identifying the Object of Negation and Enumerating the Objects of Negation

In order to generate the pure view of Madhyamaka within your continuum, it is first necessary to identify the subtle object of negation through reasoning investigating the ultimate in the Madhyamaka system. This is because, before the concept of true existence (the object to be negated) appears to cognition, emptiness (which is a non-implicative negation negating that object) does not appear to cognition. For instance, it is just like how one is unable to ascertain by a source of knowledge the lack of a vase in a certain place without first having an appearance to cognition of the concept of vase, the object to be negated. In this way, our text says:

> [IX.139ab] ***Without contacting the imputed entity,***
> ***One cannot apprehend the lack of this entity.***

Moreover, it is not sufficient merely to identify the appearance of the concept of true existence that has been imputed by a philosophical system. Everybody is engaged from beginningless time in an innate apprehension of true existence, regardless of whether one has been influenced or not by philosophies; it is necessary for this apprehension and its apprehended concept of true existence to appear clearly to cognition.

If this criterion for the object of negation is not properly understood, then either the object of negation identified is overextended—and what need not be negated is negated—causing one to fall into the extreme of denigration; or, the object of negation identified [677] is not extensive enough, and something that needs to be negated is not fully negated. Thereby, one falls into the extreme of superimposition with something extra remaining.

In general, the object of negation is twofold: (1) the objects of negation by the path and (2) the objects of negation by reason. The former are, for instance, the two obscurations. These are existent objects of knowledge; if they did not exist, all beings would automatically be liberated and striving to cultivate the path would be pointless. How to negate these is to stop them in a way that they can never arise again in one's continuum, but their existence as objects of knowledge is not negated. As for objects of negation by reason, they are identified here as what is negated by reasoning investigating the ultimate; their status as objects of negation by reasoning investigating the conventional will not be described here.

Objects of negation by reasoning are twofold: (1) misconceptions that superimpose distortions onto reality and (2) the objects of these kinds of apprehension. The former is an existent object of knowledge, like the apprehension of true existence. The latter is not existent as an object of knowledge, like true existence. Between these two, the main object of negation is the latter. This is because, if it is not seen that what a misconception takes to exist is undermined by reason, then there is no other way for that misconception to be negated. When it is seen that what a misconception takes to exist is undermined by reason, then through this one can ascertain that things do not exist in the way they are apprehended. Based on this, one can uproot the seeds of misconception.

2. Extensive Explanation of the Ways the Objects of Negation Are Respectively Identified by Prāsaṅgikas and Svātantrikas

If the distinctive criteria for the objects of negation of the Prāsaṅgikas and Svātantrikas are not known, then the distinction of their views will not be known. Therefore, one should ascertain the distinct criteria for these two systems' objects of negation. This section has two parts: (1) how Svātantrikas identify the object of negation and (2) how Prāsaṅgikas identify the object of negation.

1. How Svātantrikas Identify the Object of Negation

This section has two parts: (1) identifying true existence and the apprehension of true existence and (2) the example of an illusion to make it easy to understand.

1. Identifying True Existence and the Apprehension of True Existence

I will explain in brief here the essential points stated in the *Light of the Middle Way* in detail, which are cited in texts like Tsongkhapa's explanation of the *Introduction to the Middle Way.* Phenomena such as forms that are posited through the force of a cognition not impaired by a temporary cause of distortion are said to be conventionally existent phenomena. The opposite of these, namely, what is not posited by the force of an appearance to an unimpaired mind, but exists objectively from its own unique mode of being (*yul rang gi mthun mong ma yin pa'i sdod lugs kyi ngos nas*), is said to truly exist, ultimately exist, correctly exist, and exist in reality. These are the consummate objects of negation by reasoning investigating the ultimate, which do not exist even conventionally.

A cognition that apprehends these as existent, without relying upon analysis by reason, is said to be the "innate apprehension of true existence." The negation of its conceived object should be held to be the ultimate truth. In this Svātantrika system here, there is no such thing as this kind of truly existent phenomenon. Nevertheless, they do [678] not accept that what objectively exists, naturally exists, exists on its own, and substantially exists are objects of negation for reason investigating the ultimate. This is because they assert that phenomena must exist in these three ways (e.g., objectively) and that to be an entity is necessarily to substantially exist. Thus, although they claim that phenomena are mentally imputed and conceptually designated, they hold that the essence of those mentally imputed and conceptually designated phenomena objectively exists first.

One might wonder, "The *Light of the Middle Way* states, 'The claim, "they do not ultimately arise" is explained to mean that they do not arise to an accurate cognition.'[94] Arising, and so forth, not existing from the perspective of an intelligent cognition (*rigs shes*) is explicitly shown to be the meaning of not ultimately existing. This shows implicitly that if arising and so forth were to exist in that perspective, then it would mean that they would ultimately exist. This conflicts with the previous criterion given for what constitutes ultimate existence."

There is no problem because there are two ways of understanding the ultimate when qualifying the object of negation with "ultimately." It is important to know the difference between these two when coming to ascertain the views of both Prāsaṅgika and Svātantrika, so I will describe it briefly.

One way is to claim that the meaning of not ultimately existing refers to what is considered ultimate and does not exist from the perspective of an investigation into reality by an intelligent cognition by means of study, contemplation, and meditation. Another way is to claim that the meaning of not ultimately existing refers to what is not posited through the force of its appearance to an unimpaired cognition, and what does not exist objectively from its own mode of being. These are the dividing lines. In this context, what we really need for identifying the object of negation is the latter.

The ultimate in the former sense and the reality that is ascertained from the perspective of an intelligent cognition's ascertainment both exist. This is because an intelligent cognition investigating reality and what exists from its perspective both exist. What exists from the perspective of that intelligent cognition exists because emptiness exists from the perspective of this kind of intelligent cognition's ascertainment of reality. The ultimate in the latter sense does not exist, nor is there something that exists there. If there were something that existed there, then it would follow that this would truly exist and be an object of negation. Therefore, there is nothing that can be ultimately existent in the latter way of understanding. If there could be something truly existent there, it would necessarily have to be ultimate in the former sense as well because that kind of intelligent cognition is what investigates whether something is existent or not.

If these points are understood, then so is the essential point of why there is no conflict between the statement that the basic nature—the way things are—is the ultimate truth and the statement that the basic nature is established as the way things are, yet does not ultimately exist. The basic nature is the object warranted by an intelligent cognition investigating the ultimate and is the object it finds; nevertheless, it need not withstand analysis by that intelligent cognition. These distinctions are to be clearly differentiated. [679] Due to not differentiating these, it is said that there come to be claims such that the ultimate truth truly exists and withstands analysis or that the ultimate truth is not an object of cognition.

2. *The Example of an Illusion to Make It Easy to Understand*

An example of the way an illusion appears is used here to illustrate whether or not phenomena are considered to be posited through the force of cognition and whether or not there is appearance and conception. When a magician conjures a horse and ox from a pebble and stick, for the audience whose eyes have been influenced by the mantra substance, the pebble and stick appear as a horse and an ox, and they conceive them that way. Similarly, for ordinary beings who have not realized emptiness, phenomena appear to exist objectively by their own power without being posited through the force of cognition's appearance, and they conceive them that way. For the magician, however, the horse and ox merely appear, but are not conceived to exist that way. Similarly, for ordinary beings who have realized emptiness, phenomena appear as if they objectively existed by their own power without being posited through the force of cognition's appearance. Even so, they do not apprehend them to exist this way because they have realized that phenomena are merely posited through the force of their appearance to cognition.

Those in the audience whose eyes were not influenced by the mantra substance do not have either the appearance of the pebble and stick as a horse and ox nor do they conceive them that way. Likewise, in the perspective of the gnosis of a sublime being's meditative equipoise that directly realizes emptiness, since there is no such appearance as before of what is truly existent, then it is needless to mention that they are not conceived that way. This is because this kind of gnosis is free from the influences of predispositions for ignorance.

In brief, in this Svātantrika system it is accepted that from the side of appearance, phenomena must be both merely projected (*phar bzhag*) by the power of appearing to an unimpaired cognition and be established out there (*tshur grub*) in an objective way. This is because an entity like a sprout must be both posited by an unimpaired cognition and be established objectively by the sprout's own mode of being. The former is necessary because otherwise, a sprout would have to be established as a sprout even from the perspective of someone who did not know the term "sprout," but this is not the case. The latter is necessary because otherwise, everything would be like a nominally designated space-flower and a conceptually apprehended space-flower.

For example, when a pebble and stick are conjured as a horse and ox by a magician, the appearance of the horse and ox in the pebble and stick is projected by the force of the cognition of those whose eyes were infected by the mantra substance. Also, objectively from the pebble and stick, the horse and ox appear out there. Both must be in conjunction. The first is necessary because otherwise, those in the audience whose eyes were not infected by the mantra substance would also have to see the appearance of the horse and ox in the pebble and stick; but this is not the case. The second is necessary because otherwise, on a basis where there is no pebble or stick, this kind of appearance of a horse and ox would also have to arise [680]; but this is not the case.

From the side of emptiness, an object must be empty of being established from its own mode of being, objectively without being posited by the force of an unimpaired cognition. If it were not empty, it would be established in that way. If it were established in that way, it would have to be established in the consummate reality. If it were established in that way, it would have to be realized by the perception of a sublime being's gnosis; but it is not. As for cognition, in the claim that phenomena are posited through the force of cognition, there are two types: conceptual and nonconceptual.

It is not that everything that is posited by just any cognition is accepted as conventionally existent; rather, the understanding cognition must be an unimpaired cognition. The meaning of being unimpaired is that it is not influenced by temporary causes of distortion; that which is understood by such a cognition is said to be undistorted. As for the meaning of being undistorted, it is asserted as that which can be warranted by a cognition in the way that the object objectively exists in its own mode of being. It is not that the understanding mind must be unaffected by *fundamental* causes of distortion because the appearance of phenomena existing on their own is an appearance that is influenced by the causes of distortion. This is because it is influenced by the innate apprehension of true existence.

One might wonder what the term "merely" excludes in the phrase "merely posited by the force of appearing to an unimpaired cognition." It does not exclude objective existence that is posited by cognition, which is accepted. Rather, it excludes what is objectively existent from its own mode of being that is not posited through the force of cognition.

2. How Prāsaṅgikas Identify the Object of Negation

This section has three parts: (1) the way of conceptually posited phenomena, (2) demonstrating the opposite apprehension—how things are apprehended as truly existent, and (3) showing how everything functions while merely nominally designated.

1. The Way of Conceptually Posited Phenomena

In the Prāsaṅgika system here, nothing at all is accepted as an objective object; all phenomena are said to be merely conceptual designations and mere nominal designations. The meaning here is the viewpoint of numerous scriptures that are definitive in meaning and their commentaries. The *Inquiry of Upāli* (*Upālipariprcchā*) states:

> *I taught the mind's fear in hell, and*
> *That thousands of beings are made miserable;*
> *Yet there never existed one*
> *Who went to the lower realms after dying.*
> *There are no harmful*
> *Razors, big spears, and weapons;*
> *Through the force of conceptuality they are seen to fall upon the body in the lower realms,*
> *But there are no weapons there.*
> *The various things that bring joy to the mind,*
> *Flowers in bloom, glorious mansions of gold,*
> *These are not made this way at all;*
> *They are posited through the force of conceptuality.*
> *The world is imputed by the force of conceptuality;*
> *Immature beings discriminate by holding onto identifications. [681]*
> *There is no arising of apprehension nor lack of apprehension;*
> *They are completely conceptual, like an illusion and a dream.*[95]

This shows that everything in the world of the lower realms and higher realms is simply a conceptual designation. Another sūtra says:

This teaching has shown before that there is no self and no sentient being,
Yet they are not extinguished.
They are said to be imputed, mere designations.[96]

And,

That which is peaceful, and the completely peaceful contemplation of phenomena,
Is contemplation that never arises.
All constructions are mental concepts;
Therefore, know this to be contemplation of phenomena.[97]

Also, the *Prajñāpāramitā* states extensively:

"Bodhisattva" is merely a name. Likewise, "transcendent perfection of wisdom" is just a name. Form, feeling, identification, formation, and consciousness are just names. Form is like an illusion. Feeling, identification, formation, and consciousness are like an illusion. Illusion, too, is just a name. It does not abide anywhere or in any place.[98]

Reason in Sixty Verses says that the whole world is merely conceptual imputation:

Since the perfect Buddha taught that
The world is conditioned by ignorance,
How is it unreasonable that
This world is a conception?[99]

Also, the *Precious Garland* states:

The entities of form are mere names;
Space is also merely a name.
Without elements, how could form exist?
Therefore, even name-only does not exist.[100]

Thus, ultimately even name-only does not exist. Also, the same text says that there is nothing at all besides what is conventionally designated by a name:

Other than conventional designation,
What is this world
That really exists or does not exist?[101]

2. *Demonstrating the Opposite Apprehension—How Things Are Apprehended as Truly Existent*

To apprehend the existence of phenomena in a way that they are not merely posited by names and concepts, as explained above, is the innate apprehension of true existence. If things are established as truly existent in the way they are apprehended, they are said to truly exist, ultimately exist, correctly exist, exist in reality, intrinsically exist, objectively exist, exist on their own, and substantially exist. All these here are, without distinction, objects of negation for reason investigating the ultimate; they do not exist even conventionally. The apprehension of these objects of negation to exist with respect to persons and phenomena is the twofold apprehension of self. The objects of these two modes of apprehension is the twofold self. This will be explained extensively below.

Since Svātantrikas believe that to exist on its own is not necessarily to truly exist, [682] the difference between the degree of subtlety of the object of negation for Prāsaṅgikas and Svātantrikas is enormous. For this reason, as will be explained below, there are many differences between Prāsaṅgikas and Svātantrikas, such as whether or not intrinsic production and production from other are accepted. Thus, in Svātantrika texts, claims such as "not intrinsically existing" or "lacking essence" are not explained to mean not intrinsically existing and not existing on its own even conventionally. Rather, they are necessarily understood to mean *ultimately* lacking intrinsic nature or lacking a *truly existent* intrinsic nature.

In the context of Prāsaṅgika, every time it is said that all phenomena lack intrinsic nature even conventionally, it is not to be understood as meaning that even conventionally there are no intrinsic natures, like heat being the intrinsic nature of fire and so on. Rather, it is stated in this way to indicate that nothing exists on its own or has an objectively existent intrinsic nature even conventionally. For this reason, these two traditions have distinct criteria for positing conventional existence. In the system of Svātantrika, a conventionally existent object, like a sprout, is understood to exist by the force of its appearance to cognition in accord with its own mode of being (*rang gi sdod lugs ltar*). Moreover, prior to cognition's ascription, the cognized sprout is held to first exist with an objective mode of being (*rang ngos kyi sdod lugs*). Due to this essential point, the existence of intrinsically existent sprouts, etc. is asserted.

While Prāsaṅgikas also posit things like sprouts by the force of their appearing to cognition, the conventional existence of things like sprouts is understood to be merely a nominal and conceptual designation. Apart from this, no objects designated by words like "sprout" are accepted whatsoever to exist objectively, from their own side. Merely this is not enough for Svātantrikas to account for existence. There is a big difference in the meaning of "cognition," too, in the phrase "posited through the force of cognition": Svātantrikas accept that conventional existence must be understood exclusively by an unimpaired cognition that is not mistaken regarding the mode of being of a thing like a sprout. Prāsaṅgikas, however, accept that the conventional existence of things like sprouts can be understood even by a cognition that is mistaken with regard to the object's mode of being.

Likewise, even though both traditions are similar in just accepting the necessity of positing all warranted objects by their respective sources of knowledge, there is also a great difference here. What the term "mere" is interpreted to exclude in statements in texts such as the Perfection of Wisdom Sūtras that "all phenomena are *mere* names and *mere* designations" is also different. Svātantrikas interpret "mere" to exclude phenomena's ultimate existence, not their objective existence, whereas Prāsaṅgikas accept that all phenomena are mere names and mere designations, so the "mere" is interpreted to exclude not just true existence, but objective existence as well.

Due to the two systems of Svātantrikas and Prāsaṅgikas identifying the object of negation differently, they also have different criteria [683] for examining reality. Svātantrikas are not satisfied with simply words and conventions that "a sprout comes from a seed." They investigate whether or not there is the arising of a sprout from a seed objectively, and the process of arising. But this does not involve ultimate analysis; it is just conventional analysis. If anything is found by such an analysis, it is said to be a conventionally existent thing and something that is established unreflectively without analysis. Ultimate analysis is held to be an analysis of the status of the arising of a sprout from a seed not held to be posited by the force of cognition—an analysis of the production from a seed as the objective way of a sprout's own mode of being; they accept that no phenomenon withstands this type of analysis.

Since it involves a search for a designated object, Prāsaṅgikas also assert the former kind of analysis to be an ultimate analysis. Thus, the line between Prāsaṅgikas and Svātantrikas is also drawn in terms of the way of understanding conventional existence to the same extent as the way of understanding ultimate analysis or a search for a designated object. Nevertheless, in both systems there is no difference in reason's subtle object of negation being accepted as that which is found when a designated object is sought out according to their own respective assertions. This is because phenomena undeniably exist when they are not analyzed in both systems, and it is similarly accepted that when examined with ultimate analysis, a phenomenon withstanding this analysis is impossible, like a rabbit horn.

3. Showing How Everything Functions while Merely Nominally Designated

How all frameworks are understood based on all phenomena being merely conceptually and nominally designated is explained as follows. Through accepting and rejecting based merely on designating conventions such as "this is a form; this is feeling," "arising, ceasing," "coming, going," and so forth, purposes are accomplished. All things are possible—such as existence and nonexistence, being and not being—based on mere names. Without being satisfied with just this, when the object designated by something like "form" is sought out—in terms of its shape, color, or parts, and so on—nothing is ever found and nothing is feasible.

Therefore, there is nothing more than mere nominal designation; it is like imputing a snake onto a colored rope or a person onto a heap of stones. Nevertheless, the meanings of these examples are not the same in terms of the status of conventional existence because there is a difference as to whether an affirmed designation is undermined or not by a conventional source of knowledge. Thus, it is said that since the difference in the status of the existence of these two cannot be distinguished from the side of the object itself, one must draw a fine line by means of differentiating whether or not it is undermined by another conventional cognition. This has been said again and again to be a consummate essential point of the Prāsaṅgika view that is difficult to understand.

In this way, an unexcelled feature of this system is that while things are merely nominally designated, [684] all activities—such as cause and effect, arising and ceasing, coming and going—can be posited with respect to them. The consummate viewpoint of master Nāgārjuna, father and son [Āryadeva], was explained with many stainless scriptures and reasonings by the genuinely great chariots—master Buddhapālita, glorious Candrakīrti, and the Victor's child, Śāntideva—with one intent and one voice.

In master Buddhapālita's commentary on the *Fundamental Verses of the Middle Way,* based on the *Jewel Heap* he used the example of two villagers who visit a temple. They argue about whether a painting is the body of Īśvara or Viṣṇu, with an arbitrator making the distinction between what is true and what is false. Since no phenomenon exists objectively, nothing is found when a designated object is sought out. Nevertheless, all things can function based on merely mundane names.

The glorious Candrakīrti used the example of a chariot, based on a Hīnayāna text:

> *In dependence upon a collection of parts*
> *A chariot is designated;*
> *Likewise, based on the aggregates*
> *Conventionally, sentient beings are acknowledged.*[102]

Even though phenomena like persons are not found when analyzed, he showed that without analysis, based on merely their bases of designation, all things function while just being posited with mere designations.

Also, in accord with the intended meaning of the *Meeting of the Father and Son Sūtra*, the Victor's child, Śāntideva, showed that based on the six elements that are the basis of designation for a being, a being does not exist other than as a mere imputation; it is like an illusion. Even so, he claims that conventionally, there is a difference in the status of a mind's existence in an actual being and an illusory being, and also a difference in the status of the evil deed's existence for killing one of them. In our text here, it is shown many times that everything is merely a nominal designation, like an illusion, such as: [IX.9a] ***The illusory Victors*** . . . , [IX.9c] "***If beings are like illusions*** . . . ," and, [IX.11a] ***In killing an illusory being*** . . . . Nevertheless, he shows that everything can be distinguished, such as the difference between having a mind or not. In this one should know the essential point of there being no contradiction between the claim made above—that there is no division between a correct and incorrect conventional truth in this Madhyamaka system—and the explanation in our Prāsaṅgika system that we can understand the difference between such things as what is true and false in regard to claims about a god's body and between an illusory being and an actual being having a mind or not.

As for the meaning of nominal existence, in name only: "name only" eliminates the extreme of existence or permanence; "nominal existence" eliminates the extreme of nonexistence or annihilation. If it is merely a nominal designation, it need not exist, but if it nominally exists, in name only, it must exist. This is because [685] here (1) existence and (2) nominal existence, in name only, mean the same thing.

Next, as it is said: [IX.7] ***For the purpose of guiding the world*** . . . The intent of the scriptures that are spoken for the purpose of guiding disciples to the subtle selflessness is described here in two parts: (1) explaining the explicit teaching of our text here, showing sūtras teaching impermanence and so on to be provisional in meaning, and (2) explaining its implicit teaching, the way of classifying sūtras of the three wheels as provisional or definitive.

1. Showing Sūtras that are Provisional in Meaning

In general, there are many descriptions in the Hīnayāna canon of the coarse view of the four noble truths, including the sixteen aspects such as impermanence,[103] which are traversed until the stage of an Arhat. The Mahāyāna also describes both the sixteen aspects such as impermanence, the coarse view, as well as the way of traversing the path of realizing the lack of intrinsic nature. Other masters accept the commentaries on their viewpoints and explain them that way. However, in this Prāsaṅgika system, the actual path of liberation is exclusively the path of realizing the lack of intrinsic nature in phenomena; other than this, there is no second gateway to peace, as it is said in the *Four Hundred Verses:* "There is no second gateway to peace."[104] Therefore, we assert that merely the path that realizes the coarse view of the sixteen aspects, such as impermanence, is not able to achieve even a sublime path within any of the three vehicles. This will be explained extensively below.

One might wonder, "If the sixteen aspects such as impermanence are not the actual path of liberation, then why were they taught?" These are paths that purify the continua; by just this they are the actual path of liberation for suitable receptacles. Yet for dull Hīnayāna types who are not yet suitable receptacles, they are taught for the purpose of progressively guiding to the subtle selflessness. It is said in *Reason in Sixty Verses*:

The path of arising and ceasing
Is taught with a purpose.
By understanding arising, ceasing is understood;
Through understanding ceasing, impermanence is understood.
By applying the understanding of impermanence,
One will understand the sublime doctrine.
Those who know
Dependent arising
Abandon arising and ceasing;
They cross over the ocean of beliefs.[105]

Here is what this means: By holding onto permanence and happiness, and being completely attached in one's mind to what is conditioned, there will be no wish for liberation. As a remedy to this, impermanence and suffering are taught. Based on understanding the arising of the conditioned, conditioned phenomena are understood to be impermanent. Based on this understanding, one becomes averse to existence. Then one understands the endeavor, the wish to dispel it and achieve liberation. Based on this, one directly realizes the path of liberation, the actual sacred doctrine of interdependence, which is free from the nature of arising and ceasing. Thereby, one crosses over the ocean of existence generated by wrong views.

Also, *Praise to the Basic Field of Reality* states:

Impermanence, suffering, and emptiness –
These three purify the mind.
That which supremely purifies the mind [686]
Is the doctrine of the lack of intrinsic nature.[106]

One might wonder, "Does this not conflict with statements that claim that seeing impermanence and so forth is seeing reality?" Candrakīrti said this in his commentary on *Reason in Sixty Verses*: "Distortion is the apprehension of things like happiness, because things with this nature do not even conventionally exist. The lack of distortion is to apprehend things like suffering because things with this nature do exist conventionally."[107] The meaning intended here is that objects apprehended that do not even conventionally exist, like permanent aggregates, and objects apprehended that do conventionally exist, like impermanent aggregates, can be distinguished in terms of being distorted or undistorted *conventionally*. Yet in terms of reality, based on things like forms not existing as either permanent or impermanent, the distinction between being distorted and undistorted cannot be made. Intending this, the *Mother Sūtras* say that whoever regards forms and the like as permanent or impermanent, happiness or suffering, self or no-self, empty or non-empty is coursing in signs.[108]

The selflessness and emptiness realized in the context of the sixteen aspects is a realization of merely the lack of a self that is imputed by non-Buddhists. This is not sufficient to be the remedy to the innate apprehension of self that apprehends an intrinsically existent person. Therefore, the remedy to this is necessarily to realize the lack of intrinsic nature of persons (the selflessness of persons) in the way that the aggregates and so on lack intrinsic existence (the selflessness of phenomena). Without this understanding, as long as form is apprehended to be truly existent, the apprehension of the person as truly existent will persist as well. As long as that persists, there is no removal of the afflictions, so it is impossible to be liberated from existence. It is stated in the *Introduction to the Middle Way*:

> *Your contemplative practice (rnal 'byor, yoga) that sees selflessness*
> *Does not realize the reality of forms and so on;*
> *Since it persists when forms are perceived*
> *Attachment and the like arise, there being no realization of their nature.*[109]

And, "When you realize no-self, the permanent self is relinquished . . ."[110]

2. The Way of Classifying Sūtras as Provisional or Definitive

Here is a brief exposition of the three wheels, and ways of classifying the provisional and definitive. Among the four philosophical systems, the Vaibhāṣikas do not accept the wheel of dharma of scripture; they claim that a wheel of dharma is necessarily the wheel of dharma of realization, and for that to be exclusively the path of seeing. The Sautrāntikas accept both wheels of dharma of scripture and realization. Within the wheel of dharma of scripture, they assert nothing more than simply the words of sūtras that express the four truths. For the most part, both Vaibhāṣikas and Sautrāntikas claim that the Buddha's Word is necessarily definitive in meaning. There are also those who accept it to include both meanings that are provisional and definitive, as is said in the *Blaze of Reason* (*Tarkajvāla*).

Proponents of Mind-Only follow [687] the division of the three wheels into provisional and definitive from the *Sūtra Explaining the Intent.* The first two wheels are accepted as provisional, and the last is accepted as definitive. The reason for this is that the distinctions among the three wheels are posited based on the subject matter. In terms of the subject matter—by way of mainly teaching selflessness—the first wheel teaches merely the selflessness of persons, while phenomena's true existence is not negated. The middle wheel teaches the selflessness of phenomena through negating the true existence of all phenomena without a clear differentiation. The last wheel teaches the three natures according to Mind-Only and the selflessness of phenomena, through differentiating clearly between what is truly existent and what is not. From among the three cycles teaching selflessness, they accept that the explicit teaching of the first and second wheel is provisional in meaning because it is not suitable to be accepted literally. The explicit teaching of the last wheel is suitable to be accepted literally, and for this reason is accepted as definitive in meaning.

In the Madhyamaka system, it is said in texts such as *Clear Words* and the *Light of the Middle Way* that one must make the division between the provisional and the definitive following the *Akṣayamati Sūtra*. As for this way, it is said in the sūtra itself:

> What is a sūtra of definitive meaning and what is a sūtra of provisional meaning? Sūtras that teach the existence of conventional truth are called "provisional in meaning." Sūtras that teach the existence of ultimate truth are called "definitive in meaning."[111]

This means that the distinction between the provisional and definitive is made based on the subject matter. Those sūtras that mainly teach a conventional truth, like phenomena or persons, are provisional in meaning. Those sūtras that mainly teach the ultimate truth, like the lack of self in phenomena and persons, are definitive in meaning. This is the concise explanation of the way of classifying them. At the end of this passage it also clearly states the way of teaching the two truths by identifying sūtras that teach the two truths and the distinct ways of teaching them.

Also, the *King of Meditative Stabilizations* states:

> *Emptiness, as the Sugatas explained –*
> *Know to be a quality of sutras that are definitive in meaning.*
> *All the doctrines that teach sentient beings, persons, and individuals –*
> *Know to be provisional in meaning.*[112]

This meaning is just like the previous sūtra, as is stated in *Clear Words*.

The criteria for what is provisional in meaning are as follows: In general, a provisional meaning sūtra guides disciples. Yet it is not simply by guiding that it is provisional in meaning; here, the meaning of the sūtra must guide elsewhere. Also, within the two ways of guiding, there is one in which the explicit teaching is [688] not suitable to be apprehended literally; its explicit teaching needs to lead elsewhere, as in, "Your mother and father are to be killed."[113] This should be explained as referring to karmic existence and craving. Furthermore, in the statement, "all conditioned phenomena are impermanent," its explicit teaching can be accepted literally, yet mere impermanence is not the consummate reality of conditioned phenomena.

It must guide to another reality; it still needs to guide elsewhere, to the meaning of their reality—the emptiness of true reality.

The criteria for what is definitive in meaning are as follows: a teaching that cuts through constructs, such as the statement, "phenomena do not truly arise," having an explicit teaching of the consummate ultimate reality. Thus, it does not guide anyone anywhere else. It is classified as definitive in meaning if it also has a source of knowledge that establishes it in accord with the meaning that is taught. The *Light of the Middle Way* states: "If one wonders, 'What is definitive in meaning?' It is a statement oriented to the ultimate with the support of a source of knowledge because it cannot be guided anywhere else by another."[114] In this way, from the aforementioned two ways of guiding, since it cannot be guided elsewhere, it is called "the certain meaning" or "definitive in meaning." The *Introduction to the Middle Way* states:

> *A sūtra that has a meaning that is not reality*
> *Is said to be provisional in meaning; when understood, it is what guides.*
> *Know that what has the meaning of emptiness is definitive in meaning.*[115]

In terms of just this way of classifying what is provisional and definitive in meaning, there is no difference between Svātantrika and Prāsaṅgika. Nevertheless, according to the Svātantrika system, not only must a sūtra that is definitive in meaning mainly teach the ultimate truth, but it also must be accepted as the literal truth. For this reason, in the *Hundred Thousand Verse Mother*, for instance, when it says that "this is conventionally a truth for the world, but not ultimately,"[116] there are some times when the qualifier *ultimately* is explicitly applied to the object of negation and these are classified as sūtras that are definitive in meaning. Even though the *Heart Sūtra* mainly teaches the ultimate truth, it does not clearly apply the qualifier *ultimately* to the object of negation, so it cannot be held to be literal; thus, it is classified as provisional in meaning.

The reason for this is that in the Svātantrika system, it is not possible for any phenomenon to ultimately exist. If something did exist in this way, it would have to intrinsically exist; how they assert was explained above. Yet the *Heart Sūtra* says, "The five aggregates are empty of intrinsic existence";[117] since this cannot be taken literally, it is classified as provisional in meaning. If it were said that the five aggregates were ultimately empty of intrinsic existence, applying the qualifier *ultimately*, then it would be classified as definitive in meaning because it could be taken literally.

In the Prāsaṅgika system, there is no difference in whether qualifiers like *ultimately* or *intrinsically existent* are [689] applied to the objects of negation. Thus, in the Svātantrika system, the first wheel is provisional in meaning and the second wheel has two aspects of definitive and provisional: the extensive, middling, and condensed [Perfection of Wisdom] are definitive in meaning, whereas something like the *Heart Sūtra* is held to be provisional in meaning. They accept that the last teaching, the wheel of doctrine of clear differentiation, is provisional in meaning in terms of the framework of the three natures according to the proponents of Mind-Only's assertions. However, there are many ways of explaining their way of understanding what is provisional and definitive in meaning in the last wheel; it is a difficult point in this context here. I will also not mention here the way of explaining what is provisional and definitive in meaning based on the three criteria of having a basis in another intention, and so forth.[118]

In the Prāsaṅgika system, the first wheel spoken of in the *Sūtra Explaining the Intent* must be provisional in meaning; yet in general, the first wheel has aspects of both what is provisional and definitive in meaning. The first wheel teachings of the lack of intrinsic nature in persons and phenomena is definitive in meaning. The first wheel's teachings of merely the coarse selflessness of persons—a person being empty of existence as a self-subsisting substance (*rang skya thub pa'i rdzas yod*)—and the teaching of forms and so on existing on their own are provisional in meaning.

These are explained as provisional in meaning due to having a basis in another intention, having a purpose, and explicit invalidation of the literal meaning. The basis in another intention is its intending merely the conventional existence of forms and so on. The purpose is to teach merely a coarse selflessness of persons to progressively train the minds of those who are, for the time being, not suitable receptacles for the teaching of the subtle selflessness. Thereby, they are progressively led to the subtle selflessness. Explicit invalidation of the literal meaning is found in arguments negating anything existing on its own. The middle wheel asserts that phenomena are merely conventionally existent, having refuted any phenomenon that exists on its own. This is the consummate definitive meaning taught to those of extremely sharp faculties, those disciples with the heritage of the Mahāyāna who can understand the meaning of emptiness as dependent arising.

In the Prāsaṅgika system, the literal statements in texts like the *Hundred Thousand Verse Mother,* which explicitly apply the qualifier *ultimately* to the object of negation, are definitive in meaning. Moreover, even when the words of a qualifier *ultimately* are not applied to the object of negation, as in the

Heart Sūtra, it should be understood in these concise demonstrations as it is in the contexts of the extensive explanations, where *intrinsically* is also applied to the object of negation. Even when this is not applied, as in "no form, no feeling. . . ,"[119] there is no difference in the fact that all the sūtras that teach emptiness are definitive in meaning. This is because when a qualifier is applied in one context, as in the *Hundred Thousand Verses,* all the other sūtras with its shared subject matter also are understood perforce to make this qualification. Therefore, when a *Mother Sūtra* states, "no form, no feeling. . . ," it is not teaching that form and feeling do not exist. Rather, it is teaching that they do not *intrinsically* exist; there is a big difference.

In the last wheel, [690] it is taught that the imagined nature (*kun btags*) does not exist on its own, and that the dependent (*gzhan dbang*) and consummate natures (*yongs grub*) exist on their own. This is provisional in meaning. The basis in another intention is that it intends the mere conventional existence of the distinction between what is posited by nominal designation and what is not, in accord with the assertions of the three natures according to proponents of Mind-Only. The purpose is to prevent disciples who, even though they have the Mahāyāna heritage, would develop a view of annihilation—that holds that karmic causality, bondage, and liberation do not exist—if they were taught from the beginning the subtle selflessness of phenomena that negates phenomena's existence on their own. By training their continua through teaching the coarse selflessness of phenomena, such as the emptiness of a separate substance of the apprehended and the apprehender, later they are led to the subtle selflessness of phenomena, such as is taught in the middle wheel. Therefore, there is a difference between the disciples of the middle and last wheels in terms of the sharpness of their faculties.

As for explicit invalidation of the literal meaning, no functionality can be posited whatsoever in the position of those who assert that phenomena exist on their own. Yet the functioning of everything is suitable in the position of those who assert emptiness; the reasons for this are shown in texts like the *Fundamental Verses of the Middle Way.* In general, a sūtra that is provisional in meaning need not be provisional with another intention, but what is provisional in meaning with another intention necessarily has the threefold criteria of having a basis in another intention, etc.

Moreover, it says in the *Inquiry of King Dhāranīśvara* (*Dhāranīśvararājaparipṛcchā*), "Noble child, a skilled jeweler knows well how to clean gems . . . ,"[120] using the example of a jeweler cleaning a jewel with a threefold wash and threefold rub. This shows how the Victorious One, knowing the constituents of sentient beings, teaches in three stages to guide disciples. First, he brings them to enter the disciplinary doctrine through generating aversion for cyclic existence by means of the discourse on impermanence, suffering, and no-self. Later, through the discourse on emptiness and signlessness, he brings them to understand the way of the Tathāgatas. Then, he brings these sentient beings to the domain of the buddha through the discourse of the irreversible wheel. In this way, the three wheels have different meanings; the three wheels are based upon differences among the continua of the disciples of Mahāyāna and Hīnayāna. This is the way of guiding a single individual through the stages of the path. Thereby, this sūtra shows both the ways of guiding on the path those who are at that time possessing a Hīnayāna heritage, and the stages of the path for those who from the beginning are determined to have the Mahāyāna heritage.

One might think, "According to how proponents of Mind-Only explain, the dependent and consummate natures both truly exist; and according to Madhyamaka, they are both empty of true existence. If both of these positions must be posited as the meaning of this sūtra, then one meaning of the sūtra would negate the other, and there would be an internal contradiction on the part of the author."

[691] This is not a problem. In relation to the mind of a disciple who is a proponent of Mind-Only, the meaning of the last wheel sūtras is that the dependent and consummate natures truly exist. In relation to the mind of a Mādhyamika, these two lacking true existence is the meaning of the middle wheel. They are taught this way based on the minds of the disciples, so there is no negation of the sūtra's meaning, nor is there an internal contradiction on the part of the author. Furthermore, even though the meaning of the subject matter in the *Sūtra Explaining the Intent* teaches that the dependent nature and consummate nature truly exist, this is not the viewpoint of the author's own system; no truly existent phenomenon can be posited there in any time, place, or philosophical system. As it is said in the *Introduction to the Middle Way*: "The buddhas never taught the existence of entities."[121] No buddhas taught in any scripture the true existence of entities as their own system. The *Descent to Laṅka* is cited to establish this in the autocommentary:

> *The three existences are mere imputation,*
> *Essentially without entity.*[122]

Likewise, the *Sūtra Explaining the Intent* says that if the dependent nature is apprehended as not truly existent, then all three natures are denigrated. Even so, this is taught from the perspective of those disciples who cannot understand the meaning of emptiness as dependent arising even though they have the Mahāyāna heritage. From the perspective of disciples with supreme intelligence who can understand this, realizing the dependent nature as not truly existent is a supreme method for negating the view of denigration.

Furthermore, the middle wheel is definitive in meaning and the last wheel is provisional in meaning, but this does not contradict the fact that from the perspective of some disciples, the last wheel is definitive in meaning and the middle wheel is provisional in meaning. The *Four Hundred Verses* says:

> *For those who are not sublime, apprehending a self is supreme;*
> *They should not be taught selflessness.*[123]

It says that from among the two teachings of self and selflessness, the former is supreme for some disciples. Therefore, until one is able to understand emptiness and interdependence without contradiction, the division is made between some phenomena being truly existent and some that are not. Thereby, disciples are progressively guided through teaching selflessness partially, as was cited earlier in the verses from *Reason in Sixty Verses* and the *Precious Garland.*

One might wonder, "If the framework of the three natures as presented by proponents of Mind-Only is described as provisional in meaning, then how do Prāsaṅgikas understand the three natures in their own system?"

This is explained as follows: Phenomena such as forms are the dependent nature. Their intrinsic existence is the imagined nature. Their emptiness of intrinsic existence is the consummate nature. This framework for the three natures is reasonable because, for instance, a multicolored rope that is the basis of designation is posited as the dependent nature; the snake designated with respect to that while not existing is [692] posited as the imagined nature; and the genuine reality with respect to the actual snake is posited as the consummate nature. This is stated in the autocommentary on the *Introduction to the Middle Way*: "The snake is designated upon the dependently arisen assemblage of the rope."[124] And later in that text, "The viewpoint of the sūtras is explained after understanding the framework of the three natures."[125] Based on this explanation, the chapter of Maitreya's Inquiry in the *Mother* is shown to be definitive in meaning, and the chapter of Maitreya's Inquiry in the *Sūtra Explaining the Intent* is shown to be provisional in meaning.

To summarize the meaning of the chapter of Maitreya's Inquiry in the *Mother,* the teaching of the subtle emptiness should be applied to each part by understanding the basis of designation for a phenomenon such as a form, which is the aspect of the dependent nature; the designated phenomenon, which is the aspect of the imagined nature; and its emptiness of that, the aspect of the consummate nature. To illustrate this with a form, the form is the *designated form* (*rnam btags kyi gzugs*); the intrinsically existent form is the *imagined form* (*kun btags kyi gzugs*); and the emptiness that is the form's emptiness of intrinsic existence is the *basic nature form* (*chos nyid kyi gzugs*). The first one is a genuine form; the latter two are nominal forms. It is said to apply to other phenomena in the same way.

Therefore, in the Madhyamaka's own system, all three natures are equally without true existence, and equally conventionally existent. If you know this well, then it is easy to establish as provisional in meaning the teaching of the dependent and consummate natures truly existing in the chapter of Maitreya's Inquiry from the *Sūtra Explaining the Intent*. An elaborate treatment of this should be known from texts like the *Essence of Eloquence* that distinguish between the definitive and provisional meanings.

Next, it is said: [IX.7cd] ***One might say, "There is a contradiction [if impermanence] is conventional."*** What follows here is the way to understand the path to realize the subtle and coarse four truths and their sixteen aspects, such as impermanence. There are two paths: one is the path to realize the coarse sixteen aspects such as impermanence explained in the two Abhidharma texts according to the lower philosophical systems; the other is the path to realize the subtle sixteen aspects according to Prāsaṅgika. The Svātantrikas and below accept that one can be liberated from existence even by just the former path.

Also, they accept that after directly realizing the selflessness (among the sixteen aspects) that is the emptiness of a person existing as a self-subsisting substance, one must apply a method to cultivate a path that produces the actual path that brings liberation and other features. The *Compendium of Metaphysics* (*Abhidharmasamuccaya*) says that the mental engagement of selflessness eliminates the afflictions, and the rest of the features are methods for this complete purification.[126] The *Commentary on Epistemology* also says this: "The view of emptiness liberates; other meditations are for this purpose."[127] "Emptiness" here refers to the selflessness that is the emptiness of the existence of a self-subsisting substance. Svātantrikas and below do not understand the selflessness of persons [693] as the emptiness of existing on its own; they also do not understand that to apprehend a person existing on its own is to apprehend the self of persons. This is due to the fact that they maintain that these things do exist on their own.

Prāsaṅgikas accept that to realize the subtle selflessness of persons, it is necessary to realize the emptiness of a person's intrinsic existence. Also, Prāsaṅgikas accept that the truth of the path is the realization of this kind of subtle selflessness, and due to this, that the truth of cessation is the elimination of those potentials (*sa bon*) to be relinquished. It is through cultivation, having realized the sixteen subtle aspects with these kinds of features, that it is held to be necessary to become liberated from cyclic existence. Here, the emptiness of a person existing on its own is understood as the selflessness of persons, and apprehending a person existing on its own is understood as apprehending the self of persons. This is due to the fact that nothing is accepted to exist on its own, even conventionally. One should know that this is the meaning of the response below to disputations such as, [IX.40] ***"By seeing the [four] truths one is liberated . . ."***

One might wonder, "How are each of the sixteen aspects such as impermanence divided into two?"

The coarse truth of suffering is the contaminated aggregates produced by the apprehension of self that apprehends the person to exist as a self-subsisting substance. The karma and afflictions that are brought about by this apprehension of self is the coarse truth of origin. The coarse cessation is the relinquishment of manifest afflictions explained in the two Abhidharma texts, those that are temporarily relinquished based on cultivation after directly realizing the selflessness that is the emptiness of the existence of a self-subsisting substance. The path to the direct realization of this kind of selflessness is the coarse truth of the path. The qualities of impermanence, suffering, and so on that characterize this kind of four truths are the sixteen coarse aspects. Furthermore, one should know the subtle truth of suffering as the contaminated aggregates produced by the apprehension of a self of persons that is the apprehension of a person existing on its own. Their qualities, along with the division within sixteen subtle aspects such as impermanence, should be understood to apply as before.

Yet this kind of division made in terms of subtle and coarse is only made upon a qualified basis, like the truth of suffering; one cannot make the division between subtle and coarse in terms of qualities like impermanence and suffering on their own (*rang ngos nas*). This is because, as some intellectuals claim, the former and latter types of impermanence are both subtle impermanence. The coarse truth of cessation, as is explained in the two Abhidharma texts, is posited from the aspect of merely relinquishing manifest afflictions temporarily. While this is the truth of cessation explained in the Abhidharma, since it is not based on the elimination of any potentials to be relinquished, this is not posited as the genuine truth of cessation. It is just as it is in the case of an Arhat as explained in the two Abhidharma [694] texts.

This Prāsaṅgika system accepts that it is suitable to have yogic perception that directly realizes the coarse sixteen aspects such as impermanence in the continuum of an ordinary being prior to the attainment of the path of seeing that realizes the subtle selflessness. It is clearly said that they have it: [IX.8ab] ***There is no problem; [impermanence] is conventional for yogis; yet for the world,*** *seen to be ultimate.* This system is not like that of the Sautrāntika, Mind-Only, and Svātantrika because they claim that yogic perception is necessarily a sublime being's gnosis.

Next, [IX.13] ***"If ultimately there is nirvana . . ."*** Here is a brief explanation of the framework for cyclic existence and nirvana. "Liberation" and "nirvana" have the same meaning. One might think, "What is this cyclic existence that is to be liberated from?"

The aspect of continuously taking birth, or being born due to the force of karma and afflictions, is the actual cyclic existence. Nāgārjuna said: "The suffering in this life is called 'existence.'"[128] Also, the *Succession of Lives* says: "Liberation, with little difficulty, from the fortress of birth . . ." Further, to put forth separately the agent, action, and object in relation to cyclic existence: the ones that cycle are the sentient beings who take birth powerlessly; the place of cycling is in the appropriating aggregates; the way of cycling is to cycle without the slightest interruption—from the summit of existence to the hell of utter torment. The conditions for cycling are the forces of karma and the afflictions.

Furthermore, the cycle in the lower realms is due to the forces of actions that are unmeritorious and their afflictions. There is no effort needed for this; it proceeds naturally. The cycle in the realms of happiness is through the forces of merit, unwavering actions (*mi g.yo ba'i las*), and their afflictions; these are difficult because there is great effort necessary to accomplish their causes. A Vinaya text states that those who go to the lower realms from the higher and lower realms are as numerous as specks of dust on the great earth, whereas those who go to the higher realms from those two realms are like the dust collected on a fingernail.[129] The commentary on *Reason in Sixty Verses* says: "The essence of cyclic existence is the five appropriating aggregates."[130] The *Commentary on Epistemology* says: "The aggregates of cyclic existence are suffering . . ."[131] These texts mainly teach the appropriating aggregates that take birth and cycle through the forces of karma and afflictions to be the truth of suffering; the actual cyclic existence was explained above.

To describe again the way of cycling and its domain, the *Anthology of Training* cites the *Vast Display*:

> *The three realms are ablaze with the sufferings of aging and sickness;*
> *This is the blazing fire of death without a protector.* [695]
> *Beings are constantly bewildered about the way out of existence,*
> *Like a bee circling around inside a jar.*[132]

And,

> *Through the force of ignorance, craving existence,*
> *The unwise constantly cycle in the five classes of beings,*
> *Taking the three paths of humans, god realms, and lower realms.*
> *They spin like a potter's wheel.*[133]

It is said that beings cycle within five continua like a bee in a jar and like a potter's wheel. In the autocommentary on the *Introduction to the Middle Way,* the way that beings powerlessly circle within cyclic existence through the force of the view of the transitory collective (*'jig lta*) that apprehends me and mine is said to be like the mechanism of a pulley. There are said to be six qualities of similarity between them: As a pulley is tied with a rope, sentient beings are bound by karma and afflictions. As it depends on something to turn it, sentient beings in cyclic existence depend on a restless and untrained consciousness. As it circles all around from the top to the bottom of a well, beings circle from the summit of existence to the hell of utter torment. As it goes down naturally, but takes great effort to pull it up, beings naturally go to the lower realms, but need great effort to go to the higher realms. As it is difficult to determine the sequence of progression when it is spinning, it is difficult to determine the sequence of progression of the twelve links of dependent arising when beings cycle through existence. As it turns, there is pressure pushing on all sides; similarly, when beings cycle in existence, they are constantly afflicted by the three sufferings.

As for nirvana, the liberation from cyclic existence, Nāgārjuna said, "The cessation of this is liberation . . ."[134] The analytical cessation that has relinquished all afflictive obscurations without exception is liberation. Further, the Vaibhāṣikas consider the essence of nirvana to be an unconditioned, permanent entity and an implicative negation. The Sautrāntikas and above consider it to be unconditioned and a non-implicative negation.

Svātantrikas assert that nirvana has aspects of both of the two truths, while Prāsaṅgikas accept it to be ultimate truth exclusively.

To divide nirvana in terms of its modes of expression (*sgra brjod rigs*), there is natural nirvana, non-abiding nirvana, nirvana with remainder, and nirvana without remainder. The emptiness that is phenomena's emptiness of true existence is natural nirvana. This and the ultimate truth have the same meaning. In the Prāsaṅgika system, it is not necessarily that natural nirvana is not nirvana, because there is a common ground of the truth of cessation and the ultimate truth. The analytical cessation that has relinquished the two obscurations without exception is the non-abiding nirvana. This and Mahāyāna nirvana, as well as consummate nirvana, have the same meaning.

There are several ways of explaining the difference between nirvana with remainder and nirvana without remainder, and whether or not these are accepted as exclusively [696] Hīnayāna nirvanas. Here, to merely give a rough sketch in the system of Madhyamaka in general, nirvana with remainder is an analytical cessation that has completely relinquished afflictive obscurations and has aggregates of suffering impelled by previous karma and afflictions. Nirvana without remainder is understood as an analytical cessation that has completely relinquished afflictive obscurations and is free from aggregates of suffering impelled by previous karma and afflictions.

Most Vaibhāṣikas and Sautrāntikas, as well as the proponents of Mind-Only following scripture, accept that the engagement with conditioned phenomena ceases at the time of no remainder. The proponents of Mind-Only following reasoning accept no such cessation, since awareness has no beginning or end. Mādhyamikas do not accept that matter or awareness cease at the time of nirvana without remainder. This is because it is held that when it occurs, one is incited by light rays of the Tathāgata's speech, and is thereby brought to enter the Mahāyāna path.

In the *Golden Light Sūtra (Suvarṇaprabhāsūtra)* and the *Gateway to the Three Embodiments of Buddhahood* (*Kāyatrayāvatāramukha*) it is said that the two Form Bodies are the nirvana with remainder, and the Truth Body (*chos sku*) is the nirvana without remainder.[135] It is nirvana from the aspect of being free from the suffering of the two obscurations; it is said to be with or without remainder from the aspect of whether or not there is a remainder of manifest appearance for disciples. Yet this is not an actual nirvana because an actual nirvana must be the unconditioned truth of cessation, and the two Form Bodies are not this. Even the Truth Body is not necessarily the truth of cessation. The *Fundamental Verses of the Middle Way* says: "Nirvana is unconditioned,"[136] and the *Treasury of Metaphysics* says: "There are three types of unconditioned phenomena: space and the two cessations."[137]

The unique way of presenting the two nirvanas with and without remainder in the Prāsaṅgika system is as follows: The nirvana without the remainder of appearances as true is the nirvana without remainder from the perspective of a meditative equipoise that manifests the complete cessation of the nature of the aggregates from the beginning in a Hīnayāna Arhat who has relinquished all the afflictions. From the perspective of a postmeditation that has arisen from meditative equipoise, the nirvana that has the remainder of appearances as true is understood as the nirvana with remainder. In this way, the sequence for actualizing these two nirvanas is different from others because first one actualizes the nirvana without remainder in meditative equipoise, and then one actualizes the nirvana with remainder in the context of postmeditation.

2. Refuting the Assertions of Mind-Only in Particular

This section has two parts: (1) presenting the dispute about whether external and internal phenomena exist, and (2) the response to the debate.

1. Presenting the Dispute about Whether External and Internal Phenomena Exist

> [IX.15cd] ***"When even delusion does not exist***
> ***What is it that perceives illusion?"***

The meaning of this is a rebuke by a proponent of Mind-Only: "It is not reasonable for you Mādhyamikas to assert that all inner and outer phenomena are without true existence, like illusions. If this were the case, then even subjective cognitions would not truly exist. Given this, by what cognition would an illusory object be perceived? It couldn't be perceived."

The reason for this dispute is that the appearances of external objects like forms are held not to exist as they appear in the system of Mind-Only, but are asserted as the nature of internal consciousness itself. Also, they assert that this consciousness itself truly exists. Without knowing the philosophical system as presented by the interlocutor, a proponent of Mind-Only, one will not be able to ascertain the way that the proponents of Mind-Only criticize the Mādhyamikas, nor the ways that the Mādhyamikas respond. Therefore, even though it is difficult to comprehend the extensive ways that the threefold ground, path, and fruition are asserted in the Mind-Only system, and even though it goes beyond this explanation, I will express here merely some requisite features. This explanation has three parts: (1) the way that, in the absence of external objects, material forms are established to be the nature of mind only, (2) the way that, even while there are no external objects, they appear that way due to the force of predispositions, and (3) the way of presenting the two truths and three natures.

1. The Way That, in the Absence of External Objects, Material Forms Are Established to Be the Nature of Mind-Only

The definition of a proponent of Mind-Only is a Buddhist who refutes external objects with reason and claims that cognition truly exists. A proponent of Mind-Only (*sems tsam pa*), a proponent of Cognition (*rnam rig pa*), and a Yogācāra (*rnal 'byor spyod pa ba*) have the same meaning. The way they assert cognition only is as follows: Even though external objects like forms are not real, cognitions arise with the appearance of objects through the force of predispositions for the appearance of external objects. Since the forms that appear this way are not substantially different from cognition, they assert that all phenomena are established as mind only.

The way they refute external objects and establish mind only is twofold: by scriptures and by reasoning. As for scriptures, the *Sūtra on the Ten Grounds* says: "Hey, child of the Victors! Think like this: The three realms are mind only."[138] Also, the *Descent to Laṅka* says:

> *There are no external appearances;*
> *The mind appears in diversity.*
> *The body, material objects, and abodes are just like this;*
> *I explain this as mind only.*[139]

Furthermore, this is established based on scriptures such as the chapter of Maitreya's Inquiry from the *Sūtra Explaining the Intent* and the *Densely Arrayed*.

This is established by reasoning as follows. There are examples for the way that externality is not real at all, like a rabbit horn, while external objects appear and cognition is truly existent: the past and future appear to the present mind; a herd of elephants can appear in a dream of a person sleeping in a small room; examples like illusions and reflections; falling hairs appear to an eye with an eye disorder while there are no hairs; [698] the entire earth appears to be filled with skeletons through the power of meditative stabilization on foulness. Also, a single object like a cup full of what is wet and moistening appears as nectar, water, and bloody pus to gods, humans, and hungry ghosts due to the dominant condition of strong karma. All appearances in this way do not exist the way they appear, yet a cognition arises that apprehends them this way. Likewise, even though there appear to be external objects like material forms, they do not exist the way they appear; only the basis of appearance, cognition, truly exists.

There are several arguments refuting external objects in texts such as the *Compendium of Mahāyāna* (*Mahāyānasaṃgraha*), the *Twenty Verses* (*Viṃśatikā*), the *Compendium of Epistemology* (*Pramāṇasamuccaya*), and the *Commentary on Epistemology*. Here, the claim that there are no external objects is an assertion that there are no external objects like material forms that are established as substantially different from cognition. It is not an assertion that there are no perceived material forms. This is like the Mādhyamika's claim that there are no *truly existent* material forms, yet there are material forms that are not truly existent.

2. The Way That, Even While There Are No External Objects, They Appear That Way Due to the Force of Predispositions

One might wonder, "If there are no external objects, how does the mind arise with their form?" The way of dispensing with this problem in the Mind-Only system is stated in the *Introduction to the Middle Way*:

> *In the way that the wind agitates the ocean*
> *To produce waves on water,*
> *Likewise, from the seed of all, called "the basic consciousness" (kun gzhi),*
> *Mere consciousness arises through its power.*[140]

They assert that, for example, in the way that waves arise on the ocean through being agitated by the wind, a truly existent consciousness arises with the appearance of external objects, like material forms, from the maturation of predispositions for the appearance of external objects within the basic consciousness. The way that predispositions are infused within the basic consciousness is twofold: (1) the supporting basic consciousness of maturation, and (2) the supported basic consciousness of potentials.

1. The Supporting Basic Consciousness of Maturation

The first is the basic consciousness among the eightfold collection of consciousness. Its distinctive observation is the threefold observation of the five sense objects, the five faculties, and the predispositions for manifest conception (*mngon zhen gyi bag chags*). Its distinctive form is the appearance of an environment and an inhabitant; yet as these are very unclear, it cannot bring about their ascertainment. Its distinctive essence is to be unobscured and undetermined. Its distinctive associates are the mental states of the five omnipresent factors and the [five] concurrent factors. Furthermore, it holds all the virtuous, nonvirtuous, and undetermined potentials. It is constantly engaged without interruption until the brink of the actualization of the Hīnayāna nirvana without remainder or the *vajra*-like meditative stabilization of the Mahāyāna; it ceases in the second moment of these two. It is stated as follows in *Thirty Verses* (*Triṃśikā*):

> *Here, the basic consciousness*
> *Is maturation and the entirety of potentials.*
> *The cognitions of appropriation and place*
> *Are uncognized.*
> *It is always with contact, attention,*
> *Feeling, identification, and intention.*
> *Its feeling is indifference.*
> *It is unobscured and undetermined;*
> *Its contact and so on is, too.*
> *It is a continuity, like a stream, [699]*
> *Ceasing with Arhatship.*[141]

Here, "Cognitions of appropriations and place" shows the distinctive observation, as stated above: the five sense faculties are appropriated, and the predispositions for manifest conception are the appropriator of a body. These two are the cognition of an inhabitant or the cognition of appropriation. The five objects are the cognition of an environment or the cognition of place. "Are uncognized" is the distinctive form, as stated above. The others can be understood as explained above. The *Sūtra Explaining the Intent* also says:

> *The appropriating consciousness is profound and subtle;*
> *It is the entirety of potentials, flowing like a stream.*[142]

The basic consciousness is uniquely acknowledged in the Mahāyāna; this and "the consciousness of maturation" (*rnam smin gyi rnam shes*), "the consciousness of the entirety of potentials" (*sa bon thams cad pa'i rnam shes*), and "the appropriating consciousness" (*len pa'i rnam shes*) have the same meaning.

2. *The Supported Basic Consciousness of Potentials*

The infusers (*sgo byed*) are the sevenfold collection of consciousness together with their associated factors; the infused ground (*bsgo gzhi*) is the basic consciousness. When the infusers become oriented toward their own cessation, they are the potency that deposits predispositions according with their causes—virtue, vice, and undetermined actions. The infused ground is the support, the basic consciousness. It has these five qualities: It is not unsupported, like lightning, but is continuously supporting. It can become infused with all predispositions; it is unobscured and undetermined. It can become infused because it is impermanent. The infuser and the infused ground have a relationship of simultaneous arising and ceasing. It is the total support of predispositions.

The infusers are determined to be the sevenfold collection of engaged consciousnesses, together with their associated factors. The form of their observations needs to be clear. As for the divisions of the predispositions or potentials that are infused, there is a sixfold division, a threefold division, and two fourfold divisions. Here I will briefly explain the way they are divided into three: (1) predispositions for expression (*mngon brjod kyi bag chags*), (2) predispositions for a view of self (*bdag lta'i bag chags*), and (3) predispositions for the branch of existence (*srid pa'i yan lag gi bag chags*).

The first—the predispositions for expression—is deposited only by the depositing mental consciousness. It is the causal condition for the arising of the mental consciousness that imputes a manifold of names for the essences and qualities of all phenomena, from form to omniscience. This is the cause that projects the mind toward objects and so is also called the "predisposition for construction" (*spros pa'i bag chags*). The second, the predispositions for a view of self, is deposited by the afflictive mind (*nyon yid*) and its associated factors. It is the causal condition for the arising of cognition with the appearance of self and other. This is the cause for the arising of the view of the transitory collective so is also called the "predisposition for the view of the transitory collective" (*'jig lta'i bag chags*). The third, predispositions for the branch of existence, is any virtue or vice deposited by the six engaged consciousnesses. It is the causal condition for the arising of cognition with the appearance of the higher and lower realms, transmigration at death, and birth in cyclic existence. This is also called the "predisposition for maturation" (*rnam smin gyi bag chags*).

The basic consciousness of maturation is the basis for the depositing of the basic consciousness of potentials. [700] It is a support because it is the support for its residing. The basic consciousness of potentials is called the supported because it resides within the basic consciousness of maturation. In this system, the former [basic consciousness of maturation] is substantially existent, and the latter [basic consciousness of potentials] is nominally existent.

"Potential" (*sa bon*), "potency" (*nus pa*), and "predisposition" (*bag chags*) have the same meaning. Since these conditioned phenomena are different from cognitions and material forms, they are non-associated formations (*ldan min 'dus byad*).

The existence of this kind of basic consciousness is established by scriptures and reasoning. As for scriptures, a sūtra states:

> *The beginningless element is the abode of all phenomena.*
> *Since it exists, all beings achieve nirvana.*[143]

Further, the *Sūtra Explaining the Intent* says: "The appropriating consciousness...,"[144] and there are also passages in texts such as the *Golden Light Sūtra,* the *Descent to Laṅka,* and the *Densely Arrayed.*[145] As for reasoning, although there is a lot said in texts such as the *Compendium of Mahāyāna* and the *Principles of Elucidation,*[146] in brief, they are included for the most part in the following eight reasons. If there were no basic consciousness it would follow that (1) it would be impossible to appropriate a body, (2) it would be impossible for an initial consciousness to arise, (3) it would be impossible for a mental consciousness to clearly arise, (4) predisposition potentials would be impossible, (5) action would be impossible, (6) bodily feeling would be impossible, (7) a mindless absorption would be impossible, and (8) it would be impossible for consciousness to transmigrate at death. Even though these need to be clarified and expanded a bit more, fearing too many words, I will not elaborate. Further, expansive details of topics like the structure of the afflictive mind, the scriptures and reasoning establishing it, and the different ways of asserting the number of consciousnesses should be known from the texts of Asaṅga and his brother [Vasubandhu], such as the *Compendium of Determinations* (*Viniścayasaṃgrahaṇī*), the *Compendium of Mahāyāna, Thirty Verses,* and in particular, Tsongkhapa's root text and autocommentary on the basic consciousness.[147]

3. The Way of Presenting the Two Truths and Three Natures

This section has two parts: (1) the way of presenting the two truths and (2) the way of presenting the three natures.

1. The Way of Presenting the Two Truths

The basis of division is objects of knowledge, which are divided into two truths. The essence of the conventional truth is a convention which, when observed, can produce thorough afflictions. "The conventional truth" (*kun rdzob bden pa*), "the unreal" (*brdzun pa*), and "the customary truth" (*tha snyad bden pa*) have the same meaning. An illustration is the phenomena within the imagined and dependent natures. The essence of the ultimate truth is the phenomenon that is the consummate observation of the pure path. "The ultimate truth" (*don dam bden pa*), "the basic field of phenomena" (*chos dbyings*), "the consummate nature" (*yongs grub*), and "reality" (*de bzhin nyid*) have the same meaning. An illustration is the twofold selflessness.

In this system, an ultimate truth necessarily exists on its own, but a conventional truth does not necessarily exist this way. This is because phenomena within the dependent nature must exist on their own, but phenomena of the imagined nature do not exist on their own. What is unreal need not be established as unreal, because the dependent nature is unreal [701] yet is not established as unreal since it truly exists. Thereby, they assert that all entities share a common ground of being truly existent and unreal. They accept that the true existence of all that is the basic nature shares a common ground with the real. They assert that everything unconditioned (other than the basic nature) that is established as unreal shares a common ground with the unreal.

2. *The Way of Presenting the Three Natures*

This section has three parts: (1) the imagined nature, (2) the dependent nature, and (3) the consummate nature.

1. *The Imagined Nature*

The essence of the imagined nature is the aspect of superimposition of various linguistic concepts or nominal signs upon any phenomenon. Etymologically, it is the "imagined nature" because it is merely imputed by nominal signs, without having any of the characteristics on its own as they are imputed. There is a twofold division of the imagined nature in terms of the way it is superimposed: based on the superimposition of essence or quality. For instance, these are, respectively, like "this is form" and "this is the arising of form." There is also a twofold division in terms of its essence: the imagined nature of completely disjointed characteristics (*tshan nyid yongs chad kyi kun btags*) and the imagined nature of categories (*rnam grangs pa'i kun btags*). The first refers to what is totally nonexistent, like the twofold self. The second refers to unconditioned phenomena of the conventional, which are the bases of essences and qualities appearing to exist on their own despite not existing that way. An example of the imagined nature is stated in the *Sūtra Explaining the Intent*: it is like a space-flower.[148] That is an example of something that is a mere conceptual designation, but is not an example for what is impossible as an object of knowledge.

2. The Dependent Nature

The essence of the dependent nature is an entity arising in dependence on its causes and conditions. Etymologically, it is the "dependent nature" because it arises due the power of other causes and conditions, and having arisen, does not have its own power to remain more than an instant. When divided, it is divided into the pure and impure dependent nature (*dag ma dag gi gzhan dbang*). The first is, for instance, the gnosis of a sublime being's meditative equipoise and the pure major and minor marks. The second is, for instance, the impure world of the environment, the contaminated aggregates, and the causes of these: karma and afflictions. To give an example, it is like an illusion: when a pebble and stick are influenced by a mantra, they appear like a horse and an ox while not existing that way. Likewise, the dependent nature does not exist as a duality of an apprehended and apprehender that are distant and cut off, yet it appears that way due to the force of the imagination of the unreal (*yang dag pa ma yin pa'i kun rtog*).

3. The Consummate Nature

The essence of the consummate nature is the reality that is empty of the two selves superimposed by the twofold apprehension of self. Etymologically, it is the "consummate nature" because it is unchanging; it is the consummate observation [702] of the pure path; and it is the supreme of all virtuous phenomena. When divided, it is divided into two: the consummate nature in terms of the selflessness of persons and the consummate nature in terms of the selflessness of phenomena. Further, there are many divisions, such as the twenty emptinesses. Also, there is the twofold division of (1) the undistorted consummate nature (*phyin ci ma log pa'i yongs grub*), like the gnosis of a sublime being's meditative equipoise; and (2) the unchanging consummate nature (*'gyur med yongs grub*), like the basic nature. The former is merely presented as a division of the consummate nature, but is not the genuine consummate nature. To give an example, it is said to be like space. As space is the mere negation of obstructive contact, and pervades everywhere, the consummate nature likewise is a non-implicative negation that is the mere exclusion of the object of negation and pervades everything. These are explained in the way of the scriptures of the *Sūtra Explaining the Intent* and the *Compendium of Mahāyāna*; I fear too many words, so do not cite them here.[149]

The three natures encompass all phenomena: all conditioned phenomena are the dependent nature; all that is the basic nature is the consummate nature; and everything else is the imagined nature. These three are all asserted to be objectively existent (*rang ngos nas grub*), yet there is a difference as to whether or not they are truly existent (*bden par grub*) because the imagined nature does not truly exist whereas both the dependent and consummate natures are held to truly exist.

What follows is a brief explanation of how this tradition identifies the extremes of superimposition and denigration and how it relinquishes them. The imagined natures do not ultimately exist, nor exist on their own; superimposition is to apprehend them as if they did. The conceived object here is the extreme of superimposition. The *Bodhisattva Grounds* (*Bodhisattvabhūmi*) states: "It is a manifest conception having superimposed what does not have its own characteristics—phenomena like forms and the designated words for entities like forms."[150] Both the dependent and consummate natures ultimately exist and exist on their own; denigration is to apprehend them as nonexistent. The conceived object here is the extreme of denigration. Again, the *Bodhisattva Grounds* says:

> The inexpressible nature of what is the basis of the linguistic signs and the support of the designated words ultimately exists; to say that these genuine entities do not exist whatsoever is the extreme of denigration; it is wasteful. Know that these two fall short of the disciplining doctrine.[151]

This passage does not explicitly state that the dependent nature is the basis of denigration, but this is stated perforce from before by the way that the consummate nature is also denigrated. Also, the way the dependent nature is denigrated is not just to say that there is no dependent nature in general or that it conventionally does not exist; rather, it is to hold that it does not ultimately exist. [703] To maintain this is to hold that there is no dependent nature and thereby is to denigrate the other two natures as well. This is because the dependent nature is the basis for designation of the imagined nature, and has the quality of the consummate nature. So holding that the dependent nature does not ultimately exist is to denigrate all three natures. The general approach of realist philosophical systems is to hold that an entity that does not truly exist must not exist whatsoever; thus, if the dependent nature does not truly exist, it must be nonexistent.

Given that this is the way of identifying superimposition and denigration, one might wonder how these are relinquished. In terms of apprehending the extreme of superimposition, in general there are two types: imputed (*kun btags*) and innate (*lhan skyes*). The imputed is in the continua of both non-Buddhists and realists, and the innate is the apprehension of the self of persons and phenomena. Within the apprehension of the self of phenomena, there is the apprehension of the imagined existing on its own and the apprehension of the apprehended and apprehender as substantially different. A threefold argument refuting the apprehension of the imagined existing on its own is stated in the *Compendium of Mahāyāna*:

> *Since there is no cognition of it before a name, and*
> *Since names are many and not determined,*
> *There is conflict with*
> *Its nature being multiple and mixed with a name.*[152]

Based on the meaning and reasoning in this text, one should know elsewhere the details of negating superimpositions, such as is explained in the *Compendium of Mahāyāna*, for engaging mere cognition devoid of apprehender-apprehended duality, and engaging by means of the four thorough investigations (*yongs su tshol ba bzhi*) and the four knowledges (*shes pa bzhi*).[153]

It is not possible to have an innate apprehension of the extreme of denigration, so this exists only in the continuum of a proponent of a philosophical system. Furthermore, this cannot exist in the continuum of either those who are in non-Buddhist schools or those who are realists, because if their position does not accept the ultimate existence of any phenomenon, then it must be that they accept it to conventionally exist. For this reason, the apprehension of the extreme of denigration is present in the continuum of a proponent of essencelessness. The *Compendium of Determinations* says: "Some proponents of Mahāyāna hold on to their own faults, claiming that, 'everything exists conventionally, nothing ultimately exists.' . . .with this response."[154] This means that when a Mādhyamika is asked, "What are the two truths?" The Mādhyamika's response is that the ultimate is not truly existent, and that whatever phenomena appear to truly exist are conventional. The two truths presented in this way is then challenged again as an opposing position with many refutations. The way of asking what the two truths are and the way of responding here still needs to be fleshed out in detail, but I refrain. This is merely their way of negating denigration in brief.

2. Response to the Dispute

[IX.16ab] ***When illusion does not exist,***
What is there to be perceived?

[704] This shows how the proponents of Mind-Only are refuted with a parallel argument. I will present some requisite aspects in this context by way

of an overview in three parts: (1) how the viewpoint of sūtras that proclaim mind only is explained, (2) how external objects are asserted in the system of Prāsaṅgika, and (3) the unique way of refuting the basic consciousness.

1. How the Viewpoint of Sūtras That Proclaim Mind Only Is Explained

The "only" in the statement from the *Sūtra on the Ten Grounds* that "the three realms are mind only"[155] is not a negation of external objects. Rather, it shows that the three realms are produced by karma, as in the statement: "The various worlds arise from karma."[156] Since karma is determined within the twofold intention (*sems pa*) and intended (*bsam pa*), the three realms are created by mind. Therefore, in order to negate another creator that is different from mind, like Īśvara, the word "only" is used. This *Sūtra on the Ten Grounds* itself establishes this, saying that the twelve links depend on the mind:

> The three realms are mind only; the Tathāgatas reveal that the twelve links of existence, all the teachings, depend on the mind alone.[157]

Therefore, the word "only" does not exclude external objects; it excludes a creator other than mind. This is established by the sūtra itself. Other sūtras also refute a creator other than mind; the *Descent to Laṅka* says:

> *The person, the continuum, the aggregates,*
> *And likewise conditions and particles,*
> *The creators—the primal basis (gtso bo) and Īśvara –*
> *I assert as mind only.*[158]

Some non-Buddhists claim that things like the continuum and the person are the creator of the world; seeing that this is not the case, it is said that the creator is mind only. Also, Bhāviveka responded that in the formation of the world, among material forms and mind, the mind is most important. Yet this is not making a claim in the way that proponents of Mind-Only do, such that mind only is taught after negating external objects. Candrakīrti also responded in tune with this, addressing these topics with seven stanzas in his *Introduction to the Middle Way*, beginning with: "Bodhisattvas oriented to the manifest . . ."[159]

Also, regarding the passage in the *Descent to Laṅka* that says "there are no external appearances . . . "[160] cited by proponents of Mind-Only, Bhāviveka responded by saying that this sūtra is not teaching mind only after refuting external objects, but rather is refuting the apprehension of an external world that is featureless (*rnam med*) and showing the presence of phenomenal features (*rnam bcas*). Candrakīrti's response is different. He says that this sūtra certainly states that there is mind only after negating external objects; yet the sūtra is provisional in meaning.

Reasoning and scriptural evidence show that this sūtra is provisional in meaning. As for reasoning, there is the argument that establishes objects and cognitions as coextensively present or absent. [705] Also, if objects of knowledge are explicitly taught not to be external objects, then it is easy to establish that cognition does not intrinsically exist either. Thereby, reason establishes this. As for scriptures, the *Descent to Laṅka* itself says:

> *In the way that a physician gives medicine to patients,*
> *The Buddha taught mind only to sentient beings.*[161]

An earlier passage from the *Descent to Laṅka* said that there are no external objects, just mind alone; this latter passage explains this as provisional in meaning. Furthermore, in this context, other sūtras explained as provisional in meaning are explicitly mentioned in the autocommentary on the *Introduction to the Middle Way*; there are four kinds found in the *Sūtra Explaining the Intent*: (1) passages that teach that there are no external objects, such as "a reflection is the domain of the Blessed One's meditative stabilization";[162] (2) passages that teach the dependent and consummate natures to exist on their own, as in "if it is asked, 'What is this essencelessness that is the characteristic of phenomena?' ";[163] (3) passages that teach the existence of a basic consciousness that is essentially different from the mental consciousness, as in "the appropriating consciousness is profound and subtle";[164] and (4) passages that teach that there are three consummate vehicles, as in "those who only go to peace."[165]

The first is explained to be provisional in meaning in the text from the *Descent to Laṅka* cited above, "In the way that a physician . . ."[166] The second is explained to be provisional in meaning in the *Descent to Laṅka:* "Mahāmati, emptiness and nonarising . . ."[167] The third is explained to be provisional in meaning in the same text, which says that sūtras that teach a permanent and steadfast essence are provisional in meaning; the *Descent to Laṅka* states: "From among the sūtras spoken by the Blessed One, the Blessed One taught the buddha-nature . . ."[168] The fourth is extensively explained by Nāgārjuna to be provisional in meaning through citations in the *Anthology of Sūtras*. While not cited in the autocommentary on the *Introduction to the Middle Way*, its meaning is found in the *Lotus Sūtra* (*Saddharmapuṇḍarīkasūtra*) teaching a single consummate vehicle through the parable of a skillful captain leading a group of merchants to an island of jewels. The *Anthology of Sūtras* says: "There is only one vehicle; this is exclaimed in many sūtras."[169] These meanings are stated in three stanzas in the *Introduction to the Middle Way:* "Sūtras that teach that there are no external appearances . . ."[170]

2. How External Objects Are Asserted in the System of Prāsaṅgika

Prāsaṅgikas do not, like the proponents of Mind-Only, claim that there are no external objects even conventionally, or that cognition truly exists; rather, Prāsaṅgikas establish the coextensive presence or absence of objects and cognitions. The way this is established is by reasoning and scripture. By reasoning, the objects and cognitions within the five aggregates are [706] both acknowledged to exist in mundane convention. Neither object nor cognition can be posited when the designated object is sought with reason; and from the perspective of a sublime being training in the realization that directly realizes reality, the five aggregates equally do not appear. As for scripture, the *Mother Sūtras* say that all five aggregates are empty of intrinsic existence, and the Abhidharma texts ascertain those five aggregates equally by means of their general and specific characteristics. So it is established that it does not make sense to separate existence and nonexistence within the pair of objects and cognitions.

Furthermore, the *Introduction to the Middle Way* says:

> *In the reality of the world*
> *The five aggregates acknowledged in the world exist;*
> *For the yogis, whose desired gnosis of reality has arisen,*
> *The five do not arise.*
> *If there are no forms, do not maintain that mind exists;*
> *If the mind exists, do not say that forms do not.*
> *The Buddha said that these are equally relinquished in*
> *the sūtras teaching the mode of wisdom*
> *And equally existent in the Abhidharma doctrines.*[171]

It states the coextensive presence or absence of objects and cognitions. The *Commentary on the Spirit of Awakening* says this, too.[172] Also, the *Four Hundred Verses* states:

> *To say, "one exists and the other does not,"*
> *Is neither the way of reality nor the world.*

So one cannot say,
"This exists but that does not."[173]

It says that distinguishing existence and nonexistence within the pair of objects and cognitions is neither the framework of mundane convention nor the ultimate. Our text here as well states:

[IX.27] ***Even though an illusion is unreal, it is seen;***
The same goes for the seeing mind.

Objects and cognitions are paired; together, they do not truly exist and together they exist conventionally. This way of assertion is different from others because proponents of Mind-Only and Yogācāra-Svātantrika-Mādhyamikas do not accept external objects even conventionally, and accept that cognition exists on its own; while Sautrāntika-Svātantrika-Mādhyamikas accept that both objects and cognitions intrinsically exist.

As for the above Mind-Only examples for the nonexistence of external objects and the intrinsic existence of cognition, presenting cognitions in a dream or cognitions with the appearance of floating hairs, and so on, is not reasonable because the examples are not established. This is because these examples show the apparent existence of nonexistent external objects (such as elephants and floating hairs) to establish their unreality. Yet just like these unreal objects, the subjective cognitions are also established to be unreal, not intrinsically existent. Therefore, this argument that shows the pairing of objects and cognitions in these examples—as equally existent or not—is said to be a tremendously powerful argument that refutes the claims of the proponents of Mind-Only. This is stated in the *Introduction to the Middle Way*: "If you say, 'it is just like a dream' this should be considered . . ."[174] and [707] "If when awake the mind is remembered in the dream . . ."[175] There are many arguments that refute a truly existent cognition that is the dependent nature. In our text here as well, there are many arguments that refute truly existent phenomena.

Although Prāsaṅgikas are like Vaibhāṣikas and Sautrāntikas in merely asserting external objects, they are not at all alike in the way they assert them. Vaibhāṣikas and Sautrāntikas posit external objects through a reasoned analysis of partless particles and their aggregations. Here, this kind of partless entity is not accepted even conventionally. If this kind of entity were accepted, then one would need to accept truly existent entities, and there would be no distinction at all between Prāsaṅgikas and Svātantrikas. This is because Prāsaṅgikas do not posit external objects based on a reasoned analysis;

external objects are posited merely conventionally, without investigation or analysis.

For this reason, the arguments that refute external objects found in Mind-Only texts refute the type of external objects asserted by Vaibhāṣikas and Sautrāntikas. Nevertheless, Mind-Only arguments do not undermine the kind of external objects that are posited merely conventionally, without analysis. Furthermore, the argument that the pair of objects and cognitions are coextensively existent or nonexistent undermines the position of proponents of Mind-Only who do not accept external objects even conventionally. Not only can a conventional source of knowledge not negate external objects, but since this kind of source of knowledge undermines the nonexistence of external objects, external objects are posited here conventionally.

The distinction of whether or not external objects are accepted conventionally also comes down to whether or not one accepts something to exist on its own. Proponents of Mind-Only are not satisfied with external objects like pots and cloths that are merely acknowledged in the world. Rather, they think that if there were external objects, they would have to be the types of things that would be substantially existent and a different substance than internal cognition; they would need to be posited based on the scrutiny of analysis. This comes down to their assertion of something that exists on its own. Prāsaṅgikas posit external objects such as pillars and pots merely conventionally, just in terms of what is acknowledged in the world. This is due the fact of not accepting anything to exist on its own, even conventionally.

3. Unique Way of Refuting the Basic Consciousness

In this Prāsaṅgika tradition that does not accept the intrinsic existence of anything, even conventionally, the basic consciousness is not accepted. This is because causal relationships are completely reasonable even without accepting anything like a basic consciousness. One might wonder if this conflicts with the statements about the basic consciousness in the *Descent to Laṅka*, the *Densely Arrayed*, and the *Sūtra Explaining the Intent.* There is no conflict because in these sūtras, and others that teach the aggregates as truly existent and the existence of a self of persons, as in "Monks, the five aggregates are the burden, and the person is the bearer of this burden";[176] there is a basis in another intention. They are provisional in meaning with a purpose for teaching. The *Introduction to the Middle Way* says:

> Statements that the basic consciousness exists, that persons exist, and
> That only the aggregates exist [708] –

These are for those who
Cannot understand the most profound meaning.[177]

If one wonders what this purpose is, it is for disciples who have become habituated for a long time to wrong views and who are, for the time being, not suitable receptacles for the profound meaning. If they were taught the profound doctrine from the beginning, they would become scared; they would see the Buddha's teaching as like an abyss and turn their backs on it. Thus, there will be great benefit for them if they are first taught things like the basic consciousness as a method to progressively guide them. The *Precious Garland* states:

Saying, "there is no self, nor will it come to be;
There is nothing that is mine, nor that will become mine."
This frightens immature beings.[178]

The *Four Hundred Verses* says:

Whatever people like
Give it to them first.
By this a receptacle for the sacred doctrine
Will not be destroyed.[179]

As for the basis in another intention, the autocommentary on the *Introduction to the Middle Way* says: "Since it permeates the nature of all phenomena, one should know that the term 'basic consciousness' indicates only emptiness."[180] Candrakīrti says that the term "basic consciousness" is taught conventionally, intending the meaning of emptiness. Bhāviveka said that its basis of intention is the mental consciousness; this is different.

As for its explicit invalidation, there is scripture and reasoning. For scriptural invalidation, our teacher himself said that the basic consciousness had another intention. Invalidation by reasoning is like this: If you assert the basic consciousness, then you have to accept that there are no external objects; forms and so on are just appearances from the maturation of predispositions in the basic consciousness. This is not reasonable because of the coextensive presence or absence of the pair of objects and cognitions. Likewise, if you accept the basic consciousness, it is not something that is established by a source of knowledge that investigates the conventional, so it must be posited through a reasoned analysis into its designated object. Thereby, while not wanting to, you are forced to assert something that exists on its own. Moreover, if you accept the basic consciousness, you have to claim that it is the innate observation of the afflictive mind and the view of the transitory collective. Since the *Introduction to the Middle Way* mentions many refutations of the position of those who assert consciousness as what is observed in a view of self, it is said that the basic consciousness is not reasonable here. Bhāviveka said that claiming the basic consciousness is simply the way of asserting a person as the Naiyāyikas do, while merely changing the name. Candrakīrti said this as well in his autocommentary on the *Introduction to the Middle Way.*

The essential point of whether or not the basic consciousness is accepted is, once again, whether or not there is anything accepted that exists on its own. Those who accept the basic consciousness posit it upon seeking out its designated object with reason. Without being satisfied by the person that is merely designated upon the aggregates, they posit the basic consciousness while maintaining that it is necessary for there to be a basis for the signified (*mtshan gzhi*) person that objectively exists. Due to accepting it to exist on its own, they assert the basic consciousness as the basis for the infusion of the predispositions of karma, and maintain that appearances of external objects arise due to the force of the basic consciousness's predispositions [709] whereby they are not able to posit external objects merely conventionally.

Due to the essential point of not accepting anything that exists on its own, even conventionally, Prāsaṅgikas know how to posit a person that is merely designated upon the aggregates, the person itself as the basis for the infusion of karma, and external objects that are just conventionally separate from an internal cognition.

There are two kinds of sūtras: those that teach the basic consciousness and those that do not. The *Mother Sūtras* and texts like the *Buddha-Nature Sūtra* do not teach the basic consciousness. Texts like the *Sūtra Explaining the Intent* do teach it; likewise, the *Ornament of the Mahāyāna Sūtras,* "the two that distinguish,"[181] and the *Compendium of Mahāyāna* teach the basic consciousness and refute external objects. The *Ornament of Manifest Realization* and the *Sublime Continuum* do not speak of the basic consciousness and describe a position that accepts external objects.

Asaṅga did not explain the viewpoint of the *Sublime Continuum* in the tradition of Mind-Only or Svātantrika, but explained it in the tradition of Prāsaṅgika. He cites an Abhidharma text, "The beginningless element is the abode of all phenomena . . .,"[182] as a means of knowing the existence of buddha-nature. This accords with Candrakīrti's description of the basis of intention for the basic consciousness being emptiness. The *Compendium of Mahāyāna* cites this passage to establish the existence of the basic consciousness.[183] When the *Commentary on the Spirit of Awakening* says, "Like a magnet and nearby. . .,"[184] it uses the name "basic consciousness," but it is simply designating the mental consciousness with the term "basic consciousness." It does not teach a basic consciousness that is essentially different from the six collections of consciousness, as is stated in Tsongkhapa's explanation of the *Introduction to the Middle Way*.

Among Mādhyamikas as well, Bhāviveka and Jñānagarbha accept external objects while not accepting the basic consciousness; whereas Kamalaśīla, Śāntarakṣita, Vimuktisena, and Haribhadra have a position that accepts neither the basic consciousness nor external objects. Therefore, whereas accepting the basic consciousness entails not accepting external objects, not accepting the basic consciousness does not entail accepting external objects.

Next, after our text refutes their reply, it shows how self-awareness is refuted by way of a response to a question, stating:

> [IX.16cd-17a] ***If it is said, "They have another existence;***
> ***Their form is that of the mind itself."***
> ***When the mind itself is an illusion***
> ***What is seen by what?***
> ***The protector of the world said . . .***

On this the *Introduction to the Middle Way* says:

> *When there is nothing apprehended nor an apprehender*
> *Yet the nondual entity of the dependent nature exists,*
> *By what is its existence known?*
> *It is not appropriate to say, "It exists without being apprehended."*[185]

Proponents of Mind-Only assert the intrinsic existence of cognition without apprehender-apprehended duality. Yet without being apprehended by a source of knowledge to establish it, it is not reasonable to say that it exists. When asked the question of what source of knowledge there is for knowing this, they respond that knowing this is not apprehending another *object*; it exists because it is apprehended by self-awareness. [710] In response to this, there is a similar teaching on how self-awareness is refuted.

On this topic, I will explain here in four parts the way self-awareness is asserted and the way it is refuted: (1) identifying the position of those who accept self-awareness, (2) the meaning of self-awareness that they establish,

(3) how they establish the existence of self-awareness, and (4) the unique way of refuting self-awareness here.

1. Identifying the Position of Those Who Accept Self-Awareness

Sautrāntikas, proponents of Mind-Only, Śāntarakṣita, father and son [Kamalaśīla], Haribhadra, and others accept self-awareness. Here, the main opponent is a proponent of Mind-Only, as is known from our text in this context. However, it has also been said that some Sautrāntikas following scripture, along with some of the proponents of Mind-Only following the *Yogācāra Grounds* (*Yogācārabhūmi*) do not clearly assert self-awareness.

2. The Meaning of Self-Awareness That They Establish

The *Blaze of Reason* puts forward the position of the opponent, saying:

> Proponents of Mind-Only claim that consciousness appears dualistically: it appears as itself and it appears as an object. Consciousness that appears as an object takes on the representation of an external object that is the object of consciousness that appears as itself.[186]

What "appears as itself" (*rang snang*) is the representation of a subject (*'dzin rnam*) and what "appears as an object" is the representation of an object (*bzung rnam*). The representation of the object, which is the objective form, is explained to be the object for the representation of the subject. The experience of the objective representation by the subjective representation is said to be the meaning of self-awareness. Therefore, self-awareness is the subjective representation alone. It itself is the mere clarity and mere awareness within all object-cognitions (*gzhan rig*). Without depending on any external object, it is oriented only within; all dualistic appearances of subjects and objects are excluded from it.

The way self-awareness is held to arise is as follows. When a visual cognition apprehending blue occurs, on the one hand there is simply the clear awareness of a blue appearance, without an appearance of a subjective representation of the visual cognition that apprehends blue. On the other hand, the subjective representation appears without the objective representation of blue appearing; there is a clear appearance of the experience of the dissolution of the dualistic appearance of the cognized object and the cognizer. For example, it is like when a crystal ball is put on a blue cloth on the ground. On the one hand, there is an aspect of clarity within the crystal that has changed to blue; on the other, there is an aspect of clarity that has not transformed, the self-radiance of the crystal; both simultaneously arise. The former clear awareness is an other object-awareness (*gzhan rig*), or the objective representation. The latter is self-awareness, or the subjective representation. The *Commentary on Epistemology* says regarding the former:

> *Appearing as an object, and the cognition with that –*
> *This is an appearance oriented toward the external.*[187]

And for the latter:

> *The mind that apprehends the mind*
> *Is always oriented inwardly toward itself.*[188]

And,

> *There is no representation of either cognized object or cognizer.*[189]

3. *How They Establish the Existence of Self-Awareness*

[711] Those who assert self-awareness have many arguments for establishing self-awareness. Mainly, the reason of memory is used to establish self-awareness. The *Commentary on Epistemology* says: "Self-awareness is established from memory."[190] The way this is established is as follows. It is not established by saying, "for a visual cognition apprehending blue there is self-awareness" because from the perspective of the opponent, there is no example that has both the property of the evidence and what is to be established.

One might wonder how then it is established. The existence of this experience is established based on evidence: consider a visual cognition apprehending blue; it has an experiencer because there is a cognition that remembers its existence. After a visual cognition sees blue, there is a memory of seeing a blue object. The memory of an object is the result of having experienced an object. The experiencer of the object is an other object-awareness with respect to a visual cognition that sees blue. The memory "I saw it" is a memory of a subject, which is the result of having experienced being a subject. The experiencer of the subject is self-awareness with respect to a visual cognition that sees blue.

If a blue object had not been previously experienced, it would not be possible for a memory of blue to occur. Likewise, if there had not previously been a subjective experience of apprehending blue, it would not be possible to remember a visual cognition apprehending blue. This is what they say to establish self-awareness from the evidence of memory. Based on this evidence, the existence of an experience is established; there are only two options for an experience: a self-experience (*rang myong*) or an other-experience (*gzhan myong*). Since an other-experience is refuted by reason, nothing but a self-experience is reasonable; thereby, this argument establishes the existence of self-experience. Since it is impossible for oneself to appear to oneself as distant and cut-off, self-awareness is established as a self-experience in which dualistic appearances have dissolved.

How an other-experience is negated with reason is stated in the autocommentary on the *Introduction to the Middle Way*. If the experiencer were a different substance [from the cognition of the experience], whether it be the case that the cognition different from the experiencer were to occur simultaneously or be experienced by a later cognition, there would be two problems. Firstly, there would be the problem that the experiencer would fall into an infinite regress: If the experiencer of cognition were of a different substance from the cognition, like a visual cognition apprehending blue, would another experiencer of cognition of a different substance be necessary or not to experience that cognition? If not, then a substantially different experiencer of cognition was not necessary in the first place. If it were necessary, then that cognition would need another, and there would be the problem of an infinite regress.

Secondly, there would be the problem that a later cognition could not convey (*'pho ba*) another object. This is because, if it were the case that the experience of subsequent visual cognitions apprehending blue occurred by way of taking the former cognitions that are their primary causes (*rang gi nyer len du gyur pa*) as their apprehended objects, then it would follow that the subsequent cognitions would not convey any object (like blue) at all. This follows because it is not reasonable to take a distant external object like blue as an object, having relinquished taking the proximate cognition as an object. The *Compendium of Epistemology* says:

> *If experience occurs by another cognition*
> *There is an infinite regress; moreover, memory*
> *Would not convey another object,*
> *Even while it is seen.*[191]

[712] The *Commentary on Epistemology* says:

> *If the former cognition is there,*
> *It would not convey another object.*[192]

One might think, "If both (1) a later visual cognition of blue that discerns a former visual cognition of blue, and (2) the visual cognition of blue that discerns blue arise simultaneously, then there is no problem of not conveying another object."

It is not reasonable for two substantially different visual cognitions of a similar type to simultaneously arise in the continuum of one person. A sūtra says, "The continua of sentient beings' consciousnesses are distinct." This passage does not deny the simultaneous arising of many separate substances of dissimilar types of cognition in the continuum of one person.

4. The Unique Way of Refuting Self-Awareness Here

This section has three parts: (1) refuting what is established, (2) refuting the means of establishment, and (3) the way our system accounts for memory without appealing to self-awareness.

1. Refuting What Is Established

The way the opponents have understood self-awareness based on the previously described analysis is not reasonable. This is because scriptures that refute self-awareness, such as the *Inquiry of Ratnacūda* (*Ratnacūdasūtra*) and the *Descent to Laṅka*, have established that it does not exist. When investigated with reason, too, when objective and subjective representations are made, it is dualistic. Yet when it is held that what is cognized is not at all different from the cognizer, it is impossible for cognition to discern itself, no matter how clear it is, by way of the dissolution of dualistic appearances. For example, no matter how sharp a knife is, it cannot cut itself. No matter how long a finger is, it cannot point to itself. No matter how physically fit a person is, she cannot climb on her own shoulders. No matter how hot a fire is, it cannot burn itself. The cognized and the cognizer, the cut and the cutter, and the touched and the toucher are not established as separate. While not separate, if something were to intrinsically act upon itself, then it would absurdly follow that all agents, actions, and patients would become a singularity. This problem is described in the autocommentary on the *Introduction to the Middle Way*. In the root text it says:

> *Since the agent, patient, and action are not the same,*
> *It is not reasonable for something to apprehend itself.*[193]

Our text here says as well: [IX.17] ***The protector of the world . . .***

2. Refuting the Means of Establishment

It is not reasonable to establish self-awareness through citing memory as evidence. If the evidence of memory that exists on its own is cited, this is not correct evidence for establishing the existence of self-awareness. This is because, just as self-awareness is not established for us, neither is this kind of memory. This kind of proof commits the fallacy of begging the question: what is to be proved is the same as the means of proof. It is like citing as evidence to prove the impermanence of sound that it is apprehended by a visual cognition. [713] The *Introduction to the Middle Way* says:

> *If it is claimed to be proved by a later memory,*
> *Since what is unproven is what to be proven,*
> *There is no means of proof; what is claimed is not established.*[194]

If the evidence of memory is cited based on its mundane, conventional use, it is not a correct reason for establishing the existence of self-awareness. This is because the existence of this kind of memory does not entail the existence of self-awareness. For example, the presence of water does not entail the existence of a water-crystal, and the presence of fire does not entail the existence of a fire-crystal, as was mentioned in the autocommentary on the *Introduction to the Middle Way*.[195]

Thus, citing either of the two kinds of memory as evidence is not a correct reason for establishing self-awareness. The former [memory established on its own] has the shortcoming of not being established; and the latter [memory in its mundane, conventional use] has the shortcoming of no entailment. The evidence of a later memory establishes merely that a previous cognition was experienced; it does not establish self-awareness. This is because, being an experience is undetermined as either a self-experience or an other-experience according to the assertions of both Sautrāntikas and proponents of Mind-Only.

Here in Prāsaṅgika, experience is asserted to exist as merely a nominal designation, yet no self-experience or other-experience is asserted at all. For example, even though nominally designated production is accepted, neither self-production nor production from other is accepted. Also, a lamp is conventionally said to have the nature of luminosity, but it is not asserted to be either self-luminous or other-luminous. Here, self-experience is not accepted. Merely asserting conventionally that "I am aware myself" is not the complete meaning of self-experience; when self-experience is asserted after analyzing experience in terms of either self-experience or other-experience, then it is this kind of self-awareness that is negated in this context here. Other-experience is also nonexistent because if it did exist, there would be the problems mentioned above. Moreover, if other-experience is posited after analysis, it would necessarily be the case that other-experience would exist on its own. If that were the case, since experience and memory would be intrinsically other, then there would be the problem that it would not be possible to have a later memory like "I saw it before."

3. The Way Our System Accounts for Memory without Appealing to Self-Awareness

This section has two parts: (1) the actual explanation and (2) an appended presentation of sources of knowledge.

1. Actual Explanation

The reasoning from our text here is stated like this:

> [IX.23ab] ***"If there is no self-awareness***
> ***How is memory possible?"***

The meaning of this is that the opponent says, "It absurdly follows that the memory, 'I saw blue,' is not possible because there is no self-awareness." The response to this *reductio* shows that there is no entailment for either its consequence or its contraposition in a probative argument. Thus, our text here and the *Introduction to the Middle Way* both refute self-awareness, not only ultimately, but conventionally as well. The autocommentary on the *Introduction to the Middle Way* states: "Even in terms of mundane convention, memory that is a result of self-awareness is [714] impossible."[196]

As for the way memory actually occurs:

> [IX.23cd] ***Connected with the experience of an object,***
> ***There is memory, like poison from a rat.***

When a memory of an object previously experienced occurs later, it is not that the subjective cognition is excluded and only the object is remembered. Rather, through the connection or conjunction of an object and a subjective cognition, there is a memory with its dualistic appearance, "I saw this before." For example, when a rat bites someone in the winter and injects poison, the bite is experienced but not the poison. Later, when thunder is heard [in the spring] and the poison takes effect, there occurs the memory that "I was poisoned when I was bitten before." Thus, one does not experience being poisoned when the poison was injected, yet one remembers being poisoned when remembering the bite later. Likewise, during a previous experience of an object, the subject does not experience itself. Nevertheless, through the influence of a later memory of an object, it makes sense that the subject is remembered as well.

The way that memory occurs without self-awareness is stated in the *Introduction to the Middle Way* as well:

> *Since what experienced an object*
> *Is not different from what recalls it for me,*
> *There is the memory "I saw this."*
> *This too is the way of mundane convention.*[197]

Here is what this means: Even without self-awareness as an experiencer of an apprehension of blue, there is no conflict in the occurrence of a memory that "I previously saw blue." This is because the visual cognition that previously apprehended blue and the later memory (the memory of the visual cognition apprehending blue) are not intrinsically different; even for the innate mundane mind it is impossible for these two to be held as distinct. Also, the apprehender of blue is not the self, so that apprehension and the person who is the seer of blue are in conflict; nevertheless, based on my seeing by means of apprehending blue, we can also posit that "I saw blue." Furthermore, seeing and memory are not possible according to your reasoning; yet in mere mundane convention without investigation or analysis, the blue object apprehended as blue and the blue object remembered are the same.

As for the opponent's position, it does not make sense for a later memory of apprehending blue to remember the subject and object of a previous apprehension of blue, because the later memory and the cognition of the previous experience of the object are intrinsically different. For example, they are like the later cognitions of Maitreya not remembering a previous object experienced by Upagupta. As the *Introduction to the Middle Way* says:

> *This kind of remembering is not appropriate for memory because*
> *It is different, as if it occured in the continuum of one who did not cognize it.*[198]

The opponent might respond that the example does not apply here because there is a difference between the same continuum and distinct continua. The *Introduction to the Middle Way* says: "This argument undermines qualifications as well"[199] because of being established on their own as other. This argument also undermines the qualification of being a single continuum. [715] Previously, the phenomena supported by Maitreya and Upagupta were said to be not included in one continuum because they are different; the argument showing that it is not reasonable for what is established on its own to be a single continuum has already been explained, and it applies to memory as well.

Furthermore, arguments refuting self-awareness found in texts like the seventh chapter of the *Fundamental Verses of the Middle Way*, *Dispelling Disputes*, and the *Finely Woven* are similar to the ones stated in our text here.[200] The *Essence of Madhyamaka* (*Madhyamakahṛdaya*) and the autocommentary on *Distinguishing the Two Truths* also demonstrate ways of refuting self-awareness.[201] The *Introduction to the Middle Way* shows four ways of refuting it, with arguments that (1) it is begging the question, what is to be established is not different from the means of establishing it; (2) even with an existent self-awareness, it is impossible to remember what is intrinsically other; (3) action, agent, and patient would be one; and (4) memory occurs even without self-awareness. All these have been cited above.

One might ask, "Without self-awareness, even conventionally, how does your Prāsaṅgika system account for something like a perception that apprehends blue?"

Our account is as follows: By the power of apprehending a blue object, a visual perception apprehending blue does not need to be conjoined with another source of knowledge; the visual cognition itself can directly induce a memory of the apprehension of blue. This is because the memory eliminates superimpositions of both the blue not existing and the visual cognition apprehending blue not existing. Also, it is because memory itself is a source of knowledge for the existence of a visual cognition apprehending blue. Tsongkhapa's explanation of the *Introduction to the Middle Way* mentions additional reasons, too.

In order to establish an intrinsically existent, dependent nature consciousness, the opponents posit self-awareness, having analyzed a single consciousness into two parts of self-experience and other-experience. This is due to the fact that they accept something that exists on its own. Here in Prāsaṅgika, it is accepted that objects and subjects are mutually confirming; there is no need for a separate source of knowledge that investigates the subject apart from that which investigates objects. Thus, self-awareness is not accepted and this is due to the fact of not accepting anything that exists on its own, even conventionally.

2 Appended Presentation of Sources of Knowledge

What follows is a brief discussion of the framework of epistemology in the Prāsaṅgika system. The definition of a source of knowledge is a cognition that is non-deceptive regarding the object of its mode of apprehension. Non-deceptive in this context is posited based on the way the warranted object exists in accord with the way it is discerned by a source of knowledge; this is different from the way all conventional phenomena are said to be deceptive. The etymology here is different from others, too: it is a source of knowledge because it is a reliable warrant (*rab tu 'jal*).

There is a fourfold division of sources of knowledge: (1) perception, (2) inference, (3) testimony, and (4) analogy. The number of sources of knowledge is posited based on the warranted objects, and there are determined to be four warranted objects. They are what is evident and what is remote, and within remote objects, there are what is slightly remote, what is extremely remote, and remote phenomena [716] that are like an example. Although they are divided into four, there is a determined number of two sources of knowledge, perception and inference, because the latter two are subsumed within inference. For this reason, there are four sources of knowledge in *Clear Words*, as there are in the root text and commentary on *Dispelling Disputes*, whereas two sources of knowledge are described in the commentary on the *Four Hundred Verses*.[202]

The essence of a perceptual source of knowledge is the non-deceptive cognition of an evident warranted object that apprehends its object without relying on a sign. There is a twofold division of perceptual sources of knowledge: (1) a perceptual source of knowledge that is based on the dominant condition that is a sense-faculty with material form and (2) a perceptual source of knowledge that is based on the dominant cognition that is the mental faculty. The latter has a twofold subdivision: (1) mental perception that just comes from the dominant condition of the mental faculty without relying on the unity of calm abiding and special insight, and (2) yogic perception that comes from the dominant condition relying on the unity of calm abiding and special insight. Thereby, there are three types of perceptual sources of knowledge: sense perception, like a visual apprehension of blue; mental perception, like the memory of blue that arises after a visual cognition of blue; and yogic perception, like the cognition that directly realizes any of the subtle or coarse types of selflessness. It has already been explained that self-awareness is not accepted as a perceptual source of knowledge.

In general, a yogic perception is necessarily a mental perception, but it need not be the mental perception that is within the threefold division of perception because these two are incompatible.[203] Mental perception that experiences feelings associated with mental cognition, such as pleasure and pain, does not necessarily appear as an inward-looking dissolution of dualistic appearance; it is said that it appears to the mind as a separate experienced and experiencer, so it is not similar to self-awareness.

The essence of an inferential source of knowledge is the non-deceptive cognition of a remote warranted object that apprehends its object based directly on evidence or a reason. There is a threefold division of inference: (1) inference by the power of fact (*dngos stobs*), like an inference that realizes emptiness; (2) trustworthy inference, such as an inference that realizes the non-deceptive meaning of a scripture, like "enjoyments come from generosity and happiness from discipline," by means of scriptural evidence that is pure in terms of the threefold criteria of analysis;[204] and (3) analogical inference, such as an inference that a gayal is similar to a cow. Furthermore, there are others, such as the twofold division of inferential sources of knowledge: those that are based on a consequence and those that are based on a reason with the three modes complete.

Here in Prāsaṅgika, it is not accepted that a source of knowledge has to be a newly non-deceptive cognition, nor is it accepted that perception has to be nonconceptual. The framework for epistemology here has a lot of differences from others, such as memory and subsequent cognitions (*bcad shes*) being accepted as perceptual sources of knowledge, and a source of knowledge and a distorted cognition being accepted as non-contradictory.

Also, in the context of the verse, [IX.27c] ***If you say, "Cyclic existence is based on real entities. . . ,"*** in Gyeltsapjé's commentary and notes in the context of the opponent's disputation, it is said that "this debate comes from the *Anthology of Training*."[205] [717] It also says that "the reason is also stated in the *Anthology of Training*"[206] in the context of the response. One might wonder how it is spoken of in the *Anthology of Training*. The *Anthology of Training* itself says:

> "How is the conventional possible without a basis?" How is it not possible? It is like the way a nonexistent tree trunk is confused for a person. That with which persons are confused is said to be emptiness; how does the tree trunk ultimately exist? There is no root to any phenomenon because actually, a root is not reasonable. This is also spoken in the noble *Vimalakīrti Sūtra* (*Vimalakīrtinirdeśa*):
>
> "What is the root of the imagination of the unreal?" The root of the imagination of the unreal is distorted identification. "What is the root of distorted identification?" The root of distorted identification is baseless. "What is the root of the baseless?" Mañjuśrī, what

> is there to root the baseless? All phenomena abide upon the root of the baseless.[207]

The opponent argues about the baseless, saying, "What is unreal, distortions like cyclic existence, must have a real basis of distortion, a real root or basis—as in the case when a log is confused for a person: there is a real log." In response, it is said: "How is it not possible?" The meaning here is that it is possible for distortion to arise even without a real basis of distortion—as in the case of confusing an unreal log for a person. All phenomena are said to be emptiness, so how is a tree trunk established as real? All phenomena are rootless because there is no truly existent root. This reason is also established by the sūtra passage: "This is also spoken in the noble [*Vimalakīrti Sūtra*]."

3. Responding to the Objection That the Madhyamaka Path Is Pointless
[IX.30a] ***"Even if it is understood to be illusory . . . ,"*** and [IX.32a] ***By habituation to the predisposition for emptiness . . . .*** The latter passage shows the way of cultivation having ascertained the view. Through cultivation in this way, how the Mahāyāna path is progressively traversed through habituation with the realization of emptiness is like this: With inspired conduct (*mos spyod*), when a stable cultivation of the spirit of awakening is attained, this is said to be the path of accumulation (*tshogs lam*). The criterion for stability is that it is upheld from its onset until the accumulations are gathered for three countless eons. Stablity has four characteristics, as stated in the *Compendium of Mahāyāna*:

> *When endowed with goodness, powerful prayers,*
> *A stable mind, and the distinctive way,*
> *The bodhisattva fully initiates the endeavor*
> *For three countless eons.*[208]

The *Bodhisattva Grounds* states that the three countless eons [718] begin with inspired conduct. Its beginning is also said to be the path of accumulation. In terms of a bodhisattva with a determined heritage (*rigs nges*), the path of joining (*sbyor lam*) is understood to be from the time of a newly attained special insight that realizes emptiness. This is distinguished into four stages, such as "warmth"; these are divisions of the stages in which the constructs of dualistic appearances fade away in meditative equipoise on emptiness.

On the sublime path of Mahāyāna, the essence of the ground of the ultimate spirit of awakening is the uncontaminated gnosis that directly realizes emptiness in a sublime being's continuum that is embraced by a special method. There is a tenfold division of the grounds, such as Supreme Joy. Their essence is uncontaminated gnosis. Their accompaniment is great compassion, and being held by the spirit of awakening. They are called "grounds" because they support the many qualities that they are supporting. The meaning of "contaminated" (*zag bcas*) and "uncontaminated" (*zag med*) here is understood in terms of whether or not it is impaired by ignorance that apprehends true existence, or any of its predispositions.

There is no difference in the way the basic nature is realized by the gnosis of meditative equipoise for bodhisattvas on the ten grounds. Therefore, there are no divisions made in terms of a distinct essence. The *Sūtra on the Ten Grounds* says:

> *In the way that a trail of a bird through space*
> *Cannot be expressed by the wise, nor is seen by them,*
> *Likewise, the grounds of the bodhisattvas cannot be expressed,*
> *So how could they be heard?*[209]

Nevertheless, there is said to be a tenfold division based on the distinctions in postmeditation in terms of supporting qualities. There are four distinctions: (1) the distinction of expanding the number of qualities, such as the attainment of twelve hundred qualities on the first ground, etc.; (2) the distinction of perfect power, in terms of the power of purification increasing from the earlier to the later grounds, and the quality of expanding the power by traversing further and further on the path; (3) the distinction of the exceptional transcendent perfections, such as the attainment of the transcendent perfection of generosity on the first ground. Transcendent perfection means "gone to the other side"; the words suggest that it only applies to the stage of a buddha, not the path of training. Yet "gone to the other side by this" applies to the action; it genuinely refers to the ten transcendent perfections during the path of training as well. (4) The distinction of the way of taking mature birth, as for instance, most of the ones who take birth as kings in the world are first-ground bodhisattvas. This is just a brief description; extensive details of the common and unique frameworks of the grounds and paths should be known elsewhere.

Next, [IX.34] ***When entities and non-entities . . .*** This shows the pacification of all constructs from the perspective of the vision of a sublime being's meditative equipoise. Here and in a later [719] verse, [IX.38] ***"By making offerings to what lacks mind . . . ,"*** and others, such as in the *Introduction to the*

Middle Way: "The mind stops, there is actualization through the body,"[210] and in the autocommentary, "Since there is complete and perfect awakening, the movements of mind and mental states completely cease";[211] many different claims are made based on these passages: some claim that there is no gnosis in a sublime being's meditative equipoise, and that it has no object. Some claim that at the stage of a buddha, along with mind and mental states there is not even the movement of gnosis; and that a buddha's gnosis has no object. Nevertheless, according to the viewpoint of Tsongkhapa's explanation of the *Introduction to the Middle Way*, if the buddha's gnosis had no object, then it would absurdly follow that the buddha's gnosis is not a subject. Also, it would be unreasonable to say that there are four or two gnoses by which objects are known. Also, it would not be reasonable to say that since cognitions and objects are posited relationally, they are both equally existent or equally nonexistent. Also, if there were no mind, mental state, or gnosis whatsoever for a buddha, there would be the problems that there would not be many types of meditative stabilizations, the spirit of awakening, love, or compassion in the continuum of a buddha's mind; and there would be no gnosis with the ten powers, and so forth.

Moreover, Nāgārjuna said: "Unequalled gnosis is inconceivable."[212] Also, the hero [Mātṛceṭa] said: "Only your gnosis encompasses all objects of knowledge."[213] The *Introduction to the Middle Way* states: "Omniscient gnosis is held to have the character of perception."[214] Our text here says: [V.31ab] ***The buddhas and bodhisattvas have completely unimpeded vision.*** Many scriptures state that a buddha has gnosis, that this gnosis has an object, that this gnosis is inconceivable, that each aspect of gnosis encompasses all objects of knowledge, that it is direct vision, and that it is unimpeded vision. Furthermore, *Praise to the Basic Field of Reality* says:

> *When fireproof clothes that are soiled with lots of stains*
> *Are put into a fire, the stains are burned but not the clothes.*
> *Likewise, when the mind of luminous clarity is stained from attachment,*
> *The fire of gnosis burns the stains, but not the luminous clarity.*[215]

When stained, mineral-treated clothes are put into a fire, the stains are burned but not the clothes. Likewise, the fire of gnosis burns the stains of mind, making them nonexistent, yet the luminous clarity of mind is not burned to nonexistence. The reason for this is that even though the mind and the stains are co-emergent from the beginning, the mind is naturally luminous and clear, while the stains are adventitious without penetrating the nature of mind; they are removable. It is said to be like "the element of water, gold, and space,"[216] as pollutants [720] are removable from water, etc. Otherwise, if you accept that when the stains of mind are eliminated, the mind is eliminated, too, then there is no meaning whatsoever in the statement that "the mind is naturally luminous and clear while the stains are adventitious." Some other schools accept this, and it is said to be difficult to draw the distinction.

The previous passages showing that a buddha's gnosis does not have an object, and most of the arguments for these types of claims, are stated merely in terms of the way that an object is cognized. Each of the gnoses that knows what is and whatever there is sees all objects of knowledge. Nevertheless, from the perspective of knowing what is, the gnosis that knows what is does not see whatever there is. Also, from the perspective of knowing whatever there is, the gnosis that knows whatever there is does not see what is. This is said to be the meaning.

The meaning of the cessation of all mind and mental states at the stage of a buddha is that there is no mind or mental states that are conceptual. *Clear Words* says: "Conceptuality is the movement of mind. Since it is free from this, reality is nonconceptual."[217] It explains this, citing a sūtra that says: "That which does not have the movements of mind . . . ."[218] Also, the *Introduction to the Middle Way* says: "Without concepts, until the end of existence you . . . ."[219] In the autocommentary it frequently says that the meaning of the cessation of mind is the cessation of concepts. It also describes gnosis and wisdom that is free from the eye disease of ignorance. Nāgārjuna says:

> *The mind that has eliminated concepts*
> *Is liberated without concepts;*
> *Since cyclic existence is just a concept*
> *Infused with concepts.*[220]

He proclaims the elimination of concepts and the existence of the nonconceptual mind. Also, in the "Collection of Praises," there is a lot of praise in terms of omniscient gnosis and the domain of gnosis's vision.

Next, [IX.35] ***A wish-fulfilling gem and a wish-granting tree*** . . . This is the framework of the result. By practicing the Mahāyāna path to completion, progressively traversing from the ground of inspired conduct to the tenth bodhisattva ground, the effect of the two accumulations is the attainment of the two embodiments of buddhahood that perfect the twofold benefit. The *Precious Garland* says:

> *The Form Bodies of the Buddhas*
> *Arise here from the accumulation of merit;*
> *The Truth Body, in brief, O King,*
> *Is born from the accumulation of gnosis.*[221]

How this unexcelled state is actualized is like this: At the end of the continuum on the tenth ground, by engaging the suchness of reality on the uninterrupted path (*bar chad med lam*), which is the direct antidote for the subtle cognitive obscurations, the subtle, dualistic appearances, without interrupting, become like water placed in water. In the second instant of this, when the path of liberation (*rnam grol lam*) arises, [721] while in meditative equipoise that knows all phenomena as they are without interruptions by subtle dualistic appearances, the entirety of qualities of whatever phenomena exist are known like a fresh myrobalan placed in the palm of the hand. At the time of this direct vision, the Truth Body is actualized and one is called a complete and perfect buddha.

The way this is actualized in terms of the four embodiments of buddhahood is as follows: In the second instant of the uninterrupted path at the end of the continuum, when the path of liberation is actualized, there is the gnosis of the single essence of the gnosis of meditative equipoise and postmeditation, which becomes the Truth Body. The basic nature of the uninterrupted path itself is free from all stains, which becomes the Essential Body (*ngo bo nyid sku*). The subsequent body of similar type to the body ornamented with the major and minor marks at the end of the continuum becomes the Enjoyment Body (*longs sku*). At that time, infinite Emanation Bodies (*sprul sku*) are revealed in limitless fields, without conceptuality. This is the simultaneous actualization of the four embodiments of buddhahood.

The essence of the four embodiments of buddhahood is explained as follows: The Essential Body consists of both aspects of the purity of the basic field (*dbyings*) at the stage of a buddha: (1) the natural purity, which is pure of the pains of true existence from the beginning, and (2) the purity of the adventitious, which is the adventitious stains made pure through an antidote. The Gnosis Truth Body (*ye shes chos sku*) is the consummate vision in relation to objects of knowledge—what is and whatever there is. When divided, there are many, such as five gnoses. The Enjoyment Body is the incessant displays of body, the incessant expressions of speech, and the incessant activities of mind. All these are without effort. While it appears in a diversity of bodies due to the influence of disciples, it does not exist in diversity. It is explained in the *Sublime Continuum* to have these five qualities.[222]

An Emanation Body is the continuous activity for the benefit of others through infinite displays in accord with the continua of disciples, which is the result of the great blessings of previous aspirations. There is a threefold division of Emanation Bodies: (1) artwork Emanation Bodies (2) born Emanation Bodies, and (3) supreme Emanation Bodies.

The qualities of the three mysteries of the buddhas, who have the identity of these four embodiments, are inconceivable and inexpressible. Through enlightened activity that is spontaneously present and unceasing, they do not rely on concepts or efforts for as long as existence remains. Like a wish-fulfilling gem or a wish-granting tree, they completely fulfill the hopes of disciples in accordance with their fortunes. This has been merely a partial explanation; one should know from elsewhere the extensive details of the embodiments of buddhahood, gnoses, qualities, and enlightened activities.

Next, [IX.38] ***"By making offerings to what lacks mind..."*** Even though there is no entailment in the reply to the objection, it is a reply that says it is true that there is no mind that is conceptual, not a reply [722] that says that it is true that there is no mind. Even though the buddhas do not have concepts of wishing to accept offerings, the results of merit appear. It says so in the *Heap of Flowers Dhāraṇī* (*Puṣpakūṭadhāraṇī*):

> Siṃhavikrīḍita, whether a Tathāgata is present, or has completely passed beyond suffering, all offerings to them bring a complete cessation of suffering in one among three vehicles. Siṃhavikrīḍita, one sees a Tathāgata and becomes completely inspired, and with an inspired mind gives belongings, clothes, food, bedding, medicine, material things, and comforts—all this is done with respect, offering, and service. Know that the maturation is equal for one who offers to a stūpa with relics of only a mustard seed of a Tathāgata. There are no distinctions or divisions in offerings to a Tathāgata.[223]

The *Bodhisattva Basket* (*Bodhisattvapiṭaka*) also states:

> *One who offers to a residing Tathāgata, and*
> *One who offers to a relic of*
> *A Tathāgata who has passed away,*
> *What is only the size of a mustard seed,*
> *Will be seen to become a Tathāgata.*
> *One who offers to a residing Tathāgata, and*

One who offers to a relic of
A Tathāgata who has passed away,
What is only the size of a mustard seed,
Are equal in mind and equal in effect.[224]

The *Anthology of Training* states this extensively, citing texts like the *Lotus Sūtra.*

2. Necessity of Realizing Emptiness Even for Those Wishing for Only Liberation

This section is explained in two parts: (1) the dispute about whether or not it is absolutely necessary to realize emptiness just to become liberated, and (2) a response to this.

1. Dispute about Whether or Not It Is Absolutely Necessary to Realize Emptiness Just to Become Liberated

[IX.40ab] ***"By seeing the [four] truths one is liberated;***
What is the point of seeing emptiness?"

The meaning of this is that an opponent says, "One becomes an Arhat liberated from cyclic existence through habituation to the direct vision of the four truths, qualified by the sixteen coarse aspects such as impermanence. So what is the point [723] of seeing emptiness?"

Those who say this believe that it is not necessary to realize the subtle emptiness to attain just liberation. Furthermore, they believe that it is not necessary to realize this even to become a buddha. The main opponents here are some of those in the Disciple schools who believe that the Mahāyāna Sūtras that teach emptiness are not the Word of the Buddha.

Alternatively, there are those who accept the Mahāyāna Sūtras that teach emptiness as the Word of the Buddha, and who also accept that it is necessary to realize emptiness to become a buddha. Nevertheless, they do not accept that it is absolutely necessary to realize the subtle emptiness in order to attain just liberation. This is the position of the Svātantrikas and below, who also can be included among the opponents here. Here it is emphatically established for them that the path that realizes all phenomena as not intrinsically existent is indispensible for just liberation.

2. Response to This Dispute

[IX.40cd] ***Since the scriptures say that***
Without this path there is no awakening.

Within this set of scriptures, this is the clearest source establishing that Disciples realize the subtle selflessness of phenomena. This has already been stated in brief in Tsongkhapa's commentary on the *Fundamental Verses of the Middle Way*.[225] Here, how it is established that Disciples and Self-Realized Ones realize the selflessness of phenomena will be explained as it is stated in Candrakīrti's *Clear Words* and in his commentary on the *Introduction to the Middle Way*. This explanation has three sections: (1) a general demonstration that this is realized based on scripture and reasoning, (2) a specific explanation of the sources that proclaim this, and (3) resolving disputes regarding this explanation.

1. General Demonstration Based in Scripture and Reasoning That This Is Realized

Citing the *Sūtra on the Ten Grounds*, the autocommentary on the *Introduction to the Middle Way* says:

> Hey, children of the Victors! For example, a son who is born in the ruling caste and is the son of the king has the king's name. By merely being born he has the king's blessing that outshines the entire host of ministers, but this is not due to his mental power of discrimination. When he comes of age, his developed mental powers completely surpass all the activities of the ministers. Hey, children of the Victors! Likewise, this is the case for bodhisattvas. As soon as they generate the spirit of awakening, the immensity of their superior intention outshines all the Disciples and Self-Realized Ones. Yet this is not due to their mental powers of discrimination. When bodhisattvas reside on the seventh ground, by abiding in the greatness of the knowledge of their domain, they completely surpass all the activities of the Disciples and Self-Realized Ones.[226]

[724] The way the glorious Candrakīrti explains this passage is as follows: The autocommentary on the *Introduction to the Middle Way* says: "This sūtra states that Disciples and Self-Realized Ones also understand that all phenomena lack intrinsic nature. This is certainly clear."[227] Moreover, in what is called "the

first generation of the spirit of awakening," it is the initial context because of being the first generation of the ultimate spirit of awakening.[228] In this context, bodhisattvas can outshine those with the heritage of Disciples or Self-Realized Ones through the power of their superior intention. Nevertheless, they are not able to outshine them by their mental powers until they reach the seventh ground. Bodhisattvas residing on the sixth ground and below do not abide in the greatness of knowledge of their domain by means of directly engaging and arising in each moment within the authentic limit of cessation. From the seventh ground they achieve the distinctive qualities of being able to do this, so it is said in this sūtra that they can then outshine Arhats who are Disciples and Self-Realized Ones by means of their mental powers.

This clearly shows that the Disciples and Self-Realized Ones realize the selflessness of phenomena. Otherwise, why wouldn't bodhisattvas on the first ground be able to outshine the Disciples and Self-Realized Ones by their mental powers? It is intended for those who might think that it is because bodhisattvas on the first ground directly realize the selflessness of phenomena, whereas Arhats who are Disciples and Self-Realized Ones do not.

There are three arguments and seven scriptural passages that invalidate the position that Arhats who are Disciples or Self-Realized Ones do not realize the selflessness of phenomena. Three arguments are stated in the autocommentary on the *Introduction to the Middle Way*. As for the first argument, the text states:

> If this were not the case, they would not have the complete knowledge that entities lack intrinsic nature. Like those who are free from mundane attachments, they would also be outshined by the mental discernment of bodhisattvas who initially generated the spirit of awakening.[229]

This means that it would absurdly follow that the mental power of realizing emptiness by the first-ground bodhisattvas would outshine Arhats who are Disciples or Self-Realized Ones because they would lack the wisdom that realizes that entities lack intrinsic nature. For example, they would be like sages from the sphere of Nothing Whatsoever (*ci yang med*) on down, who are free from manifest attachments based on having the form of a coarse peace from a mundane path. These kinds of sages lack the wisdom that realizes the lack of intrinsic nature, so they are used as examples for those who are outshined by first-ground bodhisattvas. If you accept this, then [the claim that they do not realize the selflessness of phenomena] contradicts the sūtra passage.

As for the second argument, it says in the autocommentary: "They would not have eliminated all the latencies (*phra rgyas*) for action in the three realms, like non-Buddhists."[230] This means that it would absurdly follow [725] that Arhats who are Disciples or Self-Realized Ones would not have eliminated all the latencies for the three realms because they would lack the wisdom that directly realizes emptiness, like a non-Buddhist sage.

As for the third argument, the autocommentary says: "Due to a distorted observation of the essence of things like material forms, even the selflessness of persons would not be realized because the aggregates are observed, which is the cause for designating a self."[231] This means that it would absurdly follow that Arhats who are Disciples and Self-Realized Ones would not genuinely realize the selflessness of persons because they have not undermined its distorted conceived object, which is the conception of the aggregates (the basis of designation for the person) as truly existent. Without undermining the conceived object of the aggregates (the basis for designation) apprehended as truly existent, there is the apprehension that they truly exist. As long as this is the case, the conceived object of the apprehension of a person (the designated phenomenon) as truly existent cannot be undermined.

From among these three aforementioned arguments, there is an objection and a reply regarding the meaning of the second argument. First, for an objection raised by Svātantrikas and below: "It is not reasonable to say that someone who does not realize emptiness, like a non-Buddhist sage, is not able to eliminate the latencies for the three realms. This is because even without realizing emptiness, one can completely eliminate the latencies for the three realms along with their potentials based on habituating to the direct realization of the selflessness that is the emptiness of a person existing as a self-subsisting substance. This kind of selflessness is ascertained by study and contemplation; it becomes a direct realization by habituating to it for a long time. This is established through reason by way of yogic perception. The path of seeing that directly realizes this kind of selflessness is able to eliminate the potentials for the imputed afflictive obscurations; and the path of meditation that habituates to the direct realization of this can eliminate the potentials for the innate afflictive obscurations."

Secondly, the reply: Even without achieving the view of emptiness, there is yogic perception that newly and directly sees the selflessness of persons that is the emptiness of a self-subsisting, substantial existence. This occurs through habituating to the sixteen aspects [of the four truths] such as impermanence, as described in the two Abhidharma texts, that are ascertained by a source of knowledge. Also, there is a path of habituating to this vision. Nevertheless, these two paths, respectively, are not accepted as the path of seeing and the transcendent path of meditation. This is because these two paths can eliminate merely the manifest coarse latencies that are imputed and innate, as described in the Abhidharma, yet they cannot eliminate any of the potentials for what is to be removed on the path of seeing or the path of meditation. Therefore, it is reasonable here to describe as provisional in meaning the sūtras that teach these kinds of paths as the paths of seeing and meditation, as well as the sūtras that claim that all the potentials for both of these things to be removed are thereby eliminated, whereby there is attainment up to an Arhat. [726] For example, there are sūtras that claim that the ten grounds and the three later paths are traversed based on ascertaining by a source of knowledge the emptiness that negates an apprehended and apprehender as distinct substances, and by habituating to this. The proponents of Mind-Only accept them as definitive in meaning, but Mādhyamikas explain them as provisional in meaning.

The path that realizes the emptiness of the person existing as a self-subsisting substance is not able to eliminate any potentials for the afflictions. Yet it can stop some of the manifest afflictions that are described in the two Abhidharma texts. If a mundane path shared with the non-Buddhists that has the form of a coarse peace can stop some of the manifest afflictions below the sphere of Nothing Whatsoever, then it is needless to mention that a path that realizes this kind of coarse selflessness of persons can eliminate some of the manifest afflictions described in the Abhidharma. Nevertheless, in this Prāsaṅgika system, to apprehend true existence is said to be an afflictive obscuration. Thus, this kind of path cannot eliminate the ignorance that apprehends true existence, nor through its influence can even the mere manifest afflictions that are beliefs or the unique afflictions that are not beliefs be eliminated. This is because it is necessary to realize emptiness to eliminate them.

Moreover, there is a qualitative distinction between (1) a path that has the form of a coarse peace and (2) a path that realizes the emptiness of a person existing as a self-subsisting substance. This is because there is a difference between these two in terms of whether or not they are able to eliminate the manifest afflictions at the summit of existence as described in the Abhidharma; and there is a difference in terms of whether or not they can eliminate the manifest apprehension of a person held to exist as a self-subsisting substance.

Also, the meaning of the third argument shows that there can be no complete realization of the selflessness of persons until the apprehension of the true existence of the conceived object (the aggregates that are the basis for designation of the person) is undermined. Also, it shows that to completely realize the selflessness of persons entails that the conceived object of the apprehension of a self of phenomena be undermined. Yet it does not state that realizing the selflessness of persons entails realizing the selflessness of phenomena. This is because, in the process of the arising of the twofold apprehension of self, the apprehension of a self of phenomena produces the apprehension of a self of person. Even so, when engaging the reality of selflessness, first the person is realized to lack intrinsic nature, then one must later realize that phenomena like the aggregates lack intrinsic nature. The *King of Meditative Stabilizations* states:

> *In the way that you identify the self,*
> *Train the mind in knowing all cognitions that way.*[232]

And in the *Condensed Perfection of Wisdom*:

> *Know all beings in the way you know the self;*
> *Know all phenomena in the way you know all beings.*[233]

And in the *Precious Garland*:

> *Since beings are a collection of six elements,*
> *They are not real;*
> *Likewise, since each of the elements is a collection,*
> *They are not real either.*[234]

It first [727] shows that beings are not actually real. Later, it is ascertained that their bases of designation are not real either. There is no difference in terms of the subtlety of the selflessness that is to be ascertained with respect to persons and phenomena. However, there is a difference between the ease of realizing them due to the essential point of the qualified basis: it is easy to ascertain with respect to a person, but it is hard to ascertain with respect to the aggregates that are the basis of the person. For example, there is no difference in subtlety between the emptiness that is the lack of true existence of a sprout and a reflection; yet there is a difference in the ease of realizing their emptiness. For this reason, a reflection is used to establish a sprout as not truly existent, as a concordant example. There are many different ways of explaining this point.

In our text here, the selflessness of persons is ascertained first, and after this the selflessness of phenomena is ascertained. It mainly shows the process of engaging selflessness. The *Fundamental Verses of the Middle Way* states:

The view of one entity
Is the view of all of them.[235]

And the *Four Hundred Verses* says:

The one who sees the reality of one entity
Sees the reality of all entities.[236]

It says that to realize the mode of existence of one phenomenon is necessarily to realize the mode of existence of all other phenomena. When the lack of true existence with respect to one phenomenon is ascertained by a source of knowledge, by merely turning the mind to the status of true existence of another phenomenon, one can ascertain it to lack true existence without depending on setting forth another reason to establish this. This is the meaning; it does not mean that when you realize the selflessness of persons that you necessarily realize the selflessness of phenomena.

2. Specific Explanation of the Sources That Proclaim This

This section has three parts: (1) Mahāyāna Sūtras that proclaim this, (2) Mahāyāna treatises that proclaim this, and (3) Hīnayāna Sūtras that proclaim this.

1. Mahāyāna Sūtras That Proclaim This

The *Sūtra Teaching the Stable Superior Intention* (*Sthirādhyāśayasūtra*) states:

> "For example, there is a person who becomes desirous when he sees a woman conjured by a magician when the magician's music is played. As his mind is seduced by desire, his companions get anxious and worried. Getting up off their seats and going to him, they tell him to direct his mind to the ugliness of that woman, to direct his mind to the impermanence, suffering, emptiness, and selflessness of the woman. Noble child, what do you think: does such a person engage in what is correct or in what is mistaken?"
>
> "I will tell you, Blessed One. Toward a nonexistent woman, a person who makes efforts to direct his mind to her ugliness, impermanence, emptiness, and selflessness is mistaken."
>
> The Blessed One [728] spoke, "Noble child, any monks, nuns, laymen, or laywomen who, toward unborn and unarisen phenomena, direct their minds to impermanence, suffering, emptiness, and selflessness should also be viewed this way. Do not say, 'I cultivate the path of these foolish people,' for they engage in what is mistaken."[237]

This passage shows that sublime Disciples and Self-Realized Ones realize the selflessness of phenomena. It says that one cannot abandon attachment to the illusion of a woman when that woman is apprehended to be real, and the mind is directed to her impermanence and so on, as this is mistaken. Likewise, meditating on things like impermanence while fixating on truly existent aggregates is also mistaken. It is not cultivating the path to liberation; one cannot eliminate the potentials for the afflictions based on this.

Furthermore, the *Sūtra on the Fist of Concentration* states: "Mañjuśrī, due to not correctly seeing the noble truths, sentient beings with their minds distorted by the four distortions do not pass beyond this mistake that is cyclic existence."[238] It says that one will not be liberated due to apprehending the four truths as truly existent, no matter how much one meditates. Moreover, without knowing that the four truths lack intrinsic nature, based on meditating on merely a coarse selflessness of persons and having removed some manifest afflictions, some people think that they have become Arhats. It is said that when they die, they see that they take birth through the power of afflictions, and come to doubt the buddha; thereby, some of these beings even fall into the great hell. That sūtra says:

> They think thus, "I am free from all suffering!" Or, later at the time of Nothing Whatseover, they think, "I know that I have become an Arhat!" When they die, they see their birth and come to be suspicious, and doubt the awakening of the buddha. Succumbing to doubt when they die, they fall into the great hell.[239]

In agreement with these passages, our text says:

> [IX.45cd] ***Even without afflictions***
> ***They see the power of karma.***

And,

> [IX.44cd] ***For minds with reference***
> ***Nirvana is difficult.***

And,

> [IX.48ab] ***A mind without emptiness***
> ***May cease, but is born again.***

This shows that without the path that realizes emptiness, there is no attainment of any of the three types of awakening.

[729] This sūtra shows that one is liberated from cyclic existence by meditating on the four truths as not truly existent:

> Mañjuśrī, one who sees all conditioned phenomena as unborn completely knows suffering. One who sees all phenomena as unarisen abandons the origin. One who sees all phenomena as sheer nirvana actualizes the cessation. One who sees all phenomena as completely unborn cultivates the path.[240]

This sūtra also shows that sublime Disciples and Self-Realized Ones realize emptiness.

Furthermore, the *Diamond Cutter Sūtra* (*Vajracchedikāsūtra*) says: "Subhuti, consider this: stream-enterers who think, 'I have achieved the result of a stream-enterer!' . . . If a stream-enterer thinks like this: 'I have achieved the result of a stream-enterer!' then he is fixated on a self."[241] It also says this for abiding in the subsequent three results.[242] This shows that when the achiever or achievement of a stream-enterer is held to be truly existent, then there is, respectively, the apprehension of the self of persons and the self of phenomena. The wisdom that realizes the lack of intrinsic existence is said to bring about the attainment of the awakening of Disciples and Self-Realized Ones through undermining the conceived object of the two apprehensions of self. This sūtra is also cited by Prajñākaramati to make known that sublime Disciples and Self-Realized Ones realize the selflessness of phenomena.[243] The *Mother* says: "Those who wish to train in the stage of the Disciples also should train in the transcendent perfection of wisdom."[244] The *Condensed Perfection of Wisdom* says: "Those who think to become a Sugata, a Disciple . . ."[245] There are many *Mother Sūtras* that clearly proclaim this.

2. Mahāyāna Treatises That Proclaim This

The *Precious Garland* says:

> *As long as the aggregates are apprehended,*
> *There is apprehension of self;*
> *When there is apprehension of self, there is karma,*
> *And from this again, birth.*[246]

For as long as the apprehension in one's continuum of the conceived object—apprehending the aggregates as truly existent—has not been undermined, one will not be able to undermine the conceived object of the innate apprehension of self. If one cannot undermine this, by its force there will be the accumulation of karma, and thereby birth in existence again. Also:

There is no beginning, middle, and end to the three pathways,
Like the circle of a whirling firebrand
Mutually affecting each other
In cyclic existence.[247]

This describes the way of taking birth. The sequence of the three pathways of complete affliction—of afflictions, karma, and birth—has no beginning, middle, or end. There is no certainty in the temporal order of karma, which is the effect of affliction; the arising of suffering, which is the effect of karma; and from this suffering, the arising of its effects in karma, affliction, and suffering of similar type in the future. Each is the effect of the other, [730] and the wheel of cyclic existence turns like a firebrand, back and forth within the state of mutual arising. Also:

Since this is not obtained from self and other
In any of the three times.
The apprehension of self is exhausted;
Thereby, so is karma and birth.[248]

This says that the dependent arising of thorough affliction does not obtain birth from either self or other in any of the three times. Through seeing the lack of intrinsic birth, apprehension of self is exhausted. Thereby, karma and the arising of cyclic existence from karma cease. This is the meaning of what was said previously, "As long as the aggregates are apprehended . . ."[249] It is not saying that karma is accumulated by just apprehending true existence. Again, the *Precious Garland* states:

In the way that from a confusion of the eyes
A firebrand is apprehended as a wheel.[250]

At the end of eight stanzas that ascertain the aggregates, constituents, and sense-fields to lack intrinsic existence, it says:

In this way, by knowing correctly
Beings' lack of essence,

They enter nirvana without abode or appropriation,
Like a fire without its cause.[251]

This shows that sublime trainees who are Disciples and Self-Realized Ones attain nirvana through meditating on the path that realizes the lack of intrinsic existence in aggregates, constituents, and sense-fields. Among the two, (1) Disciples and Self-Realized Ones and (2) bodhisattvas, this was also stated with reference to Disciples and Self-Realized Ones because right after this it says:

In this way, bodhisattvas too
Definitely wish to awaken through seeing this;
Yet due to their compassion,
They continue in existence until awakening.[252]

These scriptures also show that Disciples and Self-Realized Ones realize the selflessness of phenomena.

3. Hīnayāna Sūtras That Proclaim This

Hīnayāna Sūtras also say this:

Material forms are like a mass of foam,
Feelings are like bubbles,
Identifications resemble mirages,
Formations are like the trunks of banana trees,
Consciousnesses resemble magical illusions.
This was spoken by the Sun Friend [Buddha].[253]

Prāsaṅgikas claim that this shows through five metaphors that material forms and so forth lack intrinsic existence. This establishes that the selflessness of phenomena is taught in the Disciples' canon as the basis upon which Disciples ascertain selflessness through what they study and contemplate. Furthermore, emptiness that is the lack of intrinsic nature in phenomena is taught in the uncommon Hīnayāna canon. The *Precious Garland* says:

The Mahāyāna teaches non-arising,
The other's exhaustion is emptiness.
The meanings of exhaustion and non-arising are the same,
So be tolerant.[254]

The Mahāyāna canon teaches conditioned phenomena to be without intrinsic arising, and the Hīnayāna canon teaches the exhaustion of conditioned phenomena. These two have the same meaning in revealing emptiness, so do not be intolerant of the Mahāyāna's teachings of emptiness. This was spoken in the context of establishing the Mahāyāna as the Buddha's Word.

The sameness of meaning of these two is stated [731] in a Hīnayāna Sūtra cited in the commentary on *Reason in Sixty Verses*:

> One who relinquishes all this suffering without exception, who definitively relinquishes it, is pure, exhausted, free from attachment, ceased, completely pacified, dissolved; who will not continue with other sufferings, is non-arising, and unborn; that one is at peace. That one is splendid. It is like this: all the aggregates have been definitively relinquished; existence is exhausted; there is freedom from attachment; there is cessation and nirvana.[255]

Here is what this means: "this suffering" delimits the aggregates to this life, which are relinquished without exception. In terms of suffering in future lives, it is said that there will be no continuing with other sufferings. This passage shows that when nirvana without remainder is actualized, all the aggregates without exception are exhausted. As is stated in the *Sublime Continuum,* "Since the afflictions are exhausted from the beginning . . . ,"[256] it is reasonable to explain this to mean the actualization of nirvana without remainder, through having actualized a cessation—which is an exhaustion of intrinsic nature from the beginning—of all conditioned phenomena and aggregates due to all constructs of dualistic appearances being pacified in the perspective of the gnosis of the path of liberation that is a Hīnayāna Arhat's meditative equipoise on emptiness. Nevertheless, it is not reasonable for the meaning of "exhaustion" to be the exhaustion of intrinsic nature because realists accept that the aggregates intrinsically exist.

Therefore, even though they accept in their system that the meaning of the exhaustion of the aggregates is the exhaustion or cessation of the continuity of aggregates due to the power of the antidotes, this is not a reasonable explanation. This is because, if that were the case, then at the time of actualizing nirvana without remainder there would be no person who actualized it. Also, it would be necessary to assert that when a person exists, there is no actualization of nirvana. This is necessary because they accept that when nirvana is actualized, the continuity of all the engagements with conditioned phenomena and aggregates cease. If there is a person, then there are necessarily aggregates as well, and these need to be conditioned phenomena, too. One is not able to explain the meaning of the sūtra correctly by explaining in this way.

Moreover, Hīnayāna Sūtras also teach emptiness. The *Discussion of Scripture* (*Āgamakṣudraka*) states: "Kātyāyana, in this world most people are fixated on existence and nonexistence, so they are born and age."[257] The meaning of this is stated in the *Fundamental Verses of the Middle Way*:

> *The Blessed One, knowing entities and non-entities,*
> *Negated both existence*
> *And nonexistence*
> *In his* Instructions to Kātyāyana.[258]

These demonstrate the selflessness of phenomena by refuting both extremes of intrinsic existence and of absolute nonexistence of phenomena.

Seven scriptures are known to invalidate the assertion that sublime Disciples and Self-Realized Ones do not realize the subtle selflessness of phenomena. The first [732] of these scriptures are the three stanzas beginning with "As long as the aggregates are apprehended . . ."[259] The second is the nine stanzas beginning with "In the way that from a confusion of the eyes . . ."[260] The third is "The Mahāyāna teaches non-arising . . ."[261] The fourth is "Forms are like a mass of foam . . ."[262] The fifth is "The Blessed One, knowing entities and non-entities . . ."[263] The sixth is "Those who wish to train in the stage of the Disciples also . . ."[264] The seventh is from the *Condensed Perfection of Wisdom*: "Whoever wants to be a Tathāgata . . ."[265] These have been mentioned above. Candrakīrti cites the first five passages in his commentary on the *Introduction to the Middle Way*. He cites the last two, as well as the *Sūtra on the Fist of Concentration* and the *Sūtra Teaching the Stable Superior Intention*, in *Clear Words*.

3. Resolving Disputes Regarding This Explanation

This section has two parts: (1) the explanation in the autocommentary on the *Introduction to the Middle Way*, and (2) how Tsongkhapa resolves disputes in his explanation of the *Introduction to the Middle Way* in ways not mentioned in the autocommentary.

1. Explanation in the *Autocommentary on the "Introduction to the Middle Way"*

In master Buddhapālita's commentary on the seventh chapter of the *Fundamental Verses of the Middle Way* he says that the meaning of the selflessness of phenomena taught in the Hīnayāna Sūtras is that phenomena lack intrinsic nature. Then Bhāviveka put forward a refutation in his *Lamp of Wisdom,* saying that if this were the case, then there would be no point for the teachings of the Mahāyāna. In response to this, explained according to Candrakīrti, a question is posed to Bhāviveka: according to your claim, is it that there is no point for the teaching of Mahāyāna in general, or is it that there is no point in the Mahāyāna teaching of the selflessness of phenomena? If it is the first, then there is no entailment because the purpose of the Mahāyāna teaching is not simply the teaching of selflessness. This follows because the Mahāyāna teaches limitless aspects of method, such as the grounds, activities, great compassion, dedication, and prayers. The autocommentary on the *Introduction to the Middle Way* says: "One who, if through the Hīnayāna . . . As is said in the *Precious Garland,*

How can one become a bodhisattva
Through the Disciple Vehicle
Without knowing the bodhisattva's prayers,
Activities, and dedications?
The meaning of bodhisattva activity
Is not explained in those sūtras;
It is explained in the Mahāyāna,
So the wise should uphold them."[266]

He replied that if it is the latter [that there is no point in the Mahāyāna teaching of the selflessness of phenomena], then there is also no entailment, because the Hīnayāna canon shows arguments for the selflessness of phenomena in brief, whereas the Mahāyāna teaches it extensively through limitless arguments. The autocommentary says: "Since the selflessness of phenomena is made clear . . . the master himself said:

You said that there is no liberation
Without realizing signlessness;
Therefore, you taught it completely
In the Mahāyāna."[267]

[733] What follows is an explanation of the differences between the selflessness of phenomena in the Mahāyāna and Hīnayāna, whether it is taught completely or not, and whether it is cultivated completely or not. In general, all sublime beings directly realize the subtle selflessness. Nevertheless, there

are differences in terms of how they ascertain it and the way they meditate on it. In the Hīnayāna, they ascertain reality with brief arguments, and then meditate on it; they do not have an expansive understanding of reality. In the Mahāyāna, as is stated in the *Fundamental Verses of the Middle Way*, there are limitless arguments that establish the lack of true existence with respect to each basis of analysis. An expansive understanding of reality occurs through meditating on this. For this reason, in the Hīnayāna one does not meditate on anything other than just antidotes to afflictive obscurations, while in the Mahāyāna, one needs to cultivate an extremely broad understanding that expands wisdom into reality in order to eliminate cognitive obscurations.

2. How Tsongkhapa Resolves Disputes in His Explanation of the *Introduction to the Middle Way* in Ways Not Mentioned in the Autocommentary

One might think, "It is not reasonable for a sublime Disciple or Self-Realized One to realize the selflessness of phenomena, nor is it reasonable to say that to apprehend true existence is an afflictive obscuration. This is because the *Ornament of Manifest Realization* says:

> *Since the concepts of apprehended objects are relinquished, and*
> *Since the apprehending subjects are not relinquished . . .* [268]

It states that the path of the Self-Realized Ones can relinquish the apprehending concepts of apprehended external objects, but cannot relinquish the apprehension of internal cognitions as truly existent. Also, it says:

> *Afflictions and cognitive [obscurations] are diminished by the three paths,*
> *So the Rhinoceros[-like] trainees . . .* [269]

This shows that apprehending an object as truly existent is a cognitive obscuration."

The way these problems are resolved is this: The earlier and later statements from this scripture, along with the claim that the three vehicles have three different views that are meditated on, are not held to be literal meanings in this context here. Also, the passage that says "since the basic field of reality is indivisible . . . ,"[270] in the context of dispelling objections states that the sublime Disciples and Self-Realized Ones realize the selflessness of phenomena; this is taken literally by both Vimuktisena and Haribhadra. Further, even though the consummate viewpoint of the root text of the *Ornament of*

Manifest Realization lies in Prāsaṅgika, this does not conflict with the fact that Vimuktisena and Haribhadra explained it to be Svātantrika; this should be known in detail from Tsongkhapa's explanation of the *Introduction to the Middle Way.* Thus, I have briefly elaborated here because the scriptures and arguments that establish that Disciples and Self-Realized Ones realize the selflessness of phenomena from Candrakīrti's texts are the same essential point as the viewpoint of the *Way of the Bodhisattva.* In this way, all the unique features of the Prāsaṅgika philosophical system, such as the way that the Disciples and Self-Realized Ones realize the selflessness of phenomena from [Khedrupjé's] *Exposition*, and the framework of the shared and unique features of the afflictions, one should know as the single voice and single viewpoint of the Victor's child, Śāntideva, and the glorious Candrakīrti.

Also, it is said, [IX.41a] ***If the Mahāyāna is not confirmed . . .*** Here, I will discuss briefly how the Mahāyāna is established as [734] the Buddha's Word. How those in the Disciple schools establish that the Mahāyāna is not the Word of the Buddha is like this: they say:

> "*Since it is not contained within the sūtras and*
> *Teaches a different path,*
> *The Mahāyāna is not spoken by the Buddha;*
> *It is like the extreme view of the Vedas.*[271]

This means that the Mahāyāna Sūtras are not the Word of the Buddha because they are not included in the three baskets, like the extreme view of the Vedas. Those with the extreme view of the Vedas say that evil deeds are purified by bathing and fasting; the Mahāyāna says this, too."

In reply, the *Essence of Madhyamaka* says:

> *The Mahāyāna is spoken by the Buddha because*
> *It teaches things like selflessness and*
> *The great identity of the three jewels,*
> *Like the vehicle of trainees.*[272]

This means that the Mahāyāna Sūtras are the Word of the Buddha because they teach the four seals of the doctrine, such as selflessness, and because they teach the identity that is the greatness of the three jewels, like the vehicle of the Disciple trainees.

Furthermore, I will unpack a bit more how they establish that the Mahāyāna is not the Word of the Buddha, and how we respond to this. Those in the Disciple schools say, "The Mahāyāna is not the Word of the Buddha because it teaches: a permanent Enjoyment Body, bodhisattvas going from one happiness to the next, an all-pervasive buddha-nature, and that the buddha does not enter nirvana. These conflict, respectively, with the four seals that signify the doctrine: all conditioned phenomena being impermanent, all contaminated things being suffering, all phenomena being selfless, and nirvana being peace."

These are not problems. The Enjoyment Body is understood to be a permanent continuity because it constantly appears to sublime bodhisattvas; it is not a permanent entity. Bodhisattvas go from one happiness to the next because of the influence of the spirit of awakening. Buddha-nature is said to be the basic nature of the continuum of a sentient being; it is not like a self that is singular and permanent. Because of the power of prayers, the buddhas do not completely pass into nirvana; nirvana is taught to be peace because all concepts are pacified. Therefore, it is not the case that the Mahāyāna is not the Buddha's Word.

Furthermore, one might say, "The Mahāyāna is not the Buddha's Word because it does not appear in the Vinaya, does not engage the sūtras, and conflicts with the basic nature. Also, the compilers did not include it, and it is not included within any of the eighteen schools."

We reply that this is not a problem because the Mahāyāna engages the sūtras by teaching the four truths, it appears in the disciplining (*'dul ba*) of the afflictions, and it does not conflict with dependent arising. There are many discrepancies within your Disciple scriptures, so there are many instances where there is no mutual engagement among the sūtras. Since the Mahāyāna is profound and vast, it may not engage with some of the Disciple sūtras, but it [735] does engage with the sūtras of the Mahāyāna itself. Also, it appears in the 700 trainings of the bodhisattvas and does not conflict with the basic nature due to teaching emptiness. Even though the compilers of the Disciple's canon did not include it, it was included by the likes of Samantabhadra, Maitreya, Mañjughoṣa, and Vajrapāni (*gsang bdag*). Also, there appear many presentations of Mahāyāna grounds and paths in texts included in the eighteen schools, such as the "Vast Foundation" (*sde snod kyi gzhi chen po*) of the Mahāsaṃghikas, the Vaipulya texts of schools such as the Pūrvaśailas, and the *Twelve Thousand* of the Aparaśailas (*'jigs med ri bo'i sde snod khri nyis stong pa*). Therefore, it is not the case that the Mahāyāna is not the Buddha's Word.

Further, one might think, "The Mahāyāna is not the Buddha's Word because it teaches a path like that of the non-Buddhists, that evil deeds are purified through bathing, reciting *dhāraṇīs,* and fasting, etc. Also, it teaches that even grave misdeeds can be purified and teaches the emptiness of all phenomena, like the nihilists. It disparages Arhats and teaches that householders are praiseworthy. It also expresses more praise for bodhisattvas than for buddhas. Since it demonstrates many contradictions like these, it is the product of demons and sophists."

These are not problems. With bathing, it is not held that the water itself purifies negative actions, but it is through the power of the Anavatapta Nāga prayer. *Dhāraṇīs* are held to have the qualities of meditative stabilization and wisdom. Fasting practices are for the purpose of accomplishing the mantra of the deity. Scripture and reasoning establish that even determined actions are purified when all four powers are present.[273] Scripture and reasoning also establish that all phenomena are empty and selfless.

Some Mahāyāna texts describe the difference between Arhats and bodhisattvas as like that between a mustard seed and Mt. Meru, but this is expressed in terms of the difference in the nature of their qualities; it is not a disparagement of Arhats. In scriptures acknowledged by the eighteen schools, householders with qualities of the spirit of awakening and so on are also praised by monastics. Further, the praise for bodhisattvas more than buddhas is for the purpose of revering the distinctive quality of the cause. Thus, your attempts to undermine the Mahāyāna cannot establish that it is not the Buddha's Word. This was a short excursus gleaned from texts like [Jamyang Shepa's] *Great Exposition of Philosophical Systems,* which presents briefly what is stated in detail in the *Blaze of Reason.*

Furthermore, it is known that early Disciple schools did not accept Mahāyāna Sūtras (such as those in the middle wheel) as the Buddha's Word. After others came, like Nāgārjuna, father and son [Āryadeva], there were said to be two factions within the eighteen schools: those that accepted the Mahāyāna as the Buddha's Word and those that did not. The detractors who said that the Mahāyāna [736] was not the Buddha's Word were some of the proponents of the Hīnayāna philosophical systems, like the Vaibhāṣikas and Sautrāntikas, acknowledged within the eighteen Disciple schools. They were not those who entered the Hīnayāna path and were placed in the Disciple Vehicle because they sought the awakening of a Disciple. Rather, they were placed in the Hīnayāna because they engaged for their own benefit due to their inferior intentions. Nevertheless, they accepted Mahāyāna Sūtras that teach emptiness as the Buddha's Word. Moreover, they understood the meaning of emptiness.

In the *Sublime Continuum,* the Mahāyāna is established as the Buddha's Word through a teaching of the faults of rejecting the doctrine. The chapter on "Establishing the Buddha's Word" in the root text and commentary of the *Ornament of the Mahāyāna Sūtras* also states this extensively.[274] Since the Mahāyāna is also established as the Buddha's Word extensively in the texts of Nāgārjuna, Bhāviveka, Asaṅga and his brother [Vasubandhu], as well as in this text, the *Way of the Bodhisattva,* it seems to be very important.

Next, it is said, [IX.46] ***"For a time, the appropriations, craving . . . "*** This shows that from among all the origins of suffering, which are karma and the afflictions, the primary one is craving. The reason for this is as follows: A sūtra says:

> One might ask, "What is the noble truth of the origin of suffering?" It arises again with craving, along with enthusiastic attachment. It has the nature of fascination for this and that. It is like this: desirous craving, existential craving, and fearful craving.[275]

The three lines where it says, "It arises again with craving . . . the nature of fascination" shows craving for objects in the future, the past, and the present. Alternatively, the first gives a brief demonstration, and the latter two respectively show craving to be not separated from an object acquired in the present, and craving that is the desire to encounter in the future what has not been acquired. The last part of the passage, following "It is like this" shows its division: (1) desirous craving, which is wanting to achieve happiness; (2) existential craving, which is the attachment to self; and (3) fearful craving, which is wanting to eliminate suffering.

The *Compendium of Metaphysics* cites the above sūtra to show that craving is primary since it encompasses everything. The *Compendium of Metaphysics* says:

> One might ask, "What is the meaning of 'encompassing everything'?" This craving follows after all things. It follows all situations. It happens in all times. It encompasses all realms. It is involved in all efforts. It takes on all forms.[276]

Here, "it follows after all things" refers to the way that the craving not to lose what one has acquired and for acquiring what has not been acquired is encompassing. "It follows all situations" of feeling refers to the feeling of craving to be free from suffering and not to part from happiness. "It happens in all times" refers to memories of the past, attachment to the present, and anticipation for the future. "It encompasses all realms" refers to craving in the three realms, such as the Desire Realm. [737] The sufferings of the Desire Realm and so on are accomplished by craving for what is desirable, and effort for existence. "It is involved in all efforts" refers to there being no liberation from existence due to craving in pursuit of perverse activities. "It takes on all forms" refers to all forms of permanence and annihilation in craving for the permanence of desirable objects and for the immediate termination of undesirable things.

The *Commentary on Epistemology* also teaches craving as primary in terms of being the main cause for taking on a future existence. The *Commentary on Epistemology* states:

> *While ignorance is the cause of existence,*
> *It is not mentioned, but craving is:*
> *Since it perpetuates the continuum*
> *And is immediately preceding; but not karma because*
> *When it is present, it is existent and nonexistent.*[277]

Here is what this means: Given that ignorance, craving, and karma are all three causes of a future existence, one might then wonder, "Why is only craving said to be the cause here?" The lack of knowledge, or ignorance, that is first among the twelve links of dependent origination is a cause that perpetuates existence in general. Nevertheless, since it is not an immediate producer, it is not mentioned here. Since craving alone is both the immediate producer and the perpetuator of the continuum for its subsequent effect, just craving is explicitly mentioned here as the cause of a future existence. Karma is also not the primary cause of a future existence because karma will naturally accumulate if craving is present, but if craving is absent, it is not certain that there will be birth in a future existence even with karma. Therefore, for the complete production of existence, between karma and afflictions, afflictions are primary; and among the afflictions, craving is primary.

Likewise, in the context of identifying the direct cause of cyclic existence, the *Commentary on Epistemology* says:

> *By attachment to the self,*
> *Not led by another sentient being,*
> *With the wish to remove suffering and achieve happiness,*
> *A decadent place is taken.*
> *A distorted mind with regards to suffering,*
> *And the strong binds of craving –*
> *Those without these causes of birth*

Will not be born.[278]

This means that ordinary beings are attached to the self; they are not led by another power, like Īśvara. Through a craving that wishes to achieve happiness and remove suffering, they take up a decadent place, like a womb. A distorted mind (apprehending suffering as happiness) and the binds of craving (wishing to achieve happiness) are causes of birth as an ordinary being in cyclic existence. Those who do not crave anything, the Arhats, will not be born. There is a lot more in this text that describes the faults of craving. Also, the *Fundamental Verses of the Middle Way* says:

Without craving, there is no appropriation;
There will be liberation, not existence.[279]

This means that without craving for feelings as mine, there is no appropriation. Thereby, there will be liberation; [738] there will be no complete production of existence.

Next, it says:

[IX.48] ***A mind without emptiness . . .***
Therefore, one should meditate on emptiness.

And, [IX.53] ***Thus, with this position of emptiness . . .*** It says several times that one should meditate on emptiness; I will say a bit here about the reason for this. Even if you wish for just liberation, then you should meditate on special insight after cultivating the wisdom that unerringly ascertains the reality of selflessness. This is because even non-Buddhists have a mere calm abiding that is nonconceptual, clear, and free from laxity and agitation. They are also able to perform minor miracles and achieve paranormal powers (*mngon shes*) based on that. Mere calm abiding just temporarily suppresses some of the manifest afflictions, but it cannot eliminate their potentials and is not able to counter in the slightest the apprehension of a self that is the root of existence. When the conditions are met with again, they will become manifest. It is said in the *Praise of Confession* (*Deśanāstava*):

The forest fire of meditative concentration again and again
Burns the underbrush of faults,
Yet it cannot destroy the firm roots of the view of self,
So they arise again when moistened by rain.[280]

Kamalaśīla said:

> Stabilize the mind on the observation in this way, then investigate it with wisdom. Thereby, an illumination of cognition will occur that will eradicate the seeds of confusion. Otherwise, a mere meditative stabilization like that of non-Buddhists will not eliminate the afflictions, as a sūtra said:
>
> *Mundane beings engage in meditative stabilization,*
> *But this will not destroy the view of self*
> *Due to being afflicted and disturbed,*
> *Like the meditative stabilization meditated on by the brahmanical teacher (lhag spyod).*[281]

Citing a sūtra, he spoke this in his first *Stages of Meditation.* One might wonder, "How then is one to meditate to become free from existence?" At the end of the previous passage, it says:

> *If you discern the lack of self in phenomena,*
> *And if you meditate on what you have discerned,*
> *That will be the cause of the effect, attaining nirvana;*
> *Other causes will not bring peace.*[282]

It is said that there is liberation from existence through habituation to the wisdom that realizes selflessness. This is because the root of existence is the apprehension of self. This is stated extensively in texts like the middle *Stages of Meditation.*

Furthermore, the main cause for attaining omniscience is the wisdom that realizes reality. Generosity, and so on, is blind without it, for wisdom is like a guide. This is stated in the *Condensed Perfection of Wisdom*:

> This transcendent perfection of wisdom of the Victors is a great awareness-mantra. It pacifies the suffering and pains of myriad realms of beings. Whoever has passed [into nirvana] and whoever is a protector of worlds in the ten directions has become an unexcelled medicine king by training in this awareness-mantra.[283]

And,

> [739] By completely knowing the nature of phenomena with wisdom, one transcends all the three realms. Becoming the mightiest among

humans and turning the precious wheel, one teaches the dharma for beings in order to eliminate suffering.[284]

And, "When completely embraced by wisdom, one gains vision, and also gains its name [transcendent perfection]."[285] There are many such passages. The *Diamond Cutter Sūtra* also says:

> For example, when a blind person enters into darkness, nothing at all is seen. You should view the bodhisattva who performs an act of generosity while falling under the influence of real entities likewise. Subhūti, consider this. For example, when the sun rises at dawn, a sighted person sees various forms. You should view the bodhisattva who performs an act of generosity without falling under the influence of real entities likewise.[286]

This applies to discipline, and so on, as well.

As in the life story of our teacher, it is reasonable to seek out the meaning of emptiness, and having sought it out, to meditate on it with great earnest. The *King of Meditative Stabilizations* states:

> *Those who meditate on phenomena as empty*
> *Constantly radiate billions of rays of light,*
> *Making the circle of the sun seem to be without splendor;*
> *These heroes will soon become guides.*[287]

And,

> *I meditated deeply before on this domain of peace*
> *For many trillions of eons.*
> *I never desisted from diligence in this path.*
> *At that time Dipañkara also prophesied becoming a Victorious One;*
> *In this sūtra, you will train following me.*[288]

And,

> *Give up completely any regard for this body and life*
> *And meditate on emptiness that is complete peace.*[289]

By meditating on emptiness you become a buddha. Since our teacher himself became a buddha by meditating on emptiness, it is said that his followers should seek out emptiness without regard for body or life, and meditate on it. Nāgārjuna said:

The great one, the buddha,
And all those with love always
Know emptiness, like space.
Thus, the ground of all phenomena is
Peaceful and like an illusion;
Always meditate on emptiness,
The groundless destroyer of existence.[290]

And *Clear Words* states: "It is reasonable for intelligent ones to seek out reality, giving up even their lives, in the way that the bodhisattva Sadāprarudita sought out the Blessed *Mother*."[291] Also, the *Lamp of the Path of Awakening* (*Bodhipathapradīpa*) says:

Through scripture and reasoning
Ascertain all phenomena
To be without arising, without intrinsic nature.
Then meditate nonconceptually.
By meditating on reality in this way
One will attain the grounds like Manifest Joy;
The buddha's awakening will not be far away.[292]

Those who wish to pursue liberation and omniscience [740] should meditate on reality.

Next, it says, [IX.54] ***The afflictions and cognitive obscurations . . .*** Here I will explain the unique framework of the two obscurations in three parts: (1) how the apprehension of true existence is presented as an afflictive obscuration, (2) how each of the two obscurations is identified, and (3) how the two obscurations are eliminated on which path.

1. How the Apprehension of True Existence Is Presented as an Afflictive Obscuration

There is a difference in how Prāsaṅgikas and Svātantrikas present the two apprehensions of self as which one of two obscurations. Svātantrikas assert that to apprehend a self of persons is an afflictive obscuration, and assert that to apprehend a self of phenomena is a cognitive obscuration. Prāsaṅgikas, however, present both apprehensions of self as afflictive obscurations. Here, due to the essential point that to apprehend a self of phenomena is understood as an afflictive obscuration, there is no difference in degree of subtlety between the two selves that are negated. Therefore, there is no difference in degree of subtlety between the twofold selflessness that negates them, either. For this reason, since no difference between the degree of subtlety is accepted within the twofold apprehension of self, then it is accepted that to apprehend a self of phenomena must be an afflictive obscuration, just like to apprehend a self of persons is an afflictive obscuration. Moreover, to apprehend a self of phenomena that apprehends the aggregates as truly existent is an afflictive obscuration because it is afflictive ignorance—which is the opposite of the gnosis-awareness (*rig pa ye shes*) that realizes the aggregates to lack true existence, for which the discordant factor is the apprehension of true existence.

How afflictive ignorance is identified in general is like this: Asaṅga and his brother [Vasubandhu] asserted it to be the ignorance that is the mental state of confusion regarding causality and reality. This is held to be different from the view of the transitory collective. Dharmakīrti and some of the masters of Mind-Only and Madhyamaka accepted that afflictive ignorance is the view of the transitory collective that apprehends the person to exist as a self-subsisting substance. Here in Prāsaṅgika, afflictive ignorance is held to be the discordant factor of the gnosis-awareness that realizes the lack of true existence. Also, afflictive ignorance is not merely the absence of this antidotal awareness, or something other than it. Rather, afflictive ignorance is understood to be the apprehension of true existence of persons and phenomena in direct contradiction to this awareness; it is also understood to be delusion (*gti mug*) within the three poisons. For this reason, to apprehend a self of phenomena is also established as afflictive ignorance.

Since this kind of apprehension of true existence is afflictive ignorance, it is clearly said by the glorious Candrakīrti to be relinquished both by Arhats who are Disciples or Self-Realized Ones and by bodhisattvas on the pure grounds. The autocommentary on the *Introduction to the Middle Way* states:

> Also, Disciples, Self-Realized Ones, and bodhisattvas relinquish afflictive ignorance. For those with vision of conditioned phenomena as [741] existing like reflections, they have a reality that is of an artificial nature, but that is not truly existent because they lack the presumption of true existence.[293]

The *Four Hundred Verses* states:

Consciousness that is the seed of existence
Has objects as its domain.
When objects are seen without a self,
The seed of existence ceases.[294]

Candrakīrti's commentary on this passage is stated similarly as above. Further, it is explained that the seed of existence is to apprehend true existence and that seeing the lack of true existence eliminates it. It is also stated this way in the sacred words of the sublime father [Nāgārjuna] and son. *Emptiness in Seventy Verses* says:

The conception that entities that arise
From causes and conditions are real
Is said by our teacher to be ignorance.
From this, the twelve links arise.
To see, as it is, the emptiness of entities
Is to know well, and ignorance does not arise.
This is the cessation of ignorance;
Due to this the twelve links cease.[295]

Conceiving entities that arise from causes and conditions to be real is taught to be the ignorance that is the root of existence—the apprehension of true existence. From this apprehension of true existence, the twelve links arise, such as the apprehension of a self of phenomena similar in type to it, and the ignorance that apprehends the person to truly exist. By knowing emptiness that is the lack of intrinsic nature, ignorance ceases and the other links cease as well.

Reason in Sixty Verses says, "If you find any basis . . . "[296] It says that if you find a basis for any intentional object (*gmigs gtad*) apprehended as real, then you are caught by the snake of the afflictions. Moreover, the *Four Hundred Verses* says:

In the way that the body faculty pervades the body,
In the same way delusion resides everywhere.
Therefore, to destroy delusion from among the afflictions
Is to destroy them all.
When interdependence is seen
Delusion does not occur.[297]

The other afflictions depend on apprehending true existence among the three poisons, and proceed without parting from it. Through seeing the meaning of interdependence, the lack of intrinsic nature, ignorance is averted. In our text here, it says:

> [IX.47cd] ***The mind that has an observation***
> ***Remains on something.***

This clearly shows that apprehending true existence is an afflictive obscuration. Thus, there is no difference on this point in the way that the three masters explain the sublime viewpoint.

It is said that there is no liberation for those with a conception of real entities. This shows that apprehending true existence makes an obstacle for liberation. There are several other scriptures that teach that to apprehend true existence is an afflictive obscuration. This kind of aprehension of true existence is said to be the root of cyclic existence and the first of the twelve links; this should primarily be understood as what is in the continua of ordinary beings.

2. How Each of the Two Obscurations Is Identified

Due to understanding afflictive ignorance in a different way, [742] the other afflictions are also presented differently here than in Svātantrika and similar positions. In Prāsaṅgika, the apprehension of self that holds onto a person existing as a self-subsisting substance, and the subsidiary and ancillary afflictions that arise from that (as mentioned in common with the two Abhidharma texts), are understood to be coarse afflictions. The apprehension of a self that is a person or phenomenon existing on its own, and the craving and so on that arise from that, are understood to be subtle afflictions mentioned only in this tradition. Understanding these kinds of subtle ignorance and craving, which are not acknowledged as afflictions in other systems, is due to the essential point that here in Prāsaṅgika, nothing is held to exist on its own and apprehending true existence is understood to be an afflictive obscuration.

Others like the Svātantrikas accept something that exists on its own, and due to this, do not accept that to apprehend a person as existing on its own is to apprehend the self of persons. For this reason, they do not understand apprehending a subtle self of person other than as a cognition that apprehends a person to exist as a self-subsisting substance. Thus, in terms of afflictions like attachment as well, they do not understand any subtle affliction other than what comes from this type of apprehension of a self of persons. In this

Prāsaṅgika system here, there needs to be both subtle and coarse types of afflictions like craving, as our text clearly says: [IX.46c] ***This craving, even though not afflictive . . .***

Here I will present the characteristics of the two obscurations for the most part in the way of [Khedrupjé's] *Exposition*. The definition of an afflictive obscuration is a type of affliction that mainly obscures the attainment of liberation. When divided, there are two: those that are imputed (*kun btags*) and those that are innate (*lhan skyes*). The definition of an imputed afflictive obscuration is any seed consisting of a producer of an affliction, or is concordant with it, that arises due to the influence of a philosophical system. The definition of an innate afflictive obscuration is any seed consisting of a producer of an affliction, or is concordant with it, that has arisen from a predisposition from beginningless habituation without depending on the influence of a philosophical system.

Each of these has two aspects: a manifest aspect and a potential aspect (*mngon gyur dang sa bon gyi cha*). A manifest afflictive obscuration that is imputed is to apprehend a person existing as a self-subsisting substance that is in disjunction with the characteristics of the aggregates; and produced from that, afflictions and that which is concordant with them. Also, it is to apprehend true existence imputed by a philosophical system, and that which is produced from this—afflictions like holding onto an extreme and that which is concordant with them. The imputed afflictive obscuration's potential aspect is the predispositions for afflictions that produce these.

Manifest innate afflictive obscurations are innate apprehensions of true existence, the afflictions (that arise from these), and that which is concordant with them. The predispositions that are placed by the power of these for [743] producing later afflictions are the innate afflictive obscuration's potential aspect. A mental consciousness that is concordant with an affliction like attachment is afflictive and an afflictive obscuration, but is not an actual affliction. Imputed afflictive obscurations (*nyon sgrib kun btags*) and afflictive obscurations that are to be removed on the path of seeing (*nyon sgrib mthong spang*) have the same meaning. Innate afflictive obscurations (*nyon sgrib lhan skyes*) and afflictive obscurations that are to be removed on the path of meditation (*nyon sgrib sgom spang*) have the same meaning.

This is how to understand cognitive obscurations: It is stated clearly in the autocommentary on the *Introduction to the Middle Way*:

> On this, the predispositions for ignorance are obstacles to discerning cognitive objects. The presence of these predispositions for attachment and the like is also the cause of the engagements of body and speech. These predispositions, for ignorance and attachment and so on, desist only in omniscience and in becoming a buddha, not otherwise.[298]

"The predispositions for ignorance" shows an illustration of a cognitive obscuration; these are the predispositions for apprehending true existence. "[Obstacle for discerning] cognitive objects" shows the definition of a cognitive obscuration. In terms of engagements of body and speech, assuming a negative state (*gnas ngan len*) of body due to a predisposition such as attachment, even for Arhats, is like jumping like a monkey. Assuming a negative state of speech due to a predisposition such as hatred is like saying to someone, "you idiot!" Assuming a negative state of mind is said to be "an obstacle for discerning cognitive objects." This is the subtle aspect of an unclear mind, such that it is difficult to realize the domain of a cognitive object; for instance, it is said that Maudgalyāyana did not know that his mother had been born in the mundane realm of the luminous hell, despite looking for a long time with his paranormal powers. The word "also" shows that these predispositions for attachment and the like are also obstacles for discerning cognitive objects.

Thus, when the apprehension of true existence and the predispositions for attachment and so on produced by it are set in place, there are two predispositions implanted in the mind: (1) one that can produce a subsequent apprehension of true existence, attachment, and so on, similar in type to it, and (2) the subtle predisposition implanted by apprehending true existence that cannot produce a manifest affliction that is an apprehension of true existence, even if it meets with conditions. It can produce merely an appearance of true existence; that is, the objects of the six engaged consciousnesses (such as forms) appearing as if they truly existed, and the potential for this kind of affliction is understood to be a predisposition for afflictions. Within these two, a cognitive obscuration is understood to be the latter predisposition for afflictions. A potential (*sa bon*) for an affliction is necessarily an afflictive obscuration, but a predisposition (*bag chags*) for an affliction is not necessarily an afflictive obscuration because there are cognitive obscurations among them as well.

Thus, the definition of a cognitive obscuration is an obscuration of the type that obstructs the simultaneous knowledge of all cognitive objects.

"Cognitive obscurations" (*shes sgrib*) and "obstructive obscurations" (*thogs sgrib*) have the same meaning. They have a twofold division: the manifest aspect and the potential aspect. The manifest aspect of a cognitive obscuration is understood to be the distorted aspect of dualistic appearance for which any of its objects, like form, appears as truly existent; it is a type of obscuration that arises in the continuum of a sublime being [744] on the path of training who has completely relinquished apprehending true existence. Cognitive obscuration's potential aspect is understood to be that which is caused by what is implanted by apprehending true existence and has as its effect the appropriating distortion of dualistic appearance; it is a type of obscuration that arises in the continuum of a sublime being on the path of training who has completely relinquished apprehending true existence. A cognitive obscuration is necessarily innate and is to be removed on the path of meditation; it has no imputed aspects or aspects that are to be removed on the path of seeing.

Some people say that there is a common ground of cognitive obscurations and cognitions, but most of the previous masters of reason say with one voice that there are no cognitive obscurations that are cognitions. It is also said that the non-afflictive ignorance is ignorance, from the aspect that it obscures the understanding of subtle reality. Yet if this were the case, it would not need to be a cognition that apprehends an object. One might wonder, "What is the essence of non-afflictive ignorance?" It is stated in the autocommentary on the *Introduction to the Middle Way*:

> That which taints or infuses the mental continuum, and proceeds along with it, is a predisposition. Other words for predispositions are that which reaches the extreme of affliction, habit, and root. When afflictions have been removed by the uncontaminated path, even these cannot be relinquished by the Disciples and the Self-Realized Ones. It is as in the case when oil, butter, or flowers have been removed, but their subtle qualities are still observed in a vase or on the clothes that have touched them.[299]

This passage shows that until the afflictions are completely removed, their predispositions have not been relinquished. The *Sublime Continuum* also says: "We assert the concepts of the three spheres to be cognitive obscuration."[300] This means that the predispositions for apprehending the three spheres as truly existent are cognitive obscurations.

3. How the Two Obscurations Are Eliminated on Which Path

The way that afflictive obscurations are eliminated is as follows: For the Hīnayāna, the removal of the afflictive obscurations begins from the forbearance of the phenomena of suffering (*sdug bsngal chos bzod*) on the Hīnayāna path of seeing. The attainment of Hīnayāna Arhatship occurs at the same time as the elimination of the afflictive obscurations. Furthermore, the imputed aspects of the afflictive obscurations are removed by the uninterrupted path of seeing. The innate apprehension of true existence that is to be removed on the path of meditation is divided into nine types, and each of the nine types removed are progressively eliminated by the appropriate stage of the uninterrupted path of meditation. As for the Mahāyāna, the removal of the afflictive obscurations begins from the forbearance of the phenomena of suffering on the Mahāyāna path of seeing. The attainment of the eighth ground, or the attainment of the first path of liberation on the eighth ground, occurs at the same time as the complete elimination of the afflictive obscurations.

The way that the things removed on the path of seeing are eliminated is as follows: [745] The uninterrupted path of seeing eliminates them by means of eliminating the potentials for the imputed afflictive obscurations that are to be removed on the path of seeing. The continua of persons in which resides the last gnosis of "the supreme quality" (*chos mchog*) on the path of joining becomes oriented (*mngon du phyogs pa*) toward the arising of the uninterrupted path on the Mahāyāna path of seeing. At the same time, the potentials in their continua for concepts that are to be removed on the path of seeing become oriented toward cessation. What is to be removed is eliminated as the uninterrupted Mahāyāna path of seeing arises in their continua at the same time as the cessation of the potentials for concepts to be removed on the path of seeing, such that they are not capable of arising again in their continua. In the second instant, the elimination of what is to be removed on the path of seeing is actualized in their continua at the same time as the attainment of the path of liberation on the path of seeing.

In the continuum of one on the uninterrupted path of the Mahāyāna path of seeing, there are no potentials for concepts that are to be removed on the path of seeing. Yet one might wonder whether potentials for what is to be removed on the path of meditation are present or not in that continuum. In the system of the Svātantrikas who do not accept the basic consciousness, they are not. Rather, the mental consciousness in this continuum is understood as an illustration (*mtshan gzhi*) of the path of seeing, which has become essentially uncontaminated. If there were potentials that remained to be eliminated within this, then there would be problems such that it would follow that it would be contaminated. In this way, these potentials to be removed are held not to arise temporarily because the conditions for their arising are not complete, not because they are not able to arise due to an antidote. Thus, even though they are held not to exist in this continuum at that time, they are not held to be eliminated.

Those who accept the basic consciousness hold that within the basic consciousness there are potentials to be removed on the path of meditation. In this Prāsaṅgika system, even though the mental consciousness of this continuum is essentially uncontaminated, it is held that there are potentials that remain to be eliminated based on the mere "I" that is imputed based on the aggregates.

The way that the things removed on the path of meditation are eliminated is explained as follows: There are two systems, in terms of whether or not what is to be removed on the path of meditation is present on the first ground. For the first in which they are present, the greater of the great of what is to be removed on the path of meditation is divided into the coarse and the subtle. The direct antidote for the coarse ones is the uninterrupted path of meditation on the first ground, and the direct antidote for the subtle greater ones to be removed is the uninterrupted path on the second ground. What is removed from the middling of the great to the lesser of the middling is progressively eliminated by the appropriate stage, from the uninterrupted path on the third ground to the uninterrupted path on the seventh ground. The three lesser ones to be removed are held to be eliminated simultaneously. There are many accounts of how they are eliminated, but mainly these three are eliminated by the uninterrupted path at the end of the seventh ground. The attainment of the path of liberation that eliminates them occurs at the same time as the attainment of the eighth ground. The eighth-ground gnosis is permeated by gnosis that is pure of afflictive obscurations. This is the intent of the words of the *Introduction to the Middle Way*:

> *Their minds without attachment are pure of faults and do not remain together with them.*
>
> *So the stains of these along with their roots are pacified on the eighth ground;*
>
> *The afflictions are exhausted and they become exalted on the three grounds.*[301]

This is one position.

Alternatively, [746] the eighth-ground gnosis includes the direct antidote for the three kinds of lesser afflictions that are to be removed on the path of meditation on the initial uninterrupted path of the eighth ground, the path of liberation that completely eliminates the afflictive obscurations brought about by that, and the uninterrupted path, and so on, on the eighth ground that is the direct antidote to the greater cognitive obscurations as well. This is because it is said that even though these cannot be eliminated for 100,000 eons on the seventh ground and below, they can be eliminated in an instant on this ground. Also, it is because the passage from the *Introduction to the Middle Way* cited above shows that apprehending true existence along with its potentials are exhausted on the eighth ground. This is a second position.

For the way that cognitive obscurations are eliminated, there is none other than a fourfold division of greater, middling, and lesser cognitive obscurations; and within the lesser ones, those that are subtle and coarse. These are eliminated like this: The greater cognitive obscurations are eliminated on the eighth ground by the uninterrupted path that is their direct antidote. The middling ones are eliminated by the uninterrupted path on the ninth ground. The coarse lesser ones are eliminated at the beginning of the uninterrupted path on the tenth ground, and the subtle lesser cognitive obscurations are eliminated on the uninterrupted path at the end of the continuum. Each of these uninterrupted paths has a path of liberation that it induces, but these are easily understood by implication. The path of liberation induced by the uninterrupted path at the end of the continuum is the Mahāyāna path of no more learning (*mi slob lam*).

These were presented in terms of those who have a determined Mahāyāna heritage. It is different for others like the Svātantrikas. According to the system of the Yogācāra-Svātantrika-Mādhyamikas, the imputed aspects of both obscurations, along with their potentials, are eliminated by the uninterrupted path on the Mahāyāna path of seeing. Also, the innate aspects of both obscurations, which are divided into nine types, are held to be progressively eliminated in nine stages of the uninterrupted path on the path of meditation. Then, one becomes a buddha when both of the subtle aspects of the two obscurations, which are to be eliminated by the uninterrupted path at the end of the continuum, are simultaneously eliminated. This is their explanation of how they are eliminated for one with a determined Mahāyāna heritage. In his *Blaze of Reason,* Bhāviveka says that those with a determined Mahāyāna heritage completely remove the afflictive obscurations when they reach the eighth ground. This is different from the description above. Also, this differs from that of the Prāsaṅgikas because this position does not accept that cognitive obscurations have yet to begin to be eliminated before afflictive obscurations have been exhausted.

One might wonder, "When Arhats who are Disciples or Self-Realized Ones enter the Mahāyāna path, they have already eliminated the afflictive obscurations. The cognitive obscurations, however, cannot be eliminated until the attainment of the eighth ground according to the position of this Prāsaṅgika system. So would it not be the case that they would have nothing to eliminate up until the seventh ground?"

When Arhats who are Disciples or Self-Realized Ones enter the Mahāyāna path, up until the seventh ground they mainly train in the accumulation of merit in postmeditation. In order to make their accumulation of gnosis powerful, they rest one-pointedly in meditative equipoise on emptiness, and so on, [747] training by alternating the practices of the two accumulations. This kind of gnosis of meditative equipoise is not distinguished in terms of being an uninterrupted path or a path of liberation. This is because, if these kinds of conventions were made in terms of the way the things to be eliminated were removed, then there would be no potentials at all to be removed for them up until the seventh ground. It is just like the case of a Hīnayāna Arhat entering the Mahāyāna path at the time of the paths of accumulation or joining. Yet by training in the two accumulations, they develop further and further the distinctive powers of these two. So they move through the higher paths and arrive to the appropriate degree of each one, in terms of dispelling conflicting factors and fulfilling conducive conditions. Through the power of this, they move from the path of accumulation to the path of joining, and move within the path of joining through the four stages, such as "warmth." Then they move progressively to the first ground and onto the higher grounds, progressively actualizing the distinctive 1,200-fold qualities, and so on. This is most reasonable and is acknowledged as a good explanation.

Also, another system based on the *Sūtra Explaining the Intent* describes twenty complete delusions (*kun rmongs*) and eleven negative states (*gnas ngan len*) that correspond to the ten grounds.[302] It is also claimed that the uninterrupted paths eliminate the obscurations that obstruct the attainments in postmeditation on the higher paths, such as the 1,200-fold qualities. Whether or not it is preceded by a lower path, no cognitive obscurations are eliminated before the eighth ground is reached.

To eliminate cognitive obscurations, if there is no accompaniment of an actual accumulation of merit gathered for two incalculable eons, or a gathering of merit equivalent to this, then cognitive obscurations cannot be eliminated solely by the antidote that is wisdom that realizes emptiness, or without having the full aspects of method in place. Therefore, to eliminate the cognitive obscurations, it is necessary for the integration of both the wisdom that meditates on the complete selflessness of phenomena and the inconceivable aspects of Mahāyāna method. The *Introduction to the Middle Way* states:

> *Since the light of the fire that burns all the kindling of*
> *cognitive objects without exception*
> *Comes from the fire on this third ground.*[303]

This means that the fire light that foretells the actual fire of gnosis, which arises on the pure grounds and burns the cognitive obscurations, arises on the third ground. There are many other differences among the systems of Svātantrika and below as to how the two obscurations are identified and how they are eliminated, and so on. These should be known elsewhere.

3. Extensive Presentation of the Arguments That Establish Emptiness

This section has two parts: (1) a general demonstration and (2) specific explanations.

1. General Demonstration

[748] Here will be explained the way the view of selflessness is ascertained and the stages of meditating on it in an integrated way without separating them. There are two parts: (1) the stages of entering the meditation on selflessness as explained in the *Anthology of Training* and (2) identifying such things as the self that is the object of negation and self-apprehension.

1. The Stages of Entering the Meditation on Selflessness as Explained in the **Anthology of Training**

The *Anthology of Training* states:

> *Seek out and study the object of forbearance,*
> *Then remain in the forest.*
> *Strive in meditative equipoise and*
> *Meditate on things like foulness.*[304]

To explain this meaning in brief, the *Anthology of Training* itself says: "On this, forebear for a while in the beginning. Since lacking forbearance is not being able to forbear sorrow, which causes your endeavor in study and so on to diminish . . . these words are a teaching."[305] To explain this in detail, the *Anthology of Training* establishes the meaning of each word through many sūtra passages, saying: "Forbearance is spoken of in the *Compendium of Dharma* (*Dharmasaṃgītisūtra*): 'Forbearance is to take up suffering'[306] . . . this summarizes the purification of delusion."[307]

To explain this meaning in brief in conjunction with the context at hand, "forbearance" is to forbear difficulties for the purpose of studying the meaning of emptiness. "Seek out and study" is to muster diligence to find discourses on emptiness. Further, one must not simply be satisfied with mere study, but one must meditate single-pointedly. With a twofold extension[308] one practices by resting the mind evenly, and the purpose of meditative equipoise is also to eliminate the afflictions. Thus, this shows the way that initially one meditates by concentrating on the antidote that suppresses the afflictions: by meditating on foulness as an antidote for attachment, love as an antidote for hatred, and interdependence as an antidote for delusion.

Then, to generate wisdom that realizes selflessness—the antidote that completely uproots the afflictions—meditation on selflessness through the fourfold application of mindfulness is explained. The *Anthology of Training* further states: "Then when the mind has become workable, engage in the applications of mindfulness . . . this was the explanation of the applications of mindfulness."[309] The individual meanings of the applications of mindfulness, to the body and so on, are established in detail through scriptures such as the *Compendium of Dharma*. Again, the *Anthology of Training* states: "Then when the mind has become suitable, engage emptiness . . ."[310] In an extensive explanation of the way of meditating on emptiness by means of the six elements, the six sense-fields of texture, and the eighteen feelings of mental movement, it cites texts like the *Meeting of the Father and Son Sūtra*.

In this way, the earlier and later ways of meditating on selflessness both teach selflessness, [749] but the notes on the *Anthology of Training* correlate the earlier one with the selflessness of persons and the later one with the selflessness of phenomena. Yet Tsongkhapa's *Notes on the Wisdom Chapter* say that the sūtras that teach the applications of mindfulness teach both selflessnesses.[311] Here, in accord with the viewpoint of the root text of the *Way of the Bodhisattva*, meditation on the selflessness of persons is taught by means of the six elements, [IX.57] ***The teeth, hair, and nails . . .***, and [IX.78] ***The body is not the feet . . .*** It teaches a meditation on the selflessness of phenomena by means of the four applications of mindfulness. The commentaries also explain it this way. These two are mutually illustrative, so there is no conflict. The basis of designation for a person is the six elements, and so on; and the lack of true existence of the body, feelings, and so on, is the selflessness of phenomena. Since the lack of true existence of the designated object—the person—is the person's lack of true existence, either way of correlating this is fine.

Tsongkhapa's notes say that the passages in the *Anthology of Training* also make known that the former selflessness of persons is also the subtle selflessness of persons.[312] This is merely stated in brief. For details, "Seek out and study the object of forbearance" mainly is to seek out a thorough study of the meaning of reality. Then it shows how afflictions are eliminated based on meditating on it: the forbearance that eliminates the discordant factors of a thorough study; the diligence that accomplishes its conducive conditions; and both the meditative concentration and the wisdom that have the nature of the antidote to the afflictions. Each of these four is separated out and many classifications of their meaning are established for each one in passages from sūtras. They are also correlated in different ways with four chapters from the *Way of the Bodhisattva,* including the Patience Chapter. Here, it is good to explain the correlations between the *Anthology of Training* and the *Way of the Bodhisattva* in just the context of the Wisdom Chapter.

2. *Identifying Such Things as the Self That Is the Object of Negation and Self-Apprehension*

One might ask, "In the ascertainment of selflessness here, what is the self that is negated with respect to persons and phenomena? What is self-apprehension? And what is selflessness that is the negation of these?"

These will be explained here. The innate apprehension of self is to apprehend any phenomenon to objectively exist without simply being conceptually posited. The conceived object of this innate apprehension of self, or the object of this mode of apprehension, is the self or intrinsic nature that is the object of negation. The existence of that with respect to a person is the self of person, and the existence of that with respect to phenomena (like the aggregates that are the basis of designation for a person) is the self of phenomena. The absence of this kind of self that is the object of negation with respect to a person is the selflessness of persons. Its absence with respect to phenomena is understood to be the selflessness of phenomena. The commentary on the *Four Hundred Verses* states:

> Here, the "self" is the intrinsic nature of an entity that does not depend on other entities. The absence of this is the lack of self. This is known to be twofold through a division into phenomena and persons; these are called "the selflessness of phenomena" and "the selflessness of persons."[313]

[750] The intrinsic nature of phenomena that does not depend or rely on a conceptual posit is the object of negation.

This passage implicitly shows that to apprehend this kind of object of negation existing with respect to persons and phenomena is the twofold apprehension of self. Therefore, the intrinsic existence of persons is the self of persons. To apprehend persons as intrinsically existing is the apprehension of the self of persons. The emptiness of a person's intrinsic existence is the selflessness of person. Likewise, the intrinsic existence of phenomena is the self of phenomena. To apprehend phenomena as intrinsically existing is the apprehension of the self of phenomena. The emptiness of phenomena's intrinsic existence is the selflessness of phenomena.

The person in the former and latter expressions of "person" and "phenomena" is a person who is designated in dependence upon its basis of designation, the aggregates, like Upagupta. "Phenomena," as phenomena bifurcated into persons and phenomena, should be understood as the basis of designation for the person, like the phenomena of Upagupta's aggregates such as his eyes and ears. The two selves that are the conceived objects (*zhen yul*) of the twofold apprehension of self are, like the horns of a rabbit, not even conventionally existent. The observed objects (*dmigs yul*) of the twofold apprehensions of self are both persons and phenomena; so those two, along with the twofold apprehension of self and the twofold selflessness, are conventionally existent.

Furthermore, Svātantrikas divide the twofold apprehension of self with respect to the mode of apprehension (*'dzin stangs*), not with respect to the observed object (*dmigs yul*). This is because they understand that apprehending the self of persons is to apprehend a person existing as a self-subsisting substance upon observing a person; and they understand that apprehending the self of phenomena is to apprehend true existence upon observing that. Prāsaṅgikas divide the twofold apprehension of self with respect to the observed object, not with respect to the mode of apprehension. This is because to apprehend intrinsic existence upon observing a person is understood to be apprehending the self of persons, and to apprehend intrinsic existence upon observing phenomena is understood to be apprehending the self of phenomena.

Similarly, Svātantrikas divide the twofold selflessness by means of the object of negation (*dgag bya*), not by means of the empty basis (*stong gzhi*). This is because they understand the selflessness of persons to be the negation of the existence of a self-subsisting substance with respect to a person; and they understand apprehending the selflessness of phenomena to be the negation of true existence with respect to persons and so on. Prāsaṅgikas divide the twofold selflessness by means of the empty basis, not by means of the object of negation. This is because a person's emptiness of intrinsic existence is understood to be the selflessness of persons, and phenomena's emptiness of intrinsic existence is held to be the selflessness of phenomena.

Further, according to Svātantrikas, there is a difference in the degree of subtlety in terms of the twofold apprehension of self because there is a difference in the degree of subtlety within the two selves that are the objects of negation. In the Prāsaṅgika system, the subtle self to be negated is understood to be [751] something that exists on its own, so there is no difference in the degree of subtlety within the twofold selves to be negated. For this reason, there is no difference in the degree of subtlety in terms of the twofold apprehension of self, either.

In general, how to understand the subtle and coarse selflessness is like this: Most Buddhist schools of the Svātantrika and below similarly maintain the coarse selflessness of persons to be the emptiness of a person that intrinsically exists as permanent and singular, and maintain the subtle selflessness of persons to be the emptiness of a person existing as a self-subsisting substance. Yet the Vātsīputrīyas do not accept this kind of subtle selflessness of persons. Vaibhāṣikas and Sautrāntikas do not accept the selflessness of phenomena, so they claim that the subtle selflessness and the subtle selflessness of persons have the same meaning. Proponents of Mind-Only claim the coarse selflessness of phenomena to be the emptiness of external objects composed of partless particles; they claim the subtle selflessness of phenomena to be the emptiness of the separate substances of a material form and the source of knowledge apprehending that form, for instance.

Yogācāra-Svātantrika-Mādhyamikas claim that the coarse selflessness of phenomena is the emptiness of the separate substances of perceived and perceiver, for instance; they assert the subtle selflessness of phenomena to be the emptiness of phenomena's true existence. Sautrāntika-Svātantrika-Mādhyamikas accept external objects, so they do not assert the emptiness of the separate substances of a material form and the source of knowledge apprehending that form. The way they understand the coarse selflessness of phenomena is similar to the way proponents of Mind-Only do, and the way that they understand the subtle selflessness of phenomena is similar to the way of Yogācāra-Madhyamaka. There are also differences among them in terms of whether or not they assert the subtle selflessness of persons as emptiness.

In the Prāsaṅgika system, the coarse selflessness of persons is the emptiness of a person existing as a self-subsisting substance and the subtle selflessness of persons is the emptiness of a person existing on its own. The coarse selflessness of phenomena is the emptiness of a separate substance of macro-objects (*rags pa*) composed of partless particles and the source of knowledge that apprehends them. The subtle selflessness of phenomena is understood to be the emptiness of the aggregates, the basis of designation for the person, existing on their own.

2. Specific Explanations

This section has two parts: (1) explaining the reasoning establishing the selflessness of persons and (2) explaining the reasoning establishing the selflessness of phenomena.

1. Explaining the Reasoning Establishing the Selflessness of Persons

This section has two parts: (1) a general presentation and (2) a presentation of specific arguments that negate the self of persons.

1. General Presentation

The root verses describe the selflessness of persons in general as follows: [IX.57] ***The teeth, hair, and nails are not the self . . .*** This shows how the innate conceived object of the apprehension of a self of persons is refuted. Later, there is a refutation of the self imputed by non-Buddhists that shows how an imputed self ascribed by philosophical systems is refuted. [752] Here I will explain a brief overview in three parts: (1) how to identify the imputed and innate apprehensions of self, (2) how to negate the self that is the conceived object of the innate apprehension of self, and (3) how to understand the self that is the observed object of the innate apprehension of self.

1. How to Identify the Imputed and Innate Apprehensions of Self

When the apprehension of a self of persons is divided in terms of its modes of expression, there is the coarse and the subtle. Within the coarse apprehension of a self of persons as well, there is the imputed and the innate. The imputed is to apprehend the existence of a self-subsisting substance that is discordant with the characteristics of the aggregates, like a master of a servant. The innate is to apprehend the existence of a self-subsisting substance that has the nature of the aggregates. The former is not different from the way that Svātantrikas and below assert the existence of a self-subsisting substance in the way that it is apprehended as permanent, singular, and independent; thus, this is only imputed. The latter must be posited as innate because it is taught that there is a view of the transitory collective like that which is the object appropriately eliminated on the fourth ground. The *Introduction to the Middle Way* states: "What is connected with a view of self is completely extinguished."[314]

Within the subtle apprehension of a self of persons, as a result of the influence of a philosophical system or having engaged in reasoned analysis, the imputed is the apprehension that holds it to be reasonable for a person to exist on its own. The innate does not rely on anything like that; it is a natural, default (*ngang ngam shugs kyis*) apprehension of a person existing on its own. The conceived object of the innate apprehension of a self is the main object of negation; negating the imputed is just ancillary because the innate is the root of existence. In this way, the *Introduction to the Middle Way* says:

> *All afflictions and faults without exception are seen by the mind*
> *To arise from the view of the transitory collective.*[315]

It says that the root of all problems—the afflictions, such as attachment, birth, and aging—is the innate view of the transitory collective.

One might think, "Does this not conflict with what was said before, that the root of cyclic existence is the apprehension of a self of phenomena that apprehends the aggregates as truly existent, as in 'As long as the aggregates are apprehended . . . '?"[316]

There is no contradiction because there is no difference between these two in terms of their mode of apprehension, and they are both the same in being innate apprehensions of true existence. Regarding this, the innate view of the transitory collective is afflictive insight (*shes rab nyon mongs can*) that, regarding one's continuum, takes either "I" or "mine" as an observed object and apprehends it to exist on its own. Thus, there are two: the view of the transitory collective that apprehends "I" and the view of the transitory collective that apprehends "mine." It is impossible for them to have a common locus. The observed object of the view of the transitory collective that apprehends "I" is the mere "I" that is imputed in dependence upon the aggregates. The observed object of the view of the transitory collective that apprehends "mine" is just the concept (*rang ldog*) "mine." A feature of both of these is that the observed object [753] is similarly apprehended as existing on its own.

To identify the basis of characteristics (*mtshan nyid gzhi*) for "mine," the eyes and ears within one's continuum are a basis of characteristics for "mine," but are explained not to be the observed object of the innate view of the transitory collective. Alternatively, the eyes and ears are the basis for designation of "mine," but are not its basis of characteristics because it is not reasonable for a basis for designation to be the designated object. Therefore, to describe the eyes and ears as the basis of characteristics for "mine" is to show a basis of characteristics for that which causes the construction of "mine," it does not show that which is "mine" itself. There are many different types of claims, and a system of four alternatives for categorizing the apprehension of a self of persons in relation to the view of the transitory collective. Nevertheless, here in Prāsaṅgika both the view of a transitory collective that apprehends "I" and "mine" are apprehensions of a self of persons, so we follow the tradition that does not accept that the view of the transitory collective is not an apprehension of a self of persons.

Observing another person that is different from one's continuum and holding this to exist on its own is apprehending a self of persons but not a view of the transitory collective. To be a view of the transitory collective, the mental idea "mine" must naturally arise upon observing either "I" or "mine" regarding one's continuum. This is stated in the autocommentary on the *Introduction to the Middle Way*. Therefore, a view of the transitory collective that apprehends "I" is necessarily both an apprehension of the self of persons and a view of the transitory collective. Yet if it is an apprehension of the self of persons and a view of the transitory collective, it is not necessarily a view of the transitory collective that apprehends "I." One should likewise know this for the view of a transitory collective that apprehends "mine" as well.

2. How to Negate the Self That Is the Conceived Object of the Innate Apprehension of Self

Having understood that the innate view of the transitory collective that apprehends this kind of "I" and "mine" is the root of existence, one must negate it. The way of doing so is first, for a person desiring liberation to acknowledge the faults of existence, and to contemplate them again and again such that one becomes disgusted by them and wants to dispel them. Then, seeing that if its cause is not removed, neither is the effect, one engages in the analysis of what is its root. Through analysis one gains certainty as to the way that ignorance, or the innate view of the transitory collective, is the root of existence and one wishes to dispel it. Then one strives in the methods for dispelling it, as is said in the *Introduction to the Middle Way:*

> *Realizing that the self is its object*
> *The yogis negate the self.*[317]

One should negate the distorted apprehension through undermining its conceived object through reason. How to undermine it is to investigate with genuine reason whether or not the self is intrinsically existent as it is apprehended to be. Thereby, it is rejected through knowing that there is no such self. The *Four Hundred Verses* says:

> *When seeing that there is no self in the object,*
> *The seed of existence ceases.*[318]

And the *Commentary on Epistemology* says:

> *Without undermining the object,*
> *It cannot be eliminated.*[319]

[754] To thereby relinquish it by undermining the conceived object of the view of the transitory collective, all problems and faults cease, just like cutting the roots of a tree. The *Anthology of Training* states:

> The emptiness of persons is fully established. By this, the entirety of afflictions will not arise because the root is cut. It states in the *Mystery of the Tathāgata Sūtra:* "Śāntimati, consider this. For example, when you cut a tree by the roots, all the branches, leaves, and stems will wither. Śāntimati, likewise when you completely pacify the view of the transitory collective, all the afflictions and the subsidiary afflictions will be pacified."[320]

The autocommentary on the *Introduction to the Middle Way* also explains in this way.

3. How to Understand the Self That Is the Observed Object of the Innate Apprehension of Self

The self or person that is the observed object of the innate view of the transitory collective conventionally exists. The way it exists is as a mere conceptual designation depending on the aggregates. The *Four Hundred Verses* states:

> *Attachment and so forth without concepts*
> *Do not exist.*[321]

In the commentary it says, "There are only concepts; without concepts there is no existence. Without a doubt they definitely do not exist essentially, like a rope imputed upon a snake."[322] As is said, all phenomena are merely conceptually designated, like a snake imputed upon a colorful rope.

For example, a colorful rope is thought to be a snake as a consequence of having a similar shape and form as a snake, and the conditions of it not being clear and so on. When this happens, the snake in the rope is merely a conceptual designation. From the side of the colorful rope itself (*rang ngos nas*), there is no snake. This is because there is no basis of characteristics for a snake that is apprehended at all in the collection of the parts, shape, and color of the colorful rope. Other than those parts as well, there is no basis of characteristics for such an apprehended snake. Likewise, when a person is designated upon the aggregates, there occurs the thought "I" or "person." When this happens, the person is designated in dependence on the aggregates; it does not exist objectively (*rang ngos nas*) other than being a mere conceptual designation. This is because there is no basis of characteristics for a person to be apprehended in each of the aggregates, in the collection, in the continuity, or in the parts; and it is not apprehended apart from the aggregates, either.

In this way, in accord with the viewpoint of the *Meeting of the Father and Son Sūtra,* the *Precious Garland* says:

> *A being is not earth and not water,*
> *Nor fire, wind, or space.*
> *Neither consciousness, nor all of them.*
> *What is a being other than these?*[323]

A being is designated based on the six elements, yet there is no being or person in each of the elements, like the earth. A being is also not the collective, "nor all of them." The last line states that a being is not found elsewhere than them, either. It says in our text here as well, [IX.57] ***The teeth, hair, and nails are not the self . . .*** It likewise states how there is no self or person to be found in each of the six elements, [755] their collection, or elsewhere. If you understand the way that a person is conceptually designated, then you can understand that all phenomena are like this, as in the above citations from the *Condensed Perfection of Wisdom* and the *Precious Garland.*

In this way, Prāsaṅgikas hold that any phenomenon that is posited cannot be found upon seeking out its designated object, so all frameworks take place by means of mere designations without investigation and analysis. Svātantrikas and below are not satisfied with mere names for positing persons and so on. Rather, they think that it must be the case that a person can be posited if its basis of characteristics can be found within the basis of designation—the aggregates—such as the collection, parts, or continuity. They think that if it is not found there then a person cannot be posited because it cannot be found elsewhere. Therefore, they understand the person as the designated object, having sought it out within the aggregates that are its basis of designation. The *Introduction to the Middle Way* says:

> *Some people claim the aggregates to be the basis for a view of self;*
> *Some assert all five, and others assert only mind.*[324]

As for the observed object of a view of self or basis of characteristics for a person, some in the Mahāsaṃmata sect within the Vaibhāṣikas posit all five aggregates. Likewise, some in the Mahāsaṃmata sect posit just the mind. The Kaśmiri Vaibhāṣikas and Sautrāntikas following scripture posit the continuity of aggregates. Further, "others assert only mind" summarizes this. Svātantrikas like Bhāviveka, who do not accept the basic consciousness, posit the mental consciousness, along with both Sautrāntikas and proponents of Mind-Only following reasoning.

Most proponents of Mind-Only posit the basic consciousness as the basis of characteristics for a person. They say that they accept that a person nominally exists, but they hold that this is the case for just the concept (*rang ldog*) of a person; they do not accept that a person is necessarily nominally existent. This is because they accept that consciousness and so on that are understood as the basis of characteristics for a person substantially exist. Even though the mere words "nominally existent person" are similar to those of the Prāsaṅgikas, the meaning is not at all alike. Although they accept that a person is designated in dependence upon the aggregates that are its basis of designation, they think that the basis of designation for a person is necessarily a person. They think that the aggregates are designated as a person. Also, they think that if there were no person within the basis of designation for a person, then there would be no person.

Prāsaṅgikas hold that a basis of designation is necessarily not the designated object. Therefore, from the side of the basis of designation, nothing at all exists as the basis of characteristics for a person, and furthermore, anything that is a person's basis of characteristics, like consciousness, is negated even conventionally. One might think then that a person would not exist [756] because it is not found anywhere else than this. This is not the case because it is accepted that without investigation and analysis, mere conventional designation is enough, such as "this is Upagupta," "this is Devadatta," "this one did this." Without being satisfied with this, if a person is posited having sought out its designated object, it comes to be objectively existent. Thereby, it is held that one falls away from the assertion of interdependence, and the meaning of a person's nominal existence becomes insufficient.

Therefore, in the Prāsaṅgika system, the observed object of the innate view of self, or the basis of characteristics for a person, is not posited as either the collection of the aggregates, each one, or anything else other than the aggregates. Rather, it is posited as just the mere convention of self or person designated in dependence on the aggregates. For example, it is like the way that neither the parts of the chariot, etc., nor anything other than those parts, is posited as the chariot's basis of characteristics. Rather, it is held that its basis of characteristics is the mere chariot that is designated in dependence on parts.

One might think, "The innate view of the self would not be the view of the transitory collective because 'the transitory collective' is the aggregates, which is not posited as the observed object of the innate view of self." This is not a problem because the "view of the transitory collective" expresses a view of a mere self that is designated in dependence on the transitory collective of aggregates. Moreover, one might wonder, "If the aggregates are not the observed object of the view of self, then this would conflict with a sūtra that says: 'Whichever mendicants or *brahmins* think "I" and follow this view, they are following the view of only the appropriating aggregates.'"

Here is what this means: The word "only" excludes an observed object that is other than the aggregates; it does not show that the aggregates themselves are the self. Another sūtra says: "Form is not the self . . ." Understood otherwise conflicts with the negation of the aggregates being the self, as is stated in the *Introduction to the Middle Way*:

> *Since our teacher said that the aggregates are the self,*
> *The self has been asserted as the aggregates.*
> *Yet that was to negate a self other than the aggregates*
> *Since other sūtras say that form is not the self.*[325]

Thus, the previous sūtra negates a self that is different from the aggregates, as non-Buddhists claim. The latter sūtra negates a self that is the aggregates as well, as most of our Buddhist schools claim. According to the Prāsaṅgikas, the import of the words "following the view of these five aggregates" is the observed object of the innate view of self that is the mere self that is designated in dependence on the aggregates. This is taught as the support of karmic causality since it presents a clear organization of the sūtras. [757] This way of assertion is a wondrous feature of Prāsaṅgika that other Buddhist schools try to achieve, but fail. By this unmistaken path of scripture and reasoning, the viewpoint of the sūtras is clearly presented.

Next, [IX.60] ***If the cognition of sound were permanent . . .*** Here is a twofold presentation of (1) the assertions of the non-Buddhist Sāṃkhya and (2) their refutation.

A1. Assertions of the Sāṃkhya

The Sāṃkhya was the first non-Buddhist school to appear. In an ageless time, there was a sage called Kapila, who had a yellowish-grey topknot and possessed the five paranormal powers. He had a great innate intellect and composed many Sāṃkhya treatises. His followers were called the Kāpilas or Sāṃkhyas. In this school, they claim that an effect is present at the time of the cause and is manifested by conditions. Also, there were atheistic Sāṃkhyas who accepted that things arise from just the primal basis (*gtso bo*) and there were theistic Sāṃkhyas who accepted that while cause and effect share the same nature, there are separate manifestations through the blessings of Īśvara. Within each of these systems, there are two accounts: one tradition describes the essential identity of cause and effect, which is unmanifest but becomes manifest through the presence of conditions—whereby it is designated with the convention of arising; another propounds transformation, in the way that milk with the nature of curd becomes curd through meeting with conditions.

They classify all phenomena within a fixed number of twenty-five categories. If these are known, then it is easy to understand their assertions, so I will state them here: The threefold primal basis (*pradhāna*), intellect (*mahat*), and ego (*ahaṃkāra*); the fivefold "basics" (*tanmātra*) of form, sound, scent, taste, texture; the fivefold mental-faculties of eye, ear, nose, tongue, and skin or body; the fivefold action-faculties of mouth or speaking, handling, walking, evacuation or buttocks, and reproduction; the eleventh faculty [i.e., *manas*] that has the nature of both [mind and action]; the five elements of earth, water, fire, wind, and space; and the spirit (*puruṣa*). "The basic materiality" (*rtsa ba'i rang bzhin*), "the universal" (*spyi*), and "the primal basis" (*gtso bo*) have the same meaning. "The intellect" (*blo*) and "the great" (*chen po*) have the same meaning. "The self" (*bdag*), "the person" (*gang zag*), and "the spirit" (*shes rig gi skyes bu*) have the same meaning. These are all said to be comprised within matter and mind; the spirit is mind, and the other twenty-four are matter. There are four alternatives for the twenty-five categories in terms of being materiality and/or a transformation: the primal basis is exclusively materiality; there are seven that are both materiality and a transformation: the intellect, the ego, and the five basics; there are sixteen that are only transformations: the eleven faculties and the five elements; and spirit is neither materiality nor a transformation. It says in Īśvarakṛṣṇa's text:

> *The basic materiality is not a transformation.*
> *The seven, including the intellect, are transformations of materiality.*
> *Sixteen are transformations.*
> [758] *The spirit is neither materiality nor transformation.*[326]

Materiality and cause have the same meaning; transformation and effect have the same meaning. Spirit is held to have the following characteristics: It is the essence of mind; it is not the creator of transformations. It is eternal since it is unborn. It is the enjoyer since it experiences happiness and sorrow. It does not have the three qualities (*guṇa*); it pervades all beings. It is singular since it is partless; and it is infinite since it has no beginning or end.

The primal basis is held to have six characteristics: It is the performer of actions; it is eternal because it is unborn; it is singular since it is partless; it is exclusively an object because it is mindless; it pervades the entirety of inhabitants and environments; and it is the equilibrium of the three qualities. The intellect is held to be like a double-mirror, in which reflections of outer transformations of objects and reflections of inner spirit arise. The intellect is pervasively material, and it is said that cognition necessitates a self.

Bondage and liberation occur like this: When the wish to participate in the domain of spirit arises, the primal basis provides transformations. Furthermore, from the basic materiality comes the intellect, and from the intellect the ego. From among three types of ego, the five basics arise from the energetic (*rajas*) ego. From those, the five elements arise. From the light (*sattva*) ego, the eleven faculties arise. The inert (*tamas*) ego is said to initiate the other two egos. This way of arising is described in Īśvarakṛṣṇa's text.

Engagement with objects is like this: Through the five faculties such as the ear being blessed by the mind, the intellect conceives objects like sound. The conceived objects are then cognized by the spirit. The primal basis is like a mute with legs; it knows how to transform but does not cognize this activity. The spirit is like a sighted lame person; it can cognize activities but cannot manifest them. There is cyclic existence for as long as the spirit partakes of objects without knowing the transformations to be manifestations of the primal basis. When certainty arises, based on a teacher's essential instructions, that the transformations are merely manifestations of the primal basis, the faults of objects are seen, and attachment to objects decreases. Based on cultivating meditative concentration, paranormal powers are attained, and when the eye with paranormal power gazes upon the primal basis, the primal basis retreats in embarrassment, like another's woman; it does not remain in proximity to the spirit, from which it separates. The transformations dissolve back into the primal basis, fading like a rainbow in the reverse process by which they evolved. When they become unmanifest, the spirit remains in isolation, without any object to behold. They claim this to be the attainment of liberation.

Moreover, it is explained as follows:

> *By knowing the twenty-five principles*
> *The one with a topknot or crown on his head,*
> *No matter what he* [759] *wears,*
> *Will no doubt be liberated.*[327]

They are called "Sāṃkhyas" ("Enumerators") because they accept the determined number of twenty-five objects of knowledge, or because they accept liberation through knowing the characteristics of the twenty-five principles. Also, they are called "Kāpilas" because they regard Kapila as their teacher, or are called "proponents of material causality" because they hold materiality to be the cause. They are also called "manifestors" (*gsal byed pa*) because they believe that the effect exists at the time of the cause and is made manifest by conditions. There are also ways of explaining the Kāpilas and the Sāṃkhyas as distinct.

A2. Refutation of the Sāṃkhya

Here I show how to refute a permanent spirit through argument: if a spirit that is the enjoyer of the five basics such as sound were permanent, it would absurdly follow that it would need to always apprehend sound even when there was no sound. Later, I will show how to refute a permanent primal basis and production from self. One should know the ways of refuting a material intellect and so on from elsewhere.

Next, [IX.67] ***What lacks mind is also not the self...*** Here, I will present the assertions of the non-Buddhist Nyāya-Vaiśeṣika followed by their refutation.

B1. Assertions of the Nyāya-Vaiśeṣika

The Vaiśeṣika teachers were a sage called Aulūkya who thought he discovered six categories from an owl that he took to be a god, and another sage, Kaṇāda, who would not eat grains dispensed by anyone else. The Vaiśeṣikas who were their followers were also known as Aulūkyas and Kāṇādas. As for the teacher of the Nyāya, when Īśvara put a handsome sage to protect the Goddess Umā, Umā became attracted to the sage, revealing many alluring expressions. Even so, his eyes fell on her feet and he practiced discipline, which pleased Īśvara. Īśvara empowered him to compose a text, and he was known as the sage Akṣapāda ("eyes on feet"). His Naiyayika followers were also known as Ākṣapādas.

Both the Vaiśeṣikas and the Naiyayikas hold Īśvara as their teacher, and believe that Īśvara is the creator of the entire world of inhabitants and environments. Among them there are some who hold Brahmā and Viṣṇu as their teacher. Since they are followers of a text composed by Kaṇāda clarifying the specifics (*viśeṣa*),[328] they are called Vaiśeṣikas. There are other ways of explaining this term as well. Since they follow the views of reason (*nyāya*) set out by Akṣapāda, they are called Naiyayikas. They accept the framework of sixteen categories from the logicians, such as the sources of knowledge and warranted objects.[329] Vaiśeṣikas accept three sources of knowledge: perception, inference, and testimony. Naiyayikas accept four, adding analogy to those three.

As for the six categories, they accept a determined number of six categories as objects of knowledge, as is said: "The sixfold substance, quality, action, universal, particularity, and inherence."[330] The definition of the first category among the six, [760] *substance*, is threefold: that which has action, quality, and is the cause of inherence. There is a ninefold division of substance: earth, water, fire, wind, space, time, direction, self, and cognition. Among these, the self is accepted to substantially exist apart from the body, faculties, and cognition. Further, it is held to be the support of the nine qualities such as cognition, and acts as the cause of the inherence of these qualities. It is held to be mindless material, permanent, unborn, an agent, an enjoyer, all-pervasive, and a partless singularity. Spirit and person have the same meaning as the self.

From among the nine substances, the four elements and cognition are held to be substances that do not pervade everywhere. The subtle particles of the four elements are permanent substances, and the macro-objects that are constituted by them are held to be impermanent substances. The self, direction, time, and space are four substances that are held to pervade everything.

As for *quality*, it has four features: it relies on substance, does not have another quality, does not act as the cause of inherence, and is independent. When divided, there are twenty-four qualities. It is said:

> There are twenty-four: form, scent, taste, texture, number, magnitude, distinctness, conjunction, separation, remoteness, nearness, cognition, happiness, suffering, desire, aversion, effort, heaviness, liquidity, heat, viscidity, conditioning, virtue, and vice.

From among these, the self has nine qualities: cognition, which is knowing an object; happiness, which is satisfaction; suffering, which is torment; desire, which is attachment; aversion, which is anger; effort, which is striving to attain a goal; virtue, which is an action that results in happiness; vice, which is the opposite of virtue; and conjunction, which arises from cognition and is the cause of cognition. These qualities are held to rely on nothing but substance; and there are no second qualities of qualities.

The third category is *action*, of which there are five: lifting, dropping, extending, retracting, and traversing. The fourth category is *universal*, which is a substance that is appealed to in language and cognition for a common property that it encompasses. For instance, "existence" is a distinct universal; "cow" and "tree" are limited universals. It is held that there is no second [higher] universal of universals. The fifth category is *particularity*, which is a phenomenon's supporting characteristic by which it is understood to be distinct from other phenomena. It is that by which, for instance, the difference between white and black is understood. The sixth category is *inherence*. This is the property of relationship that is a separate substance from the supported and support. It is the means by which something like a supported quality and its supporting substance are understood, such that it is observed that "this exists there."

[761] Thus, there are two aspects within the qualities of the six categories, what is permanent and what is impermanent. Action is exclusively impermanent; the others are permanent. This system's path of liberation is through bathing, initiations, fasting, celibacy, sacrifices, and so on. These virtues are held to bring about liberation from existence; the opposite of these are vices, the causes of existence. At some point, through meditating on yoga in accord with a teacher's essential instructions, one comes to know things like the faculties and self differently. Then one comes to see reality and understand the nature of the six categories. At that point, one does not accumulate virtue or vice; one does not accumulate new karma, and old karma becomes exhausted. Thereby, one becomes free from the former qualities of the self, such as the body, faculties, and cognition, and does not take on a new body of faculties and so on. Like a fire that has consumed its kindling, the entirety of birth is severed and only the self remains; this is held to be liberation. It is said that there is no beginning to cyclic existence, but that there is an end. There are some slight differences within the philosophical systems of the Nyāya and Vaiśeṣika as subschools, but I have explained them in common because their general structure is similar.

B2. Refutation of the Nyāya-Vaiśeṣika

They assert a self that is mindless matter, an agent, and an enjoyer. This is refuted by arguments that show that this does not make sense, for instance, just like asserting things like a pot to have these qualities. The refutation of the claim of a permanent creator of inhabitants and environments, like Īśvara, will be explained later. Also, there are many arguments in texts like the *Commentary on Epistemology* that refute the claim to a path of liberation through initiations as described in the Īśvara scriptures.

> Next, [IX.70] ***"If the self does not exist,***
> ***Then a relationship of karmic causality would not make sense . . . "***

Here I will respond to the objections of those who say that karmic causality without a permanent self makes no sense. The response has three parts: (1) showing why a causal relationship makes sense, (2) our unique way of positing the entity of disintegration (*zhig dngos*), and (3) our unique way of positing the three times.

1. Showing Why a Causal Relationship Makes Sense

Our Buddhist schools do not accept a permanent self, and we hold that all conditioned phenomena are impermanent, as is taught. A sūtra says: "The karma of embodied beings will not perish for even a hundred eons."[331] We hold that even if there are numerous eons and generations between an action and its result, the particular result will not perish, but will definitely occur.

The Sāṃkhyas and others say, "We assert the person as the support of karmic causality, a person that is singular, permanent, and independent. Thereby, the causal relation makes sense from one person coming here from a previous life and moving on to another life in the future. For you, this is not reasonable. If the person who acts is impermanent, then it would follow that the person would not be the one experiencing the effect, for the self had been annihilated at that time. [762] There would be other problems as well, such that it would follow that the results of actions would perish, and that one would meet with the results of what one did not do. Likewise, as it is expressed by an opponent in the *Fundamental Verses of the Middle Way*:

> *If it remains at the time of maturation*
> *Then the action would be permanent;*
> *If it ceases, then how can what has ceased*
> *Produce an effect?*[332]

If a virtuous or evil action remains until it produces its matured effect, then it would be permanent. Yet if the action disintegrates in the second instant of its existence, then how is it reasonable for the effect to arise if the cause had ceased long ago? It does not make sense."

This is our reply: If there is a problem for karmic causality not being reasonable because we do not assert a permanent self, then there is a similar problem in your assertion of a permanent self. This is because it is not possible for something that is permanent to be involved in activities like performing actions and experiencing results, or coming and going at all—such as coming here from the past and going there in the future. The previous explanation refutes the permanent self that you impute, and later I will explain the arguments that undermine the possibility of something permanent performing an action. Therefore, your claim to a permanent self, and your words that it is that which performs actions, comes and goes, etc., contradict themselves.

Moreover, both of us have to accept that the one that performs an action and the one that reaps the effect are distinct; the performer of an action does not exist when the matured result is experienced; and the experiencer of the result does not exist when an action is performed because this is established by reason. If you do not accept this then you contradict reason; if you do accept this then it follows that the self is annihilated. Other problems follow from this claim but there is no point to debate this here.

One might respond, "In your Buddhist system, is the person that accumulates karma the person or self that experiences the maturation or not? If it is, then it is permanent. If it is not, then the accumulator of karma does not experience the maturation. Since the experiencer of the maturation did not accumulate the karma, then the action performed would perish; the same problems remain as before, which are intractable."

This is our response: Even though the person who accumulates karma is not the one who experiences the maturation, the two persons at the time of the accumulation and at the time of maturation are held to be a single continuum of aggregates that are its basis of designation. This is the "I" that is part of the mere "I" that is designated. Therefore, since we can posit that "I performed this action, and I experienced the maturation," we do not have these problems. In the same way, we can posit youth and old age, yesterday and today, morning and afternoon, and previous and later instants. Therefore, in our system we do not accept a permanent self that moves from here to there, or anything that intrinsically exists. We can distinctly posit the one who performs an action and the one who reaps its effect by designating in dependence upon a single continuum of aggregates [763] that is its basis of designation. So there is no problem of karmic causality being unreasonable.

This is expressed in the Meditative Concentration Chapter of our text:

> [VIII.98] ***The thought, "I experienced this"***
> ***Is wrong;***
> ***For what dies is one thing***
> ***And what is born, another.***

And,

> [VIII.101] ***A continuum and a collection***
> ***Are unreal, like a garland and an army.***

The *Treasury of Metaphysics* states this as follows:

> *There is no self, only aggregates*
> *Conditioned by afflictions and karma.*
> *The continuity in the intermediate existence*
> *Enters the womb like a flame.*[333]

Other than being designated upon a mere continuum of aggregates, there is nothing that transfers from here to there as it is asserted by non-Buddhists. From a continuum of aggregates in the intermediate existence, there are aggregates in the existence of birth. From this, there is the existence of a prior time from which there is the existence of death and again the intermediate existence. The continuum of aggregates is impermanent like the wheel of a spinning firebrand. Even without a permanent self, there is no contradiction with the continuum of aggregates entering into the womb, and so forth. For example, even though a flame changes every instant, there is a continuum that goes to another place. As in the case of the flame, there is no contradiction here. In addition to the flame, other examples are stated by Nāgārjuna in his *Essence of Interdependence* (*Pratītyasamutpāda hṛdaya*):

> *Like a recitation, a flame, a mirror, a seal,*
> *A magnifying glass, a seed, sourness, and sound,*
> *The wise should know that the aggregates also do not move*
> *Even though they transmigrate.*[334]

Moreover, since each of these examples individually cannot completely illustrate the way of transmigration, the eight examples are needed. One should know this way of birth and death extensively from the sūtras themselves.

Furthermore, the *Anthology of Training* cites the *Rice Seedling Sūtra* (*Śālistambasūtra*):

> There is no phenomenon at all that moves from this world to another world. Even so, there is the manifest outcome of the effects of actions when the causes and conditions are complete. For example, the reflection of a face shines in a polished round mirror, yet it is not that the face moves into the round mirror. When the causes and conditions are complete, the face appears.[335]

It also shows the example of the reflection of the moon in water. The *Anthology of Training* states: "When the causes and conditions are complete, the seed, consciousness, karma, and afflictions make the connection to the birthplace in the mother's womb. Thereby, the sprout of name and form is established."[336] And, "When the aggregates at the time of death cease in the end, the aggregates included in birth arise like one side of a scale rising while the other falls."[337] This describes how the aggregates arise and cease at the times of birth and death. The *Sūtra of Great Emptiness* says:

> Karma exists. [764] Maturation exists. Other than the designated words upon phenomena, no other agent leaving the aggregates and transmigrating to other aggregates is observed. Designated words upon phenomena are like this: "when this is present, that arises."[338]

Also, the *King of Meditative Stabilizations Sūtra* says:

> *Someone who dies in this world*
> *Does not go on or move to another world.*
> *Even so, their committed actions never perish;*
> *They mature as positive and negative effects in cyclic existence.*
> *They are neither permanent nor annihilated.*
> *Karma is not accumulated nor does it remain;*
> *Nor is it the case that what was done is not met with later.*
> *Also, there is no experience of what others have done.*
> *There is nothing that goes or comes back;*
> *All of it neither exists nor does not exist.*
> *There is no purity in views that engage a basis.*[339]

Also, the *Praise of the Exceptional One* (*Viśeṣastava*) says: "From one body to another body . . ."[340] In short, other than the basic nature of interdependence that is free from the extremes of permanence and annihilation, and inexpressible as either the same or different, there is not even the slightest thing that transfers from one place to another. The Madhyamaka *Essence of Interdependence* says:

> *From phenomena that are only empty,*
> *None other than empty phenomena arise.*[341]

Virtuous and unvirtuous actions disintegrate in their second instant, but there is no problem with their producing effects. This is because when actions orient toward cessation, they have a basis upon which there is posited the potency of the action to elicit maturation. One might wonder how this is. Some Sautrāntikas and Kaśmīri Vaibhāṣikas posit the mental continuum (*sems kyi rgyun*). Some proponents of Mind-Only posit the basic consciousness. Svātantrikas and proponents of Mind-Only that do not accept the basic consciousness posit the mental consciousness. These three are ways of positing the person that is the support of karmic causality.

Alternatively, some Vaibhāṣikas assert "the non-perishing" (*chud mi za ba*), which is like a promissory note (*bu lon gyi dpang rgya*). Other Vaibhāṣikas assert the "acquisition" (*thob pa*) of an action. These two are posited as that which elicits the maturation of an action. These two are each held to substantially exist as non-associated formations (*ldan min 'dus byed*) that are separate from the action. These, along with the uninterrupted continuity of predispositions or potencies for action that elicit maturation within the basic consciousness, are our Buddhist traditions' assertions of the way something with the power to produce a later effect elicits maturation.

Prāsaṅgikas maintain that karma does not intrinsically exist, so karma does not intrinsically arise. Therefore, an intrinsic cessation of karma is impossible. Merely conventionally, the cessation or disintegration of an action is most reasonable to be an entity, so there is no contradiction for an action to produce its effect even after a long time passed since it had ceased. Therefore, there is no need to posit anything like what is non-perishing or a basic consciousness, having sought out a designated object. Thus, the *Fundamental Verses of the Middle Way* states:

> *Since an action does not arise*
> [765] *It does not have intrinsic existence;*
> *Its not arising is the reason for*
> *Its not perishing.*[342]

The autocommentary on the *Introduction to the Middle Way* also cites this passage to establish this meaning.[343] Here, the non-perishing is explicitly negated, and by this the basic consciousness is negated implicitly. "Will not perish for even a hundred eons"[344] is held to mean that since karma does not intrinsically arise, it will not perish. As soon as karma is held to intrinsically exist, it will remain permanently until its maturation and will be annihilated when it ceases. Thus, disintegration being an entity is not suitable for this position.

Also, the autocommentary on the *Introduction to the Middle Way* states:

> Thus, in neither of the two truths does it intrinsically exist, so this is a complete rejection of the views of permanence and annihilation. Moreover, there is a connection with the effects of actions even after a long time after an action has ceased. This is reasonable even without constructing things like the continuity of the basic consciousness, the non-perishing, or acquisition. How is this?
>
> > *Since there is no intrinsic cessation*
> > *This has power even without the basic consciousness.*
> > *Know that even after a long time after an action ceases*
> > *The precise effect will arise.*[345]

Nevertheless, conventionally as a mere basis for the infusion of predispositions of karma, it is said that the person is posited as the lasting basis and the mental continuum is posited as the temporary basis for the infusion of predispositions.

The way that an effect arises from an action that has ceased and lacks intrinsic nature is also described in the *Introduction to the Middle Way* through an example:

> *Fools become attached to objects that were observed in a dream*
> *Even while awake.*
> *Likewise, from an action that has ceased and has no intrinsic nature*
> *Results arise.*[346]

To make this understood, the autocommentary on the *Introduction to the Middle Way* cites the *Sūtra of Transmigration (Bhavasaṃkrāntisūtra)*:

> Great King, consider this. For example, a person has a dream of sleeping with a beautiful local woman. When he wakes up from sleep, he thinks of the beautiful local woman. What do you think of this, great king?

Then it connects the example to the meaning:

> Great king, immature ordinary beings that are uneducated are completely captivated by forms that make their minds happy when they see them with their eyes. They are completely captivated and then become attached.[347]

Also, it mainly shows the causal relation in terms of birth and death when it says, "When remaining there at another time, at the time of death, a time when the karma of equal fortune is exhausted and the last consciousness ceases . . ."[348] [766] Further, it shows that a transmigration of death and birth do not ultimately exist, but that they conventionally exist, and karma does not perish when it says, "Great King, there is nothing that transfers from this world to another world, yet the transmigration of death and birth is manifestly there . . . it is clear that karma does not perish."[349] Likewise, the *Anthology of Training* says:

> Even though all phenomena are selfless in this way, there is no conflict with causation; even though there is no intrinsic nature, there is no conflict with all phenomena appearing the way they do. This is taught in the *Meeting of the Father and Son Sūtra*.[350]

It cites this sūtra that says, "a person dreams of a beautiful local woman . . . ,"[351] which is no different from above. Although these earlier and later sūtra passages cited above do not explicitly address the intermediate existence between the existence at death and the existence at birth, it is certainly there. One should know the intermediate existence from this teaching of the way of appropriating the aggregates at the times of birth and death.

One might say, "If an effect arises in this way from the disintegration of an action that lacks intrinsic nature, then there would be problems such that maturations would be endless and that maturations would be inconsistent." There are no such problems, as the *Introduction to the Middle Way* says:

While both objects are equally nonexistent,
Those with an eye disorder see floating hairs but
Do not see other [nonexistent] entities.
Likewise, know that once matured, it does not reach maturation again.[352]

It says that although they are equally nonexistent, it is determined that floating hairs appear to someone with an eye disorder, but not things like rabbit horns. While an action has no intrinsic nature, after it ceases there are effects from the disintegration of actions that have not elicited maturation, but these do not come from actions that have already matured. Furthermore, this example also shows that it is completely reasonable for actions and their effects to be distinctly ascertained.

2. Our Unique Way of Positing the Entity of Disintegration

This section has three parts: (1) establishing the entity of disintegration through scripture, (2) establishing the entity of disintegration through reasoning, and (3) establishing the entity of disintegration through what is acknowledged in the world.

1. Establishing the Entity of Disintegration through Scripture

When the scriptures teach dependent arising, they say, "Based on the condition of birth, there is aging and death." Regarding death here, disintegration should be understood as the sentient being that died. That [disintegration] is said to be produced by birth, which is its condition. This shows that disintegration has a cause. Also, the *Sūtra on the Ten Grounds* says: "Dying also has two functions: it brings about the destruction of a conditioned phenomenon and it also acts as the cause for the uninterrupted continuity of ignorance."[353] It says that dying directly produces death, and dying functions to produce a subsequent ignorance. This shows that disintegration is an effect. Therefore, a phenomenon that is produced by a cause and can produce an effect should be asserted as an entity. For this reason, the *Fundamental Verses of the Middle Way* says: "Entities and [767] non-entities are conditioned phenomena . . ."[354] It says that both entities like sprouts, as well as the disintegration of a sprout that is the sprout's non-entity, are both entities. The latter [sprout's disintegration] is an entity because the sprout's entity is conditioned by causes and conditions, and because the disintegration of that sprout arises based on the sprout's entity.

2. Establishing the Entity of Disintegration through Reasoning

In some of our Buddhist traditions that accept disintegration (*zhig*) and decay (*'jig*) to be contradictory, it is held that the decay of entities in the moment they are produced, without remaining for a second instant, arises from the entities and their causes. They accept that other than their own causes, decay does not depend upon other causes that arise later. Due to this, they accept that the disintegration in the second moment is a non-entity and thus is not a cause at all. What follows is a refutation of those who claim in this way that disintegration is not a cause at all. *Clear Words* says:

> If it is claimed that decay is causeless and that conditioned phenomena are momentary, then since there is no decay without a cause, how could entities be conditioned phenomena that are momentary and without decay? Thus, all of this makes no sense.[355]

This refutes that position by showing that both the birth and dying of sentient beings, along with both the decay of entities in the second moment and the disintegration of entities in the second moment, are equal in terms of their being posited as entities or not, and in terms of their being produced from their own cause or not. If there were no cause for a sprout to have not remained for a second moment, then it would need to be the case that there would also be no cause for the sprout not to remain for a second moment. Thereby, it would not be momentary. Also, the sprout would not be a conditioned phenomenon, so it would not be reasonable to claim that conditioned phenomena are impermanent.

An implication here is that, as the decay of a sprout is produced from a cause, the disintegration of a sprout is also produced by a cause. Also, as there is a cause for the same sprout not to remain for a second instant, there is a cause for the sprout to have not remained for a second instant. The disintegration of the sprout, in relation to the sprout, is a non-entity that is the absence of the sprout that has ceased. Nevertheless, in relation to its essence, it is an entity that has not disintegrated so it is posited as an entity. Therefore, when *Clear Words* says "decay," it asserts that disintegration is also decay. *Reason in Sixty Verses* states:

> *Peace is the exhaustion of the cause;*
> *This is observed to be "exhaustion."*[356]

It mentions the cessation of oil and butter as the cause of a butter lamp's dying. This also shows causality of the past. In its commentary it says:

> When there are no conditions for the future, there is a continuity of non-arising. If it were not the case that there were no conditions, then without a doubt something would arise. Therefore, it is accepted that non-arising also has a cause.[357]

This shows that even the future is an entity because it is shown to have causes. The statement that the exhaustion of butter produces the dying of a butter lamp establishes that the disintegration of a continuum is an entity; it is similar to the disintegration [768] of the first instant in the second instant as well.

3. Establishing the Entity of Disintegration through What Is Acknowledged in the World

The commentary on *Reason in Sixty Verses* states: "Since there is no water, I can't have grain."[358] In the world it is acknowledged that something later is ruined through something prior not existing, such as, "Due to a lack of water, the plant's yield was harmed" and "My son died due to a lack of food." Moreover, water and food not being depleted must be accepted as causes for a good yield from plants and sustenance for a son. Likewise, it is reasonable to assert that the depletion of water and food are causes for the demise of their effects; there is no difference here.

This way of understanding the past and future is not reasonable in the systems of the Sautrāntika, Mind-Only, and Svātantrika that maintain what exists on its own. In their systems, the meaning of the disintegration of a sprout turns away all features of a sprout, without acquiring any other entity (such as a pot) whatsoever. Thus, it is accepted to be a non-implicative negation so is not accepted to be an entity at all. This is due to the essential point that it must be posited based on a phenomenon's designated object being sought out by reason.

In this Prāsaṅgika system that posits all causation merely nominally, without existing on its own, positing disintegration as an entity is completely reasonable. Even though the disintegration of a sprout, for instance, is posited as an entity, there is no such thing at all that is the entity that has disintegrated, or the entity that is of a similar type as it, posited through being sought out by reason in the basis of characteristics of the disintegrated entity. Rather, it is posited as an entity that merely nominally exists, in name only, arising based on the disintegration of a sprout. Therefore, positing disintegration as an entity also comes down to the fact that conventionally nothing is held to exist on its own.

Disintegration is a negation because it must be conceived through the explicit exclusion of an object of negation. Further, it is an implicative negation because it implies an entity that is excluded; it is not a non-implicative negation that merely excludes what has disintegrated. The description of disintegration as an entity, and that it has a cause, is similar to the way it was shown that a sprout is an entity and that it has a cause; it need not be posited having sought out the designated object. Texts like Tsongkhapa's great commentary on the *Fundamental Verses of the Middle Way* clearly show the way that disintegration is described as an entity in the *Fundamental Verses of the Middle Way* and *Reason in Sixty Verses,* and in Candrakīrti's commentaries on these two texts.[359]

3. Our Unique Way of Positing the Three Times

For the reason that both disintegration and the future are accepted as entities in this way, there is also a unique way of positing the three times. The commentary on the *Four Hundred Verses* states:

> Regarding this, the future does not go to the present time. The past has gone by. What occurs in the present has arisen but has not ceased. Since what occurs in the present is observed in the present, it is the main one. Both what [769] will come to pass and what has passed—posited as the future and the past—are not the main ones.[360]

The definition of the past is the aspect of the disintegration of another entity that had already arisen. The definition of the future is the aspect of what has not yet arisen due to conditions not being fully present even though there is a cause for the production of another entity. The definition of the present is held to be that which has arisen but has not ceased, and is not any aspect of another entity's future or disintegration. To illustrate this with something like a sprout, the past time of the sprout is the disintegration in the second instant of the sprout that had arisen. The future time of the sprout is that which has not yet arisen due to conditions not being fully present even though there is a cause for the production of the sprout. The present sprout is the sprout itself that has arisen but has not ceased.

Therefore, it is not sufficient for the past to simply be turned away in the present; there must be an aspect of disintegration of what happened. Texts like the Abhidharma mention "the cessation of what has arisen." "What has arisen" is, for instance, a sprout that has passed. As for the future, "it has a cause, yet it has not arisen," so there is a distinctive way in which it has not arisen. "It has a cause" excludes being the future of something like space or a rabbit horn that is not possible to be a cause that ever produces that phenomenon. It has a cause for producing that phenomenon, yet since the conditions are not all complete, it does not arise for the time being. This aspect is posited as the future. The present is the main one because it alone is that which has arisen but has not disintegrated. The other two are subsidiary because they are necessarily posited from the aspects of the present having disintegrated or having not arisen. Nevertheless, the three times are also established relationally. The way that the past and future are relational can be understood from what was just said. The present is also shown to be relational; "has arisen" excludes the future, and "has not ceased" excludes the past. Thus, whichever time is posited, it must be understood relationally.

Merely this way of understanding the three times is the same in Sautrāntika, Mind-Only, and Svātantrika, yet they assert that an entity must be in the present. Thus, they claim that the past and future are non-entities, and moreover, non-implicative negations. In this Prāsaṅgika system, the past and future are held to be entities, and moreover, implicative negations. This is because the phrase "sprout's disintegration" excludes its non-disintegration and the phrase "future sprout" excludes its occurrence. Not only are these two objects of negation merely excluded, but another entity is implied. Furthermore, it is held that the former implicates the arising of a sprout's disintegration based on the sprout. The latter implicates the entity of a future sprout that lacks the complete conditions for a sprout's arising.

A sprout's disintegration, for instance, is the past of the sprout, yet in relation to the sprout at the time of the sprout, it is the future because it is the sprout's effect. Likewise, [770] a future sprout, for instance, is the future of the sprout, yet in relation to the sprout at the time of the sprout, it is the past because it is the sprout's cause. One might say, "At the time of a sprout's disintegration, for instance, it has arisen and has not ceased, so it is present. Yet if this is the case, there would be no conflict between the past and the present."

This is not a problem. At the time of a sprout's disintegration, the sprout has disintegrated, but not the disintegration itself. Likewise, at the time of the disintegration of a sprout's disintegration as well, it is not yet the disintegration of itself; rather, it is the disintegration of the first instant of the sprout's disintegration. In general, since it is a disintegration, it is exclusively the past, not the present. Therefore, for whatever arises that has a similar type as the past, its nature should be understood from the aspect of being the disintegration of another entity; it is not like the other two times. It is similar in the case of the future as well, even though it has arisen, it should be understood as the aspect of being another entity that has not yet arisen; so it is exclusively the future, not the present. Therefore, for whatever arises that has a similar type in the future, its nature should be understood from the aspect of another entity that has not yet arisen. The present is not understood in this way; it is like a sprout that has itself arisen but has not ceased. Therefore, it is not like the past or the future. Even though they are the same in having arisen and not ceased in their own time, since they have these different qualities, the three times are in conflict.

Vaibhāṣikas and Prāsaṅgikas are similar in merely asserting the three times as entities, but their ways of assertion are completely different. Vaibhāṣikas posit each entity, such as a sprout, with each of the three times. Thereby, they claim that the sprout exists even in the past and future times; they also claim that the three times substantially exist. The *Treasury of Metaphysics* describes four distinctive features of the way the three times are understood in that system. Prāsaṅgikas do not claim that for each entity like a sprout there exists each of the three times. Nor is any substantial existence claimed whatsoever. Due to these features, this is said to be Prāsaṅgika's unique way of positing the three times.

> Next, [IX.75] ***"If there are no sentient beings,***
> ***To whom is one to be compassionate?"***

What follows dispels objections that the cultivation of compassion and the attainment of fruition are not reasonable without a self. When the intrinsic nature of phenomena is analyzed, there is no one who cultivates compassion and no one toward which to cultivate it. Nevertheless, the cultivation of compassion is reasonable conventionally. Likewise, a person who attains fruition, a fruition to be attained, and the attainment of the fruition by a person all lack intrinsic nature, yet they are reasonable merely conventionally. The *Inquiry of Upāli* states:

> *In this extremely joyous teaching*
> *It is said that by leaving home and becoming a monastic*
> [771] *There is a supreme result.*
> *This was taught by the Compassion One.*
> *While leaving home and becoming a monastic*
> *Does lead to the attainment of all results,*
> *When considering the lack of intrinsic nature in phenomena,*
> *There are no results and also nothing to attain.*
> *Yet the attainment of results is attained.*
> *Amazing! This reasoning is extremely well said*
> *By the compassionate Victorious One, the supreme person.*
> *It is awe-inspiring!*[361]

Our compassionate teacher taught the way that the result is attained conventionally but not ultimately. It says that great reverence arises for the Victorious One through being inspired by his trustworthy testimony. The scriptures cited here and above are for the purpose of our teacher's followers to dispel doubts and gain confidence; they are not cited in order to refute other traditions.

2. PRESENTATION OF SPECIFIC ARGUMENTS THAT REFUTE THE SELF OF PERSONS

This section has two parts: (1) showing the self to be without intrinsic nature and (2) establishing that the intrinsic nature of "mine" does not exist either through this.

1. Showing the Self to Be without Intrinsic Nature

There are many ways to ascertain the selflessness of persons through reason, but the main one is the sevenfold reasoning. This is said to have many distinctive qualities. Also, a sūtra states:

> *Form is not the self;*
> *The self does not possess form.*
> *The self is not in form*
> *Nor is form in the self.*"[362]

By applying this in the same way to each of the remaining four aggregates, there is a fourfold analysis for each one, which shows twenty antidotes for the view of the transitory collective. The *Fundamental Verses of the Middle Way* says:

> *It is not the aggregates, nor different from them.*
> *The aggregates are not in it, nor is it in the aggregates.*
> *The Tathāgata does not possess them.*
> *What is the Tathāgata?*[363]

The twenty-second chapter and the tenth chapter state this fivefold reasoning extensively.

One might wonder, "In terms of the self being essentially different from the five aggregates such as form, there are twenty-five by adding five more views in this way. So why is it said that there are twenty?"

The sūtras only state four. The fifth basis, which is conceiving the self as different from the aggregates, does not occur except for non-Buddhists, so this fifth alternative was not mentioned. The *Fundamental Verses of the Middle Way* mentions this fifth position in order to refute the non-Buddhist systems as well. Still, some of our realist Buddhist schools, and some Svātantrikas, explicitly posit the mind as a self that takes birth in the past and future. Furthermore, in order to refute some other qualities of a person, such as it being held to be the collection of the aggregates or a quality of their shape, the *Introduction to the Middle Way* demonstrates a sevenfold reasoning, adding two arguments that refute a self that is a mere collection and a self that is a shape. Moreover, a sūtra says:

> *The self is a demonic mind;*
> *It is a belief.*
> *These conditioned aggregates are empty;*
> *There is no sentient being in them,*
> [772] *Like a collection of parts.*[364]

As was stated in the sūtra cited above, the self is understood in a similar way as a chariot. Based on this, the sevenfold reasoning is laid out clearly.

First, I will present an example, followed by the meaning it exemplifies. The *Introduction to the Middle Way* states:

> *Like a chariot, it is not different from its parts,*
> *Nor is it the same; it does not posses them.*
> *The chariot is not in its parts nor are its parts in the chariot.*
> *It is not the mere collection nor is it the shape.*[365]

A chariot is not intrinsically the same nature as its parts nor is it intrinsically different from them. It does not essentially possess its parts. It does not essentially depend upon parts nor do the parts essentially depend on it. It is not merely a collection of parts nor is a chariot the quality of being the assembled shape of parts.

The meanings of these are progressively established as follows: A chariot is not intrinsically the same as its parts—the axle, wheels, and so forth. This is because, if it were the same, there would be the problem that as the chariot is one, the parts would also be one; and alternatively, that as the parts are many, the chariot would also be many. A chariot is not intrinsically different from its parts because, if it were, then it would be essentially different. If things that are essentially different occur at the same time, then they are other, unrelated objects—like a horse and an ox. Thus, a chariot would have to be observed separately from its parts, but it is not.

It does not make sense that a chariot intrinsically possesses its parts. This is because the two ways of possession—of what is essentially different or essentially the same, respectively like Upagupta possessing an ox and Upagupta possessing a form—are nothing other than relationships of identity and difference, and both of these have already been negated. Both the positions that the chariot intrinsically is supported by its parts and that the parts are intrinsically supported by the chariot are not reasonable because, if they were, then they would have to be intrinsically different and their essential difference has already been negated. It is also not reasonable for a chariot to be held to be the mere collection of its parts, like the wheels. If it were reasonable, then it would absurdly follow that the collection that is a pile of all the separate chariot parts—the wheels, axle, bolts, and so forth—would also be a chariot.

It is also not reasonable to posit the chariot as the quality of the shape of its parts because (1) neither the shapes of the individual parts nor (2) the shape of the collection of its parts is at all [773] reasonable to be posited as a chariot. The first is not reasonable because, if a chariot were held to be the shape that is no different from its shape at the time before it was assembled, then there would not be the slightest difference between the shapes of the wheels and so on before and after assembly. Thereby, as there is no chariot before assembly, there would be no chariot after assembly, either. If the chariot had a different shape than its parts before assembly, then the existence of a new and different shape of the wheels and so on that did not exist before the assembly would have to be observed, but this is not the case.

The second alternative, that a chariot is held to be the shape of its collected parts, is not reasonable. This is because in realist systems it is not reasonable for its shape to substantially exist while a collection does not substantially exist. Also, realists claim that a chariot substantially exists because they assert it to substantially exist as the basis of designation for what nominally exists. In the Prāsaṅgika system, there is no claim to a basis for nominal existence in what substantially exists; rather, the shape of the collection of parts is the basis of designation (*gdags gzhi*) for a chariot, but is not its basis of characteristics (*mtshan gzhi*).

One might think, "If a chariot sought out through this sevenfold reasoning is not found in this way, then a chariot must not exist. In that case, all conventions such as 'bring the chariot' would not make sense." There is no such problem. When sought out by the sevenfold reasoning there is no chariot found in either of the two truths. Nevertheless, it is not that the chariot does not exist. A chariot is not posited upon being found after its designated object is sought out; it is understood without analysis, based on mundane convention. Also, it is understood to exist merely nominally, designated in dependence upon its parts. The *Introduction to the Middle Way* states:

> *In terms of reality or the world,*
> *It is not established in these seven ways.*
> *Without analysis, in terms of the world only*
> *It is designated in dependence upon its parts.*[366]

Secondly, I will explain the exemplified meaning. The "I" or self that is the observed object of the innate view of the transitory collective should be investigated as to whether it is the same or different from the aggregates that are its basis of designation. This is because, if it did exist, it would have to be either the same or different from them. When examined in this way—as when a chariot and its parts are sought out by means of the sevenfold analysis—it is not found. Likewise, the designated object that is a person and the aggregates that are its basis of designation are not intrinsically the same. The self is not intrinsically different from the aggregates. The self does not essentially possess the aggregates. Neither the self nor the aggregates are intrinsically supported by or the support of the other. The mere collection of aggregates is also not the self. The distinctively assembled [774] shape of the aggregates is not the self, either.

The meanings of these are progressively established as follows: The self is not intrinsically the same as the aggregates because, if it were, there would be three problems: It would absurdly follow that (1) there would be no point to claiming a self; (2) the self would be subject to arising and ceasing; and (3) there would be many selves. For the first, the *Fundamental Verses of the Middle Way* states:

> *If the self were just the appropriation*
> *Your self would not exist.*[367]

If the self were the same as the aggregates, there would be no self apart from the aggregates. Thus, it would be pointless to claim a self because the self would just be a synonym for the aggregates, like "the moon" and "the rabbit one."[368] For the second, the *Fundamental Verses of the Middle Way* states:

> *If the aggregates were the self*
> *The self would be subject to arising and ceasing.*[369]

If these two were intrinsically the same, then there is the problem that it would absurdly follow that the self would also be subject to arising and ceasing as the aggregates are subject to arising and ceasing. Moreover, even though there is no problem in being subject to arising and ceasing merely conventionally, if it were intrinsically established to be subject to arising and ceasing, then selves in past and future lives would be intrinsically distinct. Thereby, they would necessarily be other, unrelated objects. If this were the case, it is said that there would be three problems; it would absurdly follow that (1) it would not be possible to remember [past] lives; (2) actions performed would perish; and (3) the effects of what one had not done would be encountered.

One might think, "There would not be these three problems because of being a single continuum." The problems cannot be fixed this way because it is not reasonable for what is intrinsically distinct to be a single continuum. The *Fundamental Verses of the Middle Way* states:

> *If a god and a human were distinct*
> *It would not be reasonable that they are a continuum.*[370]

As for the third problem [that there would be many selves], the *Introduction to the Middle Way* states:

> *If the aggregates were the self,*
> *Then since they are many, the self would also be many.*[371]

If the self and the aggregates were intrinsically the same, it is said that there would be three problems; it would absurdly follow that (1) the self would be many, and so forth; (2) it would be reasonable for the undetermined questions to be answered;[372] and (3) seeing the nonexistence of the aggregates would be the meaning of realizing selflessness. Within the first, there are five root arguments; it is said that there would be problems such that it would absurdly follow that: the self would be many, the self would substantially exist, the apprehension of self would be undistorted, the self would be annihilated upon the attainment of nirvana without remainder, and the self would arise and cease prior to the attainment of nirvana without remainder.

The self and the aggregates are not intrinsically different because, if they were, as the *Fundamental Verses of the Middle Way* states:

> *If it were different from the aggregates*
> *It would not have the characteristics of the aggregates.*[373]

Since it would be another object, unrelated to the aggregates, there would be problems such that the self would not have the characteristics of the aggregates—like arising, abiding, and ceasing. There is no conflict with the self and the aggregates being merely conventionally distinct.

When intrinsic identity and difference are negated in this way, the position that the self intrinsically possesses [775] the aggregates is also refuted because the two ways of possession—of what is the same and different—are no different from this. The *Introduction to the Middle Way* says:

> *The self is not accepted as possessing form,*
> *Since it does not exist.*[374]

In the same way, the two positions holding that the self and aggregates are mutually the support and supported are also refuted by the earlier reasoning. If the two were intrinsically different, then the two positions that one is the support of the supported other would make sense, but the intrinsic difference of these two has already been refuted. The *Introduction to the Middle Way* states:

> *The self is not in the aggregates*
> *Nor are the aggregates in the self.*[375]

It is also not reasonable for the mere collection of aggregates to be the self. The *Introduction to the Middle Way* states:

> *The sūtras say that it depends on the aggregates,*
> *So the mere collection of aggregates is not the self.*[376]

It says that the self is designated based on the aggregates. Thus, the aggregates are the basis of designation, and the person is the designated object; it does not make sense for a basis of designation to be the designated object.

It is not reasonable to maintain that the shape of the aggregates is the self. It says in the *Introduction to the Middle Way*:

> *If you say that it is the shape, then since it has material form*
> *For you these are said to be the self.*
> *Yet the collection of mind and so on would not be the self*
> *Because they do not have shape.*[377]

A shape is a property of only that which has material form. If only a shape were the self, then since the collection of mind and mental states does not have shape, it is not reasonable to posit them as the self. Furthermore, it would absurdly follow that the self would be material and that there would be no self when born in the Formless Realm. When sought out through analysis by this sevenfold reasoning, there is no person to be found in either of the two truths.

One might think, "Then a person does not exist." This is not a problem. It means that an intrinsically existent person is not found, but it does not mean that a person does not exist even conventionally. Without investigation or analysis, a person that is merely designated in dependence upon its aggregates is undeniably established by a source of knowledge. The *Introduction to the Middle Way* says: "In reality or . . . are designated in dependence upon their bases of designation."[378] The earlier reasoning also should be applied here as well.

This scripture shows that the essential point of the sevenfold reasoning comes down to the reasoning of interdependence. This is because certainty is induced in a person being merely designated in dependence upon its basis of designation by not being found in these seven ways. Also, by understanding it to be a mere designation, confidence arises that the designated object is not findable through analysis, that it is dependently arisen without intrinsic nature, a mere illusion. In short, the basis for the thought "I" is conventional usage based on its basis of designation, the aggregates; that is the "person." Names like "person" (*gang zag*), "self" (*bdag*), and "being" (*skyes bu*) have the same meaning. I have just written briefly here in this context of the aforementioned example and the meaning it exemplifies [776] from the passages in the *Fundamental Verses of the Middle Way* and the *Introduction to the Middle Way*.

2. Establishing That the Intrinsic Nature of "Mine" Does Not Exist Either through This

The *Fundamental Verses of the Middle Way* states:

> *When there is no self*
> *How can there be "mine"?*[379]

When an intrinsically existent person is negated through an analysis by the sevenfold reasoning, an intrinsically existent "mine" is also completely negated. Furthermore, a cognition that realizes that the self does not intrinsically exist does not apprehend the lack of an intrinsically existing "mine." Nevertheless, based on the activity of a cognition that realizes the self not to exist intrinsically, by merely orienting cognition to an analysis of the status of an intrinsically existing "mine," it is easily found to lack intrinsic existence. For this reason, this reasoning is not mentioned separately. Moreover, in analysis applying the aforementioned sevenfold reasoning to what is acknowledged in the world, entities like pots and cloths, and phenomena that are causes and effects like karma, are not found. All of it can be established to lack intrinsic existence, yet when not analyzed, their existence as merely acknowledged in the world is not negated.

2. *Explaining the Reasoning Establishing the Selflessness of Phenomena*

This section has three parts: (1) explaining the selflessness of phenomena through the fourfold application of mindfulness, (2) dispelling disputes about the two truths being unreasonable, and (3) explaining the reasoning that negates the self of phenomena.

1. Explaining the Selflessness of Phenomena through the Fourfold Application of Mindfulness

[IX.78] ***The body is not the feet or the legs . . .***

This describes meditation on selflessness having negated the apprehension of the self of phenomena together with its conceived objects. There is also a twofold division within "the apprehension of the self of phenomena" in terms of its mode of expression: the coarse and the subtle. Within the coarse apprehension of the self of phenomena as well, there are imputed ones (like apprehending temporally partless moments that are the smallest instants of time, and spatially partless minute particles), and there are innate ones (like apprehending as separate substances the macro-objects that are constituted by partless minute particles, which are asserted by the two realist schools, and the sources of knowledge that apprehend them). Within the subtle apprehension of the self of phenomena, too, there is the imputed, which is an apprehension that holds it to be reasonable for forms and so on to exist on their own having been analyzed by reason; and the innate, which is apprehending forms and so on to exist on their own naturally or by default, without relying upon an engaged reasoned analysis. The imputed is present in the continua of only those whose minds have been influenced by philosophical systems. The innate is present in both those whose minds have been influenced by philosophical systems and those whose minds have not. Here, mainly the conceived objects of the innate apprehension of the self of phenomena are negated among these, then the way to meditate on the selflessness of phenomena is explained. This has two parts: (1) the actual way of meditating on the fourfold application of mindfulness and (2) the way of meditating on calm abiding and special insight.

1. Actual Way of Meditating on the Fourfold Application of Mindfulness

The observations of the fourfold application of mindfulness are the fourfold contaminated body, feelings, mind, and phenomena. [777] This is because immature beings apprehend a self after conceiving, respectively, the bases of: a self's abode, a self's enjoyments, a self's essence, and a self's thorough affliction and complete purity. For this reason, these are negated.

The essence of the fourfold application of mindfulness is an understanding that engages the path of either mindfulness or meta-awareness (*dran shes gang rung*); upon observing the body and so on, it is a meditation that investigates the features of both the general and specific characteristics. Although mindfulness and meta-awareness are mainly mentioned, it is also said in the *Compendium of Metaphysics* and the *Treasury of Metaphysics* to include with these the concordant mind and mental states. The way of meditating is to meditate on the specific characteristics of the body as unclean, feelings as suffering, the mind as impermanent, and phenomena as thorough affliction to be rejected and complete purity to be adopted. The general characteristics are meditated on in this way: conditioned phenomena are impermanent; contaminated phenomena are suffering; and phenomena are empty and selfless. This is described in the *Treasury of Metaphysics*.

The *Treasury of Metaphysics* describes the purpose as follows: to act as antidotes to the four distorted apprehensions of purity, happiness, permanence, and self. *Distinguishing the Middle and the Extremes* says that the purpose is to engage in rejecting and adopting with respect to the four truths. It is posited with this term "application of mindfulness" because the meaning of the term is understood from apprehending, without forgetting—like a small child holding a tree branch—through being mindful with wisdom's discernment into what is to be adopted or rejected.

These mainly show how to meditate on the application of mindfulness with respect to just the common selflessness of persons. In general, all practices of the path have this kind of meditation, but they have different qualities, such as what is observed. Nevertheless, through meditating on the specific characteristics of the body and feelings (uncleanliness, suffering, and so on) and their general characteristics (a mere lack of self that negates the coarse self of persons), their lack of true existence cannot be ascertained whereby a fixated apprehension of their true existence collapses. Therefore, in order to dismantle apprehending the true existence of body, feelings, and so on, it is necessary to meditate having ascertained their lack of intrinsic existence that is their general characteristic. By meditating in this way, all phenomena come to be realized as lacking true existence. Thereby, this will act as an antidote to apprehending the body and so forth as truly existent, and will act as an antidote to apprehending their cleanliness and so forth as well.

Therefore, in the *Anthology of Training*, in the context where many sūtras are cited while the way of meditation on the application of mindfulness is explained, two ways of meditation are taught: the conventional features of body and feelings and so on are meditated on as unclean and suffering, etc.; and the ultimate features of body and feelings and so on are meditated on as emptiness, lacking intrinsic nature. Here, to state this briefly in the context of the application of mindfulness on body, the *Inquiry of Vīradatta* (*Vīradattagṛhapatiparipṛcchā*) says:

> *In this way the body of unclean aggregates*
> *Is held to be precious by those with pride in forms.*
> *Those with immature minds, without evidently knowing,*
> *Take up this pot of vomit*
> *With noses dripping with mucus and*
> *Mouths [778] constantly emitting a foul odor.*[380]

Also, the *Compendium of Dharma* says: "Thinking, 'this body is like space' is the application of mindfulness on the body as like space . . ."[381] and "This body has not come from any prior limit nor goes to any later limit. It is not located in either a prior or later limit."[382]

Likewise, for the application of mindfulness on feelings, he cites the *Inquiry of Ratnacūda*:

> When bodhisattvas experience happiness, they discover great compassion for sentient beings who are attached. They relinquish their latent attachment. Likewise, when they experience suffering, a great compassion arises for those who are angry, and when they experience a neutral feeling, a great compassion arises for those who are stupid. They know the feelings of happiness to be impermanent and the feelings of suffering to be painful.[383]

Also, the *Compendium of Dharma* says:

> *A teaching on the experience of feeling:*
> *There is no other feeler than the feeling.*
> *If it is not separate,*
> *What is it that is feeling?*
> *Awakening is also like this.*
> *The wise apply mindfulness in this way*
> *On the feeling of luminous clarity*
> *Within peace and purity.*[384]

In the context of the application of mindfulness on mind, he cites the *Jewel Heap:* "Kāśyapa, the mind is like the flow of a river; without abiding, it arises, decays, and disperses. The mind is like the wind; traveling far and moving without being apprehended."[385] Also: "Kāśyapa, the mind is not inside nor is it outside. It is not in both nor is it observed. Kāśyapa, the mind is formless, indemonstrable, unobstructed . . ."[386]

For the application of mindfulness on phenomena, he cites the *Vast Display:*

> *Conditioned phenomena are impermanent and unreliable,*
> *They are subject to decay, like an unfired clay pot.*
> *They are just like things on loan from others;*
> *Like a city made of sand, they don't last long.*[387]

Also:

> *Thus, some who are wise investigate,*
> *"From where did this come and to where does it go?"*
> *Having looked in all directions,*
> *This has not been seen to come or go.*[388]

In the explicit teaching of the words of the root text of the Wisdom Chapter, it teaches the way of meditating on the lack of true existence of body, feelings, and so forth. In this way, the lord of doctrine, Gyelsé Rinpoché, cited a sūtra in his commentary:

> To engage the selflessness of phenomena, the *Instruction on the Non-Arising of All Phenomena* (*Sarvadharmāpravṛttinirdeśa*) says:

> "Mañjuśrī, to see the body as like space is the application of mindfulness on body. Likewise, not to observe feelings . . . to know the mind as a mere name . . . not to observe virtuous or unvirtuous phenomena is the application of [779] mindfulness on phenomena." These are the teachings of the four applications of mindfulness.[389]

2. Way of Meditating on Calm Abiding and Special Insight

In general, the meditations on repulsiveness and the applications of mindfulness have aspects of both calm abiding and special insight. Nevertheless, as was mentioned above in the *Anthology of Training,* the meditations on repulsiveness and so forth mainly demonstrate calm abiding, and the meditations on the applications of mindfulness mainly demonstrate special insight. This is stated in the *Treasury of Metaphysics* as well. There is also a semblance (*rjes mthun pa*) of the four applications of mindfulness in those who have not entered the path; they are genuinely (*mtshan nyid pa*) present from the lesser path of accumulation in the three vehicles. There is also genuine calm abiding and special insight in those who have not entered the path. At the time of the path of accumulation, in general there is attainment of the unity of calm abiding and special insight that observes emptiness. Yet on the path of accumulation of one who has a determined Mahāyāna heritage, there is a unity of calm abiding and special insight that arises from a meditation that observes whatever there is, and there is calm abiding that arises from a meditation that observes emptiness. Nevertheless, there is no special insight that observes emptiness then because, if this were the case, then that attainment would be posited as one that had moved onto the Mahāyāna path of joining.

The observation of emptiness is also the main part (*dngos gzhi*) of a meditative concentration that realizes emptiness in the continuum on the Mahāyāna path of accumulation. It also is the yoga of the union of calm abiding and special insight. Nevertheless, by just this it is not understood to be the yoga that is the union of calm abiding and special insight that observes emptiness. This is because special insight observing emptiness is attained when pliancy (*shin sbyangs*) arises that is induced by the force of reasoned analysis into emptiness within the state of meditative equipoise on calm abiding that observes emptiness. At this time, it must be understood to be the yoga that is the union of calm abiding and special insight that observes emptiness.

The essences of calm abiding and special insight are identified in accord with the *Sūtra Explaining the Intent* like this: The essence of calm abiding is a meditative stabilization that one-pointedly observes its object while being held with pliancy; the essence of special insight is discerning wisdom held with pliancy that is induced through the force of an analysis of the observation within the state of calm abiding. These are their distinctive qualities, but each of them has observations of what is and whatever there is, so calm abiding and special insight are not distinguished based on their observed objects, and so on. The *Cloud of Jewels* (*Ratnamegha*) states: "Calm abiding is one-pointed mind. Special insight is genuine discernment."[390] The *Ornament of the Mahāyāna Sūtras* says:

> *Since based on genuine abiding,*
> *The mind is placed within mind, and*
> *Since phenomena are completely discerned,*
> *These are calm abiding and special insight.*[391]

The reason why it is necessary to have both calm abiding and special insight that realizes selflessness is this: If there is [780] just calm abiding without special insight, then it is impossible to see the way things are, like being without the eyes of the view. If there is just the view that realizes selflessness without a firm meditative stabilization, then it is impossible to clearly see the way things are due to being disturbed by the winds of concepts. Thus, the middle *Stages of Meditation* states:

> Through the power of calm abiding, the winds of concepts will not agitate the mind, like a butter lamp placed where there is no wind. Through special insight, the bad views of philosophical systems are rejected, so others will not divide you. As the *Moon Lamp Sūtra* (*Candrapradīpasūtra*) states:
>
> *The power of calm abiding brings non-agitation*
> *Through special insight, one becomes like a mountain.*[392]

The *Anthology of Training* also says:

> *The Sage said that meditative equipoise*
> *Genuinely knows things as they are.*[393]

Citing sūtras, the *Compendium of Dharma* says: "A mind placed in meditative equipoise genuinely knows things as they are."[394] Moreover, when there is calm abiding with an undistracted mind, all virtues of meditations that analyze things like impermanence, the spirit of awakening, and selflessness become powerful. When the mind is distracted, all virtuous practices are weak. In our text here it says, [V.16] ***Recitations and all austerities . . .*** , and:

> [VIII.1] ***A person with a distracted mind***
> ***Dwells within the fangs of affliction.***

The sequence of these two is like this: In the beginning, when it is newly engendered, calm abiding must be accomplished first. Then based on this, special insight must be accomplished. This is stated in the *Sūtra Explaining the Intent* and the *Stages of Meditation.* It is explained this way in the contexts of all the explanations on the sequence of the latter two of the six transcendent perfections [meditative concentration and wisdom] and the latter two of the three trainings [meditative stabilization and wisdom]. It is also explained that later, calm abiding can be cultivated based on special insight. In our text here, both of these are taught: [VIII.4] ***First, seek out calm abiding . . .***, and [IX.92] *Meditative concentration that grows from the field of investigation . . .* Moreover, when calm abiding is not attained, one cannot generate pliancy even by doing analytic meditation. Since it can be produced at the end of an analytic meditation that has achieved calm abiding, calm abiding is necessary before special insight. Yet being preceded by calm abiding is not necessary otherwise for an understanding (*go ba*) of the view that realizes selflessness to arise, or for just a mentally transformative experience (*myong ba*) of that to arise.

What follows is how to cultivate calm abiding and special insight.

1. How to Cultivate Calm Abiding

For calm abiding, there are two parts: (1) the way to generate a flawless meditative stabilization in the context of an actual meditation based on the prerequisites for calm abiding (such as initially remaining in a conducive place and so on[395]); and (2) the stages in the development of mental abiding based on this. For the first, *Distinguishing the Middle and the Extremes* states:

> *The five flaws are relinquished by the eight applications;*
> *This arises through relying on the cause.*[396]

Calm abiding is accomplished through relying on the eight applications that are the antidotes to the five flaws. The five flaws are stated in *Distinguishing the Middle and the Extremes:*

Laziness, forgetting the practical instructions,
Laxity and agitation,
Application, and over-application –
These are held to be the five flaws.[397]

[782] How these are flaws is this: When practicing meditative stabilization, laziness is a flaw because one will not practice it. When engaging in meditative stabilization, forgetting the practical instructions is a flaw because there is no meditative equipoise on the observed object in mind when the observation is forgotten. When cultivating meditative stabilization, laxity and agitation are flaws because these two cause the mind to be unworkable. When laxity and agitation occur, not applying the antidote is a flaw because thereby these two will not be pacified. When abiding in flawless meditative stabilization without laxity or agitation, over-application of the antidote is a flaw because one will become too agitated by tightening again, and one will become too lax by loosening the sharpness of the mode of apprehension.

Laxity and agitation are also treated individually in the *Stages of Meditation*, making six flaws. Regarding this, laziness is not to delight in the cultivation of meditative stabilization and to enjoy what is unconducive to it. Forgetfulness is to give up the observation of a meditative stabilization. Laxity is to have slight clarity with regard to the object of one's attention, but without a very clear or firm apprehension of the observation because the mode of apprehension is lax; this comes from dullness, yet can also be virtuous so it is different from dullness. Agitation is a mind not at ease; it is included within attachment that follows after attractive characteristics; it functions to obstruct calm abiding. The latter two can be understood as explained above.

The eight applications that are their antidotes are as follows: *Distinguishing the Middle and the Extremes* states:

The basis and what is based in that,
Cause and effect,
Not forgetting the observation,
Noticing laxity and agitation,
Application to relinquishing those, and
Letting be when they are pacified.[398]

How these are antidotes is this: The antidote for laziness is diligence and the fourfold cause and effect: faith, aspiration, diligence, and pliancy. Next, the antidote for forgetfulness is mindfulness; the antidote for laxity and agitation is meta-awareness that notices laxity and agitation; the antidote for non-application is the intention to apply; and the antidote for over-application is to let be in equanimity.

Regarding these, faith is seeing the qualities of meditative stabilization. Aspiration is to pursue meditative stabilization. Diligence is to continually endeavor out of delight for meditative stabilization; this is the actual antidote to laziness. Pliancy is being workable in body and mind; it functions to eliminate obscurations like laziness. Further, "the basis" is aspiration, the basis of diligence; what is "based in that" is diligence. The "cause" of aspiration is faith. The "effect" of the effort is pliancy. These four precede and follow one another as cause and effect.

Mindfulness has three qualities: it functions to observe what one has familiarized oneself with, not to forget it, and not to be drawn away from it. Meta-awareness is to notice the presence or absence of laxity and agitation. Intention is a mental state that moves toward a mental object, inciting the mind. If there is laxity or agitation, it is the intention to apply the mind to relinquish them.

How to relinquish them is like this: When lax, bring to mind a joyous object that causes excitement in the mind; when agitated, bring to mind a somber object, causing the mind to become drawn within. The *Anthology of Training* states: "When disheartened, cultivate joy and raise your spirits. When agitated, think of impermanence and quell the mind."[399] The application of equanimity is to leave be when laxity and agitation have subsided, relaxing the efforts to raise the spirits or draw within, etc. Among the three types of equanimity (*btang snyoms*)—the indifferent feeling, the immeasurable impartiality, and the application of equanimity—this one is the latter. In short, look again to the mind; turn within to see if it is agitated or lax and seek out the quality of abiding. When this quality of abiding is there, alternate between loosening up and inducing the sharpness of the quality of clarity. A flawless meditative stabilization is accomplished by sustaining these two in alternation. Otherwise, when too tight, there will be a quality of clarity but it will be difficult for abiding to occur because of being too agitated. When too loose, there will be a quality of abiding but there will be no sharpness of clarity because of being too lax. Therefore, there needs to be an equal balance of the qualities of tightness and looseness. Since this is difficult to maintain, Candragomin said:

By relying on effort, there is agitation;
When giving this up, there is dullness.

Thus, it is difficult to find an equipoise that is appropriate.
Since my mind is disturbed, what shall I do?[400]

Secondly, the actual stages of development of mental abiding: From among the nine mental abidings, the first is *setting* the mind appropriately. This is to withdraw the mind from an external focus and direct the mind to an internal support of observation. The *Ornament of the Mahāyāna Sūtras* states: "Direct the mind to an observed object . . ."[401] *Continuous setting* is to continually set the mind on the observation, without getting distracted from the continuity of the mind's earlier focus: "Do not get distracted from its continuity."[402] *Re-setting* is to immediately notice when the mind becomes outwardly distracted, and to bring it back again, or bind it, to the previous observation: "Swiftly notice distraction, and bring it back again."[403] *Close setting* is to again and again bring the mind back within a wide open mind, making it subtle and settled further: "Intelligent ones further and further bring their minds back within."[404]

[783] *Disciplining* is to reflect on the qualities of meditative stabilization and bring forth joy: "Then from seeing the qualities, the mind becomes disciplined in meditative stabilization."[405] *Pacifying* is to see the faults of distraction and pacify the distaste for meditative stabilization: "From seeing the faults of distraction, distaste for it will be pacified."[406] *Thorough pacification* is to pacify with effort the arising of afflictions like mental attachment, unhappiness, lethargy, and sleep: "The arising of things like mental attachment and unhappiness are pacified as well."[407] *Single-pointedness* is to put effort into becoming naturally effortless: "Then the ones who endeavor with discipline apply the mind and attain its occurrence naturally."[408] Alternatively, this is called *streamlining,* which is to continuously engage without interruption. *Setting in equipoise* is a natural, spontaneous engagement, without needing effort due to habituation with the previous ones: "Through habituation, there is no application."[409] Here, there is no effort needed to depend on an antidote; this is the same essential point as the equanimity of application mentioned above.

How these are accomplished by the six powers is like this: The power of study accomplishes the *setting* of mind. This is because it is just the initial directing of mind by simply following what was heard from another's instructions for setting the mind on the observation; there has been no habituation through consistent contemplation. The power of contemplation accomplishes the *continuous setting* of mind. This is because one attains the beginning of an ability to maintain a slight continuity through sustaining a consistent contemplation of the mind upon the initial directed observation. The power of mindfulness establishes the mind of both *re-setting* and *close setting*. This is because there is mindfulness of the former observation that is reset when there is distraction from the observation, and because cultivating the power of mindfulness deters distraction from the onset. The power of meta-awareness accomplishes both the mind of *disciplining* and *pacifying*. This is because noticing the faults of concepts and subsidiary afflictions with meta-awareness does not allow them to proliferate. The power of diligence accomplishes both the mind of *through pacification* and *single-pointedness*. This is because even when subtle concepts and subsidiary afflictions occur, they are not taken up; they are rejected with effort. Thereby, a continuous meditative stabilization is accomplished that cannot be disrupted by laxity or agitation. The power of familiarization accomplishes the mind of *setting in equipoise*. This is because there naturally arises meditative stabilization without effort through the power of strong habituation to the previous ones.

[784] Within these there are four mental engagements (*yid byed*). There is a tightened mental engagement because there needs to be concentrated effort in the first two mental abidings. Then there is an interrupted mental engagement because one cannot sustain the mind for a long time without being interrupted by laxity or agitation at the time of the fifth mental abiding. There is an uninterrupted mental engagement at the time of the eighth mental abiding because one can sustain the mind for a long time without the interruptions of laxity and agitation. There is an effortless mental engagement at the time of the ninth mental abiding because there is neither disruption nor need to rely on continuous effort. This is explained in accord with the way the six powers and four mental engagements are described in the *Disciple Grounds* (*Śrāvakabhūmi*).

These are the ways of accomplishing calm abiding in general, without separating the observations of what is and whatever there is. The Meditative Concentration Chapter of our text here designates love and compassion, or the mind that exchanges self and other, as the spirit of awakening, teaching this itself as the observation for calm abiding. Even while practicing the essence of a meditative stabilization on love and so on, it must be practiced by directing the mind to the appropriate observation, then setting, followed by re-setting, and so forth. Specifically, in the practice of calm abiding that observes emptiness as well, the mind is initially directed to the emptiness that is the lack of the objective existence of phenomena and persons, then it is done as before with setting, then re-setting, and so on. Thereby, the ninth mental abiding that observes emptiness is achieved when an effortless, spontaneously present engagement with emptiness is attained.

In short, there are common observations, like the fourfold pervasive observation[410] and so on, and specific observations, like the observation of something like a Tathāgata's body, for instance. In either case, the meditative stabilization to be achieved has two qualities: it has a sharpness of strong mental clarity and it has the quality of abiding single-pointedly on the observation without conceptualization. Furthermore, it must remain on the observation continually. For this, it is extremely important to rely on both mindfulness, which prevents distraction elsewhere from the fundamental observation, and meta-awareness, which properly notices whether or not there is distraction.

By relying on mindfulness and meta-awareness in this way, one will sustain well and attain the ninth mental abiding as described above, which is called "the meditative stabilization of a single-pointed mind of the Desire Realm." It is a semblance of calm abiding until the attainment of pliancy. When pliancy is attained, it is a genuine calm abiding or the initial attainment of the mental engagement (*yid byed*) of one on the ground of meditative equipoise. The *Ornament of the Mahāyāna Sūtras* states: "Then, their bodies and minds attain a great pliancy; this is together with mental engagement."[411]

In this way, the first mental engagement that is included within the previous preparations (*nyer bsdogs*) cannot eliminate any afflictions without the cultivation [785] of special insight, so it is necessary to cultivate special insight. Also, there are two kinds of special insight: (1) one with the form of a coarse peace and (2) one with the form of selflessness. The former is shared among Buddhists and non-Buddhists; it is a special insight that observes whatever there is, and is an antidote that eliminates just the manifest afflictions. It has also been explained before as an antidote that suppresses manifest afflictions in calm abiding, and is included within calm abiding.

2. How to Cultivate Special Insight

How to cultivate this kind of special insight is like this: Based on the previously accomplished calm abiding, the main part (*dngos gzhi*) must be engaged through cultivating calm abiding and special insight in alternation at the times of knowing the individual characteristics (*mtshan nyid so sor rig pa*) and so forth. The *Ornament of the Mahāyāna Sūtras* states: "Through developing this, it expands and goes afar; abiding in the main part is achieved by this."[412] The way this occurs is that in the preparation for the first concentration, one is freed from attachment to the manifest afflictions of the lower ground (the Desire Realm) based on the six mental engagements of knowing the individual characteristics and so forth. At the time of the seventh mental engagement, one enters the main part of the first concentration. Through this, based on the preparation for the summit of existence, one is freed from attachment at Nothing Whatsoever. Then one progressively traverses the eight concentrations and formless absorptions until engaging in the main part of the absorption at the summit of existence. However, if this is without the path that realizes selflessness, it will not be able to eliminate even the manifest afflictions at the summit of existence, so one will not be able to go beyond existence. The *Praise Honoring the Honorable One* (*Varṇārhavarṇastotra*) states:

> *Beings who have turned away from your teachings*
> *Are blinded by delusion.*
> *Although they go to the summit of existence*
> *They again suffer and establish existence.*[413]

There is a lot that can be said about this way of traversing the path of special insight with the form of coarse peace.

Special insight with the form of selflessness is a special quality of Buddhists. Within this as well, there are two forms: (1) special insight with simply a common feature of selflessness and (2) special insight with the feature of selfless reality that eliminates the potentials for afflictions from the root. The latter one may lack the attainment of concentration and formless absorption, but it can achieve sheer liberation, freedom from existence, through meditation based on just the calm abiding that is included within the preparation for the first concentration. The *Praise Honoring the Honorable One* states:

> *By following your teaching,*
> *Even if the main part of concentration is not attained,*
> *Like removing a demonic blindfold,*
> *Existence can be overturned.*[414]

In short, there are two paths: the former is a mundane path, through which one can traverse up to the summit of existence; the latter is the transcendent path, based on which one can traverse all the way up to omniscience.

How to cultivate special insight with the form of the subtle selflessness is like this: The *Sūtra Explaining the Intent* states: "It comes from the cause of a [786] pure view arising from study and contemplation."[415] By relying on a learned protector, one seeks out the Madhyamaka view through study and contemplation of the stainless scriptural tradition of Madhyamaka. This is indispensable for amassing special insight. If one has not determined the view with certainty, no understanding of special insight will occur that realizes emptiness.

Therefore, when cultivating the view that one has discovered within the state of a previously achieved calm abiding, analyze again and again with discerning wisdom the meaning of selflessness, which is the lack of intrinsic nature in phenomena and persons. Undermine the mode of apprehension that holds onto a self. At the end of analysis, settle without dispersion within a fierce certainty of selflessness. Within this view one should meditate by alternating analysis and settling. Simply summoning a mental engagement without any analysis of objects whatsoever cannot eliminate the apprehension of self. This is because this is merely not conceiving the existence of self; it is not realizing the nonexistence of self.

Discriminating analysis is conceptual, but there is no conflict in nonconceptual gnosis arising from it. Fire comes from two sticks rubbing together in the wind, and burns the sticks. Likewise, the fire of wisdom comes from discerning concepts, and burns the conceptual wood. This example is taught in sūtras and is explained in the *Stages of Meditation*.[416] The statement, "Thinking that material forms and so on are empty and selfless is to engage in signs," negates the apprehension of emptiness as truly existent; it does not negate discernment. The *Condensed Perfection of Wisdom* says: "When the conditioned and the unconditioned, and virtuous and unvirtuous phenomena, have been deconstructed by wisdom, and there is not the slightest thing observed, the world moves into the transcendent perfection of wisdom."[417] It says that when the weapon of wisdom deconstructs phenomena as not existing in the slightest way essentially, a lack of intrinsic existence is seen, which becomes the transcendent perfection of wisdom. The *Cloud of Jewels* says: "Through investigation by special insight, essencelessness is realized and signlessness engaged."[418]

Until pliancy arises that is induced through the power of analysis by practicing analytic and settling meditations in alternation, it is only a semblance of special insight. When pliancy arises that is induced through the power of that analysis itself, a genuine special insight that observes emptiness is accomplished. When special insight is achieved in this way, it becomes a unity of calm abiding and special insight that observes selflessness. Before special insight is achieved, one must rely on effort for both analysis and settling. When it is achieved, calm abiding can be induced simply through analytic meditation. All meditative stabilizations are included within calm abiding and special insight, and all the qualities of the path are also products of these two. This is stated in the *Sūtra Explaining the Intent.*[419]

2. Dispelling Disputes about the Two Truths Being Unreasonable

[IX.106] ***"If in this way there is no conventional . . ."*** [787] Prāsaṅgikas ascertain all phenomena—comprised within the body, feelings, mind, and phenomena—as not existing on their own even conventionally. Realists and Svātantrika-Mādhyamikas dispute this by saying, "If this were the case there would be no place for any phenomena. Conventional truth also becomes nonexistent even though you say that all phenomena do not ultimately exist, but conventionally do. Thus, your system does not have two truths." To resolve these objections, there are two parts: (1) explaining the reason for the opponent's objection and (2) showing that these problems do not apply to the Prāsaṅgika system.

1. Explaining the Reason for the Opponent's Objection

Realists claim that entities ultimately exist on their own, and Svātantrikas assert that phenomena exist on their own conventionally. If it were not asserted in this way, they would not know how to posit any framework whatsoever. For this reason, they hold that Prāsaṅgikas not accepting phenomena to exist on their own conventionally is a problem. Even though some people say that there is no difference between a Prāsaṅgika and a Svātantrika in terms of not accepting phenomena to exist on their own, there are many reasons why Svātantrikas do accept phenomena to exist on their own.

In the context of negating phenomena existing on their own in the *Introduction to the Middle Way*, the opponent's position is presented: "Because when analyzing these entities . . ."[420] In the autocommentary, it says:

> Since ultimately there is no arising, arising from itself and from another is certainly negated. The natures of observed phenomena like forms and feelings by perception and inference without a doubt arise from another. If you do not accept this, then why do you say there are two truths? There would only be one. Therefore, there is arising from other.[421]

In this way the objector denies arising from other ultimately, but singularly claims both arising from other conventionally and intrinsic arising. Thus, the objector is none other than a Svātantrika. The objector argues that it makes sense to negate the arising from other that is ultimate and existing on its own, but that it is not appropriate to negate the arising from other that intrinsically exists conventionally. This is because there would be no correct conventional truth if this were negated, for intrinsic arising would not exist even conventionally. Thus, without the conventional truth, the two truths would not exist. Here, the objection is made that in the Prāsaṅgika system, the two truths are not feasible given that neither what exists on its own nor arising from other exist even conventionally; thus, these are accepted in their own system.

Also, proponents of Mind-Only explain the meaning of the *Sūtra Explaining the Intent's* statement that the imagined nature has the characteristics of essencelessness as the imagined nature's not existing on its own.[422] Bhāviveka refuted this, and explained the meaning of the sūtra in his system as the imagined nature not existing on its own ultimately. Others, like [788] Śāntarakṣita, were also in accord with him. Moreover, it is clear that Svātantrikas maintain that phenomena exist on their own conventionally because they understand the *Heart Sūtra* to be provisional in meaning, and maintain a correct conventional truth. Further, they also accept this because they accept autonomous reasons and theses. This is because the meaning of "autonomous argument" refers to just an instantiation (*gzhi ldog*) of the triad of logical subject, predicate, and reason (*rtags chos don gsum*) that is understood to objectively exist; it is not posited as merely a nominal designation. The *Lamp of Wisdom* explains the meaning of autonomous as existing independently. The *Immortal Treasury* (*Amarakośa*) says: "Autonomous, independent, self-powered . . ."[423] For this reason, *Clear Words* states: "While claiming the Madhyamaka view, to express autonomous probative arguments is understood to be the domain of several major problems . . ."[424] There is an extensive refutation of Svātantrika here.

The basis of the dispute between Prāsaṅgika and Svātantrika is whether or not anything exists on its own. The system of Prāsaṅgika does not accept autonomous probative arguments, but does accept reasons for which the three modes are established by a source of knowledge. Further, drawing upon the assertions of an opponent, and based on what is widely acknowledged in their position, Prāsaṅgikas put forward arguments acknowledged by others. Otherwise, there are no commonly appearing logical subjects held between a Prāsaṅgika and Svātantrikas and below. This is because there is no appearance in common between these debaters concerning any warranted object that exists from the side of the object (*yul steng nas grub pa*) without being drawn out from another's claim.

2. Showing That These Problems Do Not Apply to the Prāsaṅgika System

This section has two parts: (1) showing that an assertion of something existing on its own contradicts scripture and reasoning, and (2) showing that all frameworks are possible for this system that does not accept anything that exists on its own.

1. Showing That an Assertion of Something Existing on Its Own Contradicts Scripture and Reasoning

In the Prāsaṅgika system, nothing is held to exist on its own, even conventionally. Moreover, for the perspective of an objector like a Svātantrika, who makes the claim that the two truths are not feasible if conventionally nothing arises that exists on its own, Candrakīrti specifically refutes anything existing on its own in both of the two truths. There are three arguments in the root text of the *Introduction to the Middle Way* that negate what exists on its own, and in the autocommentary there is an argument that it would contradict scripture, so there are four. First, for the three arguments; they are arguments that it would absurdly follow that (1) a sublime being's meditative equipoise would be a cause for the destruction of entities, (2) the conventional truth would be immune to reasoned analysis, and (3) ultimate arising would not be negated. These are shown in three stanzas: "If they were based on what exists on its own . . ."[425] I will not elaborate further here.

As for the argument that it would conflict scripture, when presenting the first argument it says: "Kāśyapa, also through correctly discerning all phenomena on the path of the middle way, those phenomena are not made to become empty; they are simply empty (*stong pa nyid*)."[426] [789] If something existed on its own, it would conflict with this statement that all phenomena are empty of existing on their own. The way this sūtra teaches the meaning of self-emptiness (*rang stong*) is clear in Tsongkhapa's explanation of the *Introduction to the Middle Way*.[427]

Moreover, the autocommentary on the *Introduction to the Middle Way* also responds to the charge that the aforementioned two truths would not be reasonable. To summarize its meaning, it responds by saying that if phenomena existed on their own, then there would be no conventional truth because conditioned phenomena would not be unreal, deceptive phenomena. Thus, according to their system, there would not be two truths, but the two truths are most reasonable in our system of Prāsaṅgika, which does not accept anything that exists on its own, even conventionally. If something is accepted to exist on it is own, there is the problem that the two truths would not be reasonable.

In short, once something is held to intrinsically exist—whether it be held to be permanent or impermanent, etc.—one is not able to go beyond the extremes of permanence and annihilation. The *Fundamental Verses of the Middle Way* states:

> *What intrinsically exists*
> *Would be permanent because it is not nonexistent;*
> *What existed before and is now nonexistent*
> *Would be annihilated.*[428]

In this way, when the existence of phenomena on their own is negated, even conventionally, an opponent objects, "If forms and so forth do not exist, even conventionally, then how does a cognition that perceives them arise?" This objection is dispelled in the *Introduction to the Middle Way:*

> *Empty entities, like reflections,*
> *Depend upon an assemblage [of conditions]; they are not unacknowledged.*
> *In the way that from empty reflections*
> *Cognitions with their forms arise;*
> *Likewise, while all entities are empty,*
> *They arise from within emptiness.*[429]

In the way that from an unreal reflection, an unreal cognition with its form arises, it says that an effect that is empty of existing on its own arises from a cause that is empty of its own existence; there is no conflict. This argument—that it all is possible when emptiness is possible—shows that all the frameworks of the two truths and so on are reasonable when phenomena are empty of existing on their own.

2. Showing That All Frameworks Are Possible for This System That Does Not Accept Anything That Exists on Its Own

This section has two parts: (1) how there are many distinctive features when nothing is accepted to exist on its own, and (2) debates about what is possible and impossible concerning efficacy while empty.

1. How There Are Many Distinctive Features When Nothing Is Accepted to Exist on Its Own

The *Introduction to the Middle Way* states: "Since nothing intrinsically exists in either of the two truths, things are neither permanent nor annihilated."[430] Since anything existent on its own is negated in both of the two truths, this does not fall to the extreme of permanence. Since it is able to posit all causality and so on while lacking intrinsic nature, it does not fall to the extreme of annihilation. When existence on its own is negated in this way, there is the quality of being able to eliminate the extreme views of permanence and annihilation easily. Moreover, there are many other unique features, such as karmic causality being most reasonable. For this reason, the autocommentary on the *Introduction to the Middle Way* states: [790] "Scholars should ascertain what are the unique features of this system."[431] It states this immediately after refuting the Svātantrikas. By means of the profound viewpoint of the sublime beings, the way of explanation in this system is said to have many unique features that are different from other systems of Madhyamaka and Mind-Only.

One might wonder how this is. Some Indian masters explained the *Fundamental Verses of the Middle Way* and the *Four Hundred Verses* as Mind-Only texts. Also, others explained their viewpoint as Madhyamaka from the aspect of the view, yet they described some of the ways of understanding the conventional truth in accord with Mind-Only—not accepting external objects and positing self-awareness. Also, other Mādhyamikas asserted that phenomena exist on their own conventionally, and accepted autonomous arguments and theses. They understood that to apprehend true existence is a cognitive obscuration and did not accept that it was necessary for those traversing the sublime path of Hīnayāna to definitely realize the subtle emptiness. There are many ways of commentary, yet all of them appear to be ways of explaining the viewpoint of sublime beings.

Nevertheless, the perfect explanation of the consummate viewpoint of the sūtras and sublime beings was put forth by three great chariots: Buddhapālita, Candrakīrti, and Śāntideva. They have a unique way of explanation that stands apart from those other Mādhyamikas and proponents of Mind-Only. Their way of explanation—conventionally accepting external objects and not accepting the basic consciousness or self-awareness—is not shared with proponents of Mind-Only. Their way of explanation—not accepting phenomena existing on their own conventionally nor accepting autonomous arguments, while understanding that to apprehend true existence is an afflictive obscuration and saying that even sublime beings in the Hīnayāna definitely realize the subtle emptiness—is also not shared with other Mādhyamikas.

In general, there are many unique features, but it is acknowledged that there are mainly eight. Regarding this, Tsongkhapa's explanation of the *Introduction to the Middle Way* says:

> To state the main ones here, there are the unique ways of negating (1) a basic consciousness that is different from the six collections, and (2) self-awareness, along with a third claim that an autonomous argument cannot generate a view of reality in the continuum of an opponent. As cognitions are accepted, external objects also must be accepted. Disciples and Self-Realized Ones have the realization of the lack of intrinsic nature in entities. Apprehending the self of phenomena is understood to be an affliction. Disintegration is an entity, and for this reason, there is a unique way of positing the three times.[432]

Also, "There are many features, such as when cognitive obscurations are eliminated."[433] To expand upon this, there are many distinctive features that come up at the time of the path and fruition. The features "such as when cognitive obscurations are eliminated" are not distinctions from the aspect of view, like the previous ones. Rather, these are unique features that stand apart from other Madhyamaka and Mind-Only traditions from the [791] essential profound point of the way of traversing the Mahāyāna path.

Further, one might wonder, "There are other philosophical systems that do not accept the basic consciousness and self-awareness. They refute them, and assert external objects and things like the entity of disintegration. So why are these held to be unique features of Prāsaṅgika?"

It is like this: due to not accepting anything that exists on its own, even conventionally, the features of not accepting things like the basic consciousness and accepting external objects are posited. Thus, these are different from others. For this reason, the words state that these are features of a unique way of negating and a unique way of positing. Therefore, it is extremely important to recognize that the root of all these distinctive features comes down to not accepting anything to exist on its own. For this reason, several other qualities have already been stated. Yet here I will add a bit about the way that all frameworks are laid out upon that which is merely nominally existent, without the slightest thing existing on its own. Our own text here responds to the objection about the aforementioned two truths not being reasonable:

> [IX.107cd] ***After it is ascertained, it exists;***
> ***If not, there is no conventional.***

It clearly demonstrates how to understand the conventional in the Prāsaṅgika system.

Furthermore, the mode of existence—reality—is difficult to realize. It is likewise extremely difficult to draw the line in this system between not the slightest thing being accepted to exist objectively, which is the object of negation, and all conventions being established by a source of knowledge upon that which is merely nominally designated. Therefore, it is necessary to find certainty in the way that the framework of dependent arising is reasonable within that which is empty of intrinsic nature. Otherwise, it does not make sense for the two truths to be separated and have varying degrees of value. When either of the two truths is lost, it is like falling to the extremes of permanence and annihilation. It is like one who falls to ruin. If neither of the two truths is lost, and they are a unity, then it will be as if the two accumulations are perfected at the time of the path, and the two embodiments of buddhahood attained at the time of the fruition.

Therefore, in this Prāsaṅgika system, when the Madhyamaka view of the unity of emptiness and dependent arising is ascertained upon a single basis, there is no conflict between the two truths. Moreover, as will be explained later as contrary to the way that realists understand, for the reason that all phenomena lack intrinsic natures, the complete functioning of causality is possible. Through finding certainty in the way that phenomena lack intrinsic nature for the reason that the complete functioning of causality is reasonable, the two truths are known in a way that they are mutually supportive. This is the unexcelled unique feature of this system.

2. Debates about What Is Possible and Impossible Concerning Efficacy While Empty

Realists think, "If phenomena lack intrinsic natures that objectively exist, what else can there be?" Understanding the lack of intrinsic existence to be utter nonexistence, they do not know how to understand things like causality whatsoever. They think, "If there is the production of an effect from its cause, and a cause produces its effect, then what else is there besides [792] objective (*rang ngos nas*) arising?" They maintain that phenomena have natures that objectively exist. They say that if phenomena were empty, then causality would not be possible, and that emptiness would not be possible if there is an invariant causal relation. Thus, they hold the two truths to be a mass of contradictions, and stray far from a view of their unity. For these reasons, realists say, "If phenomena were empty of objective existence, then it would absurdly follow that in your Madhyamaka system there would be no causality at all—no arising or ceasing, and no four truths." The *Fundamental Verses of the Middle Way* says:

If all this were empty,
Then there would be no arising and no ceasing;
It would follow that for you
The four noble truths would not exist.[434]

Dispelling Disputes states:

If there were no intrinsic nature
In any entities,
Then your words, which also lack intrinsic nature,
Would not be able to negate intrinsic nature.[435]

They argue that, if there were no intrinsic nature, then, since your words also lack intrinsic nature, they would not be able to negate the existence of intrinsic nature, nor establish that phenomena lack intrinsic nature.

The Mādhyamikas reply to them, turning around the aforementioned consequences. The *Fundamental Verses of the Middle Way* says:

If all of this were not empty
There would be no arising and no ceasing. . .[436]

Dispelling Disputes also replies to that passage, stating:

Entities that are dependently arisen
Are themselves called "emptiness."
That which is dependently arisen
Is said to lack intrinsic nature.[437]

In its autocommentary, it says that since pots and cloths dependently arise, they also lack intrinsic natures. Nevertheless, they are able to hold things like honey and protect from the cold; likewise, these words, even without intrinsic nature, can negate and affirm.

The debate with this unique philosophical system is a debate exclusively about whether or not it is possible for things to function while empty of intrinsic nature. The problems expressed by the realists do not apply to Mādhyamikas. Furthermore, all frameworks are suitable in a system for which emptiness is suitable. Nothing is suitable for those for whom emptiness is unsuitable. Realists project their own problems onto Mādhyamikas, but these problems are their own, as stated in the *Fundamental Verses of the Middle Way*:

> *Those for whom emptiness is possible*
> *Everything is possible.*
> *Those for whom emptiness is impossible*
> *Nothing is possible.*
> *You have completely projected*
> *Your own problems onto me,*
> *Like the one riding a horse*
> *Forgetting that horse.*[438]

How everything is possible for whom emptiness is possible is like this: *Clear Words* states extensively: "We say that whatever is dependently arisen is emptiness. Therefore, those for whom emptiness is suitable, dependent arising is [793] suitable; those for whom dependent arising is suitable, the four noble truths are suitable."[439] Also, those who regard what exists to intrinsically exist fall to the extreme of permanence because they do not make a distinction between existence and intrinsic existence. Likewise, those who regard what lacks intrinsic existence to be totally nonexistent fall to the extreme of annihilation because they do not make a distinction between the absence of intrinsic existence and absence. The commentary on the *Four Hundred Verses* states:

> According to realists, to the extent that entities exist, they do so by their own essences. When they lose their essence, then the entities are totally nonexistent, like a donkey's horn. Since they do not depart from these two positions, it is difficult to coordinate all their claims.[440]

For this reason, Buddhapālita and the commentary on the *Four Hundred Verses* make a distinction between existence and intrinsic existence, and *Clear Words* also describes a clear distinction between the absence of intrinsic existence and absence.

A realist might object, "Since you Mādhyamikas speak of the absence of intrinsic existence, you are the same as the nihilists" (*med pa ba*). Proponents of the absence of intrinsic nature are distinct from nihilists, the proponents of absence; they are not the same. Also, Mādhyamikas say that there is no intrinsic nature because of the dependent arising of things like past and future lives; it is not said that these do not exist. Nihilists do not speak like this; since they do not see anything coming from a past life to this one and leaving to a future life, they say these do not exist. There are said to be many distinctions, such as the way Mādhyamikas are different from nihilists based on the different reasons for their claims. The commentary on the *Four Hundred Verses* also states:

> I am not an anti-realist (*dngos por med par smra ba*) because I proclaim dependent arising. One might think, "So you are a realist?" No, because I proclaim dependent arising. "What do you claim?" I proclaim dependent arising.[441]

One might ask, "What is the meaning of dependent arising?" It means the lack of intrinsic nature. It means the absence of intrinsic arising. It means that effects arise with natures like an illusion, a mirage, a reflection, a city of *gandharvas,* an apparition, and a dream. It means emptiness and selflessness. By asserting dependent arising, the two extremes of claiming existent and nonexistent entities are dispelled. By asserting the meaning of dependent arising to be the lack of intrinsic arising, the claims of existence like those of the realists are dispelled. By showing that while lacking intrinsic existence, causality exists like an illusion, the claims of nonexistence like those of the nihilists are dispelled. Likewise, the *Heap of Collected Jewels Sūtra* cited in the *Anthology of Sūtras* says:

> Blessed [794] One, all phenomena are dependently arisen, so there is no essence. Blessed One, that which is thoroughly afflictive or completely pure is the meaning of dependent arising; it is the meaning of nonexistence. Blessed One, the wise understand that the meaning of nonexistence is the meaning of dependent arising.[442]

As scriptures explain, the meaning of dependent arising is to appear in manifold conventions while lacking intrinsic nature. This is what it means; it does not mean anything like true existence. Also, the meaning of emptiness that is the emptiness of intrinsic nature is also the meaning of dependent arising; it does not mean a void emptiness that is nothing whatsoever. *Reason in Sixty Verses* states:

> *Those who fixate on a self or a world*
> *That does not depend on anything -*
> *Alas, they have been hijacked by a view*
> *Of permanence and impermanence.*

Those who claim that dependent entities
Exist in reality
Have the problems of permanence and so on –
How will they not arise?
Those who claim dependent entities
To be like a moon reflected in water,
Neither true nor false,
Are not hijacked by a view.[443]

The first stanza shows how other schools that do not accept phenomena to be dependently arisen, but claim that they truly exist, fall into the abyss of the views of permanence and annihilation. The second stanza shows how some in our Buddhist schools, even though they accept entities to be dependently arisen, accept them to be real for the reason that they are dependently arisen; thus, they fall under the power of permanence and annihilation. The last stanza shows how Mādhyamika scholars understand the meaning of dependent arising as the emptiness of intrinsic nature for the reason that phenomena dependently arise based on causes and conditions. Asserting that while empty, there is a manifold display of conventions like the moon reflected in water, they are not hijacked by the views of permanence and annihilation; they do not fall under their power. Like this last stanza, a sūtra says: "The wise realize dependently arisen phenomena; they do not rely on extreme views."[444]

Other schools do not accept dependent arising; they claim that phenomena truly exist. Since this is the tradition of their teachers, it is not so strange. Yet when some in our Buddhist schools claim unexcelled dependent arising—the means to establish the emptiness of intrinsic nature—yet proclaim that phenomena truly exist without being able to bear the word "emptiness," this is very strange. This is stated in *Reason in Sixty Verses*.

The profound unity of appearance and emptiness that is the Madhyamaka path is extremely difficult to understand. For this reason, in addition to saying that things are empty, the Buddha said, "Profound, peaceful, luminous, unconditioned . . ."[445] claiming that it was difficult to turn the wheel of doctrine. This is stated in the *Fundamental Verses of the Middle Way*, the *Precious Garland*, and the *Four Hundred Verses*.

[795] In short, when the Madhyamaka view is ascertained at the time of the ground, one discovers certainty in the way that phenomena are empty of objective existence. Thereby, there is the gathering of a fully qualified accumulation of gnosis. When one discovers certainty in the way that dependently arisen conventions are reasonable due to their being empty of intrinsic

nature, there is the proper training in the accumulation of merit. When the two accumulations are integrated in this way, and method and wisdom are not separate at the time of the path, then at the time of the consummate fruition one will arrive at the unity of the two embodiments of buddhahood—the Truth Body and the Form Body. *Reason in Sixty Verses* states: "The two excellences are attained through merit and gnosis."[446]

3. Explaining the Reasoning that Negates the Self of Phenomena

This section has three parts: (1) explaining the argument of the diamond shards, (2) explaining the argument of great interdependence, and (3) explaining the argument that negates the production of an existent or a nonexistent thing.

1. Explaining the Argument of the Diamond Shards

This section has two parts: (1) a general explanation in accord with the root verses, and (2) a specific explanation of how arising from the four extremes is negated.

1. General Explanation in Accord with the Root Verses

[IX.116] ***In the perception of the world . . .*** What follows is how causeless arising is asserted, which is what the non-Buddhist Cārvākas claim. The roots of the Cārvāka philosophical system stem from a person named Lokacakṣu, who studied logic (*rtog ge*). He composed 100,000 texts on there being no karmic causality, and no past or future lives, because he wanted to have sex with his daughter, etc. His followers are called Cārvākas or "proponents of annihilation." There are many divisions among them, but in the *Grounds* (*sa sde*) it is said that there are two: "the sophists" (*rtog ge ba*) and "the absorptionists" (*snyoms 'jug pa*). Within each one of these, there are also annihilationists who accept past and future lives, but not karmic causality, and annihilationists who accept neither past and future lives nor karmic causality.

The sophists rely on bogus arguments, and say that there is no karmic causality because they see people who are generous in this life who are poor, some who are stingy yet rich, some who do not kill yet have short lives, and some who kill yet live long. They say that there are no past or future lives because they are not established by perception. The absorptionists achieve a concentration of formless absorption and presume they have attained Arhatship. When they die, their meditative stabilization fades; and upon seeing their next birth, they think that there is no Arhatship in this world, so they denigrate it.

How they establish that there are no past or future lives is like this: They say, "There is nothing that comes here from a previous life. An accidental mind comes from the accidental body of this life, just like an accidental light comes from an accidental butter lamp. There is also nothing that goes to the future from here. Since the mind and body are one substance, at the time of death the body becomes dormant in the four elements, and the faculties become dormant in space. When the body decays, the mind decays as well, as when a wall disintegrates, the mural disintegrates, too."

[796] They accept the way that mind depends on the body with three distinct features: as beer has the power to intoxicate, the mind is the nature of the body; like a butter lamp and its light, the mind is a product of the body; like a wall and a mural on it, the mind is a quality of the body. Some of them say:

> *Pursue happiness until death!*
> *There is no such opportunity after death.*
> *After the body has turned to dust,*
> *How can it live again?"*

Also, others propound nonexistence. In this way, they say, "The softness, shape, and various colors of the petals and stamen of a lotus flower; the roundness of a pea; the sharpness of a thorn; and the various colors of the eye of a peacock's feather—these are not caused. Nobody sees them to be produced from effort, so they come from their own natures."

Most of them denigrate, saying that there is no karmic causality, and no past or future lives, so there is no habituation to a path over many lives, and thus no liberation or omniscience. In their system, it is accepted that warranted objects are necessarily particulars and that sources of knowledge are necessarily perceptions; thus, they do not accept universals or inference.

Furthermore, their texts state:

> *Beings exist only to the extent*
> *Of the range of their faculties.*
> *Whatever is eloquently said by the highly educated*
> *Is just like the tale of a coyote!*

And,

> *Sleep with beauties and eat well!*
> *When the supreme body passes, you will be no more.*

Most of their philosophical system is motivated by passionate desire; they also presume this to be beneficial. Other names for this school are: "this-worldly beauty" because they claim that truth is whatever is beautiful in this world; "annihilationists" because they claim that the self is annihilated at the time of death; "nihilists" because they say there is no karmic causality; and "Cārvākas" ("Far-Throwers") because they throw the future far away, or because they have gone far from the correct view.

Āryadeva said: "Whether without karma or without results, bad texts are the tradition of the Cārvākas."[447] Among the non-Buddhist schools, the Cārvākas are said to be the absolute worst. To refute them, and to refute those who accept causeless arising, our text here undermines their position with an appeal to mundane perception, which will also be explained later. One should know the assertion of those who do not accept a future world, the refutation of the way the mind depends on the body, and the ways of establishing past and future lives and omniscience from texts such as the root text and autocommentary of the *Introduction to the Middle Way*, the *Blaze of Reason*, and the *Commentary on Epistemology*.

Next, [IX.118] ***If Īśvara were the cause of beings . . .*** Here is a presentation of the ways of assertion and refutation of the proponents [797] of Īśvara in two parts: (1) the assertions and (2) their refutation.

A1. Assertions of the Proponents of Īśvara

Their teacher is the great god Īśvara; Akṣapāda and Kaṇāda also accepted him as their teacher. There are many other names for Īśvara, such as Śiva and "the Primordial" (*ye srid*). For this reason, the followers of Īśvara are called proponents of Īśvara, Śaivas, and proponents of the Primordial, etc. In general, the theistic Sāṃkhyas accept Īśvara as their teacher, and there are Vaiśeṣikas and Naiyāyikas who accept him as their teacher, too. These were described separately before; here, for the actual division of the proponents of Īśvara, there are two: "the manifestors" (*gsal byed pa*) and "unpierced ears" (*rna ba ma phug pa*). They hold the texts of the *Proclamation of Īśvara Tantra* and the *Bhurkuṃkūṭa Tantra* to be warranted testimony. They hold that Īśvara lives on Mt. Kailāśa with spirit ladies (*ma mo*), like Lady Umā and Durgā. He stays with his retinue, including thousands of spirits (*'byung po*), such as Gaṇeśa and the Ṣaṇmukha. This was explained in master Prajñāvarman's two commentaries on praises.[448]

They accept that Īśvara has eight qualities. This is stated by Avalokitavrata: "Subtle, light, the object of worship, master, controller, pervader, having all that is desired, and remaining satisfied . . ."[449] The proponents of Īśvara, the theistic Sāṃkhyas, along with the Naiyāyikas and Vaiśeṣikas who hold Śiva and Brahmā as gods, all maintain that Īśvara is the creator of the entire world of the environment and inhabitants. Non-Buddhist followers of Brahmā maintain that the entire world is Brahmā's emanation. What follows is an explanation of how this is for proponents of Brahmā and the Vaiśeṣikas.

When the world disintegrates and is empty, there only remain partless, subtle particles, alone in space. At some point, Īśvara becomes motivated, wanting to make a gift of an environment and inhabitants. Because of this, and the power of sentient beings' karma, two minute wind-particles join first, then a third minute wind-particle joins. In this way, in the moment of a finger snap, a great circle of wind moves, becoming a reality. Upon this, in a process like before, from water-particles a circle of water forms and swirls. Upon this, like before, a solid mass of a circle of earth forms from earth-particles. Upon this, like before, a great heap of fire blazes from fire-particles, becoming a single tongue of a flame. In the middle of the fire, through the power of Īśvara's desire, a blazing, great egg of Brahmā manifests. When it matures and breaks, the great Brahmā, patriarch of the world, emerges from the womb of a lotus. With four faces, he sits on a lotus; he is the one held to be the creator of the entire world. This also shows how permanent minute particles are the creator of the world. Alternatively, it is also explained by proponents of Brahmā that he was born from a lotus from Viṣṇu's navel, [798] or that Brahmā was born from an egg that was emanated from the mind of Īśvara.

Also, the Nyāya-Vaiśeṣikas say, "The creation of all abodes, bodies, and enjoyments is preceded by a being's thought. Like a hatchet, he abides and engages in actions. Like pots and so on, he has features of shape. Like a battle-ax, he is efficacious. Since no one other than Īśvara can do this, all of this is the creation of Īśvara. Therefore, Īśvara is omniscient, too." Further, they say, "Īśvara is the creator of the various states of sentient beings—the high and low, happiness and suffering. This is because we can see the muddle of evildoers who live long, stingy people who are wealthy, and benefactors who are poor. For example, it is like the way some kings will bring favor to their friends and bring suffering to enemies." For their path of liberation, they say it is to practice vase-breathing, to experience the bliss of ejaculation by consorting with a woman, and to receive initiations from the tip of Īśvara's *liṅgaṃ*. They consider liberation to be—from among the four gnoses at the time of waking, dreaming, sleep, and sex—the fourth gnosis that arises from the bliss of ejaculation during sex.

A2. Refutation of the Proponents of Īśvara

In our text, a question about the meaning of Īśvara is posed, and then it is refuted. Also, it is refuted by the argument that it is not possible for what is permanent to be a cause for something that arises. The *Commentary on Epistemology* says:

> *What has the characteristics of abiding, engaging, and a shape,*
> *And is efficacious and so on,*
> *Is established by assertion, not by example,*
> *Or, there is doubt.*[450]

There are many arguments that refute the opponent's assertion above. There are also several refutations in the *Essence of Madhyamaka*.[451]

Next, in the contexts of, [IX.126c] ***The permanent primal basis . . .*** and, [IX.134c] ***If you claim that from what does not exist, nothing . . .***, our text states that it is not reasonable for a partless primal basis to have three natures. Also, there are arguments that refute an effect that is intrinsically the same as a cause—such as the absurd consequence that eating grain would entail eating excrement, and so on. These are described in the root verses and also in the refutation of arising from self, which will be explained below.

Next, it says, [IX.141d] ***. . . Individually or in conjunction.*** Here our text shows that both causes and conditions—individually or in conjunction or combination—do not intrinsically reside in their effects. One should know this as it is described extensively in the twentieth chapter of the *Fundamental Verses of the Middle Way*, "Investigation of Combination." Alternatively, this can be applied to a summation of the meaning of the refutation of three possibilities for production: *individually* referring to arising each from self and from another, and *in conjunction* referring to arising from both. Or, it is also fine to apply this as the way of refuting the assertion of arising from both. [799] Thus, here is a twofold explanation of the assertions of the Nigranthas, who assert arising from both, and a refutation of them.

B1. Assertions of the Nigranthas

As for their teachers, there were said to be twenty-five, such as Mahāvīra, the sage Arhat, and Ṛṣabha. They go by many other names including Jains, Ārhatas, Nigranthas, Parivrajakas, and so on. The texts they consider authoritative include the *Expanding Star*.[452] They assert all objects of knowledge to be included in nine categories: life, contaminations, stoppage, perishing, bondage, karma, evil, merit, and liberation. Regarding these, *life* is held to be the self. It only extends through the body of a living being; it has the identity of mind and a permanent nature, while in an impermanent state. The *Praise of the Exceptional One* states:

> *The Nigranthas claim that to the extent of the body*
> *Life expands and contracts.*[453]

Other names for the self include the sustained, an individual, a being, and a person. *Contaminations* are the outflows in cyclic existence from virtuous and unvirtuous actions. *Stoppage* prevents the outflows and does not accrue new actions. *Perishing* is to abstain from food and drink and to undergo austerities of meditative concentration and bodily penance, by which previously accumulated karma is exhausted. *Bondages* are that which obstructs liberation, such as the 360 wrong views. *Karma* is fourfold: feeling-producing karma, body-determining karma, status-determining karma, and lifespan-determining karma. *Evil* is bad actions, those on the side of untruth. *Merit* is good actions, those on the side of truth. As for *liberation,* the path of liberation is austerity: the vows of body, such as being naked; the disciplines, such as nonviolence; gnosis, such as intelligence; and relying on the five fires. Based on these, through the exhaustion of previous karma and not producing any new karma, they assert that there is liberation from cyclic existence.

Furthermore, they claim that above all worlds and beyond the three realms there is a "combination world" with an area of 4,500,000 fathoms. It is shaped like an upside-down parasol, and its color is white like a water lily. Going there is said to be going to liberation. Moreover, the Great Jina said:

> *The Victors say that liberation*
> *Has a vast fragrance of incense and the color of a flower;*
> *With a color like that of curds, frost, and pearls,*
> *And a shape like an upside-down parasol.*

They claim that effects arise from both self and other because a cause and an effect are intrinsically the same, but in different states. They have a lot to say, including arguments to establish that there is no omniscience and that plants have minds.

B2. Refutation of the Nigranthas

The assertion of the intrinsic identity of cause and effect is refuted in the *Commentary on Epistemology:*

> *[800] When asked to have curd,*
> *Why don't you take milk?*[454]

It is refuted with the absurd consequence that there would be confusion in the pursuit of objects. How arising from both is negated will be explained below. Their arguments to establish the nonexistence of omniscience are shown to be bogus arguments, and become arguments for establishing omniscience. Also, their arguments to establish that plants have minds are shown to be inconclusive. Arguments that show that plants do not have minds are stated extensively in the *Commentary on Epistemology* and in the *Essence of Madhyamaka.*[455]

In general, there are many divisions within non-Buddhist philosophical systems, but they can be comprised within the eternalists and the annihilationists. The annihilationists are the Cārvākas, and there are many among the eternalists, such as the Sāṃkhyas. Here I have only written a bit to summarize the claims of just those mentioned in the root verses.

Also, the *Praise of the Exceptional One* states:

> *The more I consider the*
> *Scriptural traditions of non-Buddhists,*
> *The more it is you, Protector, that*
> *I have complete faith in mind.*[456]

Arguments refuting the way non-Buddhists proclaim eternalism and annihilationism appear in the scriptures of the great chariots. By understanding them, there arises an uncontrived faith induced by reason in the stainless teachings and teacher of our tradition. There are many other purposes served as well: the entirety of misconceptions is dispelled, such as apprehending suffering to be causeless; holding that suffering has a cause, but apprehending it to arise from a discordant cause; and holding to what is not the path and not liberation to be the path and liberation. Also, the potentials for predispositions, embedded from previous lives through the power of hearing the scriptural traditions of bad philosophical systems like that of the Cārvāka, are weakened. In future lives, all wrong views are turned away, and a predisposition is infused in the continuum for the authentic view to take birth quickly. For these purposes, there are many presentations of refutation and proof; do not think that these are unnecessary for the essence of practice. The lords of reason say this.

2. *Specific Explanation of How Arising from the Four Extremes Is Negated*

This section has three parts: (1) the thesis of not arising from the four extremes, (2) establishing this through reasoning, and (3) the meaning thereby established.

1. The Thesis of Not Arising from the Four Extremes

In general, among arguments ascertaining selflessness, there are many formulated as *reductios* and many formulated as probative arguments. From among these, the main argument to ascertain the selflessness of phenomena is this: the argument negating arising from the four extremes, or "the argument of the diamond shards." Moreover, as was explained before, one must negate objective existence with respect to all phenomena, [801] but first one should negate it with respect to conditioned phenomena. This is because entities that are efficacious are major grounds for the confusion of realism; unconditioned phenomena, which are not efficacious in this way, are minor grounds for the confusion of apprehending true existence.

For this reason, Buddhist realist schools assert that entities truly exist for the reason that they are seen to arise, abide, and cease. The expression of praise in the *Fundamental Verses of the Middle Way* ascertains the lack of intrinsic nature in the eight extremes of ceasing and so on.[457] Thus, if intrinsic existence with respect to conditioned phenomena is negated, it is easy to negate it with respect to unconditioned phenomena. With this in mind, the *Fundamental Verses of the Middle Way* first negates the true existence of conditioned phenomena in earnest:

> *When conditioned phenomena are not established at all*
> *How could unconditioned phenomena be established?*[458]

Within conditioned phenomena as well, when intrinsically existent *arising* is negated among the threefold arising, abiding, and, ceasing, the intrinsic existence of the other two are negated along with it. Therefore, first one should ascertain the lack of intrinsic arising. For this reason, the master Nāgārjuna, father and son [Candrakīrti], first explained the equality of non-arising from among ten equalities mentioned in the *Sūtra on the Ten Grounds.* The autocommentary on the *Introduction to the Middle Way* says:

> Therefore, through showing the reasoning of only the equality of non-arising here, the other equalities are easily demonstrated. Intending this, in the beginning of the master's treatise on Madhyamaka, he states:
>
> *Not from self, nor from other,*
> *Not from both, nor without cause;*
> *No entity whatsoever*
> *Has ever arisen anywhere.*[459]

The root text of the *Introduction to the Middle Way* also says:

> *It does not arise from itself, nor does it arise from another.*
> *It does not arise from both, either, nor does it arise causelessly.*[460]

These passages do not explicitly establish the lack of intrinsic arising of entities through formulating a reason that there is no intrinsic arising from the four extremes. Yet here, by explicitly presenting the mere thesis that there is no arising from the four extremes, the meaning of the thesis is exclusively a non-implicative negation that does not imply any other affirmed phenomenon. This is because it says that there is no entity at all—be it external or internal, in any time, place, or philosophical system—that ever arises from itself, from another, from both, or causelessly.

The meaning of this thesis being delimited to four is this: For the reason that being an intrinsic arising entails arising from one of these four extremes, there is determined to be two ways for intrinsic arising to take place: with a cause or causelessly. If it has a cause, then there are only three alternatives: it could arise from itself, for which the cause and effect would have the same nature; it could arise from another, for which itself and its other would each have distinct natures; or it could arise from the collective of both itself and another. When this fourfold thesis is established, it is established perforce that there is no [802] intrinsic arising.

One might think, "Then it would follow that these theses are implicative negations."

This is not a problem. An implicative negation needs to imply another affirmed phenomenon or affirmation. Yet these theses are non-implicative negations. *Clear Words* states: "Due to accepting the expression as a non-implicative negation, the meaning of the absence of entities is the meaning of the absence of intrinsic nature."[461] Bhāviveka also said several times that it is a non-implicative negation.[462]

In general, a negation—whether or not the expressed words explicitly eliminate an object of negation—is what occurs in the form of a negation when it appears to a cognition that accords with fact (*blo don mthun*). There are two types of negations: non-implicative and implicative. A non-implicative negation is a negation that does not imply another phenomenon upon negating its object of negation. For example, when asked whether or not *brahmins* are permitted to drink alcohol, it is like the response: "They are not permitted to drink."

An implicative negation is a negation that implies another phenomenon upon negating its object of negation. How a phenomenon is implied can be done in four ways: explicit implication, implicit implication, both explicit and implicit implication, and circumstantial implication. Explicit implication is like saying: "The absence of self exists." Implicit implication is like saying: "The fat Devadatta does not eat food during the day." Both explicit and implicit implication is like saying: "The fat Devadatta does not eat food during the day, and he is not emaciated." Circumstantial implication is like saying, to one who is not certain about a man who is known to be either a *kṣatriya* or a *brahmin,* "He is the non-*brahmin.*"

2. Establishing This through Reasoning

This section has four parts: (1) negating arising from self, (2) negating arising from other, (3) negating arising from both, and (4) negating causeless arising.

1. Negating Arising from Self

As was explained before, the Sāṃkhyas assert arising from self. The way they do so is that they say, "All entities that have arisen, such as sprouts, have existed from the time of their causes. This is because they exist in the nature of their causes at the time of their causes. For example, at the time of clay, the cause for an earthen pot, the pot resides in the nature of the clay, and a sprout resides in the nature of the seed at the time of the seed, its cause. If something were to newly arise that did not exist at the time of its cause, then it would absurdly follow that even horns of a rabbit could arise."

The meaning of arising from self here is that they accept that a seed and a sprout are intrinsically the same. Thus, when a sprout arises from the nature of a seed, the nature of the seed is also the nature of the sprout. Thereby, this comes to mean that a sprout arises from its own nature; this is the meaning of arising from self. For them, arising from self does not mean that a sprout arises from a sprout, for instance; this is because they claim that a seed and sprout are mutually distinct, and that a sprout arises from a seed.

For them, that which pervades and encompasses all causes, conditions, and effects is singularly the primal basis, [803] the universal, or the basic materiality. They think that if this did not exist, then causal relationships would not be possible, whereas many causes and conditions come together in what is observed to be a common effect. As for the way things are intrinsically the same, they accept that the nature of all causes, conditions, and effects is intertwined. Some Sāṃkhyas do not accept arising from the universal or primal basis; they accept that effects that exist at the time of their causes are manifested due to conditions. Thereby, an unmanifest sprout that exists at the time of a seed is considered to be the cause of its arising; it is manifested through the cause of a seed and conditions like water and manure. Thus, they accept the arising of a sprout to be essentially manifestation.

What follows is a refutation of this. In general, a nonexistent phenomenon does not arise; something existent needs to arise. Also, Buddhist schools accept that before something arises, it is nonexistent and needs to arise in order to achieve its essence or nature. Yet as the Sāṃkhyas assert, what arises does so from its own nature; it arises again. This is not accepted by anyone. For this reason, the way that Sāṃkhyas assert is not reasonable. Buddhapālita said:

> Entities do not arise from their own natures because their arising would thereby be pointless and absurd. There is no point for entities with their own natures to arise again because if they did arise even though they already existed, they would never not arise.[463]

Here is what this means: Take a sprout that is asserted to exist in the way of being unmanifest at the time of its cause. It absurdly follows that it would be pointless for it to arise again because its nature has already been established. If they respond here that there is no entailment, then consider that kind of sprout. It absurdly follows that its arising would be endless because, even while its nature has already been established, there is a purpose for it to arise again. These two absurd consequences expressing contradiction—that its arising again would be pointless and endless—undermine the Sāṃkhya's claim of arising from self.

The Sāṃkhyas say, "We hold that even though it exists, there is arising in that the unmanifest becomes manifest, so the entailment of the first consequence does not hold. Since there is no need for what has become manifest to arise, there is also no entailment for the second consequence."

Both of these responses miss the mark. If its manifestation existed before, then it would not need to arise. If it existed before and arises, then it would be endless; our points hold. Also, if its manifestation did not exist before, the assertion that there is only what already exists in the cause would collapse. This is stated in Tsongkhapa's *Ocean of Reason*.[464] Thus, when the nature or essence of a sprout exists at the time of the seed, yet the manifestation of the sprout (which is not that) is not present, there must then be the sprout itself at the time of the cause. Yet even though it existed, when this is not enough and it needs to arise again, then we express the contradictions that it would absurdly follow that its arising would be pointless and endless. Likewise, the *Introduction to the Middle Way* states:

> *If it arises from itself, there is no value there;*
> *The arising of what has already arisen* [804] *also makes no sense.*
> *If it is thought that there is the arising again of what has already arisen,*
> *Then the arising of things like sprouts would not occur;*
> *There would be the arising of seeds until the end of existence.*[465]

This shows an argument refuting anything arising from a cause that is essentially the same as itself. This is what it means: The first line says that if the essence of a sprout is completely established at the time of its cause, then there is no point or value in it arising again. This is because arising is for the purpose of attaining its own essence or nature, so there is the absurd consequence that it would be pointless for it to arise again, like before. The remaining four lines show that the repeated arising of what has already arisen does not make sense. They express that arising again contradicts reason: that if something like a seed that has already arisen had to repeat and arise again, then there would be no opportunity for results of similar types to arise, such as sprouts and stalks. It would absurdly follow that the cause, the seed of similar type, would arise without interruption until the end of existence.

In general, to exist and to arise are not in contradiction, but to exist and to arise again is said to be a contradiction. Likewise, to exist and to arise with an end is not a contradiction, but to exist and to arise again with an end is said to be a contradiction. Therefore, the passages cited from Buddhapālita and from the *Introduction to the Middle Way* clearly express the word *again* (*yang*), before and after. In Buddhapālita's text, there is a short demonstration and an extensive explanation, and it is important to know that *again* applies to both. Although the short demonstration does not have the word *again,* it should be applied there from the extensive explanation.

Furthermore, the *Introduction to the Middle Way* refutes this with the following arguments: It would follow that a cause and effect that have the same identity would not have differences in shape, color, taste, and power. Also, it would follow that the single nature of seeds and sprouts would desist if they relinquished their former states. It would also follow that in each of their two states of being a seed and being a sprout, the existence and nonexistence of both would be equally apprehended. Also, it would follow that the intrinsic identity of seeds and sprouts would be undermined by mundane convention. The *Fundamental Verses of the Middle Way* says:

If cause and effect were one,
Producer and produced would be the same.[466]

If cause and effect were one, then there would be the problem that cause and effect—like the producer-father and the produced son—would be the same. Also, there is a second problem expressed:

If wood were fire,
Agent and object would be the same.[467]

There would be another problem that all the functions of wood (which is the object burned) and fire (which is the agent that burns) would be the same. On this point, the *Introduction to the Middle Way* says: "If you assert arising from self, then producer and produced, and object and agent would be the same."[468] In this way, the negation of arising from self is a negation [805] in both of the two truths, so there is no need to apply the qualifier *ultimately* to the negation. Therefore, "Not from itself . . ."[469] is a general negation of arising from itself. The *Introduction to the Middle Way* says: "For this reason, designating that an entity arises from itself does not make sense in reality or in the world."[470]

2. Negating Arising from Other

Those who accept arising from other include most of the non-Buddhist schools, such as the Vaiśeṣikas, and our Buddhist schools from the Svātantrika on down. They say that there is arising from other because it is established by mundane perception. Also, realists assert that there is arising from other ultimately, while Svātantrikas claim that conventionally there is arising from an other that exists on its own. Thus, realists say, "Self-arising is pointless, so it does not make sense. Without this, arising from both also is not reasonable, and causeless arising is totally absurd. It makes sense to refute these, but it does not make sense to refute arising from other. This is because scriptures say that entities that arise come about from four conditions, which exist on their own as other. Thus, to refute arising from other contradicts scripture and reasoning."

Regarding this, in the context of presenting an objection that otherwise it would contradict scripture, the *Fundamental Verses of the Middle Way* says:

There are four conditions: the causal,
The objective support, the immediately preceding, and
Likewise, the dominant;

There is no fifth condition.[471]

The *Treasury of Metaphysics* identifies each condition, and also expresses the position of opponents when comprising the conditions into four; it states that there is no fifth condition, refuting some other non-Buddhist systems and any condition like Īśvara.[472] Tsongkhapa's two great commentaries on the *Fundamental Verses of the Middle Way* and the *Introduction to the Middle Way* extensively describe this similarly.[473] Moreover, the *other* in "arising from other" does not simply refer to the cause of an effect being conventionally other. Rather, it must refer to the arising of an effect that exists *on its own* as other from a cause that exists *on its own* as other. It is established this way in the statement cited above in the autocommentary on the *Introduction to the Middle Way*, in the context of presenting the assertion of the opponent that their natures "without a doubt arise from another."[474]

To refute arising from other, Buddhapālita says, "Entities also do not arise from what is other. Why? Because if they did, it would absurdly follow that everything would arise from everything."[475] The *Introduction to the Middle Way* also says:

If something can arise based on what is other than itself
Then thick darkness could also arise from the tongue of a flame, and
Anything could arise from anything because
All that is not a producer is the same in being other.[476]

This means that entities not only do not arise from themselves, but do not arise from what is other, either. This is because the *other* of "arising from other" [806] necessarily refers to cause and effect existing on their own as other. Once something is other in this way, its mode of existence must be other, in which case it must be other such that it does not rely on any mutual relation whatsoever. This is shown to result in extremely absurd consequences: If such an effect were produced from its cause, then it would follow that any non-cause could also produce it; if such a cause could produce its effect, then it would follow that it could produce all entities that are not its effect as its effect.

Furthermore, the opponent would have to accept that as a rice seed is, on its own, other than the rice sprout that is its effect, things like fire and charcoal also are the same in being, on their own, different from a rice sprout. In that case, it would follow that there could arise a thick darkness illuminated from the blazing tongue of an illuminating fire. It would follow that anything could arise from anything, regardless of whether it was or was not its cause or effect, because they are the same in existing on their own as other. The *Fundamental Verses of the Middle Way* also says:

> *If cause and effect were other,*
> *Cause and non-cause would be the same.*[477]

Since the arguments stated in the *Introduction to the Middle Way* extensively expose the absurd consequences of arising from other, I elaborate here upon the *Introduction to the Middle Way.*

When refuted in this way, the opponent's response to this problem is stated in the *Introduction to the Middle Way:* "Since it can be produced, it is said to be an effect."[478] To summarize this meaning, they say, "Even though a cause and effect exist on their own as other, since determinate causes and effects are seen separately, this does not entail that anything could arise from anything, whether or not it be its cause or its effect. This is because the entity that has the potential to be produced from a cause is determined as its effect, and the entity that has the potential to produce an effect is determined as its cause; cause and effect are simply qualified by being other. For example, it is like the way that a barley seed is the cause of a barley sprout that has its same continuum, but it is not the cause of a rice sprout."

In response, the *Introduction to the Middle Way* says, "Barley, lotuses, and cyprus . . ."[479] I will summarize what this means: Just as things like barley and the anthers of a lotus are not the cause of a rice sprout, similarly, a rice seed is also not the cause of a rice sprout because it is intrinsically other. This shows that it is not possible to be the same continuum while existing on its own as other.

Furthermore, whatever arises, whether it be held that cause and effect are intrinsically other or the collective of two intrinsic arisings, each one of them is refuted so a collective arising from other is refuted. When arising from other is specifically refuted in the *Introduction to the Middle Way*, it shows two arguments that refute arising from other in the case of a cause and effect occurring in a temporal sequence [807] and in the case of a cause and effect occurring simultaneously. As for the first argument, the arising of an effect from a cause is possible, but it is not possible for them to be intrinsically other. Therefore, arising from other is impossible. As for the second argument, while what is asserted to be cause and effect are other, since intrinsic arising is impossible, arising from other is impossible. In this way, it refutes arising from other. Further, it also refutes arising from other through analyzing an effect in four alternatives.

Svātantrikas might say, "This negation of arising from other is fine ultimately, but it is not so in the case of negating arising from other according to mundane convention. This is because conventionally entities are directly perceived to arise objectively (*rang ngos nas*). Also, it is because the *Rice Seedling Sūtra* says that there is a simultaneous arising from other, an objective arising of a sprout when a seed ceases like the two sides of a scale seen to rise and fall simultaneously."[480]

The intent of this sūtra is to show that merely conventionally there is an illusion-like dependent arising of the simultaneous activity of arising and ceasing; it is not making a claim to arising that exists on its own. This is because the sūtra says: "The sprout in name and in form is not created by itself, nor from another, nor from both, and not from Īśvara."[481] This refutes the realist's explanation of the intent of the *Rice Seedling Sūtra*, saying that there is a truly existent other and that the activity of arising and ceasing is simultaneous.

Likewise, sūtras that describe arising from the four conditions are merely showing that conventionally entities arise from other causes and conditions; they are not claiming arising from other. In the Prāsaṅgika system, not only is arising from other not accepted even conventionally, but it is accepted that even to apprehend cause and effect as existing on their own as other is not innate to a mundane mind. The *Introduction to the Middle Way* states: "Arising from other is not accepted even in the world."[482] This also refutes the claim that arising from other is established by mundane perception.

3. Negating Arising from Both

The Sāṃkhyas who claim Īśvara assert that a sprout arises from its cause (a seed), arising from its own nature, while also claiming that it arises from other things (conditions such as water and manure). The Nigranthas assert arising from self, as in the case of an earthen pot arising from clay, which is its nature, in light of it depending on clay; while also claiming that it arises from other, in light of it depending upon things like a potter and a potter's wheel. Also, in the case of someone like Devadatta, for instance, they claim arising from self, in light of his depending on a life that arises from a previous life that had his own nature; and they claim arising from another, in light of his depending on his parents and his previous karma. In this way, they say, "We accept that entities arise from self and other, so the previous arguments that refute arising from self and other individually do not [808] invalidate our position."

To refute this, Buddhapālita says, "There is also no arising from both self and other because in that case it would follow that the problems of both would ensue."[483] The *Introduction to the Middle Way* also says:

> *It also does not make sense to arise from both*
> *Because of the problems already mentioned.*

> *This is not accepted in reality or in the world;*
> *Therefore, in neither one can arising be established.*[484]

This means that arising from both is not reasonable because the argument negating self-arising refutes the aspect of arising from self and the argument negating other-arising refutes the aspect of arising from other. As arising from both self and other is negated in both of the two truths, this does not exist in the world nor does it exist in ultimate reality.

4. Negating Causeless Arising

The Cārvākas say, "If you assert that effects arise from causes, they need to arise either from themselves, others, or both. Since there are problems with all of these, as stated before, we accept causeless arising so these problems do not apply."

To refute them, Buddhapālita said, "Entities also do not arise without cause, because if they did, there would be the problems that anything would constantly arise from anything and that there would be no point in making any effort."[485] Also, the *Introduction to the Middle Way* says:

> *If things were to arise without cause,*
> *Then everything would constantly arise from anything,*
> *In order to produce crops, this world would not endure*
> *The hundredfold activities of gathering seeds and so on.*[486]

This means that if there were arising without cause, there would be no way to determine anything to arise in this or that time or place because there would be no determining that this effect arises from this cause and not that one. It would follow that in all places and in all times any effect could arise from any cause, regardless of whether or not it was or was not its cause or effect. Also, there would be the problem that all the efforts of the world, such as planting seeds for producing crops, would be pointless. Thus, this reveals two problems: that it would conflict with reason and that it would conflict with what is seen. The *Four Hundred Verses* also says:

> *There would be no point in embellishments*
> *Like pillars for homes.*[487]

3. The Meaning Thereby Established

If entities were to intrinsically arise, they would have to arise in one of these four ways of arising. Buddhist and non-Buddhist schools that accept intrinsic arising do so in one of these four ways of arising. Here, the refutation of arising from the four extremes [809] is also a refutation of intrinsic arising. One might wonder, "In which category do those who accept Īśvara as a cause fall?" Master Bhāviveka made a distinction within those who accept causeless arising between two types. One type accepts a cause, but a cause that does not perform a function. So he said that those who claim Īśvara, Viṣṇu, spirit, and time, etc., as causes are included within those who claim causeless arising, and refuted them.[488] Yet Candrakīrti said in his [auto-]commentary on the *Introduction to the Middle Way* that they are included within the first three claims of arising.[489] By negating arising from the four extremes, arising is shown not to occur through any of them; thereby, entities are established as not intrinsically arising. The *Introduction to the Middle Way* says:

> *Since there is no arising from self, other, both,*
> *Nor without relying on a cause, entities have no intrinsic nature.*[490]

In this way, consider entities that arise: they do not intrinsically arise because they do not arise through any of the four extremes, like a reflection.

One might think, "Then entities would not arise at all." This is not a problem because to negate arising from the four extremes is to negate *intrinsic* arising, not arising *merely conventionally*. This is because arising that is merely conventional does not need to arise from any of the four extremes. Moreover, since the conventional arising of things like seeds are dependent arisings in dependence upon causes and conditions, they do not arise from the four extremes. As a consequence of the fact that nothing arises through the four extremes when a designated object is sought out, it is said to be established that merely conventionally there is relational, dependent arising. *Praise to the Transcendent* (*Lokātītastava*) says:

> *Sophists accept that suffering is created by itself,*
> *Created by another, created from both,*
> *Or created without cause;*
> *You taught dependent arising.*[491]

The *Introduction to the Middle Way* says:

> *Since entities do not arise causelessly,*
> *Nor from a cause like Īśvara,*
> *Nor from themselves, others, or both,*

They dependently arise.[492]

These scriptures show that the essential point of the argument refuting arising from the four extremes comes down to the argument of interdependence.

2. Explaining the Argument of Great Interdependence

[IX.142c] ***What delusion holds to be real...*** Here the king of reasoning, the argument of interdependence, will be explained in two parts: (1) a general demonstration of the meaning of the argument of interdependence, and (2) a specific explanation of the way of formulating the argument and the way of eliminating the two extremes.

1. General Demonstration of the Meaning of the Argument of Interdependence

The *Inquiry of Anavatapta* (*Anavataptaparipṛcchā*) states:

> *That which arises from conditions does not arise;*
> *It does not have the* [810] *nature of arising.*
> *That which depends on conditions is said to be empty;*
> *Those who know emptiness are conscientious.*[493]

The words "arises from conditions" presents the reason; "does not arise" presents what is established (*bsgrub bya*). One might think, "Does non-arising mean the lack of mere arising, too?" The fact that this is not the case is shown in the second line, which shows that not intrinsically arising is not a negation of mere arising. To make this known, *Clear Words* cites the *Descent to Laṅka:* "Mahāmati, with the intent of no intrinsic arising, I said that all phenomena are non-arising."[494] Thus, our teacher himself says that statements of non-arising intend no intrinsic arising. Therefore, the first two lines show that being a dependent arising—arising from conditions—entails not intrinsically arising.

The third line shows the meaning of being a dependent arising—arising from conditions—as the meaning of being empty of intrinsic nature. "That which . . ." presents the logical subject (*chos can*), namely, outer and inner entities like sprouts and conditioned phenomena. The fourth line presents the benefits. The *Inquiry of Sāgaramati* (*Sāgaramatiparipṛcchā*) states:

> *That which arises in dependent relation*
> *Is free of essential existence.*[495]

It states that dependently arisen phenomena are empty of essential existence. *Reason in Sixty Verses* states:

> *That which arises in dependence upon this and that*
> *Does not arise with its own essence.*
> *How can that which does not arise with its own essence*
> *Be said to arise?*[496]

The word for dependent arising, *pratītyasamutpāda,* is explained in many ways. *Clear Words* says: "*prati* means 'meet' and *iti* means 'go.'"[497] To summarize what this means, the meaning of dependent arising is that entities depend or rely on causes and conditions for their *arising, establishment,* and *existence. Clear Words* states: "For this reason, the meaning of dependent arising is that the arising of entities depends on causes and conditions."[498]

Therefore, the meaning of dependent arising can be explained in the three ways of meeting (*phrad*), relying (*ltos*), and depending (*brten*). These three are in general said to be synonymous, but here they can be described separately to identify three distinctive arguments. *Meeting* presents the meaning of an argument that there is arising through meeting: conditioned phenomena merely *arise* (*skye ba tsam*) when meeting with their particular causes and conditions. Also, the meaning of *meeting* is the meeting of a cause like a seed oriented toward cessation and an effect like a sprout oriented toward arising. This is the meaning of *meeting;* it does not refer to the meeting of cause and effect, which is impossible.

Asserting the meaning of dependent arising as merely this is similar to how realists assert, so it is referred to as an assertion in common with them, which is fine. Yet Prāsaṅgikas do not accept true existence, whereas realists claim that being a dependent arising entails being a conditioned phenomenon and being truly existent. Thus, there is a big difference in meaning because they accept that dependent arising is formulated [811] as evidence that entails being in conflict with establishing a lack of true existence, and that it is also not a means to establish a lack of true existence.

Relying presents the meaning of an argument that things are established in relation: all phenomena rely upon their parts to *establish* (*grub pa*) their own essence. Here, all phenomena—conditioned and unconditioned—are shown to be dependent arisings. Thereby, this is even more comprehensive than the previous argument, and its mere explicit teaching is held in common with Svātantrikas. Yet there is a big difference in whether or not it is held to be necessary for phenomena to objectively rely upon their parts and so on.

Depending presents the meaning of an argument that things are dependently designated: all phenomena *exist* (*yod pa*) as mere designations in dependence upon their bases of designation. This is a distinctive feature of only Prāsaṅgika, which is not held in common with Svātantrikas and those below. This is because it shows that phenomena do not exist objectively other than being merely conceptual designations. These three arguments correlate with the meaning of the passage from *Clear Words* cited above concerning the meaning of arising in "the arising of entities," respectively in terms of mere arising (*skye ba tsam*), establishment (*grub pa*), and existence (*yod pa*).

Also, the passage says "causes and conditions," which respectively shows the causes and conditions of the three arguments: it refers to the cause of a sprout, the seed, and the conditions of water and manure and so forth; it refers to the parts of the cause that establish its essence; and it refers to the concept that designates it. Thus, in the words of the root text, [IX.144] ***What is seen when together . . .***," a phenomenon is seen when causes and conditions come together. In the context of this statement, one should know the way to apply each cause and condition from the respective three arguments. Thereby, "relying on causes and conditions" does not at all times refer to the causes and conditions of conditioned phenomena being only things like seeds, water, and manure, as was just explained. In this Prāsaṅgika system, it should be understood to mainly refer to the designating concept.

In this way, all phenomena depend on causes and conditions, and arise in reliance on causes and conditions. Other than this, there is no independent foundation (*rang tshugs thub pa'i rang dbang ba*) that exists through its own essence. The *Four Hundred Verses* states:

> *That which dependently arises*
> *Is not independent.*
> *None of this is independent;*
> *Therefore, there is no self.*[499]

The meaning of this is explained extensively in its commentary. With the intention of this meaning, a sūtra says: "Consider this: when this is there, that arises. When this has arisen, that arises. Conditioned phenomena that are conditioned by ignorance . . ."[500] The *Precious Garland* also says:

> *When this is present, that comes to be,*
> *Like there is short when there is long.*
> *When this has arisen, that arises,*
> *Like light when there is a lamp.*[501]

Also, the *Fundamental Verses of the Middle Way* says:

> *An agent depends on the patient,*
> *And* [812] *a patient also depends on the agent itself;*
> *Other than what is dependently arisen*
> *No cause for establishment is seen.*[502]

The autocommentary on the *Introduction to the Middle Way* also cites these three scriptures in order, presenting the first two to show how existence is understood to be dependent existence and how arising is understood to be dependent arising.[503] The last passage is a means to show how things are mutually established in relation, that there is no way to be essentially established. This is explained as the meaning in Tsongkhapa's *Ocean of Reason.*[504]

Here, all phenomena are understood to be the conceptual designations that impute them; there is nothing that is not a dependent arising. This is because, if it exists, it is established in relation and is without intrinsic nature. On this, a sūtra says: "There are no phenomena in the absence of causes and conditions."[505] Additionally, the *Fundamental Verses of the Middle Way* says:

> *Other than what is dependently arisen,*
> *There are no phenomena whatsoever.*[506]

Also, *Clear Words* says: "In this way, there are no phenomena whatsoever that are not dependently arisen. While dependently arisen, they are empty; therefore, there are no phenomena whatsoever that are not empty."[507]

2. *Specific Explanation of the Way of Formulating the Argument and the Way of Eliminating the Two Extremes*

How to formulate the argument of interdependence is like this: consider a sprout, it does not intrinsically exist because it is a dependent arising, like a reflection. To distinctively identify the parts (such as the logical subject) in this formulation of the argument: its logical subject (*chos can*) is a sprout. Another word for the logical subject is "basis of debate" (*rtsod gzhi*). Also, it the logical subject because it has two properties: the property to be established (*bsgrub bya'i chos*), which is the lack of intrinsic existence, and the property of the subject (*phyogs kyi chos*), which is dependent arising. What is established (*bsgrub bya*) by this is that a sprout lacks intrinsic existence. Just this is called "what is established" because only what is established is done so by means of the argument, through dependent arising. What is established and "the twofold position" (*phyogs gnyis*) have the same meaning.

Its property to be established (*bsgrub bya'i chos*) is the lack of intrinsic existence. This is called the "property to be established" because it is the property that is to be established with reference to a logical subject, such as a sprout. The logical subject and the property to be established separately are called "positions" (*phyogs*), but merely nominally, not actually. The actual name for the position is the collective of these two that is what is established. Other names for "what is established" (*bsgrub bya*) are "thesis" (*dam bca'*) and "what is inferred" (*rjes su dpag bya*). Its evidence (*rtags*) is dependent arising. "Evidence," "argument" (*gtan tshigs*), "reason" (*rgyu mtshan*), and "means of establishment" (*sgrub byed*) have the same meaning. The "position" (*phyogs*) in the term "property of the position" (*phyogs chos*) refers to the first property of what is established—the logical subject. "Subject" in the term "logical subject" is, among its two properties, a property of the evidence (*gtan tshigs kyi chos*).[508]

How to formulate a concordant example (*mthun dpe*) is as follows. It accords with both the property to be established (the lack of intrinsic existence) and the property of the means of establishment (dependent arising) with reference to an object that is a logical subject (a sprout). [813] An example of a subject (a reflection) that shares the two properties of lacking true existence and being dependently arisen is called a "concordant example."

The way the argument of interdependence is established is as follows. Establishing the property of the position [a sprout being a dependent arising] is not necessary other than for non-Buddhist schools, because it has already been established in Buddhist schools. The entailment is established through the fact that being intrinsically existent and being dependently arisen are in contradiction. This is because what is intrinsically existent must be established without relying on anything else, and being dependently arisen entails being established relationally.

How this argument eliminates the two extremes is like this: Based on ascertaining the reason, the view of denigration (which holds that the framework of dependently arisen causality is not possible if there is no intrinsic nature) is eliminated, and a certainty in dependently arisen causality is discovered. Based on ascertaining what is established, the view of superimposition (which holds that phenomena are intrinsically existent) is eliminated, and a certainty in the lack of intrinsic nature is discovered. In this way, this argument directly and simultaneously eliminates both extremes—which are the main obstacles for, and the main places of going astray from, the discovery of a pure Madhyamaka view. There are no other arguments that formulate evidence from the side of emptiness in this way that can simultaneously elicit certainty in both appearance and emptiness. Also, within them, this dependently designated argument itself is extremely powerful in being able to cut the entire web of wrong views. The *Introduction to the Middle Way* says:

> *Since entities arise dependently,*
> *These concepts cannot hold.*
> *Thus, this reasoning of dependent arising*
> *Cuts through the entire web of wrong views.*[509]

Furthermore, based on the meaning of dependent arising being ascertained as the meaning of the lack of intrinsic nature, appearance eliminates the extreme of existence. Also, based on the meaning of the lack of intrinsic nature being ascertained as the meaning of dependent arising, emptiness eliminates the extreme of nonexistence. Thereby, both extremes are eliminated through the ascertainment of the evidence and what is established individually as well; such a gift of the integrated ascertainment of appearance and emptiness is a distinctive feature of Prāsaṅgika.

Moreover, it is said that emptiness—as the meaning of dependent arising—is for Mādhyamikas who negate intrinsic existence with a source of knowledge; it is not just for anybody. Further, dependent arising—as the meaning of emptiness—is difficult for just anyone; for realists it is a cause for being bound up by holding onto extremes, such as apprehending intrinsic existence due to the dependent arising of an effect from a cause. For Mādhyamikas, emptiness can be understood by virtue of interdependence, so it becomes a cause for cutting the binds of holding onto extremes.

As was mentioned before, the essential point of the other Madhyamaka arguments comes down to this argument of interdependence itself. The main purpose of the other Madhyamaka arguments is to eliminate the two extremes and generate the Madhyamaka view in [814] one's continuum. There is nothing better than the argument of interdependence for accomplishing this purpose, so it is praised as "the king of reasoning."

The good qualities of knowing the reality of dependent arising are stated in the *Condensed Perfection of Wisdom:*

> *Bodhisattvas know what is dependently arisen,*
> *With the wisdom of what is non-arising and unceasing.*
> *Like the radiant light rays of a cloudless sun dispelling darkness,*
> *They destroy the dense ignorance and obtain what is self-existing.*[510]

The *Rice Seedling Sūtra* states: "Monks, the one who sees dependent arising sees the truth. The one who sees the truth sees the buddha."[511] Nāgārjuna also said:

This dependent arising is
The profound and cherished treasury of the Victorious One's speech;
Whoever genuinely sees it
Sees the supreme knowledge of the Buddha.[512]

It says that by knowing the meaning of dependent arising, one knows the path of Madhyamaka free from extremes. Based on this, one becomes a buddha.

3. Explaining the Argument That Negates the Production of an Existent or a Nonexistent Thing

[IX.145] ***When an entity exists...*** This means that if an effect to be produced were to exist at the time of its cause, then it must always exist. Thereby, it would not need to be produced by its producing cause. If it did need to be produced, then it would absurdly follow that there would again be the arising of what had already arisen. Also, if an effect to be produced were completely nonexistent at all times, then there would be nothing at all that causes and conditions could do to produce it. If there were, then it would absurdly follow that a space-flower could arise, too. The *Fundamental Verses of the Middle Way* states:

If an effect were essentially existent,
Then what would a cause produce?
If an effect were essentially nonexistent,
Then what would a cause produce?[513]

The last two lines show that a cause does not produce what is *essentially* established as nonexistent, but it does not show that things like sprouts that lack essential existence are not produced from causes. Here, the negation of the arising of an existent thing is a negation of the arising of what is intrinsically existent, not the negation of the arising of what merely exists. Also, the negation of the arising of a nonexistent thing is a negation of the arising of what is utterly nonexistent, not the negation of the arising of what is merely nonexistent at the time of a cause.

In this way, consider a sprout: it does not intrinsically arise because it is neither the arising of what is intrinsically existent nor is the arising of that which is utterly nonexistent. Thus, *Emptiness in Seventy Verses* states:

Since what exists exists, it does not arise;
Since what does not exist does not exist, it does not arise.
Since these are discordant properties, what both exists and does not exist does not arise either;
Since it does not arise, it does not abide or cease.[514]

The *Introduction to the Middle Way* says:

If it exists, what is the use of its production? If it does not exist, what could a producer do?
If both, what is the use? And again, what is the use if neither?[515]

This analysis of the four alternatives for an effect applies to the negation of arising from other. Also, the *Lamp of the Path of Awakening* states:

The arising of what exists does not make sense;
The arising of what does not exist is like a space-flower.[516]

These simultaneously [815] demonstrate the negation of the arising of an existent or nonexistent thing and the negation of arising from the four extremes or in four alternatives. Moreover, the first two alternatives were stated before, and since the other two alternatives (both existent and nonexistent, and neither) are impossible, production from a cause does not make sense.

The earlier passage not only negates intrinsic arising, but also negates intrinsic abiding and cessation, too. In our text here just below, right after negating intrinsic arising, it says:

[IX.149] ***Thus, there is no cessation and***
No entities either . . .

It says that there is no intrinsic arising in the beginning, and that intrinsic cessation is also impossible in the end. Therefore, an intrinsic abiding in the middle of these two is impossible, so an entity that is intrinsically existent in the triad of arising, abiding, and ceasing is similarly shown to be impossible, too. Likewise, the *Fundamental Verses of the Middle Way* states:

Since arising, abiding, and ceasing are not established,
There are no conditioned phenomena.[517]

It similarly shows that since arising and so on are not intrinsically established, then conditioned phenomena have no intrinsic existence.

Ascertaining that all phenomena are free from an intrinsically existent triad of arising, abiding, and ceasing is the outcome of all of the analyses of Madhyamaka reasoning. This is also established by scriptures that are definitive in meaning: "That which arises from conditions . . ."[518] and "with the intent of no intrinsic arising . . . ,"[519] which were cited above. Also, the *Compendium of Dharma* states:

> All phenomena are non-arising and unceasing . . . with great compassion the Tathāgata, in order to dispel what was fearful for the world, spoke of arising and cessation due to the force of convention. There is nothing at all that arises or ceases here.[520]

This is cited in the *Anthology of Training*.[521] Also, a sūtra says, "Monks, the arising of the eyes does not come from anywhere. In ceasing it does not go anywhere."[522] There is no essential abiding either, as the *King of Meditative Stabilizations* says:

> *These phenomena do not abide;*
> *They do not have an abode.*
> *Even though the word "abode" is used for the abodeless,*
> *It cannot be found with an essence.*[523]

The *Condensed Perfection of Wisdom* states: "That which does not abide in form does not abide in feeling . . ." up until, "that which abides in non-abiding is said to abide by the Victorious Ones."[524] These scriptures show that arising and so on lack intrinsic nature. Previously:

> [IX.105cd] ***In this way, all phenomena***
> ***Are not conceived to arise.***

And, [IX.102a] ***The mind does not reside in the faculties . . .***, and:

> [IX.142ab] ***It does not come from elsewhere***
> ***Abide, or leave . . .***

The triad of arising, abiding, and ceasing lacking intrinsic nature applies to all these statements.

These statements of arising and ceasing lacking an intrinsic nature with regards to essence can negate the intrinsic nature of everything, in terms of such notions as permanence and annihilation with regards [816] to time, coming and going with regards to space, and identity and difference with regards to dichotomous pairs. For this reason, the *Fundamental Verses of the Middle Way* first negated the intrinsic existence of arising. In this way, while there is no intrinsic arising or ceasing, they exist merely conventionally, as was cited before in the *Compendium of Dharma*. Also, the *Fundamental Verses of the Middle Way* states:

> *Like a dream and an illusion,*
> *Like a city of gandharvas,*
> *In this way there is said to be arising and abiding, too,*
> *And likewise, ceasing.*[525]

Moreover, all phenomena arise and cease merely conventionally; they appear to have their own essences but are essentially empty, like an illusion and a dream. This is firmly established in passages like this from the *King of Meditative Stabilizations:*

> *In the way of a city of gandharvas, a mirage,*
> *An illusion, and a dream,*
> *Know all phenomena in this way;*
> *Meditation on signs is also essentially empty.*[526]

3. *Summary*

[IX.151] ***With entities empty in this way . . .*** This shows that disregard for the eight mundane concerns is a function of realizing emptiness. As Nāgārjuna said: "The knower of the world taught gain and loss . . ."[527] The eight are the pairs of gain and loss, praise and rebuke, pleasure and pain, and pleasant and unpleasant words. The root verses say, [IX.152b] ***What is to be happy about and what is to be unhappy about?*** It is easy to apply this to pleasant and unpleasant words; the other ones are explicit.

Through realizing emptiness, one knows the equivalence of these, and is not made happy or unhappy by them. On this point, the *Anthology of Training* cites the *Compendium of Dharma*:

> Proponent of emptiness are not disturbed by mundane concerns because they are non-abiding. There is neither joy in gain nor sorrow in

> loss. There is neither inflation with fame nor dejection with disgrace. There is neither disheartenedness with rebuke nor an elated mind with praise. There is neither attachment to pleasure nor depression in suffering. Those who are not disturbed by mundane concerns know emptiness; they realize emptiness without these disturbances.[528]

This shows a disregard for these eight concerns in terms of the nature of reality. Later in the *Anthology of Training*, it says, "Since sounds do not have minds . . . ,"[529] and in our text here in the Patience Chapter, the words show a disregard for the eight concerns in terms of the nature of conventional truth. [817] Also, the *Compendium of Dharma* says: "Proponents of emptiness have no attachment or non-attachment to anything."[530] This can be applied to [IX.152d] ***Who is craving and what is craved?*** This shows that when analyzed, all the beings in the living world and the rest—those who are born and are dying, beings who have arisen and who will come—lack intrinsic nature. This is stated in a sūtra:

> *Everything is unborn and non-arising;*
> *There is no transmigrating at death nor growing old,*
> *The Lion Among Men taught this, and*
> *Brought hundreds of beings to it.*[531]

> [IX.154ab] ***May beings like myself hold***
> ***Everything to be like space . . .***

This offers advice for later followers on the need to uphold the meaning of emptiness. The reason why it makes sense to seek out the meaning of emptiness has already been stated above; here I will explain in two parts: (1) the benefits of aspiring to emptiness and (2) identifying suitable recipients for the teaching of emptiness.

1. Benefits of Aspiring to Emptiness

Immeasurable merit comes from properly explaining and studying texts that teach emptiness. Also, this purifies karmic obscurations and blocks the lower realms. Nāgārjuna said: "By aspiring to the profound truth, all merits are gathered; until becoming a buddha, all excellences—of this world and beyond—are thereby accomplished."[532] Then he cites the *Sūtra Delivered by the Precious Boy*:

> A bodhisattva without skillful means may practice the six transcendent perfections for 100,000 eons, yet one who listens to this doctrine of

> emptiness with doubts gets more merit. Even more so is the merit of one who listens to and writes it, etc., without doubting.[533]

He also cites the *Diamond Cutter Sūtra*:

> There is a lot of merit in filling with seven precious substances as many worlds as there are grains of sands in as many Ganges Rivers as there are grains of sands in the Ganges River, and offering them to the buddha. Yet there is more merit in taking up just a verse of this doctrine and teaching it to others.[534]

The *Tathāgata's Treasury Sūtra* mentions ten momentous, unvirtuous deeds and says that even those who have done them will not go to the lower realms if they have an interest in, and engagement with, the doctrine of selflessness.[535] In the chapter on taming demons, it says that if a monk who knows such things as the complete taming of all phenomena overcomes even the heinous crimes with immediate retribution, then it is needless to mention that he overcomes minor infractions of rituals and discipline.[536] The *Ajātaśatru Sūtra* states: "If one becomes inspired by this doctrine by hearing it from doing a heinous crime with immediate retribution, [818] I do not say that there is a karmic obscuration from that deed."[537] These are cited in the *Anthology of Sūtras* and appear in the commentaries on the *Fundamental Verses of the Middle Way* and the *Introduction to the Middle Way* as well.

The *Anthology of Training* states:

> There are limitless beneficial qualities from meditating on emptiness. On this here, the *Moon Lamp Sūtra* says:
>
> > *This one will never reject the Sugata's trainings;*
> > *This hero will never be seduced by women;*
> > *This one will find joy in the Sugata's teaching;*
> > *This one will know the completely peaceful nature of phenomena;*
> > *This one, before long, will be a biped master.*[538]

It also cites the *Mother*: "Śāripūtra, the great bodhisattvas, the great beings, who want to achieve the embodiment of buddhahood should train in the transcendent perfection of wisdom."[539] It is like what was said before, and there are many others as well. The *Four Hundred Verses* also says:

Those with little merit
Do not even have doubts about this doctrine.
Merely having a doubt about it,
Tears existence to shreds.[540]

When explaining and listening to the doctrine as well, it is said that the one explaining it must do so properly, and the one listening must not misunderstand it. Also, both need to have a pure motivation. When these are present, it is said that beneficial qualities will definitely ensue; yet when these are inverted, there will be no new merit accrued and merit from the past will deteriorate.

Furthermore, there are two lines from the *Introduction to the Middle Way*: "The treatises were not composed for the love of debate [but were taught for the purpose of liberation]."[541] And in its commentary, it cites texts such as the *King of Meditative Stabilizations*:

One who hears this doctrine and becomes attached
Hears what is not doctrine and becomes angry.
Being puffed up with pride is the opposite of discipline;
Through the force of pride one will experience suffering.[542]

It also cites the *Four Hundred Verses*:

When you are attached to your own side
And averse to the side of others,
You don't come to nirvana;
When acting out duality, no peace comes about.[543]

Also, the *Essence of Madhyamaka* says:

Through being tormented in mind by partiality,
Peace will never be realized.[544]

Also, *Distinguishing the Two Truths* states:

Completely relinquish the mind disrupted by partiality
And investigate.[545]

Tsongkhapa's explanation of the *Introduction to the Middle Way* says:

> It is said that if you don't give up partiality and investigate with an honest mind, then based on the meditative analysis of a philosophical system itself, you will be bound to cyclic existence. Know this to be a special quintessential instruction for us, bestowed with great love.[546]

[819] In short, it does not make any sense to apprehend without any discrimination what is poorly stated and what is well said; one needs to investigate well the respective flaws and good qualities of each and adopt and reject them accordingly. Also, it is said that in doing so one needs a pure motivation, unsullied by attachment and aggression.

2. Identifying Suitable Recipients for the Teaching of Emptiness

Furthermore, emptiness should be taught to a suitable recipient of the teachings; it is a big mistake to teach it to those who are not suitable recipients. The *Fundamental Verses of the Middle Way* says:

> *When the view of emptiness is mistaken,*
> *Those with little intelligence will be destroyed.*[547]

Some people who may seem to be interested in the teachings apprehend the meaning of emptiness as nothing whatsoever when taught it. Then they fall into the extreme of annihilation with the denigration of saying, "There are no causal processes at all." The *Precious Garland* says:

> *When this doctrine is misapprehended,*
> *The unwise become corrupted;*
> *Thereby, they sink into the filth*
> *Of the view of absence.*[548]

Also, some people who are taught emptiness reject it without interest, thinking, "How could these things be empty while they are perceived?" By apprehending phenomena to truly exist, they fall into the extreme of eternalism. The *Precious Garland* says:

Further, fools misapprehend as well,
Presuming to be wise.
Through rejecting it, their nature is intractable;
They go headfirst into the hell of utter torment.[549]

In this way, both of these types will be destroyed through a mistaken view of emptiness leading them to the lower realms.

Therefore, one should teach after determining a disciple's quality of interest. One might wonder, "By what kinds of signs can this be known?" The *Introduction to the Middle Way* says:

Even when ordinary beings hear of emptiness,
If they experience a persistent, swelling joy within,
Their eyes become filled with tears of great joy,
And the hairs on their body stand on end,
Then they have the seed of the mind of a perfect buddha.
They are suitable recipients of the teachings;
The ultimate truth should be taught to them.[550]

Upon hearing the meaning of emptiness and understanding it well: they have a joy like discovering a treasure, their eyes are moved to tears by this amazing thought, and the hairs on their body stand on end. By these three signs, they are supreme recipients because they have the signs of having activated the predisposition for the view of emptiness. Also, even if those kinds of special signs do not occur, if they have an understanding that does not fall into the two extremes, and [820] have not transgressed the command of a sacred teacher, they are suitable recipients with a lot of ripe potential for realizing emptiness.

One might think, "What kinds of qualities ensue from teaching emptiness to a supreme recipient?" It says in the *Introduction to the Middle Way*:

There will be many qualities that will ensue from this;
One will take up discipline and abide in it constantly;
One will be generous and compassionate;
One will cultivate patience, and completely dedicate one's virtues
to awakening
For the liberation of all beings.
One will also venerate all the perfect bodhisattvas.[551]

This means that an immense respect for the accumulation of merit will arise through penetrating the essential point of understanding the meaning of emptiness. Also, once the view of emptiness arises, one will enact methods to ensure that it will not fall away in future lives: One will take up discipline and guard it well, thinking, "If my discipline lapses, I will fall into the lower realms and this view will be interrupted." One will be generous, thinking, "Even if I go to the higher realms, if I am deprived of provisions, I won't be able to continually study and meditate on emptiness." One will cultivate great compassion, thinking, "If not embraced by great compassion, the view will not be a cause for becoming a buddha." One will cultivate patience, thinking, "Anger destroys virtue and leads to the lower realms; even if I go to higher realms, due to the condition of having a very ugly body, sublime beings will not be pleased." One will dedicate virtues to great awakening, seeing that discipline and so on that is not dedicated to omniscience will not be a cause for becoming a buddha. One will also be extremely reverential, seeing as supreme the spiritual friend who teaches the spirit of awakening and emptiness.

> [IX.154cd] ***Those who wish for happiness***
> ***By means of fighting or enjoyments . . .***

Most of these are faults of not realizing emptiness. The *Anthology of Training* cites a sūtra: "Likewise, those who fight and argue do not understand emptiness."[552]

> [IX.160b] ***Discernment is extremely rare . . .***, and,
> [IX.162ab] ***It will be difficult to find this opportunity again, and***
> ***The appearance of a buddha is extremely rare . . .***

It is difficult to find a situation like now, with the outer and inner conditions for practicing the dharma present; thus, it is taught that one should strive now. The *Meeting of the Father and Son Sūtra* says:

> *It is difficult for a buddha to appear, for his teachings to endure, and*
> *Likewise, for there to be those with faith in the teaching.*
> *It is also difficult to find a human life –*
> *So strive well in the teachings of the Victorious Ones.*
> *It is difficult to completely relinquish the eight unfree states*

And find perfect opportunity.
The wise with faith in the Sugata's teaching
Practice the yoga of reason.
Don't remain fixated on words:
After studying, consistently make efforts
To always rely on a solitary place;
But that is not enough: become a sublime [821] *being.*[553]

These eight stanzas are cited in the commentary on the *Fundamental Verses of the Middle Way, Clear Words.* The *Anthology of Training* also cites the *Densely Arrayed*:

If it is extremely rare to hear the word "buddha"
Even in a billion eons,
Then needless to mention about seeing what is supreme
For cutting through all doubts.[554]

For those who wish to develop merit, meeting with a buddha is very important. If merely seeing his body has limitless effects, then needless to mention seeing the essence of a buddha. Therefore, consider how difficult it is to find opportunity and fortune, meet with the teachings, and be looked after by a sacred spiritual friend. With a basis in pure discipline one should, in general, engage in the practices of a bodhisattva, the meaning that one has studied a lot, and in particular, familiarize oneself with the profound meaning in a solitary place. Don't just focus on the mere spoken words; this is an essential point of the practical instructions of the scriptures stated in Tsongkhapa's explanation of the *Fundamental Verses of the Middle Way.*[555]

[IX.163cd] ***Those who are carried by the river of suffering –***
Alas! There is such pain!

And, [IX.166a] ***Tormented by the blaze of suffering in this way . . .*** It shows the way that when emptiness is realized, there naturally arises a great compassion for sentient beings who are tormented by suffering. Great compassion is the root of the Mahāyāna path. The *Anthology of Training* says:

Make compassion foremost, and
Strive to develop virtue.[556]

The *Compendium of Dharma* says:

> Avalokiteśvara spoke to the Blessed One: "Bodhisattvas do not train in a lot of things. If you uphold one thing well and realize it, you have all of the qualities of the buddhas in the palm of your hand. What is the one thing? It is great compassion."[557]

There are many occassions where sūtras extol great compassion. The *Introduction to the Middle Way* states:

> *Since this love is the seed of the abundant crop of the Victorious Ones,*
> *It is like water that brings increase*
> *And the desired maturation of lasting enjoyment;*
> *Therefore, I first pay homage to compassion.*[558]

For example, it is important in the production of an abundant crop to have a seed in the beginning, to have water in the middle, and to have a ripened fruit in the end. Similarly, to produce the abundant crop of the Victorious Ones, it is important to have just great compassion itself in the beginning, which is like a seed. It is also said to be, like water, important in the middle, and important in the end, like the ripened fruit. These are, respectively, like the compassion in the continua of those who have not entered the Mahāyāna path, that of ordinary and sublime beings who have entered the path, and the great compassion of sublime buddhas.

> [IX.167] ***When, in a non-referential way***
> ***With an accumulation of merit respectfully gathered,***
> ***Will I teach emptiness***
> ***To those who are smothered by reference?***

To gather the accumulation of gnosis is to understand in a non-referential way, [822] without clinging to the true existence of the three spheres [of agent, object, and action] regarding anything. It functions to gather the accumulation of merit out of respect for karmic causality. Then an aspiration prayer is made: having trained in the path that is the unity of these two accumulations, when will I teach the ultimate emptiness to those who are smothered by a view of reference that apprehends true existence?

This shows the condensed essential point of the practice because all the bodhisattva practices are included within the six transcendent perfections, and these are further comprised within the practice of the two accumulations. The *Sublime Continuum* explains the way that the six transcendent perfections are included within the two accumulations: "The five transcendent perfections of merit."[559] It describes the first five transcendent perfections as the accumulation of merit. This is in terms of the first five transcendent perfections not being embraced by the view of emptiness. The *Introduction to the Middle Way* says:

> *These three practices such as generosity are mostly*
> *Praised by the Sugatas for householders.*
> *These are accumulations called "merit" and*
> *Are the cause of a buddha's Form Body.*[560]

In this context, the first three transcendent perfections are the accumulation of merit; the last two are the accumulation of gnosis; and diligence is said to be included in both. The first three are mainly included in the accumulation of merit, and meditative concentration is included in the accumulation of gnosis because it is the distinctive support for it. Nevertheless, this is not saying that the first three do not have any aspect of the accumulation of gnosis, nor does it say that meditative concentration is necessarily the accumulation of gnosis. The *Ornament of the Mahāyāna Sūtras* states:

> *Generosity and discipline are the accumulation of merit, and*
> *Wisdom is the accumulation of gnosis.*
> *The other three are both;*
> *All five also are the accumulation of gnosis.*[561]

This shows that the first two have the essence of the accumulation of merit and the last one has the essence of the accumulation of gnosis. The middle three have aspects of both accumulations; this is stated in general. Yet when embraced by the view of emptiness, the first five are also taught to have aspects of the accumulation of gnosis. In this way, the accumulation of merit structures the progression of the vast path of conventional truth, and the accumulation of gnosis structures the progression of the profound path of realization of reality.

The great bodhisattva, the Victor's heir, is like the swan king with two broad, white wings—the path complete with both the vast and profound, or method and gnosis—leading an assembly of many other swan disciples. From the powerful force of the wind of virtuous goodness, he takes up a straight path on the middle way, without erring to the two extremes of existence or peace. Thereby, they are brought without obstruction to the supreme other shore of the vast and profound, oceanic qualities of the Victorious Ones, the perfect buddhas. The *Introduction to the Middle Way* says:

Leading the other swans, the swan king spreads [823]
Broad white wings of the conventional and the ultimate, and
Through the force of the wind of virtue
Takes them to the supreme other shore of the oceanic qualities of the Victorious Ones.[562]

Conclusion

[824] The sprout of the Victors, the essential nectar of the speech
Of inexhaustible intelligence, is the Way of the Bodhisattva.
It is a text that is famous like the sun and moon;
It comprises the essence of all the Mahāyāna scriptures.

Previously there were lush lotus groves of teaching and practice,
Accompanied by the splendor of millions of accomplished scholars
Filling the vast lands of both India and Tibet;
Yet this has waned at the end of these degenerate times.

When there is the power of prayer from those upholding the sacred dharma, and
The force of compassion from great, accomplished bodhisattvas,
The radiant light that never ceases will spread again
Over the garden of joy that sustains the sacred dharma.

When this happens, at the gateway to the Mahāyāna
The never-setting light will shine in the faces of fortunate beings, and
The good harvest of benefit and happiness will flourish everywhere.
This illustrates the appearance here of the sun of the Victors.

Through the great blessings of cultivating the spirit [of awakening] at the end of the teachings,
There is effort in the explanation and practice that benefits the teaching.

Through fearlessly raising the victory banner of the teaching,
There is mastery in the dharma, the splendor of the teaching.

The dharma center renowned as the Glorious Lion (Śrī Siṃha),
Is an expansive hub of many sacred beings worthy of praise.
Seated with toenails arrayed like a precious lotus
Bestowing wonderous dharma offerings for a long time.

While your cultivation of the spirit of awakening is inseparable from that of Śāntideva,
Your kindness exceeds that of a peaceful mother.
In the presence of you, supreme bodhisattva,
I heard this supreme treatise, the Way of the Bodhisattva, *several times.*

The essence of its subject matter is the spirit of awakening,
Which you, lord, saw as the supreme practical instruction.
Making this your heart-practice, you advised others
In this essential practice with great perseverence.

With each dewdrop of the nectar of your speech
The hunger of being deprived of the dharma is completely dispelled.
Giving a supreme feast that comes from the dharma,
Those who are strickened like me are brought to relief.

Even though I have little fortune to practice in accordance with your words,
I saw the maṇḍala *of your body again and again with my eyes,*
Heard the nectar of your speech stream into my ears many times, and
Received great blessings in mind through your engaged compassion.

The open treasury of the qualities of these three mysteries
Comes from the power of merit from many eons, a fortune
To see, hear, and aspire to this domain, and
Venerate your pure feet with the top of the head.

Although you have completed the path,
You show a common form in the perspective of ordinary beings;
With activities of skillful means guided by the intention to accomplish the welfare of others,
You maintain the form of gradually training on the path.

All your activities, inner and outer, are pleasing and pure,
[825] Like a lotus in full, beautiful bloom.
Enchanting all those who see and hear you,
You rely on the stainless life examples (rnam thar) of the Kadampas who acted in virtue and goodness.

Any practitioner of the dharma who enters the door of the doctrine
Knows that senseless evil contradicts the dharma.
You, the lord of dharma, see as futile some of what merely appears to be dharma,
You also reject pretense in dharma.

Even though you are renowned as a learned master of exposition,
You strive to accomplish the meaning of what you have studied.
Dharma that is not practiced, but is pleasing to say,
Has no power, and brings many faults of pride.

You give up mundane actions with little profit and practice the divine dharma.
You cut the ties of clinging to appearances, and are indifferent to the eight mundane concerns.
Whatever you do, partaking or abstaining, is in accord with the Buddha's Word.
Seeing the pleasures of existence as poison, you pursue true happiness.

Regarding all beings like your children, through the force of compassion
You fill the excellent vase of heart with the spirit of awakening's nectar.
Realizing reality, you see all phenomena as illusory, and
Accomplish only the benefit of beings through the great blessings of your activities.

Around the one whose lotus feet is a place of rest
Everyone circles around, though not summoned,
To the honey nectar of explanation and practice;
Fortunate bees gather even when they are not called.

Through training in conscientiousness, you accomplished the discipline
That does not transgress the precepts.
Whoever you accompany follows in a dignified way;
It is evident that many have been perfumed with your sweet scent.

In short, the Way of the Bodhisattva *treatise and your mental continuum*
Have both been completely purified by your practice;
You also lovingly instruct others accordingly.
This itself comprises the life story of a great bodhisattva.

The sun of your body is a source of virtue.
When it set, I became incredibly sad.
When I remember your kindness, my mind becomes fervently devoted.
I would like to repay just a fraction of your limitless kindness.

"In return for benefit,
The offering is to practice as commanded."
As is said, I know that to be able to practice accordingly
Is the supreme offering to repay kindness.

As for an inferior one like me to train
According to the life stories of sacred beings and the Buddha's Word,
I am overwhelmed with trepidation,
Yet could not just remain dejected.

So, illustrated by this flower of good explanation
That arose from the ocean water of my pure resolve,
An array of offering clouds upholding it
Greatly expanded by this complelely pure, superior intention.

In order to please those in the supreme fields
Who have pure minds and miraculous intentions
I respectfully offer this, accept it with love.
Look after me, without separation, throughout a garland of lives.

Now I pray that by taking up undivided faith,
I will drink without satiation the stream of nectar
Of practical instructions that emerge from your heart essence, and
Aspire to train in your life example of excellent activity.

To the ones who turned my mind slightly toward the pursuit of the [826] sacred dharma through kindness,
The virtuous spiritual friends who taught me the authentic path, I bow down to these sacred beings.

I also prostrate to the ones whose kindness brings out just the key points of the practice of the activities of the Victor's heirs,
And to the dharma of scriptures as well, those texts like the Way of the Bodhisattva *that demonstrate the vast and profound meaning.*

My venerable teacher, a great treasury of compassion and unequaled in kindness, is Paltrül Rinpoché, Orgyen Jikmé Wangpo; remembering just the common part of his life, and the kindness of the dharma and teachers, I pay homage to them before now turning to the following discussion.

The *Way of the Bodhisattva* previously had flourished widely in both India and Tibet. Later, its teaching and study had slowly declined. Based on Paltrül Rinpoché's activities to widely propogate its study, from the great blessings of the mind of this chief teacher himself, now the teaching, study, meditation, and accomplishment of this treatise is spreading widely in many places.

Further, previously in the presence of Panglo Lodrö Tenpa,[563] it was discussed who was learned in the *Way of the Bodhisattva*. Panglo said, "There is no one in Tibet, the Land of Snows, more learned than Götsangwa[564] and Guru [Gyelsé] Tokmé. These two have in their continua the entire meaning of the *Way of the Bodhisattva*." As proclaimed, the chief teacher [Paltrül Rinpoché] also focused on the study, contemplation, and meditation of this text, mixing the dharma and his mental continuum and making all the practices of the Victor's heirs come into his own practice. He later gave instructions to others. Thus, this instruction lineage is not merely a lineage of explanation, but a distinctive lineage by way of teaching as practical instruction.

As for myself, an inferior subject, I heard the transmitted instructions (*khrid lung*) many times in the presence of this teacher [Paltrül Rinpoché] himself. In particular, each time he taught the *Way of the Bodhisattva* for about two months, explaining it in depth and detail. He would repeat the instructions three or four times each session, and in this way taught it thoroughly to me four times. At the end of a teaching session, he would go over various points, and I also studied it this way several times. On those occasions, he based his teaching on the commentary of the lord of doctrine, Gyelsé Rinpoché Tokmé, and from explanations of various other commentaries.

In contexts like those of the Wisdom Chapter, there is a tradition of saying that there are some excellent things that come from its teaching when known in accord with how it is explained in Gyeltsapjé's commentary. Following this, I compiled this appropriately by way of an overview in accord with the great commentary on the Wisdom Chapter by Prajñākaramati, the commentary by Gyelsé Rinpoché, and the long and short explanatory notes in Gyeltsapjé's commentary on the Wisdom Chapter. Also, I drew from many Madhyamaka treatises, such as the "Collection of Reasonings," including the *Fundamental Verses of the Middle Way* and its commentaries, the *Anthology of Sūtras,* the root text and commentary on the *Four Hundred Verses,* and the *Anthology of Training.* In particular, I compiled it to accord with the root text and commentaries on the *Introduction to the Middle Way.*

In general, I have received the nectar of dharma [827] from many learned and accomplished spiritual friends. Among all other sacred beings, the kindness of these teachers—through the wonderous impact of each of their manifold actions to bear the burden of accomplishing the benefit of the teachings and beings—each exceeds that of the others; each of them is extremely kind. Yet in terms of the instruction lineage of the *Way of the Bodhisattva* in this context, it was spoken as follows by Rendawa:[565]

> When I was first studying, there were many in Sakya and so on who made the mistake of saying that there was just Madhyamaka text. These days there is a high regard for Madhyamaka texts. This too is the activity of my teachings. The great scholar Karmapa Könzhön[566] also said:
>
> > These days all the wise and foolish people in this snowy mountain range are said to have Madhyamaka coming out of their mouths and Madhyamaka coming out their noses. This is due to the kindness of Rendawa. Before him, Tangsak[567] said that Madhyamaka was a corpse. I did not hear any other talk about it.[568]

As is exemplified by this text, now the *Way of the Bodhisattva* is said to come out of everybody's mouths and come out of everybody's noses: "the teaching of the *Way of the Bodhisattva,*" "the study of the *Way of the Bodhisattva,*" "the worship of the *Way of the Bodhisattva.*" Everybody values and prints this *Way of the Bodhisattva* text; it is propogated by the young and old, and by those in the old and new schools. Moreover, in contexts such as teaching, studying, and worshiping this text, simply hearing one stanza, or simply offering a prostration, circumambulation, flower, or lamp to it, all of these roots of virtue come from the kindness of this great compassionate one [Rendawa].

The ones who resolve, "I will not deviate from
The essential points of the middle path, definitive in meaning,"
Are the great chariots who opened an unprecedented, wonderous tradition,
Sealed with millionfold paths of reasoning.

Then there are the supreme scholars who uphold this tradition of explanation.
They are innumerable, with perfect discernment,
Radiating 100,000 suns of scripture and reasoning
To completely elucidate the excellent path, free from extremes.

"The supreme summit of all the philosophical systems
Is simply the excellent tradition of Prāsaṅgika-Madhyamaka."
In one voice those highest among the proponents of reason,
Strew flowers of praise in front of many scholars.

Those with unparalleled, supreme intellects,
Those with the good path of stainless reason that stems from
Reliable sources of knowledge and the scriptural traditions that are thereby established and renowned,
Engage good sayings and elegant discourses based on this.

I have weak intelligence and meager training, and
In particular the constitution of my heart is faulty, which has obscured my discernment.
I have little authority, so whatever positive deeds I do
Cannot take place without obstacle.

Needless to mention that for supreme activities like composing treatises
I have extremely little fortune to take part;
With this kind of thought as a spur,
I shrugged off effort enmeshed in weariness.

[828] Yet because some friends with supreme intellects incited me,
In order to turn my own and others' minds toward
The meaning of this treatise, which is difficult for the mind to fathom,
I, one who is thoroughly obscured and with inferior intellect, put this together.

By this virtue may the single basis from which all benefit and happiness springs,
The supreme jewel-lamp of the Sage's teachings,
Expand and flourish for a long time
To dispel the darkness in the hearts of all beings!

I received the kindness of this dharma from those such as the master of dharma,
Lords of dharma and kind teachers
Who displayed the manner of resting in the expanse of the basic nature,
May the basic field of reality and their uncontaminated intentions be fulfilled!

May those who are now beautifying ornaments of the teachings and beings,
All who are upholding the teachings,
Keeping steady the victory banner of the Emanation Bodies,
May they all live long, never desist, and may their activities flourish!

In particular, boundless conquerers like Mañjughoṣa (Jamyang), whose wisdom and love (Khyentsé) fill the expanse of space, and
Whose amazing and supreme emanations arise from the display of the cloud formations of the magical net,
May the inconceivable lives of these great beings, the powerful (Wangpo), miraculous ones,
Remain to teach the dharma for an ocean of eons!

May the spiritual communities, the supreme fields for the faithful to accumulate merit,
Be harmonious, pure in discipline, and learned;
May the teachings and practice of scripture and realization flourish,
With assemblies swelling like a summer lake!

By the power of the firm roots and branches of benefit and happiness,
May all beings be sustained with joy, happiness, and glory;
May they have the fortune to cultivate the activities of the Victor's heirs
Through training in the precious spirit of awakening!

May I, too, in my lives have renunciation and discipline, and
Uphold the complete sacred dharma, with the ability to explain it with retention and eloquence;
May compassion, the spirit of awakening, and the authentic view also arise in my continuum,
So that I quickly traverse the grounds and paths!

Born from the milk-ocean of the two accumulations of a completely positive, superior intention, and fashioned out of a heap of precious qualities of the three mysteries;
May I become supreme, a great reliquary of the Victors, worthy to be venerated as exalted in the realms of existence and peace!
With the blazing splendor of enlightened activity, may I dispel the mental darkness of all beings, fulfilling all their wishes!
May an ocean of goodness and virtue pervade everywhere and always, constantly bestowing supreme glory and happiness in existence and peace!

Previously, the sacred teacher, [Nyoshül] Lungtok,[569] said that we need a commentary on the Wisdom Chapter. When I began composing it, some other sacred spiritual friends added, "Write an extensive one with an overview." In particular, I was strongly encouraged throughout the beginning and the end in the presence of one with the eye of dharma, the master Jamyang Loter Wangpo.[570] I was likewise encouraged by a teacher from Nyakrong, Pema Gyeltsen. [829] I received further encouragement from a teacher who upholds the profound treasures, Sögyel,[571] who directly said, "We need an overview of the Wisdom Chapter," and also wrote this down in a letter. I, Künzang Sönam, who is also called by my monastic name, "Tupten Chökyi Drakpa," composed this.

In the presence of those who are honest and sacred beings, those with careful and discerning intellects regarding the meaning of this text, I confess any distorting errors that I made due to the defilements of my immature mind. Based on anything that is positive here, in the beginning may it be an eye for viewing this profound text for bright-minded novices who are starting to study it. In the end may it uphold the qualities that are difficult to fathom, like an ocean. May it quickly serve clear and profound wisdom that engages unobstructed explanation, debate, and composition; and may it serve as a cause for attaining inexhaustible confidence! May it be virtuous! May it be virtuous!

Notes

INTRODUCTION

1. Tenzin Lungtok Nyima, *Great History of Dzokchen*, 614.
2. Dodrupchen, *Brief Biography of Paltrül Rinpoché*, 473.
3. Khenpo Künpel, *Biography of Paltrül Rinpoché*, 35–36.
4. Smith, *Among Tibetan Texts*, 23–24.
5. Patrul Rinpoché, *Words of My Perfect Teacher*, trans. Padmakara Translation Group.
6. Khenpo Künpel, *Biography of Paltrül Rinpoché*, 34–35.
7. Paltrül, *Mirror Illuminating the Meaning*, 294–295. See also Künzang Sönam, *Excellent Vase*, chap. 1.
8. Khenpo Künpel, *Nectar of Mañjuśrī's Speech* (*byang chub sems dpa'i spyod pa la 'jug pa'i tshig 'grel 'jam dbyangs bla ma'i zhal lung bdud rtsi'i thig pa*); English trans. by Padmakara Translation Group, *Nectar of Manjushri's Speech*.
9. See Jamgön Mipham, *Wisdom Chapter*.
10. Annabella Pitkin, "Cosmopolitanism in the Himalayas," 18. Pitkin cites an interview with Tulku Pema Wangyel, who claimed that Künzang Sönam was also Khunu Lama's teacher (17–18). This must be false since Khunu Lama was only eleven years old in 1905 when Künzang Sönam died, and he had yet to travel to Tibet.
11. Śāntideva, *Way of the Bodhisattva*, trans. Padmakara Translation Group, 28.
12. Dalai Lama, *Practicing Wisdom*, xi, 4.
13. Künzang Pelden, *Nectar of Manjushri's Speech*, xix.
14. Tsongkhapa, *Thoroughly Illuminating the Viewpoint*, 585. Tsongkhapa also lists a different set of unique assertions in *bka' gnas brgyad kyi zin bris*. See Ruegg, *Two Prolegomena to Madhyamaka*, 144–147. For a discussion of the unique assertions of Prāsaṅgika according to the Geluk tradition, see Cozort, *Unique Tenets of the Middle Way*.
15. Minyak Gönpo, *Garland of Nectar Beads*, 1:668.
16. Ngakchang Pema Dorjé, *Biography of Künzang Sönam*, 2.

17. Tenzin Lungtok Nyima, *Great History of Dzokchen*, 614.
18. Khedrup Gyatso et al., *Treasury of Catalogues*, 2:435.
19. Minyak Gönpo, *Garland of Nectar Beads*, 1:669. See also biography in Nyoshül Khenpo, *Marvelous Garden of Rare Gems*, trans. Barron, 466–467; and Karma Phuntsho, *Mipham's Dialectics*, 250n120.
20. It is said that when he was asked what monastery he belonged to, he identified himself as from Rashel (*r[w]a shel*), "the largest of the four branches of Kagyü monasteries in the area . . . He was thus called the 'pundit from Rashel.'" Ngakchang Pema Dorjé, *Biography of Künzang Sönam*, 2. Despite this attribution, Rashel (*rwa shel*) monastery is not a Kagyü monastery, but a branch monastery of Dzokchen, a Nyingma institution. See Jikmé Samdrup, *History of Kardzé Monasteries*, 2:575.
21. Minyak Gönpo, *Garland of Nectar Beads*, 1:669; and Khedrup Gyatso et al., *Treasury of Catalogues*, 2:435.
22. Tenzin Lungtok Nyima, *Great History of Dzokchen*, 613–614.
23. Ngakchang Pema Dorjé, *Biography of Künzang*, 3.
24. Tenzin Lungtok Nyima, *Great History of Dzokchen*, 613.
25. See Ricard, *Enlightened Vagabond*, 27–28. See also Tulku Thondup, *Masters of Meditation and Miracles*, 209–210.
26. Ngakchang Pema Dorjé, *Biography of Künzang Sönam*, 6.
27. Tenzin Lungtok Nyima, *Great History of Dzokchen*, 614. Nyoshül Khenpo relates that Tenzin Drakpa was greater than Paltrül Rinpoché in epistemology (*tshad ma*); Nyoshül Lungtok exceeded him in view; Orgyen Tenzin Norbu was greater in explanation; and Künzang Sönam was greater in conduct. See Nyoshül Khenpo, *Marvelous Garden of Rare Gems*, trans. Barron, 227.
28. Ngakchang Pema Dorjé, *Biography of Künzang Sönam*, 4–5.
29. Ngakchang Pema Dorjé, *Biography of Künzang Sönam*, 5.
30. Tenzin Lungtok Nyima, *Great History of Dzokchen*, 614. See also Ricard, *Enlightened Vagabond*, 28–29.
31. Tenzin Lungtok Nyima, *Great History of Dzokchen*, 612.
32. Ngakchang Pema Dorjé, *Biography of Künzang Sönam*, 3.
33. Ngakchang Pema Dorjé, *Biography of Künzang Sönam*, 3.
34. Khedrup Gyatso et al., *Treasury of Catalogues*, 2:436; and Minyak Gönpo, *Garland of Nectar Beads*, 1:670.
35. Khedrup Gyatso et al., *Treasury of Catalogues*, 2:436.
36. Tenzin Lungtok Nyima, *Great History of Dzokchen*, 614.
37. Künzang Sönam, *Nectar of an Excellent Vase*; English trans. by Heidi Köppl in Chökyi Dragpa, *Uniting Wisdom and Compassion*.
38. Künzang Sönam's three commentaries on the *Way of the Bodhisattva* were published together in Beijing in a single volume, *Excellent Vase*. A close runner-up for longest commentary on the *Way of the Bodhisattva* is Lozang Dorjé's *Circle of the All-Illuminating Sun*, published recently in four volumes in Chengdu. I didn't compare a word count for these commentaries, so I don't know for sure which is the

longest, but it looks to be Künzang's Sönam's commentaries. Another noteworthy contender is the 975-page commentary by Pawo Tsuklak Trengwa, *Essence of the Infinite*.

39. Śāntideva, *Way of the Bodhisattva*, IX.1.
40. Künzang Sönam, *Overview of the Wisdom Chapter*, 668.
41. Künzang Sönam, *Overview of the Wisdom Chapter*, 662.
42. Künzang Sönam, *Overview of the Wisdom Chapter*, 669.
43. Künzang Sönam, *Overview of the Wisdom Chapter*, 677.
44. Künzang Sönam, *Overview of the Wisdom Chapter*, 673.
45. Künzang Sönam, *Overview of the Wisdom Chapter*, 673.
46. See Duckworth, *Tibetan Buddhist Philosophy of Mind and Nature*, 100–102.
47. Künzang Sönam, *Overview of the Wisdom Chapter*, 665.
48. Künzang Sönam, *Overview of the Wisdom Chapter*, 665–667.
49. Künzang Sönam, *Overview of the Wisdom Chapter*, 684.
50. Künzang Sönam, *Overview of the Wisdom Chapter*, 683.
51. Śāntideva, *Way of the Bodhisattva*, IX.110–113.
52. Künzang Sönam, *Overview of the Wisdom Chapter*, 706–707.
53. Künzang Sönam, *Overview of the Wisdom Chapter*, 707.
54. Künzang Sönam, *Overview of the Wisdom Chapter*, 707.
55. Künzang Sönam, *Overview of the Wisdom Chapter*, 707.
56. Künzang Sönam, *Overview of the Wisdom Chapter*, 707.
57. Śāntideva, *Way of the Bodhisattva*, V.7–8.
58. Śāntideva, *Way of the Bodhisattva*, IX.17–24.
59. Künzang Sönam, *Overview of the Wisdom Chapter*, 715. Tsongkhapa also states that things not existing on their own even conventionally is the basis of unique Prāsaṅgika assertions, such as there being no basic consciousness or self-awareness, even conventionally. He also links Śāntideva and Candrakīrti on this point. See Tsongkhapa, *Thoroughly Illuminating the Viewpoint*, 585, 747.
60. Śāntideva, *Way of the Bodhisattva*, IX.9ab.
61. Śāntideva, *Way of the Bodhisattva*, IX.17cd–18ab.
62. Śāntideva, *Way of the Bodhisattva*, IX.6.
63. Künzang Sönam, *Overview of the Wisdom Chapter*, 665.
64. See Cabezón, *A Dose of Emptiness*.
65. Also, the status of the highest mind, the Buddha mind, as having deceptive yet "correct" content remains a theological (not a pragmatic) concern for Geluk (and other) interpreters of the *Way of the Bodhisattva*. Yet because the tenor of Śāntideva's text remains pragmatic—it does not directly participate in these scholastic concerns; it is only ever pulled into these issues by doxographers who want to co-opt it to support a particular agenda, such as to interpret Buddhism as a seamless whole.
66. Śāntideva, *Way of the Bodhisattva*, IX.10ab.
67. Künzang Sönam, *Overview of the Wisdom Chapter*, 740–741.
68. Künzang Sönam, *Overview of the Wisdom Chapter*, 665.

69. Hopkins, *Maps of the Profound.*
70. See, for instance, Mipam, *Light of the Sun* (*nyin byed snang ba*), 489; English trans. in Padmakara Translation Group, *The Wisdom Chapter*, 292.
71. Śāntideva, *Way of the Bodhisattva,* IX.57.
72. Künzang Sönam, *Overview of the Wisdom Chapter,* 813.

THE TRANSLATION

1. *Jewel Lamp* (*Ratnolkādhāraṇīsūtra,* H. 100, vol. 48), 499b.
2. *Condensed Perfection of Wisdom* (*Prajñāpāramitā-sañcayagāthā,* H. 17, vol. 34), 198b.
3. Nāgārjuna, *Praise to the Inconceivable,* v. 1 (*Acintyastava,* D. 1128), 76b–77a.
4. Nāgārjuna, *Praise to the Inconceivable,* vv. 54–56b (D. 1128), 78b.
5. Nāgārjuna, *Fundamental Verses of the Middle Way,* opening homage. See 272n61.
6. Nāgārjuna, *Reason in Sixty Verses*, opening homage (*Yuktiṣaṣṭikā,* D. 3825), 20b.
7. Nāgārjuna, *Dispelling Disputes* (*Vigrahavyāvartanī,* D. 3828), 29a.
8. *Root Tantra of Mañjuśrī* (*Mañjuśrīmūlatantra,* H. 501, vol. 88), 408a.
9. *Descent to Laṅka Sūtra* (*Laṅkāvatārasūtra,* H. 110, vol. 51), 265a.
10. See Tsongkhapa, *Ocean of Reason*, 5; English trans. in Garfield and Ngawang Samten, *Ocean of Reasoning*, 11.
11. Candrakīrti, *Commentary on the "Illuminating Lamp"* (*Pradīpoddyotanaṭīkā,* D. 1785), 200a–200b.
12. *Root Tantra of Mañjuśrī,* 408a–408b.
13. See Dharmamitra, *Clarifying Words* (*Prasphuṭapadā,* D. 3796), 8b–9a.
14. Butön, *Butön's History*, 166; English trans. in Obermiller, *History of Buddhism in India and Tibet*, 161–162.
15. One who just "eats" (*bhu*), "sleeps" (*su*), and "wanders" (*ku*).
16. Prajñākaramati, *Commentary on the "Way of the Bodhisattva"* (*Bodhicaryāvatārapa ñjikā,* D. 3872), 41b.
17. Vibhūticandra, *Especially Clear Commentary on the "Way of the Bodhisattva"* (*bodhicaryāvatāratātparyapañjikāviśeṣadyotanī,* D. 3880), 193a.
18. Butön, *Butön's History*, 169; English trans. in Obermiller, *History of Buddhism in India and Tibet,* 166.
19. Künzang Sönam's text simply says "the explanation of the *Introduction to the Middle Way*," without identifying the author. I have supplied the author "Tsongkhapa" here and in references to his texts to assist the reader.
20. Tsongkhapa, *Thoroughly Illuminating the Viewpoint*, 443.
21. Tsongkhapa, *Thoroughly Illuminating the Viewpoint*, 750.
22. See Tsongkhapa, *Thoroughly Illuminating the Viewpoint*, 476–477.
23. Gyeltsapjé, *Gateway to the Bodhisattvas*, 452.
24. Nāgārjuna, *Precious Garland,* v. 3.
25. Nāgārjuna, *Precious Garland,* v. 4.
26. Nāgārjuna, *Precious Garland,* v. 5.

27. Nāgārjuna, *Precious Garland*, v. 175.
28. Nāgārjuna, *Precious Garland*, v. 378.
29. Nāgārjuna, *Precious Garland*, vv. 435, 439d.
30. Aśvaghoṣa, *Lotus Grove: A Text on the Cultivation of the Conventional Spirit of Awakening* (*Saṃvṛtibodhicittabhāvanopadeśavarṇasamgraha*, D. 3911), 13b–14a.
31. See Candrakīrti, *Introduction to the Middle Way*, I.1–2. The threefold practice is compassion, nondual mind, and the spirit of awakening.
32. Śāntideva, *Anthology of Training Verses*, v. 2abc (*Śikṣāsamuccayakārikā*, D. 3939), 1b; English trans. in Goodman, *Training Anthology of Śāntideva*, lxxiii.
33. *Jewel Lamp*, 492b; Śāntideva, *Anthology of Training* (*Śikṣāsamuccaya*, D. 3940), 3b–4a; English trans. in Goodman, *Training Anthology of Śāntideva*, 3.
34. Śāntideva, *Anthology of Training Verses*, v. 2d (D. 3939), 1b; English trans. in Goodman, *Training Anthology of Śāntideva*, lxxiii.
35. Gyelsé Tokmé, *Ocean of Good Explanation*, 105.
36. Nāgārjuna, *One Hundred Verses of Wisdom* (*Prajñāśataka*, D. 4328), 99b.
37. Āryaśūra, *Condensed Transcendent Perfections* (*Pāramitāsamāsa*, D. 3944), 233b.
38. Āryaśūra, *Condensed Transcendent Perfections*, 234a.
39. Āryaśūra, *Condensed Transcendent Perfections*, 234a.
40. Maitreya, *Sublime Continuum* (*Uttaratantra*, D. 4024), 72b; English trans. in Fuchs, *Buddha-Nature: The Mahayana Uttaratantra Shastra with Commentary*, 290.
41. *King of Meditative Stabilizations Sūtra* (*Samādhirājasūtra*, H. 129, vol. 55), 141b.
42. *Inquiry of Rāṣṭrapāla* (*Rāṣṭrapālaparipṛcchā*, H. 62, vol. 38), 499b.
43. Kamalaśīla, *Stages of Meditation* (*Bhāvanākrama II*, D. 3916), 48a.
44. Nāgārjuna, *Reason in Sixty Verses*, v. 4 (*Yuktiṣaṣṭikā*, D. 3825), 20b.
45. Nāgārjuna, *Precious Garland*, vv. 56–57.
46. Maitreya, *Sublime Continuum*, 56a; English trans. in Fuchs, *Buddha-Nature*, 121–122.
47. I did not locate this passage in the *Densely Arrayed*.
48. Vasubandhu, *Treasury of Metaphysics*, VI.4 (*Abhidharmakośa*, D. 4089), 18b.
49. Dharmakīrti, *Commentary on Epistemology* III.3 (*Pramāṇavārttika*, D. 4210), 118b.
50. *Meeting of the Father and Son Sūtra* (*Pitāputrasamāgamasūtra*, H. 60, vol. 38), 182a; Śāntideva, *Anthology of Training* (*Śikṣāsamuccaya*), 142b; English trans. in Goodman, *Training Anthology of Śāntideva*, 244.
51. See Kamalaśīla, *Light of the Middle Way* (*Madhyamakāloka*, D. 3887), 177a–177b.
52. *Meeting of the Father and Son Sūtra*, 183b.
53. Nāgārjuna, *Fundamental Verses of the Middle Way*, XXIV.8: "The Buddhas taught the dharma in reliance on two truths: the conventional truths of the world and the ultimate truth."
54. Nāgārjuna, *Fundamental Verses of the Middle Way*, XXIV.10ab.
55. Candrakīrti, *Introduction to the Middle Way*, VI.80ab.
56. Candrakīrti, *Introduction to the Middle Way*, VI.23ab.

57. Nāgārjuna, *Commentary on the Spirit of Awakening* (*Bodhicittavivaraṇa,* D. 1801), 40b–41a.
58. *Heart Sūtra* (*Bhagavatīprajñāpāramitāhṛdaya,* H. 499, vol. 88), 45b.
59. The two sets of four problems are mentioned in chapter 3 of the *Sūtra Explaining the Intent.* See English language version of the Tibetan edition, in Powers, *Wisdom of the Buddha,* 36–45.
60. *Sūtra Explaining the Intent,* chap. 3. See Powers, *Wisdom of the Buddha,* 48–49.
61. This is from the homage in the prologue of Nāgārjuna's *Fundamental Verses of the Middle Way,* which states: "I pay homage to the best of speakers, the perfectly awakened one who taught dependent arising—the pacification of conceptual constructs—without ceasing or arising, not annihilated nor eternal, neither coming nor going, and neither different nor the same." (D. 3824), 1b.
62. Candrakīrti, *Introduction to the Middle Way,* VI.23cd.
63. Jñānagarbha, *Distinguishing the Two Truths* (*Satyadvaya,* D. 3881), 2a.
64. Candrakīrti, *Introduction to the Middle Way,* VI.24–25.
65. Jñānagarbha, *Distinguishing the Two Truths* v. 9ab (D. 3881), 2a. Künzang Sönam's third line is not found the Degé edition of the Tibetan translation of Jñānagarbha's.
66. Candrakīrti explains three meanings of *saṃvṛti* as "concealing/obscuring," "relative/dependent," and "convention/custom." See Candrakīrti, *Clear Words* (*Prasannapadā,* D. 3860), 163a.
67. Candrakīrti, *Introduction to the Middle Way,* VI.28abc.
68. Candrakīrti, *Autocommentary on the "Introduction to the Middle Way"* (*Madhyamakāvatārabhāṣya,* D. 3862), 255a.
69. Candrakīrti, *Clear Words,* 163b.
70. Nāgārjuna, *Fundamental Verses of the Middle Way,* XXIV.9.
71. Candrakīrti, *Introduction to the Middle Way,* VI.80cd.
72. Jñānagarbha, *Distinguishing the Two Truths,* v. 2 (D. 3881), 1b.
73. Kalyāṇadeva, *Companion to the "Way of the Bodhisattva"* (*Bodhicaryāvatārasaṃskāra,* D. 3874), 67a–67b.
74. Candrakīrti, *Introduction to the Middle Way,* VI.27.
75. Nāgārjuna, *Reason in Sixty Verses,* v. 30 (*Yuktiṣaṣṭikā,* D. 3825), 21b.
76. Candrakīrti, *Commentary on "Reason in Sixty Verses"* (*Yuktiṣaṣṭikāvṛtti,* D. 3864), 20a.
77. Nāgārjuna, *Precious Garland,* vv. 394–396.
78. Nāgārjuna, *Fundamental Verses of the Middle Way,* XVIII.6a.
79. Āryadeva, *Four Hundred Verses* (*Catuḥśataka*), VIII.15a (D. 3846), 9b; English trans. in Sonam, *Āryadeva's Four Hundred Stanzas on the Middle Way,* 193.
80. Nāgārjuna, *Fundamental Verses of the Middle Way,* XV.10.
81. Vasubandhu, *Principles of Elucidation* (*Vyākhyayukti,* D. 4061), 34b.
82. *Kāśyapa Chapter* (*Kāśyapaparivarta,* H. 87, vol. 40), 229b.
83. Bhāviveka, *Blaze of Reason* (*Madhyamakahṛdayavṛttitarkajvāla,* D. 3856), 329a.
84. *King of Meditative Stabilizations Sūtra,* 43b.

85. Nāgārjuna, *Fundamental Verses of the Middle Way*, XXIV.18.
86. Candrakīrti, *Clear Words*, 167b.
87. Candrakīrti, *Clear Words*, 93a.
88. Nāgārjuna, *Precious Garland*, vv. 61–62.
89. Candrakīrti, *Autocommentary on the "Introduction to the Middle Way,"* 252b.
90. *Condensed Perfection of Wisdom*, 190a.
91. I did not find this passage in Āryadeva's texts, but Bhāviveka also attributes this quote to him in *Precious Lamp of Madhyamaka* (*Madhyamakaratnapradīpa*, D. 3854), 272a.
92. Candrakīrti, *Introduction to the Middle Way*, VI.21c.
93. Nāgārjuna, *Fundamental Verses of the Middle Way*, XXII.11.
94. Kamalaśīla, *Light of the Middle Way*, 229b.
95. *Inquiry of Upāli* (*Upālipariprcchā*, H. 68, vol. 39), 243b; see also, The Cowherds, *Moonshadows*, 190–191.
96. *King of Meditative Stabilizations Sūtra*, 231b.
97. *Inquiry of Upāli*, 242b.
98. Similar passages are found, in various places, throughout the *Perfection of Wisdom in One Hundred Thousand Stanzas* (*Śatasāhasrikā-prajñāpāramitā*).
99. Nāgārjuna, *Reason in Sixty Verses*, v. 37 (*Yuktiṣaṣṭikā*, D. 3825), 21b.
100. Nāgārjuna, *Precious Garland*, v. 99.
101. Nāgārjuna, *Precious Garland*, v. 114.
102. Candrakīrti, *Autocommentary on the "Introduction to the Middle Way,"* 299b. These verses are also cited in Vasubandhu, *Autocommentary on the "Treasury of Metaphysics"* (*Abhidharmakośabhāṣya*, D. 4090), 86a.
103. The sixteen aspects of the four truths are as follows: for the truth of suffering, there are the four aspects of (1) impermanence, (2) suffering, (3) emptiness, and (4) selflessness; for the truth of origin, there are the four aspects of (5) cause, (6) origin, (7) complete production, and (8) condition; for the truth of cessation, there are the four aspects of (9) cessation, (10) peace, (11) perfection, and (12) definite emergence; and for the truth of the path, there are the four aspects of (13) path, (14) suitability, (15) accomplishment, and (16) deliverance.
104. Āryadeva, *Four Hundred Verses*, XII.13a (D. 3846), 13b; English trans. in Sonam, *Āryadeva's Four Hundred Stanzas on the Middle Way*, 245.
105. Nāgārjuna, *Reason in Sixty Verses*, vv. 21cd–23 (*Yuktiṣaṣṭikā*, D. 3825), 21a.
106. Nāgārjuna, *Praise to the Basic Field of Reality* (*Dharmadhātustotra*, D. 1118), 64b.
107. Candrakīrti, *Commentary on "Reason in Sixty Verses,"* 7b.
108. For instance, *The Condensed Perfection of Wisdom* says: "Even if bodhisattvas conceive 'this aggregate is empty,' they are coursing in signs and do not have faith in the domain of the unborn." *Condensed Perfection of Wisdom*, 189b–190a.
109. Candrakīrti, *Introduction to the Middle Way*, VI.131.
110. Candrakīrti, *Introduction to the Middle Way*, VI.130.
111. *Akṣayamati Sūtra* (*Akṣayamatisūtra*, H. 176, vol. 60), 231a–231b.

112. *King of Meditative Stabilizations Sūtra*, 33b.
113. *Tantra Explaining the Four Seats* (*Caturpīṭha-vikhyāta-tantrarāja*, H. 406, vol. 82), 219b.
114. Kamalaśīla, *Light of the Middle Way*, 148b.
115. Candrakīrti, *Introduction to the Middle Way*, VI.97bcd.
116. I did not find this passage in a Perfection of Wisdom Sūtra.
117. *Heart Sūtra*, 45a.
118. Along with having a basis in another intention (*dgongs gzhi*), the other two criteria are having a purpose (*dgos pa*) and explicit invalidation (*dngos la gnod*).
119. *Heart Sūtra*, 45b.
120. See *Sūtra Teaching the Tathāgata's Great Compassion* = *Inquiry of King Dhāraṇīśvara* (*Tathāgatamahākaruṇānirdeśasūtra*, P. 814, vol. 32), p. 300, 176b.4–177a.3.
121. Candrakīrti, *Introduction to the Middle Way*, VI.68.
122. *Descent to Laṅka Sūtra*, 259b. Candrakīrti, *Autocommentary on the "Introduction to the Middle Way,"* 270a.
123. Āryadeva, *Four Hundred Verses*, XII.12ab (D. 3846), 13b; English trans. in Sonam, *Āryadeva's Four Hundred Stanzas on the Middle Way*, 244.
124. Candrakīrti, *Autocommentary on the "Introduction to the Middle Way,"* 282b.
125. Candrakīrti, *Autocommentary on the "Introduction to the Middle Way,"* 238a.
126. See Asaṅga, *Compendium of Metaphysics* (*Abhidharmasamuccaya*, D. 4049), 85a.
127. Dharmakīrti, *Commentary on Epistemology*, II.255 (D. 4210), 117a.
128. Nāgārjuna, *Letter to a Friend* (*Suhṛllekha*, D. 4182), 46a.
129. See *Foundations of Vinaya* (*Vinayavastu*, H. 1, vol. 1), 122a–124b.
130. Candrakīrti, *Commentary on "Reason in Sixty Verses,"* 6a.
131. Dharmakīrti, *Commentary on Epistemology*, II.147 (D. 4210), 113a.
132. *Vast Display* (*Lalitavistara*, H. 96, vol. 48), 142b, cited in Śāntideva, *Anthology of Training*, 114b; English trans. in Goodman, *Training Anthology of Śāntideva*, 201.
133. *Vast Display*, 142b, cited in Śāntideva, *Anthology of Training*, 114b; English trans. in Goodman, *Training Anthology of Śāntideva*, 201.
134. Nāgārjuna, *Letter to a Friend*, 46a.
135. See *Golden Light Sūtra* (*Suvarṇaprabhāsūtra*, H. 514, vol. 89), 238b. Nāgamitra's *Gateway to the Three Embodiments of Buddhahood* does not explicitly mention nirvana without remainder, but it does describe the Truth Body as unconditioned. See Nāgamitra, *Gateway to the Three Embodiments of Buddhahood* (*Kāyatrayāvatāramukha*, D. 3890), 4a.
136. Nāgārjuna, *Fundamental Verses of the Middle Way*, XXV.13c.
137. Vasubandhu, *Treasury of Metaphysics*, I.5 (*Abhidharmakośa*, D. 4089), 2a.
138. A variation on this citation can be found in *Sūtra on the Ten Grounds* (*Daśabhūmikasūtra*, H. 94, vol. 43), 145b.
139. *Descent to Laṅka Sūtra*, 397b.

140. Candrakīrti, *Introduction to the Middle Way*, VI.46.
141. Vasubandhu, *Thirty Verses*, vv. 2–5 (*Triṃśikā*, D. 4055).
142. *Sūtra Explaining the Intent* (*Saṃdhinirmocanasūtra*, H. 109, vol. 51), 21b; English trans. in Powers, *Wisdom of the Buddha*, 76–77.
143. Cited under Asaṅga, *Compendium of Mahāyāna*, I.1 (*Mahāyānasaṃgraha*, D. 4048), 3a; see also Waldron, *The Buddhist Unconscious*, 129.
144. *Sūtra Explaining the Intent*, 21b; English trans. in Powers, *Wisdom of the Buddha*, 77.
145. See *Golden Light Sūtra*, 239a; *Descent to Laṅka Sūtra; Densely Arrayed* (*Gaṇḍavyūhasūtra*, P. 778, vol. 29), 152.
146. While Vasubandhu's *Principles of Elucidation* does not explicitly discuss the basic consciousness, he does so in other texts, such as the *Thirty Verses* and *Treatise on the Three Natures*. A presentation of arguments for the basic consciousness can be found in the first chapter of Asaṅga's *Compendium of Mahāyāna*; see also the discussion in Griffiths, *On Being Mindless*, 97–104.
147. See Tsongkhapa, *Explanation of the Difficult Points of the Mind and Basic Consciousness* (*yid dang kun gzhi dka' ba'i gnas rgya cher 'grel pa*); Tibetan edition and English trans. in Sparem, *Ocean of Eloquence*.
148. *Sūtra Explaining the Intent*, 27a; English trans. in Powers, *Wisdom of the Buddha*, 101.
149. See Tibetan edition and English translation of the *Sūtra Explaining the Intent* in Powers, *Wisdom of the Buddha*, 81–89, 129–135; Asaṅga, *Compendium of Mahāyāna*, chap. 3.
150. Asaṅga, *Bodhisattva Grounds* (*Bodhisattvabhūmi*, D. 4037), 25b; English trans. in Engle, *Bodhisattva's Path to Unsurpassed Enlightenment*, 77.
151. Asaṅga, *Bodhisattva Grounds*, 25b; English trans. in Engle, *Bodhisattva's Path to Unsurpassed Enlightenment*, 77.
152. Asaṅga, *Compendium of Mahāyāna*, II.24 (D. 4048), 18b.
153. The four thorough investigations and knowledges are those of name (*ming*), meaning (*don*), essence (*ngo bo nyid*), and specific designation (*bye brag tu btags pa*). See Asaṅga, *Compendium of Mahāyāna*, 24a. See also discussion in English translation of Asaṅga's *Bodhisattva Grounds* by Engle, *Bodhisattva's Path to Unsurpassed Enlightenment*, 96–97.
154. Asaṅga, *Compendium of Determinations* (*Yogācārabhūmi Viniścayasaṃgrahaṇī*, D. 4038), 42b.
155. *Sūtra on the Ten Grounds*, 145b.
156. This passage is cited in Sthiramati, *The Meaning of Reality: An Extensive Commentary on the "Treasury of Metaphysics"* (*Abhidharmakoṣabhāṣyaṭīkātattvā rtha*, D. 4421), 97b.
157. *Sūtra on the Ten Grounds*, 145b.
158. *Descent to Laṅka Sūtra*, 137a.
159. Candrakīrti, *Introduction to the Middle Way*, VI.84–90.

160. *Descent to Laṅka Sūtra*, 185b.
161. *Descent to Laṅka Sūtra*, 116a.
162. *Sūtra Explaining the Intent*, 50b; English trans. in Powers, *Wisdom of the Buddha*, 151. The passage in the *Sūtra Explaining the Intent* does not mention "Blessed One" (*bcom ldan 'das*).
163. *Sūtra Explaining the Intent*, 26b; English trans. in Powers, *Wisdom of the Buddha*, 99.
164. *Sūtra Explaining the Intent*, 21b; English trans. in Powers, *Wisdom of the Buddha*, 77.
165. *Sūtra Explaining the Intent*, 30b; English trans. in Powers, *Wisdom of the Buddha*, 113.
166. *Descent to Laṅka Sūtra*, 116a. See above p. 102.
167. *Descent to Laṅka Sūtra*, 135a.
168. *Descent to Laṅka Sūtra*, 135b.
169. Nāgārjuna, *Anthology of Sūtras* (*Sūtrasamuccaya*, D. 3934), 188b.
170. Candrakīrti, *Introduction to the Middle Way*, VI.94–96.
171. Candrakīrti, *Introduction to the Middle Way*, VI.91–92.
172. See Nāgārjuna, *Commentary on the Spirit of Awakening* (D. 1800), 39b; (*Bodhicittavivaraṇa*, D. 1801), 44a.
173. Āryadeva, *Four Hundred Verses*, XVI.24 (D. 3846), 18a; English trans. in Sonam, *Āryadeva's Four Hundred Stanzas on the Middle Way*, 299.
174. Candrakīrti, *Introduction to the Middle Way*, VI.64. The last part of the citation, "this should be considered," is not in the *Introduction to the Middle Way*.
175. Candrakīrti, *Introduction to the Middle Way*, VI.66.
176. *Connected Discourses* (*Saṃyutta Nikāya*), III.22; English trans. in Bhikkhu Bodhi, *Connected Discourses of the Buddha*, 952–953.
177. Candrakīrti, *Introduction to the Middle Way*, VI.43.
178. Nāgārjuna, *Precious Garland*, v. 26.
179. Āryadeva, *Four Hundred Verses*, V.10 (D. 3846), 6b; English trans. in Sonam, *Āryadeva's Four Hundred Stanzas on the Middle Way*, 139.
180. Candrakīrti, *Autocommentary on the "Introduction to the Middle Way,"* 261b.
181. This refers to Maitreya's *Distinguishing the Middle and the Extremes* and the *Distinguishing Phenomena and the Basic Nature* (*Dharmadharmatāvibhāga*).
182. Cited under Asaṅga, *Compendium of Mahāyāna*, I.1 (D. 4048), 3a.
183. Cited under Asaṅga, *Compendium of Mahāyāna*, I.1 (D. 4048), 3a. See also Waldron, *The Buddhist Unconscious*, 129.
184. Nāgārjuna, *Commentary on the Spirit of Awakening* (D. 1800), 39b.
185. Candrakīrti, *Introduction to the Middle Way*, VI.72.
186. This passage with slightly different wording can be found in Bhāviveka, *Blaze of Reason*, 205a; see English trans. in Eckel, *Bhāviveka and His Buddhist Opponents*, 234.
187. Dharmakīrti, *Commentary on Epistemology*, III.427ab (D. 4210), 134b.

188. Dharmakīrti, *Commentary on Epistemology,* III.427cd (D. 4210), 134b.
189. Dharmakīrti, *Commentary on Epistemology,* III.330 (D. 4210), 131a.
190. Dharmakīrti, *Commentary on Epistemology,* III.485 (D. 4210), 137a.
191. Dignāga, *Compendium of Epistemology* (*Pramāṇasamuccaya*) I.11–12 (D. 4203), 2a; English trans. in Hattori, *Dignāga on Perception,* 30.
192. Dharmakīrti, *Commentary on Epistemology,* III.513 (D. 4210), 138a.
193. Candrakīrti, *Introduction to the Middle Way,* VI.76cd.
194. Candrakīrti, *Introduction to the Middle Way,* VI.73.
195. See Candrakīrti, *Autocommentary on the "Introduction to the Middle Way,"* 273a.
196. Candrakīrti, *Introduction to the Middle Way,* VI.74ab.
197. Candrakīrti, *Introduction to the Middle Way,* VI.75.
198. Candrakīrti, *Introduction to the Middle Way,* VI.74bc.
199. Candrakīrti, *Introduction to the Middle Way,* VI.74d.
200. See Nāgārjuna, *Fundamental Verses of the Middle Way,* VII.8–12; Nāgārjuna, *Dispelling Disputes,* vv. 34–39; and Nāgārjuna, *Finely Woven* (*Vaidalyasūtra,* D. 3826), 23a.
201. See Bhāviveka, *Essence of Madhyamaka* (*Madhyamakahṛdaya,* D. 8355), 23b; Jñānagarbha, *Autocommentary on "Distinguishing the Two Truths"* under v. 6 (D. 3882), 4b.
202. See Candrakīrti, *Clear Words,* 25b; Nāgārjuna, *Autocommentary on "Dispelling Disputes"* (*Vigrahavyāvartanīvṛtti,* D. 3832), 132b; Candrakīrti, *Commentary on the "Four Hundred Verses"* (*Catuḥśatakaṭīkā,* D. 3865), 186b.
203. That is, yogic perception can be considered to be a subset of mental perception, but when categorized separately, as one of three perceptual sources of knowledge, it is in a different (and incompatible) category from mental perception.
204. This refers to the process of determining the validity of a scripture. The three analyses are (1) that what is evident (*mngon gyur*) is not invalidated by perception (*mngon sum*), (2) that what is remote (*lkog gyur*) is not invalidated by inference (*rjes dpag*), and (3) that what is extremely remote (*shin tu lkog gyur*) is not contradicted (internally) by previous or later statements.
205. Gyeltsapjé, *Gateway to the Bodhisattvas,* 367.
206. Gyeltsapjé, *Gateway to the Bodhisattvas,* 367.
207. Śāntideva, *Anthology of Training,* 146b; *Vimalakīrti Sūtra* (*Vimalakīrtinirdeśasūtra,* H. 177, vol. 60), 328a; English trans. in Goodman, *Training Anthology of Śāntideva,* 251.
208. Asaṅga, *Compendium of Mahāyāna,* 31b.
209. A close variant of this passage is found in the *Sūtra on the Ten Grounds,* 78b.
210. Candrakīrti, *Introduction to the Middle Way,* XI.17.
211. Candrakīrti, *Autocommentary on the "Introduction to the Middle Way,"* 255a.
212. Nāgārjuna, *Praise to the Inconceivable,* v. 1 (D. 1128).
213. Mātṛcera, *Praise Honoring the Honorable One* (*Varṇārhavarṇastotra,* D. 1138), 89b.
214. Candrakīrti, *Introduction to the Middle Way,* VI.214.

215. Nāgārjuna, *Praise to the Basic Field of Reality* (D. 1118), 64b.
216. Maitreya, *Distinguishing the Middle and the Extremes*, I.16 (D. 4021), 41a; English trans. in Dharmachakra Translation Group, *Middle beyond Extremes*, 39.
217. Candrakīrti, *Clear Words*, 120a.
218. *Bodhisattva Basket* (*Bodhisattvapiṭaka*, H. 56, vol. 37), 320a; Candrakīrti, *Clear Words*, 120a.
219. Candrakīrti, *Introduction to the Middle* Way, XI.27.
220. Nāgārjuna, *Praise to the Vajra-Mind*, v. 5 (*Cittavajrastava*, D. 1121), 69b–70a. The Degé edition of the Tibetan translation of Nāgārjuna's *Praise to the Vajra-Mind* reads "transferred" (*bsngos*) where Künzang Sönam's reads "infused" (*bsgos*).
221. Nāgārjuna, *Precious Garland*, v. 212.
222. See Maitreya, *Sublime Continuum*, 118b; English trans. in Fuchs, *Buddha-Nature*, 206–207.
223. *Heap of Flowers Dhāraṇī* (*Puṣpakūṭadhāraṇī*, H. 605, vol. 90), 467a–467b.
224. *Bodhisattva Basket*, 379a.
225. See Tsongkhapa, *Ocean of Reason*, 8; English trans. in Garfield and Ngawang Samten, *Ocean of Reasoning*, 14.
226. Candrakīrti, *Autocommentary on the "Introduction to the Middle Way,"* 226b; *Sūtra on the Ten Grounds*, 164a–164b.
227. Candrakīrti, *Autocommentary on the "Introduction to the Middle Way,"* 226b.
228. The chapters of Candrakīrti's *Introduction to the Middle Way* are consecutively titled "generation of the spirit of awakening," and the context of this discussion is the autocommentary on the first chapter.
229. Candrakīrti, *Autocommentary on the "Introduction to the Middle Way,"* 226b.
230. Candrakīrti, *Autocommentary on the "Introduction to the Middle Way,"* 226b.
231. Candrakīrti, *Autocommentary on the "Introduction to the Middle Way,"* 226b.
232. A verse closely parallels this one in *King of Meditative Stabilizations Sūtra*, 71a.
233. *Condensed Perfection of Wisdom*, 191a.
234. Nāgārjuna, *Precious Garland*, v. 81.
235. This passage is not found in Nāgārjuna's *Fundamental Verses of the Middle Way*, but in Āryadeva's *Four Hundred Verses*, VIII.16ab (D. 3846), 9b; English trans. in Sonam, *Āryadeva's Four Hundred Stanzas on the Middle Way*, 194.
236. This passage is not found in Āryadeva's *Four Hundred Verses*, but in Bodhibhadra's *Explanation of "Compendium of Wisdom's Essence"* (*Jñānasārasamuccaya-nāma-nibandhana*, D. 3852), 33b.
237. *Sūtra Teaching the Stable Superior Intention* (*Sthirādhyāśayasūtra*, H. 225, vol. 63), 269b–270a.
238. Candrakīrti cites this sūtra in *Clear Words*, 171b. This sūtra is not in the translated Word (*bka' 'gyur*), but a close variant can be found in the *Teaching the Aspects of Awakening* (*Bodhipakṣanirdeśa*, H. 179, vol. 60), 378a.
239. Candrakīrti cites this passage in *Clear Words*, 172b.
240. Candrakīrti cites this passage in in *Clear Words*, 172b.

241. *Diamond Cutter Sūtra* (*Vajracchedikāsūtra,* H. 18, vol. 34), 220a.
242. After stream-enterer, the subsequent three results are once-returner, non-returner, and Arhat.
243. Prajñākaramati, *Commentary on the "Way of the Bodhisattva,"* 223b.
244. A close variant of this passage can be found in the *Perfection of Wisdom in One Hundred Thousand Stanzas* (*Śatasāhasrikā-prajñāpāramitāsūtra,* H. 9, vol. 14), 460a.
245. *Condensed Perfection of Wisdom*, 191b.
246. Nāgārjuna, *Precious Garland,* v. 35.
247. Nāgārjuna, *Precious Garland,* v. 36.
248. Nāgārjuna, *Precious Garland,* v. 37.
249. Nāgārjuna, *Precious Garland,* v. 35; see above p. 133
250. Nāgārjuna, *Precious Garland,* v. 357ab.
251. Nāgārjuna, *Precious Garland,* v. 365.
252. Nāgārjuna, *Precious Garland,* v. 366.
253. *Connected Discourses* (*Saṃyutta Nikāya*), III.22; English trans. in Bhikkhu Bodhi, *Connected Discourses of the Buddha,* 952–953.
254. Nāgārjuna, *Precious Garland,* v. 386.
255. Candrakīrti, *Commentary on "Reason in Sixty Verses,"* 10a.
256. Maitreya, *Sublime Continuum,* v. 14 (*Uttaratantra,* D. 4024), 55b; English trans. in Fuchs, *Buddha-Nature,* 110.
257. A similar passage can be found in Śīlapālita, *Discussion of Scripture* (*Āgamakṣudraka,* D. 4115), 99b.
258. Nāgārjuna, *Fundamental Verses of the Middle Way,* XV.7.
259. Nāgārjuna, *Precious Garland,* v. 35.
260. Nāgārjuna, *Precious Garland,* vv. 357–365.
261. Nāgārjuna, *Precious Garland,* v. 386.
262. *Connected Discourses* (*Saṃyutta Nikāya*), III.22; English trans. in Bhikkhu Bodhi, *Connected Discourses of the Buddha,* 952–953.
263. Nāgārjuna, *Fundamental Verses of the Middle Way,* XV.7.
264. *Perfection of Wisdom in One Hundred Thousand Stanzas,* 460a.
265. *Condensed Perfection of Wisdom*, 191b.
266. Candrakīrti, *Autocommentary on the "Introduction to the Middle Way,"* 227b–228a; Nāgārjuna, *Precious Garland,* vv. 390, 393.
267. Candrakīrti, *Autocommentary on the "Introduction to the Middle Way,"* 228a; Nāgārjuna, *Praise to the Transcendent*, v. 27.
268. Maitreya, *Ornament of Manifest Realization* (*Abhisamayālaṃkāra,* D. 3786), 5a.
269. Maitreya, *Ornament of Manifest Realization,* 6a.
270. Maitreya, *Ornament of Manifest Realization,* 3b.
271. Bhāviveka, *Essence of Madhyamaka,* 17b.
272. Bhāviveka, *Essence of Madhyamaka,* 18b.
273. The four powers that remedy negative actions are the powers of (1) the support, (2) remorse, (3) resolve, and (4) the applied antidote. See Dungkar Lozang Trinlé, *Dungkar's Dictionary* (*dung dkar tshigs mdzod chen mo*), 1018.

274. See *Ornament of the Mahāyāna Sūtras*, chap. 2; in English: Dharmachakra Translation Committee, *Ornament of the Great Vehicle Sūtras*, 21–40.
275. A close parallel to this passage is found in *Foundations of Vinaya*, 4:64a.
276. Asaṅga, *Compendium of Metaphysics*, 78b.
277. Dharmakīrti, *Commentary on Epistemology*, II.190–191a (D. 4210), 110b.
278. Dharmakīrti, *Commentary on Epistemology*, II.81–82 (D. 4210), 138a.
279. Nāgārjuna, *Fundamental Verses of the Middle Way*, XXVI.7cd. The Degé edition of the Tibetan for Nāgārjuna's text differs slightly in the first line: *gal te nye bar len med na* (D. 3829), 94b.
280. Candragomin, *Praise of Confession* (*Deśanāstava*, D. 1159), 205b.
281. Kamalaśīla, *Stages of Meditation* (*Bhāvanākrama I*, D. 3915), 32b–33a; *King of Meditative Stabilizations Sūtra*, 44a–44b. The "brahmanical teacher" (*lhag spyod*) apparently refers to Āḷāra Kāḷāma or Uddaka Rāmaputta, Śākyamuni's meditation teachers before he became a buddha.
282. *King of Meditative Stabilizations Sūtra*, 44b.
283. *Condensed Perfection of Wisdom*, 193a.
284. *Condensed Perfection of Wisdom*, 214b.
285. *Condensed Perfection of Wisdom*, 195b.
286. *Diamond Cutter Sūtra*, 225b.
287. *King of Meditative Stabilizations Sūtra*, 164a–164b.
288. *King of Meditative Stabilizations Sūtra*, 164b.
289. *King of Meditative Stabilizations Sūtra*, 235a.
290. Nāgārjuna, *Commentary on the Spirit of Awakening* (D. 1800), 40a.
291. Candrakīrti, *Clear Words*, 122a.
292. Atiśa, *Lamp of the Path of Awakening* (*Bodhipathapradīpa*, D. 3947), 240b. One line in Atiśa's text is slightly different than what Künzang Sönam cites.
293. Candrakīrti, *Autocommentary on the "Introduction to the Middle Way,"* 255a.
294. Āryadeva, *Four Hundred Verses* XIV.25 (D. 3846), 16a; English trans. in Sonam, *Āryadeva's Four Hundred Stanzas on the Middle Way*, 275.
295. Nāgārjuna, *Emptiness in Seventy Verses*, vv. 64–65 (*Śūnyatāsaptati*, D. 3827), 26b. There are slight differences in the passage cited from the Degé edition of the Tibetan translation of Nāgārjuna's text.
296. Nāgārjuna, *Reason in Sixty Verses*, v. 51a (*Yuktiṣaṣṭikā*, D. 3825), 22a.
297. Āryadeva, *Four Hundred Verses* VI.10–11ab (D. 3846), 7b; English trans. in Sonam, *Āryadeva's Four Hundred Stanzas on the Middle Way*, 156–157.
298. Candrakīrti, *Autocommentary on the "Introduction to the Middle Way,"* 342b–343a.
299. Candrakīrti, *Autocommentary on the "Introduction to the Middle Way,"* 342b.
300. Maitreya, *Sublime Continuum*, 72b.
301. Candrakīrti, *Introduction to the Middle Way*, VIII.2.
302. See *Sūtra Explaining the Intent*, chap. 9, where the twenty-two complete delusions (*kun tu rmongs ba*) and eleven negative states are mentioned. See Powers, trans., *Wisdom of the Buddha*, 228–233.

303. Candrakīrti, *Introduction to the Middle Way,* III.1.
304. Śāntideva, *Anthology of Training Verses,* v. 20 (D. 3939), 2b; English trans. in Goodman, *Training Anthology of Śāntideva,* lxxv.
305. Śāntideva, *Anthology of Training,* 100b; English trans. in Goodman, *Training Anthology of Śāntideva,* 177–178.
306. *Compendium of Dharma* (*Dharmasaṃgītisūtra,* H. 239, vol. 65), 57a.
307. Śāntideva, *Anthology of Training,* 100b–128a; English trans. in Goodman, *Training Anthology of Śāntideva,* 178–221.
308. The twofold extension is to distance one's body from commotion and one's mind from thoughts. Khenpo Tsöndrü Zangpo, personal comm., April 2017.
309. Śāntideva, *Anthology of Training,* 128a–133a; English trans. in Goodman, *Training Anthology of Śāntideva,* 221–232.
310. Śāntideva, *Anthology of Training,* 133a; English trans. in Goodman, *Training Anthology of Śāntideva,* 232.
311. See Tsongkhapa, *Notes on the Wisdom Chapter,* 615; see also Tsongkhapa, *Bright Mind: Commentary on the Wisdom Chapter of the "Way of the Bodhisattva,"* 886–888.
312. See Tsongkhapa, *Bright Mind,* 886–887; Tsongkhapa, *Notes on the "Anthology of Training,"* 571.
313. Candrakīrti, *Commentary on the "Four Hundred Verses,"* 190b.
314. Candrakīrti, *Introduction to the Middle Way,* IV.2.
315. Candrakīrti, VI.120ab.
316. Nāgārjuna, *Precious Garland,* v. 35.
317. Candrakīrti, *Introduction to the Middle Way,* VI.120cd.
318. Āryadeva, *Four Hundred Verses,* XIV.25cd (D. 3846), 16a; English trans. in Sonam, *Āryadeva's Four Hundred Stanzas on the Middle Way,* 275.
319. Dharmakīrti, *Commentary on Epistemology,* II.223cd (D. 4210), 116a.
320. Śāntideva, *Anthology of Training,* 133a–133b; English trans. in Goodman, *Training Anthology of Śāntideva,* 233.
321. Āryadeva, *Four Hundred Verses* VIII.3ab (D. 3846), 9a; English trans. in Sonam, *Āryadeva's Four Hundred Stanzas on the Middle Way,* 186.
322. Candrakīrti, *Commentary on the "Four Hundred Verses,"* 133a.
323. Nāgārjuna, *Precious Garland,* v. 80.
324. Candrakīrti, *Introduction to the Middle Way,* VI.126cd.
325. Candrakīrti, *Introduction to the Middle Way,* VI.132.
326. Īśvarakṛṣṇa, *Sāṃkhyakārikā,* v. 3.
327. This appears to be a verse frequently cited in Sāṃkhya literature that is attributed to Pañcaśikha. See Larson and Bhattacharya, *Encyclopedia of Indian Philosophy,* 4:121. Thanks to Andrew Nicholson for drawing my attention to this source.
328. *Vaiśeṣikasūtras.*
329. For a list of these sixteen categories in the Nyāya tradition, following *Nyāya Sūtra* 1.1.1, see Hiriyanna, *Outlines of Indian Philosophy,* 245.

330. See Kaṇāda, *Vaiśeṣikasūtra,* 1.1.5.
331. *One Hundred Verses on Karma* (*Karmaśataka,* H. 346, vol. 73), 15b.
332. Nāgārjuna, *Fundamental Verses of the Middle Way,* XVII.6.
333. Vasubandhu, *Treasury of Metaphysics,* III.18 (*Abhidharmakośa,* D. 4089), 7b.
334. Nāgārjuna, *Essence of Interdependence,* v. 5 (*Pratītyasamutpādahṛdaya,* D. 3836), 146b.
335. Śāntideva, *Anthology of Training,* 126b; *Rice Seedling Sūtra* (*Śālistambasūtra,* H. 211, vol. 62), 190a; English trans. in Goodman, *Training Anthology of Śāntideva,* 219. Goodman's translation diverges from the Tibetan here.
336. Śāntideva, *Anthology of Training,* 126a; English trans. in Goodman, *The Training Anthology of Śāntideva,* 218; *Rice Seedling Sūtra,* 190b.
337. Śāntideva, *Anthology of Training,* 127a; English trans. in Goodman, *The Training Anthology of Śāntideva,* 220; *Rice Seedling Sūtra,* 191a.
338. This passage is cited in Vasubandhu, *Autocommentary on the "Treasury of Metaphysics,"* 122b.
339. *King of Meditative Stabilizations Sūtra,* 152b.
340. Udbhaṭasiddhasvāmin, *Praise of the Exceptional One* (*Viśeṣastava,* D. 1109), 3b.
341. Nāgārjuna, *Essence of Interdependence,* v. 4 (*Pratītyasamutpādahṛdaya,* D. 3836), 146b.
342. Nāgārjuna, *Fundamental Verses of the Middle Way,* XVII.21.
343. Candrakīrti, *Autocommentary on the "Introduction to the Middle Way,"* 260a.
344. *One Hundred Verses on Karma,* 15b.
345. Candrakīrti, *Autocommentary on the "Introduction to the Middle Way,"* 260a; Candrakīrti, *Introduction to the Middle Way,* VI.39.
346. Candrakīrti, VI.40.
347. *Sūtra of Transmigration* (*Bhavasaṃkrāntisūtra,* H. 227, vol. 63), 285a–285b.
348. *Sūtra of Transmigration,* 285b.
349. *Sūtra of Transmigration,* 286a.
350. Śāntideva, *Anthology of Training,* 134a; English trans. in Goodman, *Training Anthology of Śāntideva,* 234.
351. Śāntideva, *Anthology of Training,* 140a; English trans. in Goodman, *Training Anthology of Śāntideva,* 240–241.
352. Candrakīrti, *Introduction to the Middle Way,* VI.41.
353. *Sūtra on the Ten Grounds,* 146b.
354. Nāgārjuna, *Fundamental Verses of the Middle Way,* XXV.13d.
355. Candrakīrti, *Clear Words,* 59a.
356. Nāgārjuna, *Reason in Sixty Verses,* v. 20ab (*Yuktiṣaṣṭikā,* D. 3825), 21a. Künzang Sönam reads "observed" (*dmigs*) where the Degé edition of Nāgārjuna's text reads "understood" (*rtog*).
357. Candrakīrti, *Commentary on "Reason in Sixty Verses,"* 15b–16a.
358. Candrakīrti, *Commentary on "Reason in Sixty Verses,"* 16a.

359. See Tsongkhapa, *Ocean of Reason*, 187–191; English trans. in Garfield and Ngawang Samten, *Ocean of Reasoning*, 212–216.
360. Candrakīrti, *Commentary on the "Four Hundred Verses,"* 171b.
361. *Inquiry of Upāli*, 244b.
362. *Foundations of Vinaya*, 4:211a.
363. Nāgārjuna, *Fundamental Verses of the Middle Way*, XXII.1
364. I could not locate this passage in a sūtra, but it is cited in Candrakīrti, *Autocommentary on the "Introduction to the Middle Way,"* 299b.
365. Candrakīrti, *Introduction to the Middle Way*, VI.151.
366. Candrakīrti, *Introduction to the Middle Way*, VI.158.
367. Nāgārjuna, *Fundamental Verses of the Middle Way*, XXVII.5cd.
368. Like the expression, "the man in the moon," Tibetans use an expression referring to the rabbit in the moon; hence, a synonym for the moon is "the rabbit one."
369. Nāgārjuna, *Fundamental Verses of the Middle Way*, XVIII.1ab.
370. Nāgārjuna, *Fundamental Verses of the Middle Way*, XXVII.15cd.
371. Candrakīrti, *Introduction to the Middle Way*, VI.127.
372. On the Buddha's silence on fourteen "undetermined questions," mentioned in the *Middle Length Discourses* (*Majjhima Nikāya*), see Siderits, *Buddhism as Philosophy*, 70–72.
373. Nāgārjuna, *Fundamental Verses of the Middle Way*, XVIII.1cd.
374. Candrakīrti, *Introduction to the Middle Way*, VI.143.
375. Candrakīrti, *Introduction to the Middle Way*, VI.142.
376. Candrakīrti, *Introduction to the Middle Way*, VI.135cd.
377. Candrakīrti, *Introduction to the Middle Way*, VI.136.
378. Candrakīrti, *Introduction to the Middle Way*, VI.158. The Degé edition of the Tibetan of Candrakīrti's text reads "parts" (*yan lag*) rather than "bases of designation" (*gdags gzhir*). Candrakīrti, *Introduction to the Middle Way* (*Madhyamakāvatāra*, D. 3861), 212a.
379. Nāgārjuna, *Fundamental Verses of the Middle Way*, XVIII.2ab.
380. *Inquiry of Vīradatta* (*Vīradattagṛhapatiparipṛcchāsūtra*, H. 72, vol. 39), 345b–346a, cited in Śāntideva, *Anthology of Training*, 129b; English trans. in Goodman, *Training Anthology of Śāntideva*, 224.
381. *Compendium of Dharma*, 71b, cited in Śāntideva, *Anthology of Training*, 128a–128b; English trans. in Goodman, *Training Anthology of Śāntideva*, 222.
382. *Compendium of Dharma*, 70b, cited in Śāntideva, *Anthology of Training*, 128b; English trans. in Goodman, *Training Anthology of Śāntideva*, 222.
383. See *Inquiry of Ratnacūda* (*Ratnacūdasūtra*, H. 91, vol. 40), 374a–374b, cited in Śāntideva, *Anthology of Training*, 130a; English trans. in Goodman, *Training Anthology of Śāntideva*, 225–226.
384. *Compendium of Dharma*, 85b, cited in Śāntideva, *Anthology of Training*, 130b; English trans. in Goodman, *Training Anthology of Śāntideva*, 226.

385. *Kāśyapa Chapter,* 241a, cited in Śāntideva, *Anthology of Training,* 130b–131a; English trans. in Goodman, *Training Anthology of Śāntideva,* 227.
386. *Kāśyapa Chapter,* 240b, cited in Śāntideva, *Anthology of Training,* 130b; English trans. in Goodman, *Training Anthology of Śāntideva,* 226–227.
387. *Vast Display,* 144b, cited in Śāntideva, *Anthology of Training,* 132b; English trans. in Goodman, *Training Anthology of Śāntideva,* 229.
388. *Vast Display,* 145b, cited in Śāntideva, *Anthology of Training,* 133a; English trans. in Goodman, *Training Anthology of Śāntideva,* 231.
389. Gyelsé Tokmé, *Ocean of Good Explanation,* 121; *Instruction on the Non-Arising of All Phenomena* (*Sarvadharmāpravṛttinirdeśa,* H. 181, vol. 60), 438a.
390. *Cloud of Jewels Sūtra* (*Ratnameghasūtra,* H. 32, vol. 64), 146a–146b.
391. Maitreya, *Ornament of the Mahāyāna Sūtras,* XIX.67 (*Mahāyānasūtrālaṃkāra,* D. 4020), 31a; English translation by Dharmachakra Translation Committee, *Ornament of the Great Vehicle Sūtras,* 707.
392. The *Moon Lamp Sūtra* is another name for the *King of Meditative Stabilizations Sūtra.* This passage, with slight variation, can be found in Kamalaśīla, *Stages of Meditation II,* 45a–45b.
393. Śāntideva, *Anthology of Training Verses* v. 9 (D. 3939), 2a; English trans. in Goodman, *Training Anthology of Śāntideva,* lxxiv.
394. Śāntideva, *Anthology of Training,* 68b; *Compendium of Dharma,* 80a; English trans. in Goodman, *Training Anthology of Śāntideva,* 117.
395. On the prerequisites for calm abiding, see Geshe Gendün Lodrö and Hopkins, *Calm Abiding and Special Insight,* 19–23.
396. Maitreya, *Distinguishing the Middle and the Extremes,* IV.3cd (*Madhyāntavibhāga,* D. 4021), 43a; English trans. in Dharmachakra Translation Group, *Middle beyond Extremes,* 105.
397. Maitreya, *Distinguishing the Middle and the Extremes,* IV.4 (D. 4021), 43a; English trans. in Dharmachakra Translation Group, *Middle beyond Extremes,* 106.
398. Maitreya, *Distinguishing the Middle and the Extremes,* IV.5 (D. 4021), 43a; English trans. in Dharmachakra Translation Group, *Middle beyond Extremes,* 107.
399. Śāntideva, *Anthology of Training,* 114a; English trans. in Goodman, *Training Anthology of Śāntideva,* 200.
400. Candragomin, *Praise of Confession,* 205b.
401. Maitreya, *Ornament of the Mahāyāna Sūtras,* XV.11a (D. 4020), 19a; English trans. in Dharmachakra Translation Committee, *Ornament of the Great Vehicle Sūtras,* 462.
402. Maitreya, *Ornament of the Mahāyāna Sūtras,* XV.11b (D. 4020), 19a; English trans. in Dharmachakra Translation Committee, *Ornament of the Great Vehicle Sūtras,* 462.
403. Maitreya, *Ornament of the Mahāyāna Sūtras,* XV.11cd (D. 4020), 31a; English trans. in Dharmachakra Translation Committee, *Ornament of the Great Vehicle Sūtras,* 462.

404. Maitreya, *Ornament of the Mahāyāna Sūtras,* XV.12ab (D. 4020), 31a; English trans. in Dharmachakra Translation Committee, *Ornament of the Great Vehicle Sūtras,* 462.
405. Maitreya, *Ornament of the Mahāyāna Sūtras,* XV.12cd (D. 4020), 31a; English trans. in Dharmachakra Translation Committee, *Ornament of the Great Vehicle Sūtras,* 462.
406. Maitreya, *Ornament of the Mahāyāna Sūtras,* XV.13ab (D. 4020), 31a English trans. in Dharmachakra Translation Committee, *Ornament of the Great Vehicle Sūtras,* 462.
407. Maitreya, *Ornament of the Mahāyāna Sūtras,* XV.13cd (D. 4020), 31a; English trans. in Dharmachakra Translation Committee, *Ornament of the Great Vehicle Sūtras,* 462.
408. Maitreya, *Ornament of the Mahāyāna Sūtras,* XV.14ab (D. 4020), 31a; English trans. in Dharmachakra Translation Committee, *Ornament of the Great Vehicle Sūtras,* 463.
409. Maitreya, *Ornament of the Mahāyāna Sūtras,* XV.14cd (D. 4020), 31a; English trans. in Dharmachakra Translation Committee, *Ornament of the Great Vehicle Sūtras,* 463.
410. The fourfold pervasive observation (*khyab pa'i dmigs pa bzhi*) is (1) the conceptual image, (2) the nonconceptual image, (3) the extent of entities, and (4) the consummate purpose. See Dungkar Lozang Trinlé, *Dungkar's Dictionary*, 326.
411. Maitreya, *Ornament of the Mahāyāna Sūtras,* XV.15abc (D. 4020), 31a; English trans. in Dharmachakra Translation Committee, *Ornament of the Great Vehicle Sūtras,* 463.
412. Maitreya, *Ornament of the Mahāyāna Sūtras,* XV.16ab (D. 4020), 31a; English trans. in Dharmachakra Translation Committee, *Ornament of the Great Vehicle Sūtras,* 463.
413. Mātṛcera, *Praise Honoring the Honorable One*, 96a.
414. Mātṛcera, *Praise Honoring the Honorable One*, 96a.
415. *Sūtra Explaining the Intent,* 54a; English trans. in Powers, *Wisdom of the Buddha,* 195.
416. Kamalaśīla, *Stages of Meditation II*, 49b.
417. *Condensed Perfection of Wisdom*, 195b.
418. A similar meaning is expressed in a passage found in the *Cloud of Jewels Sūtra*, 146a.
419. See *Sūtra Explaining the Intent*, 54a; Tibetan edition and English translation in Powers, *Wisdom of the Buddha,* 194–195.
420. Candrakīrti, *Introduction to the Middle Way,* VI.35.
421. Candrakīrti, *Autocommentary on the "Introduction to the Middle Way"* (*Madhyamakakāvatārabhāṣya,* D. 3862), 258a–258b.
422. See *Sūtra Explaining the Intent*, 36a; Tibetan edition and English translation in Powers, *Wisdom of the Buddha,* 128–129.
423. Amarasiṃha, *Immortal Treasury* (*Amarakośa,* D. 4299), 207a.

424. Candrakīrti, *Clear Words*, 8b.
425. Candrakīrti, *Introduction to the Middle Way*, VI.34–36.
426. Candrakīrti, *Autocommentary on the "Introduction to the Middle Way,"* 258a.
427. See Tsongkhapa, *Thoroughly Illuminating the Viewpoint*, 576–577.
428. Nāgārjuna, *Fundamental Verses of the Middle Way*, XV.11.
429. Candrakīrti, *Introduction to the Middle Way*, VI.37–38ab.
430. Candrakīrti, *Introduction to the Middle Way*, VI.38cd.
431. Candrakīrti, *Autocommentary on the "Introduction to the Middle Way,"* 347a.
432. Tsongkhapa, *Thoroughly Illuminating the Viewpoint*, 585.
433. Tsongkhapa, *Thoroughly Illuminating the Viewpoint*, 586.
434. Nāgārjuna, *Fundamental Verses of the Middle Way*, XXIV.1.
435. Nāgārjuna, *Dispelling Disputes*, v. 1 (*Vigrahavyāvartanī*, D. 3828), 27a.
436. Nāgārjuna, *Fundamental Verses of the Middle Way*, XXIV.1.
437. Nāgārjuna, *Dispelling Disputes*, v. 22 (*Vigrahavyāvartanī*, D. 3828), 27b.
438. Nāgārjuna, *Fundamental Verses of the Middle Way*, XXIV.14–15.
439. Candrakīrti, *Clear Words*, 166a. Read *rung* for Künzang Sönam's *rig*..
440. Candrakīrti, *Commentary on the "Four Hundred Verses,"* 175b.
441. Candrakīrti, *Commentary on the "Four Hundred Verses,"* 220b.
442. Nāgārjuna, *Anthology of Sūtras*, 200b.
443. Nāgārjuna, *Reason in Sixty Verses*, vv. 43–45 (D. 3825), 22a.
444. Candrakīrti cites this (otherwise unidentified) passage in *Clear Words*, 168a.
445. *Vast Display*, 305b.
446. Nāgārjuna, *Reason in Sixty Verses*, v. 60 (D. 3825), 22b.
447. Āryadeva, *Compendium of Wisdom's Essence* (*Jñānasārasamuccaya*, D. 3851), 27a.
448. Prajñāvarman's *Commentary on "Praise of Divine Excellence"* (*Devātiśāyastotraṭikā*, D. 1113) and *Commentary on "Praise of the Exceptional One"* (*Viśeṣastavaṭikā*, D. 1110).
449. Avalokitavrata, *Commentary on the "Lamp of Wisdom"* (*Prajñapradīpaṭikā*, D. 3859), 122b.
450. Dharmakīrti, *Commentary on Epistemology*, II.10 (D. 4210), 108a.
451. See Bhāviveka, *Essence of Madhyamaka*, 11b.
452. Jeffrey Hopkins suggests, as a possible Sanskrit title, the *Bhāratatārakaśāstra* for the Tibetan *rgyas byed skar ma'i bstan bcos*. See Hopkins, *Maps of the Profound*, 179.
453. Udbhaṭasiddhasvāmin, *Praise of the Exceptional One*, 3b.
454. Dharmakīrti, *Commentary on Epistemology*, I.182bc (D. 4210), 101b.
455. See Dharmakīrti, *Commentary on Epistemology*, II.17; Bhāviveka, *Essence of Madhyamaka*, 39a.
456. Udbhaṭasiddhasvāmin, *Praise of the Exceptional One*, 4b.
457. The praise in the prologue of Nāgārjuna's *Fundamental Verses of the Middle Way* states: "I pay homage to the best of speakers, the perfectly awakened one who taught dependent arising—the pacification of conceptual constructs—without ceasing or arising, not annihilated nor eternal, neither coming nor going, and neither different nor the same" (D. 3824), 1b.

458. Nāgārjuna, *Fundamental Verses of the Middle Way,* VII.33cd. Künzang Sönam cites a version of the verse with a slight difference from the first line of the Degé edition of the Tibetan translation of Nāgārjuna's verses.
459. Candrakīrti, *Autocommentary on the "Introduction to the Middle Way,"* 246b; Nāgārjuna, *Fundamental Verses of the Middle Way,* I.1.
460. Candrakīrti, *Introduction to the Middle Way,* VI.8.
461. Candrakīrti, *Clear Words,* 93b.
462. See, for instance, Bhāviveka, *Lamp of Wisdom* (*Mūlamadhyamakavṛttiprajñāpradīpa,* D. 3853), 62a.
463. Buddhapālita, *Buddhapālita's Commentary on the "Fundamental Verses of the Middle Way"* (*Buddhapālitamūlamadhyamakavṛtti,* D. 3842), 161b.
464. See Tsongkhapa, *Ocean of Reason*, 35–36; English trans. in Garfield and Ngawang Samten, *Ocean of Reasoning*, 61.
465. Candrakīrti, *Introduction to the Middle Way,* VI.8cd–9abc.
466. Nāgārjuna, *Fundamental Verses of the Middle Way*, XX.20ab.
467. Nāgārjuna, *Fundamental Verses of the Middle Way*, X.1ab. Künzang Sönam cites a slight variant in the first line from the Degé edition of the Tibetan translation of Nāgārjuna's text, which reads: *bud shing gang de me yin na.*
468. Candrakīrti, *Introduction to the Middle Way,* VI.13ab.
469. Nāgārjuna, *Fundamental Verses of the Middle Way*, I.1.
470. Candrakīrti, *Introduction to the Middle Way,* VI.12cd.
471. Nāgārjuna, *Fundamental Verses of the Middle Way*, I.2.
472. Vasubandhu, *Treasury of Metaphysics,* II.64 (*Abhidharmakośa,* D. 4089), 6b.
473. See Tsongkhapa, *Ocean of Reason,* 65; English trans. in Garfield and Ngawang Samten, *Ocean of Reasoning,* 74.
474. Candrakīrti, *Autocommentary on the "Introduction to the Middle Way,"* 258b. See p. 210.
475. Buddhapālita, *Buddhapālita's Commentary on the "Fundamental Verses of the Middle Way,"* 161b.
476. Candrakīrti, *Introduction to the Middle Way,* VI.14.
477. Nāgārjuna, *Fundamental Verses of the Middle Way*, XX.20cd.
478. Candrakīrti, *Introduction to the Middle Way,* VI.15.
479. Candrakīrti, *Introduction to the Middle Way,* VI.16a.
480. See *Rice Seedling Sūtra*, 184a.
481. *Rice Seedling Sūtra*, 189a.
482. Candrakīrti, *Introduction to the Middle Way,* VI.32d.
483. Buddhapālita, *Buddhapālita's Commentary on the "Fundamental Verses of the Middle Way,"* 161b.
484. Candrakīrti, *Introduction to the Middle Way,* VI.98.
485. Buddhapālita, *Buddhapālita's Commentary on the "Fundamental Verses of the Middle Way,"* 161b.
486. Candrakīrti, *Introduction to the Middle Way,* VI.99.

487. Āryadeva, *Four Hundred Verses,* XI.15cd (D. 3846), 12b; English trans. in Sonam, *Āryadeva's Four Hundred Stanzas on the Middle Way,* 233.
488. Bhāviveka, *Lamp of Wisdom,* 50b–51a.
489. Candrakīrti, *Autocommentary on the "Introduction to the Middle Way,"* 287a.
490. Candrakīrti, *Introduction to the Middle Way,* VI.104.
491. Nāgārjuna, *Praise to the Transcendent,* v. 21 (D. 1120), 69a.
492. Candrakīrti, *Introduction to the Middle Way,* VI.114.
493. *Inquiry of Anavatapta* (H. 157, vol. 58), 349a–349b.
494. Candrakīrti, *Clear Words,* 167b.
495. A variant of this quoted passage, which suggests the same meaning, can be found in the *Inquiry of Sāgaramati* (*Sāgaramatiparipṛcchā,* H. 153, vol. 158), 73b–74a.
496. Nāgārjuna, *Reason in Sixty Verses,* v. 19 (D. 3825), 21a.
497. Candrakīrti, *Clear Words,* 2b.
498. Candrakīrti, *Clear Words,* 2b.
499. Āryadeva, *Four Hundred Verses,* XIV.23 (D. 3846), 16a; English trans. in Sonam, *Āryadeva's Four Hundred Stanzas on the Middle Way,* 274.
500. *Sūtra Teaching Interdependence* (*Pratītyasamutpādādi-vibhaṅga-nirdeśa-sūtra,* H. 212, vol. 62), 192b.
501. Nāgārjuna, *Precious Garland,* v. 48.
502. Nāgārjuna, *Fundamental Verses of the Middle Way,* VIII.12.
503. See Candrakīrti, *Autocommentary on the "Introduction to the Middle Way,"* 290b.
504. See Tsongkhapa, *Ocean of Reason,* 14; English trans. in Garfield and Ngawang Samten, *Ocean of Reasoning,* 26–27.
505. *chos nyid* read *chos.* The *Inquiry of Anavatapta* reads: "There are no phenomena (*chos*) in the absence of causes and conditions." Both editions of Künzang Sönam's text, however, read *chos nyid* rather than *chos.* See *Inquiry of Anavatapta,* 349a.
506. Nāgārjuna, *Fundamental Verses of the Middle Way,* XXIV.19.
507. Candrakīrti, *Clear Words,* 168a.
508. Its second property is being a property of what is established (*bsgrub bya'i chos*).
509. Candrakīrti, *Introduction to the Middle Way,* VI.115.
510. *Condensed Perfection of Wisdom,* 210a–210b.
511. *Rice Seedling Sūtra,* 180b.
512. Nāgārjuna, *Letter to a Friend,* 45b–46a.
513. Nāgārjuna, *Fundamental Verses of the Middle Way,* XX.21.
514. Nāgārjuna, *Emptiness in Seventy Verses,* v. 4 (*Śūnyatāsaptati,* D. 3827), 24b. Künzang Sönam's *chos min mthun* read: *chos mi mthun.*
515. Candrakīrti, *Introduction to the Middle Way,* VI.21.
516. Atiśa, *Lamp of the Path of Awakening* (D. 3947), 240a.
517. Nāgārjuna, *Fundamental Verses of the Middle Way,* VII.33.
518. *Inquiry of Anavatapta,* 349a. See above p. 239.
519. *Descent to Laṅka Sūtra,* cited in Candrakīrti, *Clear Words,* 167b. See above p. 239.
520. *Compendium of Dharma,* 66b.

521. Śāntideva, *Anthology of Training*, 145b; English trans. in Goodman, *Training Anthology of Śāntideva*, 250.
522. This (unidentified) text is cited by Prajñākaramati in *Commentary on the "Way of the Bodhisattva,"* 478a.
523. *King of Meditative Stabilizations Sūtra*, 73a.
524. *Condensed Perfection of Wisdom*, 191b.
525. Nāgārjuna, *Fundamental Verses of the Middle Way*, VII.34.
526. *King of Meditative Stabilizations Sūtra*, 42b.
527. Nāgārjuna, *Letter to a Friend*, 42a.
528. Śāntideva, *Anthology of Training*, 146b–147a; *Compendium of Dharma*, 23b; English trans. in Goodman, *Training Anthology of Śāntideva*, 251.
529. Śāntideva, *Anthology of Training*, 147a; English trans. in Goodman, *Training Anthology of Śāntideva*, 252.
530. Śāntideva, *Anthology of Training*, 147a; *Compendium of Dharma*, 24a; English trans. in Goodman, *Training Anthology of Śāntideva*, 251.
531. These lines, with slight variation, can be found in the *Jewel Mine Sūtra* (*Ratnākarasūtra*, H. 126, vol. 54), 397a. It appears that Künzang Sönam is citing this passage from *Clear Words*, which uses his wording. See Candrakīrti, *Clear Words*, 30b.
532. Nāgārjuna, *Anthology of Sūtras*, 205a.
533. Nāgārjuna, *Anthology of Sūtras*, 205a.
534. Nāgārjuna, *Anthology of Sūtras*, 205a–205b; *Diamond Cutter Sūtra*, 219a–219b.
535. Nāgārjuna, *Anthology of Sūtras*, 206a.
536. Nāgārjuna, *Anthology of Sūtras*, 206b.
537. Nāgārjuna, *Anthology of Sūtras*, 207a; *Ajātaśatru Sūtra* (*Ajātaśatrusūtra*, H. 217, vol. 62), 411b.
538. Śāntideva, *Anthology of Training*, 133b; English trans. in Goodman, *Training Anthology of Śāntideva*, 233.
539. Śāntideva, *Anthology of Training*, 133b–134a; English trans. in Goodman, *Training Anthology of Śāntideva*, 234; *Perfection of Wisdom in One Hundred Thousand Stanzas*, 59b.
540. Āryadeva, *Four Hundred Verses*, VIII.5 (D. 3846), 9a; English trans. in Sonam, *Āryadeva's Four Hundred Stanzas on the Middle Way*, 188.
541. Candrakīrti, *Introduction to the Middle Way*, VI.118.
542. *King of Meditative Stabilizations Sūtra*, 111a–111b, cited in Candrakīrti, *Autocommentary on the "Introduction to the Middle Way,"* 292a.
543. Āryadeva, *Four Hundred Verses*, VIII.10 (D. 3846), 9b; English trans. in Sonam, *Āryadeva's Four Hundred Stanzas on the Middle Way*, 190. Künzang Sönam cites these verses beginning with *rang gi phyogs* rather than *khyod la rang phyogs*, evidently citing this passage from Candrakīrti's citation in *Autocommentary on the "Introduction to the Middle Way,"* 292a, which begins this way, rather than from the text of Āryadeva's *Four Hundred Verses* itself.

544. Bhāviveka, *Essence of Madhyamaka*, 4b.
545. Jñānagarbha, *Distinguishing the Two Truths*, 15a.
546. Tsongkhapa, *Thoroughly Illuminating the Viewpoint*, 667.
547. Nāgārjuna, *Fundamental Verses of the Middle Way*, XXIV.11.
548. Nāgārjuna, *Precious Garland*, v. 119.
549. Nāgārjuna, *Precious Garland*, v. 120.
550. Candrakīrti, *Introduction to the Middle Way*, VI.4–5ab.
551. Candrakīrti, *Introduction to the Middle Way*, VI.5d–7a.
552. Śāntideva, *Anthology of Training*, 147a; English trans. in Goodman, *Training Anthology of Śāntideva*, 251; *Compendium of Dharma*, 24a.
553. This passage is not in the *Meeting of the Father and Son Sūtra*. It is found in the *Inquiry of Susthitamati* (*Susthitamatidevaputraparipṛcchā*, H. 80, vol. 40), 26a–26b.
554. *Flower Garland Sūtra* (*Avataṃsakasūtra*, H. 94, vol. 45), 61a, cited in Śāntideva, *Anthology of Training*, 167a; English trans. in Goodman, *Training Anthology of Śāntideva*, 287.
555. Künzang Sönam paraphrases and directly quotes Tsongkhapa here. See Tsongkhapa, *Ocean of Reason*, 216; English trans. in Garfield and Ngawang Samten, *Ocean of Reasoning*, 389.
556. Śāntideva, *Anthology of Training Verses*, v. 24 (D. 3939), 2b; English trans. in Goodman, *Training Anthology of Śāntideva*, lxxvi.
557. *Compendium of Dharma*, 130a–130b, cited in Śāntideva *Anthology of Training*, 157b; English trans. in Goodman, *Training Anthology of Śāntideva*, 271.
558. Candrakīrti, *Introduction to the Middle Way*, I.2.
559. Maitreya, *Sublime Continuum*, 72b; English trans. in Fuchs, *Buddha-Nature*, 289.
560. Candrakīrti, *Introduction to the Middle Way*, III.12.
561. Maitreya, *Ornament of the Mahāyāna Sūtras* XIX.40 (D. 4020), 30a; English trans. in Dharmachakra Translation Committee, *Ornament of the Great Vehicle Sūtras*, 671.
562. Candrakīrti, *Introduction to the Middle Way*, VI.226.
563. *dpang lo blo gros brtan pa* (1276–1342).
564. *rgod tsang ba* (1189–1258).
565. *red mda' ba* (1349–1412).
566. *kar ma pa dkon gzhon* (b. 1333).
567. *thang sag* (eleventh c.).
568. This text is found in Rendawa's biography, *dpal ldan red mda' ba chen po'i mam thar ngo mtshar rmad byung*. See Tibetan edition in Carola Roloff, *Red mda' ba, Buddhist Yogi-Scholar of the Fourteenth Century*, 95–96; English trans. in Roloff, 211–212; see also 359n340, 360n344. Roloff translates "just [one] Madhyamaka text". It does not appear to be the case that the number of texts is at issue here, nor is there historical evidence that anyone in the Sakya tradition ever held that there was only one Madhyamaka text. Rather, Künzang Sönam suggests by his

citation of this passage that before Rendawa, in Tibet Madhyamaka was just text (i.e., mere book learning). Then, Rendawa (and later Patrül Rinpoché) rejuvenated the instruction lineage that embodies the meaning of Madhyamaka (and the *Way of the Bodhisattva*) texts as practical instruction.

569. *smyo shul lung rtogs* (1829–1901/2).
570. *blo gter dbang po* (1847–1914).
571. *bsod rgyal* (a.k.a. Lerap Lingpa, 1856–1926).

Bibliography

CANONICAL SOURCES

D. *sde dge mtshal par bka' 'gyur: a facsimile edition of the 18th century redaction of Situ chos kyi 'byung gnas prepared under the direction of H.H. the 16th rgyal dbang karma pa.* Delhi: Delhi Karmapae Chodhey Gyalwae Sungrab Partun Khang, 1977.

H. *lha sa bka' 'gyur.* Lhasa edition of the Translated Word (*bka' 'gyur*), vols. 1–97. Zhol, 1934.

P. Suzuki, Daitetz T., ed. *The Tibetan Tripitika.* Peking edition, vols. 1–168. Tokyo: Tibetan Tripitika Research Institute, 1957.

TRANSLATED WORD (*BKA' 'GYUR*)

Ajātaśatru Sūtra (*Ajātaśatrusūtra, 'phags pa ma skyes dgra'i 'gyod pa bsal ba zhes bya ba theg pa chen po'i mdo*). H. 217, vol. 62.

Akṣayamati Sūtra (*Akṣayamatisūtra, 'phags pa blo gros mi zad pas bstan pa zhes bya ba theg pa chen po'i mdo*). H. 176, vol. 60.

Bodhisattva Basket (*Bodhisattvapiṭaka, 'phags pa byang chub sems dpa'i sde snod ces bya ba theg pa chen po'i mdo*). H. 56, vol. 37.

Cloud of Jewels Sūtra (*Ratnameghasūtra, 'phags pa dkon mchog sprin ces bya ba theg pa chen po'i mdo*). H. 32, vol. 64.

Compendium of Dharma (*Dharmasaṃgītisūtra, 'phags pa chos yang dag par sdud pa zhes bya ba theg pa chen po'i mdo).* H. 239, vol. 65.

Condensed Perfection of Wisdom (*Prajñāpāramitā-sañcayagāthā, 'phags pa shes rab kyi pha rol tu phyin pa sdud pa tshigs su bcad pa).* H. 17, vol. 34.

Connected Discourses (*Saṃyutta Nikāya*). In English: *The Connected Discourses of the Buddha: A Translation of the Saṃyutta Nikāya.* Translated by Bhikkhu Bodhi. Boston: Wisdom Publications, 2003.

Densely Arrayed (*Gaṇḍavyūha, rgyan stug po bkod pa*). P. 778, vol. 29; also in *Avataṃsakasūtra*. H. 94, vol. 45.

Descent to Laṅka Sūtra (*Laṅkāvatārasūtra, 'phags pa lang kar gshegs pa'i theg pa chen po'i mdo*). H. 110, vol. 51.
Diamond Cutter Sūtra (*Vajracchedikāsūtra, 'phags pa shes rab kyi pha rol tu phyin pa rdo rje gcod pa zhes bya ba theg pa chen po'i mdo*). H. 18, vol. 34.
Flower Garland Sūtra (*Avataṃsakasūtra, sangs rgyas phal po che zhes bya ba shin tu rgyas pa chen po'i mdo*). H. 94, vol. 45.
Foundations of Vinaya (*Vinayavastu, 'dul ba gzhi*). H. 1, vols. 1–4.
Golden Light Sūtra (*Suvarṇaprabhāsūtra, 'phags pa gser 'od dam pa mdo sde'i dbang po'i rgyal po zhes bya ba theg pa chen po'i mdo*). H. 514, vol. 89.
Heap of Flowers Dhāraṇī (*Puṣpakūṭadhāraṇī, 'phags pa me tog brtsegs pa zhes bya ba'i gzungs*). H. 605, vol. 90.
Heart Sūtra (*Bhagavatīprajñāpāramitāhṛdaya, bcom ldan 'das ma shes rab kyi pha rol tu phyin pa'i snying po*). H. 499, vol. 88.
Inquiry of Anavatapta (*Anavataptaparipṛcchā, 'phags pa klu'i rgyal po ma dros pas zhus pa zhes bya ba theg pa chen po'i mdo*). H. 157, vol. 58.
Inquiry of Rāṣṭrapāla (*Rāṣṭrapālaparipṛcchā, 'phags pa yul 'khor skyong gis zhus pa zhes bya ba theg pa chen po'i mdo*). H. 62, vol. 38.
Inquiry of Ratnacūda (*Ratnacūdasūtra, 'phags pa gtsug na rin po ches zhus pa zhes bya pa theg pa chen po'i mdo*). H. 91, vol. 40.
Inquiry of Sāgaramati (*Sāgaramatiparipṛcchā, 'phags pa blo gros rgya mtshos zhus pa zhes bya ba theg pa chen po'i mdo*). H. 153, vol. 158.
Inquiry of Susthitamati (*Susthitamatidevaputraparipṛcchā, 'phags pa lha'i bu blo gros rab gnas kyis zhus pa zhes bya ba theg pa chen po'i mdo*). H. 80, vol. 40.
Inquiry of Upāli (*Upāliparipṛcchā, 'phags pa 'dul ba rnam par gtan la dbab pa nye bar 'khor gyis zhus pa zhes bya ba theg pa chen po'i mdo*). H. 68, vol. 39.
Inquiry of Vīradatta (*Vīradattagṛhapatiparipṛcchāsūtra, 'phags pa khyim bdag dpas byin gyis zhus pa zhes bya ba theg pa chen po'i mdo*). H. 72, vol. 39.
Instruction on the Non-Arising of All Phenomena (*Sarvadharmāpravṛttinirdeśa, 'phags pa chos thams cad 'byung ba med par bstan pa zhes bya ba theg pa chen po'i mdo*). H. 181, vol. 60.
Jewel Lamp (*Ratnolkādhāraṇīsūtra, 'phags pa dkon mchog ta la la'i gzungs zhes bya ba theg pa chen po'i mdo*). H. 100, vol. 48.
Jewel Mine Sūtra (*Ratnākarasūtra, 'phags pa dkon mchog 'byung gnas zhes bya ba theg pa chen po'i mdo*). H. 126, vol. 54.
Kāśyapa Chapter (*Kāśyapaparivarta, 'phags pa 'od srung gi le'u zhes bya ba theg pa chen po'i mdo*). H. 87, vol. 40.
King of Meditative Stabilizations Sūtra (*Samādhirājasūtra, 'phags pa chos thams cad kyi rang bzhin mnyam pa nyid rnam par spros pa ting nge 'dzin gyi rgyal po zhes bya ba theg pa chen po'i mdo*). H. 129, vol. 55.
Meeting of the Father and Son Sūtra (*Pitāputrasamāgamasūtra, 'phags pa yab dang sras mjal ba zhes bya ba theg pa chen po'i mdo*). H. 60, vol. 38.
One Hundred Verses on Karma (*Karmaśataka, las brgya tham pa*). H. 346, vols. 73–74.

Perfection of Wisdom in One Hundred Thousand Stanzas (*Śatasāhasrikā-prajñāpāramitāsūtra, shes rab kyi pha rol tu phyin pa stong phrag brgya pa*). H. 9, vol. 14.

Rice Seedling Sūtra (*Śālistambasūtra, 'phags pa sā lu'i ljang pa zhes bya ba theg pa chen po'i mdo*). H. 211, vol. 62.

Root Tantra of Mañjuśrī (*Mañjuśrīmūlatantra, 'phags pa 'jam dpal gyi rtsa ba'i rgyud*). H. 501, vol. 88.

Sūtra Explaining the Intent (*Saṃdhinirmocanasūtra, 'phags pa dgongs pa nges par 'grel pa zhes bya ba theg pa chen po'i mdo*). H. 109, vol. 51; Tibetan edition and English trans. in John Powers, *Wisdom of the Buddha: The Saṃdhinirmocana Mahāyāna Sūtra*. Berkeley, CA: Dharma Publishing, 1995.

Sūtra Teaching Interdependence (*Pratītyasamutpādādi-vibhaṅga-nirdeśa-sūtra, rten cing 'brel bar 'byung ba dang po dang rnam par dbye ba bstan pa zhes bya ba'i mdo*). H. 212, vol. 62.

Sūtra Teaching the Stable Superior Intention (*Sthirādhyāśayasūtra, 'phags pa lhag pa'i bsam pa brtan pa'i le'u zhes bya ba theg pa chen po'i mdo*). H. 225, vol. 63.

Sūtra Teaching the Tathāgata's Great Compassion (*Tathāgatamahākaruṇānirdeśasūtra, de bzhin gshegs pa'i snying rje chen po nges par bstan pa'i mdo*). P. 814, vol. 32.

Sūtra on the Ten Grounds (*Daśabhūmikasūtra, sangs rgyas phal po che zhes bya ba las sa bcu'i le'u ste sum cu rtsa gcig pa'o*). H. 94, vol. 43.

Sūtra of Transmigration (*Bhavasaṃkrāntisūtra, 'phags pa srid pa 'pho ba zhes bya ba theg pa chen po'i mdo*). H. 227, vol. 63.

Tantra Explaining the Four Seats (*Caturpīṭha-vikhyāta-tantrarāja, dpal gdan bzhi pa'i rnam par bshad pa'i rgyud kyi rgyal po zhes bya ba*). H. 406, vol. 82.

Teaching the Aspects of Awakening (*Bodhipakṣanirdeśa, 'phags pa byang chub kyi phyogs bstan pa zhes bya ba theg pa chen po'i mdo*). H. 179, vol. 60.

Vast Display (*Lalitavistara, 'phags pa rgya cher rol pa zhes bya ba theg pa chen po'i mdo*). H. 96, vol. 48.

Vimalakīrti Sūtra (*Vimalakīrtinirdeśasūtra, 'phags pa dri ma med par grags pas bstan pa zhes bya ba theg pa chen po'i mdo*). H. 177, vol. 60.

TRANSLATED TREATISES (*BSTAN 'GYUR*)

Amarasiṃha. *Immortal Treasury* (*Amarakośa, mngon brjod kyi bstan bcos 'chi ba med pa'i mdzod ces bya ba skad gnyis sbyar ba*). D. 4299.

Āryadeva. *Compendium of Wisdom's Essence* (*Jñānasārasamuccaya, ye shes snying po kun las btus pa zhes bya ba*). D. 3851.

Āryadeva. *Four Hundred Verses* (*Catuḥśataka, bstan bcos bzhi brgya pa zhes bya ba'i tshig le'ur byas pa*). D. 3846. In English: *Āryadeva's Four Hundred Stanzas on the Middle Way*. Translated by Ruth Sonam. Ithaca, NY: Snow Lion, 2008.

Āryaśūra. *Condensed Transcendent Perfections* (*Pāramitāsamāsa, pha rol tu phyin pa bsdus pa zhes bya ba*). D. 3944.

Asaṅga. *Bodhisattva Grounds* (*Bodhisattvabhūmi, rnal 'byor spyod pa'i sa las byang chub sems dpa'i sa*). D. 4037. In English: *The Bodhisattva's Path to Unsurpassed Enlightenment*. Translated by Artemus Engle. Boulder, CO: Snow Lion, 2016.

Asaṅga. *Compendium of Determinations* (*Yogācārabhūmi Viniścayasaṃgrahaṇī, rnal 'byor spyod pa'i sa rnam par gtan la dbab pa bsdu ba*). D. 4038.

Asaṅga. *Compendium of Mahāyāna* (*Mahāyānasaṃgraha, theg pa chen po'i bsdus pa*). D. 4048.

Asaṅga. *Compendium of Metaphysics* (*Abhidharmasamuccaya, chos mngon pa kun las btus pa*). D. 4049.

Aśvaghoṣa. *Lotus Grove: A Text on the Cultivation of the Conventional Spirit of Awakening* (*Saṃvṛtibodhicittabhāvanopadeśavarṇasamgraha, kun rdzob byang chub kyi sems bsgom pa'i yi ge padma spungs pa zhes bya ba*). D. 3911.

Atiśa. *Lamp of the Path of Awakening* (*Bodhipathapradīpa, byang chub lam gyi sgron ma*). D. 3947.

Avalokitavrata. *Commentary on the "Lamp of Wisdom"* (*Prajñapradīpaṭīkā, shes rab sgron ma rgya cher 'grel pa*). D. 3859.

Bhāviveka. *Blaze of Reason* (*Madhyamakahṛdayavṛttitarkajvāla* (*dbu ma'i snying po'i 'grel pa rtog ge 'bar ba*). D. 3856.

Bhāviveka. *Essence of Madhyamaka* (*Madhyamakahṛdaya, dbu ma'i snying po'i tshig le'ur byas pa*). D. 3855.

Bhāviveka. *Lamp of Wisdom* (*Mūlamadhyamakavṛttiprajñāpradīpa, dbu ma rtsa ba'i 'grel pa shes rab sgron ma*). D. 3853.

Bhāviveka. *Precious Lamp of Madhyamaka* (*Madhyamakaratnapradīpa, dbu ma rin po che'i sgron ma zhes bya ba*). D. 3854.

Bodhibhadra. *Explanation of "Compendium of Wisdom's Essence"* (*Jñānasārasamuccaya-nāma-nibandhana, ye shes snying po kun las btus pa zhes bya ba'i bshad sbyar*). D. 3852.

Buddhapālita. *Buddhapālita's Commentary on the "Fundamental Verses of the Middle Way"* (*Buddhapālitamūlamadhyamakavṛtti, dbu ma rtsa ba'i 'grel pa buddha pā li ta*). D. 3842.

Candragomin. *Praise of Confession* (*Deśanāstava, bshags pa'i bstod pa*). D. 1159.

Candrakīrti. *Autocommentary on the "Introduction to the Middle Way"* (*Madhyamakāv-atārabhāṣya, dbu ma la 'jug pa'i bshad pa zhes bya ba*). D. 3862.

Candrakīrti. *Clear Words* (*Prasannapadā, dbu ma rtsa ba'i 'grel pa tshig gsal ba zhes bya ba*). D. 3860.

Candrakīrti. *Commentary on the "Four Hundred Verses"* (*Catuḥśatakaṭīkā, byang chub sems dpa'i rnal 'byor spyod pa bzhi brgya pa'i rgya cher 'grel pa*). D. 3865.

Candrakīrti. *Commentary on the "Illuminating Lamp"* (*Pradīpoddyotanaṭīkā, sgron ma gsal bar byed pa zhes bya ba'i rgya cher bshad pa*). D. 1785.

Candrakīrti. *Commentary on "Reason in Sixty Verses"* (*Yuktiṣaṣṭikāvṛtti, rigs pa drug cu pa'i 'grel pa*). D. 3864.

Candrakīrti. *Introduction to the Middle Way* (*Madhyamakāvatāra, dbu ma la 'jug pa zhes bya ba*). D. 3861.

Dharmakīrti. *Commentary on Epistemology* (*Pramāṇavārttika, tshad ma rnam 'grel gyi tshig le'ur byas pa*). D. 4210.

Dharmamitra. *Clarifying Words* (*Prasphuṭapadā, shes rab kyi pha rol tu phyin pa'i man ngag gi bstan bcos mngon par rtogs pa'i rgyan gyi tshig le'ur byas pa'i 'grel bshad tshig rab tu gsal ba zhes bya ba*). D. 3796.

Dignāga. *Compendium of Epistemology* (*Pramāṇasamuccaya, tshad ma kun las btus pa zhes bya ba'i rab tu byed pa*). D. 4203.

Jñānagarbha. *Autocommentary on "Distinguishing the Two Truths"* (*bden pa gnyis rnam par 'byed pa'i 'grel pa*). D. 3882.

Jñānagarbha. *Distinguishing the Two Truths* (*Satyadvaya, bden pa gnyis rnam par 'byed pa'i tshig le'ur byas pa*). D. 3881.

Kalyāṇadeva. *Companion to the "Way of the Bodhisattva"* (*Bodhicaryāvatārasaṃskāra, byang chub sems dpa'i spyod pa la 'jug pa'i legs par sbyar ba*). D. 3874.

Kamalaśīla. *Light of the Middle Way* (*Madhyamakāloka, dbu ma snang ba zhes bya ba*). D. 3887.

Kamalaśīla. *Stages of Meditation I* (*Bhāvanākrama I, bsgom pa'i rim pa*). D. 3915.

Kamalaśīla. *Stages of Meditation II* (*Bhāvanākrama II, bsgom pa'i rim pa*). D. 3916.

Maitreya. *Distinguishing the Middle and the Extremes* (*Madhyāntavibhāga, dbus dang mtha' rnam par 'byed pa'i tshig le'ur byas pa*). D. 4021. In English: *Middle beyond Extremes*. Translated by Dharmachakra Translation Group. Ithaca, NY: Snow Lion, 2006.

Maitreya. *Ornament of the Mahāyāna Sūtras* (*Mahāyānasūtrālaṃkāra, theg pa chen po mdo sde'i rgyan zhes bya ba'i tshig le'ur byas pa*). D. 4020. In English: *Ornament of the Great Vehicle Sūtras*. Translated by Dharmachakra Translation Committee. Boston: Snow Lion, 2014.

Maitreya. *Ornament of Manifest Realization* (*Abhisamayālạmkāra, shes rab phyi pha rol tu phyin pa'i man ngag gi bstan bcos mngon par rtogs pa'i rgyan zhes bya ba'i tshig le'ur byas pa*). D. 3786.

Maitreya. *Sublime Continuum* (*Uttaratantra, theg pa chen po rgyud bla ma'i bstan bcos*). D. 4024. In English: *Buddha-Nature: The Mahayana Uttaratantra Shastra with Commentary*. Translated by Rosemarie Fuchs. Ithaca, NY: Snow Lion, 2000.

Mātṛcera. *Praise Honoring the Honorable One* (*Varṇārhavarṇastotra, sangs rgyas bcom ldan 'das la bstod pa bsngags par 'os pa bsngags pa las bstod par mi nus par bstod pa zhes bya ba*). D. 1138.

Nāgamitra. *Gateway to the Three Embodiments of Buddhahood* (*Kāyatrayāvatāramukha, sku gsum la 'jug pa'i sgo*). D. 3890.

Nāgārjuna. *Autocommentary on "Dispelling Disputes"* (*Vigrahavyāvartanīvṛtti, rtsod pa bzlog pa'i 'grel pa*). D. 3832.

Nāgārjuna. *Commentary on the Spirit of Awakening* (*Bodhicittavivaraṇa, byang chub sems gyi 'grel pa*). D. 1800, 1801.

Nāgārjuna. *Anthology of Sūtras* (*Sūtrasamuccaya, mdo kun las btus pa*). D. 3934.

Nāgārjuna. *Dispelling Disputes* (*Vigrahavyāvartanī, rtsod pa bzlog pa'i tshig le'ur byas pa zhes bya ba*). D. 3828.

Nāgārjuna. *Emptiness in Seventy Verses* (*Śūnyatāsaptati, stong pa nyid bdun cu pa'i tshig le'ur byas pa zhes bya ba*). D. 3827.

Nāgārjuna. *Essence of Interdependence* (*Pratītyasamutpādahṛdaya, rten cing 'brel bar 'byung ba'i snying po'i tshig le'ur byas pa*). D. 3836.

Nāgārjuna. *Finely Woven* (*Vaidalyasūtra, zhib mo rnam par 'thag pa zhes bya ba'i mdo*). D. 3826.

Nāgārjuna. *Fundamental Verses of the Middle Way* (*Mūlamadhyamakakārikā, dbu ma rtsa ba'i tshig le'ur byas pa shes rab ces bya ba*). D. 3824.

Nāgārjuna. *Letter to a Friend* (*Suhṛllekha, bshes pa'i sbring yig*). D. 4182.

Nāgārjuna. *One Hundred Verses of Wisdom* (*Prajñāśataka, shes rab brgya pa zhes bya ba'i rab tu byed pa*). D. 4328.

Nāgārjuna. *Praise to the Basic Field of Reality* (*Dharmadhātustotra, chos kyi dbyings su bstod pa*). D. 1118.

Nāgārjuna. *Praise to the Inconceivable* (*Acintyastava, bsam gyis mi khyab par bstod pa*). D. 1128.

Nāgārjuna. *Praise to the Transcendent* (*Lokātītastava, 'jig rten las 'das par bstod pa*). D. 1120.

Nāgārjuna. *Praise to the Vajra-Mind* (*Cittavajrastava, sems kyi rdo rje'i bstod pa*). D. 1121.

Nāgārjuna. *Precious Garland* (*Ratnāvalī, rgyal po la gtam bya ba rin po che'i phreng ba*). D. 4158. In English: *Nāgārjuna's Precious Garland: Buddhist Advice for Living and Liberation*. Translated by Jeffrey Hopkins. Ithaca, NY: Snow Lion, 1998.

Nāgārjuna. *Reason in Sixty Verses* (*Yuktiṣaṣṭikā, rigs pa drug cu pa'i tshig le'ur byas pa zhes bya ba*). D. 3825.

Prajñākaramati. *Commentary on the "Way of the Bodhisattva"* (*Bodhicaryāvatārapañji kā, byang chub kyi spyod pa la 'jug pa'i dka' 'grel*). D. 3872.

Prajñāvarman. *Commentary on "Praise of Divine Excellence"* (*Devātiśāyastotraṭikā, lha las phul du byung bar bstod pa'i rgya cher 'grel pa*). D. 1113.

Prajñāvarman. *Commentary on "Praise of the Exceptional One"* (*Viśeṣastavaṭikā, khyad par du 'phags pa'i bstod pa'i rgya cher bshad pa*). D. 1110.

Śāntideva. *Anthology of Training* (*Śikṣāsamuccaya, bslab pa kun las btus pa*). D. 3940. In English: *The Training Anthology of Śāntideva*. Translated by Charles Goodman. Oxford: Oxford University Press, 2016.

Śāntideva. *Anthology of Training Verses* (*Śikṣāsamuccayakārikā, bslab pa kun las btus pa'i tshig le'ur byas pa*). D. 3939. In English: *The Training Anthology of Śāntideva*. Translated by Charles Goodman. Oxford: Oxford University Press, 2016.

Śāntideva. *Way of the Bodhisattva* (*Bodhicaryāvatāra, byang chub sems dpa'i spyod pa la 'jug pa*). P. 5272, vol. 99; D. 3871. In English: *The Way of the Bodhisattva*. Translated by Padmakara Translation Group. Boston: Shambhala, 2011.

Śīlapālita. *Discussion of Scripture* (*Āgamakṣudraka, lung phran tshegs kyi rnam par bshad pa*). D. 4115.

Sthiramati. *The Meaning of Reality: An Extensive Commentary on the "Treasury of Metaphysics"* (*Abhidharmakośabhāṣyaṭīkātattvārtha, chos mngon par mdzod kyi bshad pa'i rgya cher 'grel pa de kho na nyid kyi don*). D. 4421.

Udbhaṭasiddhasvāmin. *Praise of the Exceptional One* (*Viśeṣastava, khyad par du 'phags pa'i bstod pa*). D. 1109.

Vasubandhu. *Autocommentary on the "Treasury of Metaphysics"* (*Abhidharmakośabhāṣya, chos mngon pa'i mdzod kyi bshad pa*). D. 4090.

Vasubandhu. *Principles of Elucidation* (*Vyākhyāyukti, rnam par bshad pa'i rigs pa*). D. 4061.

Vasubandhu. *Thirty Verses* (*Triṃśikā, sum cu pa'i tshig le'ur byas pa*). D. 4055.

Vasubandhu. *Treasury of Metaphysics* (*Abhidharmakośa, chos mngon pa'i mdzod kyi tshig le'ur byas pa*). D. 4089.

Vibhūticandra. *Especially Clear Commentary on the "Way of the Bodhisattva"* (*Bodhicaryāvatāratātparyapañjikāviśeṣadyotanī, byang chub kyi spyod pa la 'jug pa'i dgongs pa'i 'grel pa khyad par gsal byed ces bya ba*). D. 3880.

OTHER SOURCES

Butön (*bu ston rin chen grub*, 1290–1364). *Butön's History* (*bu ston chos 'byung*). Xining: Nationalities Press, 1987. In English: *The History of Buddhism in India and Tibet.* Translated by Eugene Obermiller. Delhi, India: Paljor, 1999.

Cabezón, José. *A Dose of Emptiness: An Annotated Translation of the sTong thun chen mo of mKhas grub dGe legs dpal bzang.* Albany, NY: State University of New York Press, 1992.

The Cowherds. *Moonpaths: Conventional Truth in Buddhist Philosophy*. Oxford: Oxford University Press, 2011.

Cozort, Dan. *Unique Tenets of the Middle Way Consequence School.* Ithaca, NY: Snow Lion, 1998.

Dalai Lama. *Practicing Wisdom.* Boston, MA: Wisdom Publications, 2005.

Dodrupchen, the Third (*rdo grub chen 'jigs med bstan pa'i nyi ma*, 1865–1926). *Brief Biography of Paltrül Rinpoché* (*mtshungs med rgyal ba'i myu gu o rgyan 'jigs med chos kyi dbang po'i rtogs brjod phyogs tsam gleng ba bdud rtsi'i zil thigs*). In *Dodrupchen Jikmé Tennyi's Collected Works,* vol. 5, 451–481. Chengdu, China: Nationalities Press, 2013 [2003].

Duckworth, Douglas. *Tibetan Buddhist Philosophy of Mind and Nature.* Oxford: Oxford University Press, 2019.

Dungkar Lozang Trinlé (*dung dkar blo bzang phrin las*, 1927–1997). *Dungkar's Dictionary* (*dung dkar tshig mdzod chen mo*). Beijing, China: krung go'i bod rig pa spe skrun khang, 2002.

Eckel, David. *Bhāviveka and His Buddhist Opponents.* Cambridge, MA: Harvard University Press, 2008.

Geshe Gendün Lodrö and Jeffrey Hopkins. *Calm Abiding and Special Insight: Achieving Spiritual Transformation through Meditation.* Ithaca, NY: Snow Lion, 1998.

Griffiths, Paul. *On Being Mindless.* La Salle, IL: Open Court, 1986.

Gyelsé Tokmé (*rgyal sras thogs med*, 1295–1369). *Ocean of Good Explanation* (*byang chub sems dpa'i spyod pa la 'jug pa'i 'grel ba legs par bshad pa'i rgya mtsho*). Serta: Larung Five Sciences College, 2005.

Gyeltsapjé (*rgyal tshab rje dar ma rin chen,* 1364–1432). *Gateway to the Bodhisattvas* (*byang chub sems dpa'i spyod pa la 'jug pa'i rnam bshad rgyal sras 'jug ngogs*). In *spyod 'jug rtsa 'grel,* 100–454. Xining, China: Nationalities Press, 2001.

Hattori, Masaaki. *Dignāga on Perception*. Cambridge: Harvard University Press, 1968.

Hiriyanna, M. *Outlines of Indian Philosophy*. Delhi: Motilal Banarsidass, 1993.

Hopkins, Jeffrey. *Maps of the Profound*. Ithaca, NY: Snow Lion, 2003.

Īśvarakṛṣṇa. *Sāṃkhyakārikā*. In *Sāṃkhya Kārikā of Īśvarakṛṣṇa*. Translated and edited by Swami Virupakshananda. Chennai, India: Sri Ramakrishna Math Printing Press, 1995.

Jamgön Mipham. *The Wisdom Chapter: Jamgön Mipham's Commentary on the Ninth Chapter of the Way of the Bodhisattva*. Translated by the Padmakara Translation Group. Boulder, CO: Shambhala, 2017.

Jikmé Samdrup, ed. *History of Kardzé Monasteries* (*dkar mdzes khul gyi dgon sde so so'i lo rgyus gsal bar bshad pa*). Vols. 1–3. Beijing, China: China's Tibetology Publishing House, 1995.

Kaṇāda. *Vaiśeṣikasūtras*. Translated by Nandalal Sinha. Allahabad, India: Sudhindra Nath Basu, 1923.

Khedrup Gyatso (*mkhas grub rgya mtsho*) et al. *Treasury of Catalogues* (*mi rigs dpe mdzod khang gi dpe tho las gsung 'bum skor gyi dkar chag shes bya'i gter mdzod*). Vols. 1–3. Chengdu, China: Nationalities Press, 1984–1997.

Khedrupjé (*mkhas grub rje dge legs dpal bzang,* 1385–1438). *Opening the Eyes of the Fortunate: A Treatise That Completely Clarifies the Reality of Profound Emptiness* (*zab mo stong pa nyid kyi de kho na nyid rab tu gsal bar byed pa'i bstan bcos skal bzang mig 'byed*). In *Stoṅ mthun chen mo of mkhas grub dge legs dpal bzang and other texts of mādhyamika philosophy*. Edited by Lha mkhar yongs 'dzin bstan pa rgyal mtshan. Mādhyamika Texts Series 1. New Delhi, India, 1972.

Khenchen Kunzang Pelden and Minyak Kunzang Sonam. *Wisdom: Two Buddhist Commentaries*. Translated by Padmakara Translation Group. St. Leon sur Vezere, France: Editions Padmakara, 1993.

Khenpo Künpel. *Biography of Paltrül Rinpoché* (*o rgyan 'jigs med chos kyi dbang po'i rnam thar dad pa'i gsos sman bdud rtsi'i bum bcud*). In *Paltrül Rinpoché's Collected Works*, vol. 1, 1–87. Chengdu, China: Nationalties Press, 2013 [2009].

Khenpo Künpel (*kun bzang dpal ldan,* 1870/2–1943). *Nectar of Mañjuśrī's Speech* (*byang chub sems dpa'i spyod pa la 'jug pa'i tshig 'grel 'jam dbyangs bla ma'i zhal lung bdud rtsi'i thig pa*). In *Byang chub sems dpa'i spyod pa la 'jug pa rtsa ba dang 'grel ba*. Chengdu, China: Nationalities Press, 1990. In English: Kunzang Pelden. *The Nectar of Manjushri's Speech*. Translated by the Padmakara Translation Group. Boston: Shambhala, 2007.

Künzang Sönam (*mi nyag kun bzang bsod nams,* 1823–1905). *Excellent Vase* (*byang chub sems pa'i spyod pa la 'jug pa'i 'grel bshad rgyal sras rgya mtsho'i yon tan rin po che mi zad 'jo ba'i bum bzang*). In Tupten Chödrak (*thub bstan chos kyi grags pa*), *spyod 'jug gi 'grel bshad rgyal sras yon tan bum bzang,* 2nd. ed., 1–548. Beijing, China: China's Tibet Publishing House, 2007 [1993].

Künzang Sönam. *Nectar of an Excellent Vase* (*rgyal sras lag len gyi 'grel pa gzhung dang gdams ngag zung 'jug bdud rtsi'i bum bzang*). In Tupten Chökyi Drakpa (*thub bstan chos kyi grags pa*), *rgyal sras lag len rtsa 'grel.* Chengdu: Nationalities Press, 2005. In English: Chökyi Dragpa. *Uniting Wisdom and Compassion.* Translated by Heidi Köppl. Boston, MA: Wisdom Publications, 2014.

Künzang Sönam. *Overview of the Wisdom Chapter: A Lamp Completely Illuminating the Profound Reality of Interdependence* (*spyod 'jug shes rab le'u'i spyi don rim par phye ba zab mo rten 'byung gi de kho na nyid yang gsal sgron me*). In Tupten Chödrak (*thub bstan chos kyi grags pa*), *spyod 'jug gi 'grel bshad rgyal sras yon tan bum bzang*, 645–829. Beijing, China: China's Tibet Publishing House, 2007 [1993].

Künzang Sönam. *Tupten Chökyi Drakpa's Collected Works,* vols. 1–3. Degé: Degé Publishing House, 2000.

Künzang Sönam [Tupten Chökyi Drakpa]. *The Wisdom Chapter of the Way of the Bodhisattva, Overview and Word Commentary.* Lhun grub steng: Degé, 2010.

Künzang Sönam. *Word Commentary on the Wisdom Chapter: A Lamp Illuminating the Profound Reality of Interdependence* (*spyod 'jug shes rab le'u'i gzhung 'grel zab mo rten 'byung gi de kho na nyid gsal ba'i sgron me*). In Tupten Chödrak (*thub bstan chos kyi grags pa*), *spyod 'jug gi 'grel bshad rgyal sras yon tan bum bzang*, 549–643. Beijing, China: China's Tibet Publishing House, 2007 [1993].

Larson, G., and R. S. Bhattacharya. *Encyclopedia of Indian Philosophies.* Vol. 4, *Sāṃkhya.* Princeton, NJ: Princeton University Press, 1987.

Lozang Dorjé (*a kyong mkhan chen blo bzang rdo rje,* 1893–1983). *Circle of the All-Illuminating Sun* (*byang chub semse pa'i spyod pa la 'jug pa'i gzhung bsdus don me long ltar rnam par bshad pa kun gsal nyi ma'i dkyil 'khor*). In *Collected Works of Lozang Dorjé,* vols. 1–4. Chengdu, China: Nationalities Press, 2004.

Minyak Gönpo (*mi nyag mgon po*). *Garland of Nectar Beads* (*gangs can mkhas dbang rim byon gyi rnam thar mdor bsdus bdud rtsi'i thigs phreng*). Vols. 1–2. Beijing, China: Krung go'i bod kyi shes rig dpe skrun khang, 1996–2000.

Mipam. *Light of the Sun* (*brgal lan nyin byed snang ba*). Published in *spyod 'jug sher 'grel ke ta ka.* Sichuan, China: Nationalities Press, 1993; English trans. in Padmakara Translation Group, *The Wisdom Chapter.* Boulder, CO: Shambhala Publications, 2017.

Ngakchang Pema Dorjé (*sngags 'chang pad ma rdo rje*). *Biography of Kunzang Sönam* (*go shul kun bzang bsod nams kyi rnam thar*). In Tupten Kongchen Dorjé (*thub bstan kong chen rdo rje*), *Golden Mirror* (*dpe rgyun dkon pa'i bla ma 'ga'i rnam thar dang gnas ri ngo sprod mdor bsdus gser gyi me long*), 1–17. *sngags 'chang pad rdor gyi dpe tshogs* 6, 2008.

Nyoshül Khenpo (*smyo shul mkhan po 'jam dbyangs rdo rje,* 1931–1999). *Garland of Lapis* (*rang bzhin rdzogs pa chen po'i chos 'byung rig 'dzin brgyud pa'i rnam thar ngo mtshar nor bu baidurya'i phreng ba*). Vols. 1–2. Thimphu, Bhutan: Indraprastha Press, 1996. In English: *A Marvelous Garden of Rare Gems.* Translated by Richard Barron. Junction City, CA: Padma, 2005.

Paltrül Rinpoché (*dpal sprul o rgyan 'jigs med chos kyi dbang po*, 1808–1887). *Mirror Illuminating the Meaning* (*byang chub sems pa'i spyod pa la 'jug pa'i sa bcad don gsal me long*). In *Paltrül's Collected Works*, vol. 2, 293–322. Chengdu, China: Nationalities Press, 2013 [2009].

_____. *Words of My Perfect Teacher* (*rdzogs pa chen po klong chen snying tig gi sngon 'gro'i khrid yig kun bzang bla ma'i zhal lung*). In *Paltrül's Collected Works*, vol. 7. Chengdu: Nationalities Press, 2013. In English: *Words of My Perfect Teacher*. Translated by Padmakara Translation Group. Boston, MA: Shambhala, 1994.

Pawo Tsuklak Trengwa (*dpa' bo gtsug lag phreng ba*, 1504–1566). *Essence of the Infinite, Vast and Profound Ocean of Great Vehicle Doctrine* (*byang chub sems dpa'i spyod pa la 'jug pa'i rnam par bshad pa theg chen chos kyi rgya mtsho zab rgyas mtha' yas pa'i snying po*). Sikkim, India: Rumtek Dharma Chakra Centre, 1975.

Phuntsho, Karma. *Mipham's Dialectics and the Debates on Emptiness*. London: RoutledgeCurzon, 2005.

Pitkin, Annabella. "Cosmopolitanism in the Himalayas." *Bulletin of Tibetology* 40, no. 2 (2004): 5–24.

Ricard, Matthieu. *Enlightened Vagabond*. Boulder, CO: Shambhala, 2017.

Roloff, Carola. *Red mda' ba, Buddhist Yogi-Scholar of the Fourteenth Century*. Wiesbaden, Germany: Dr. Ludwig Reichert Verlag, 2009.

Ruegg, David S. *Two Prolegomena to Madhyamaka Philosophy*. Vienna: Arbeitskreis für Tibetische und Buddhistische Studien, 2002.

Siderits, Mark. *Buddhism as Philosophy: An Introduction*. Indianapolis, IN: Hackett, 2007.

Smith, E. Gene. *Among Tibetan Texts*. Boston, MA: Wisdom Publications, 2001.

Tenzin Lungtok Nyima (*bstan 'dzin lung rtogs nyi ma*, b. 1974). *The Great History of Dzokchen* (*snga 'gyur rdzogs chen chos 'byung chen mo*). Beijing, China: Nationalities Press, 2004.

Tsongkhapa (*tsong kha pa blo bzang grags pa*, 1357–1419). *Bright Mind: Commentarial Notes on the Wisdom Chapter of the "Way of the Bodhisattva"* (*spyod 'jug shes rab le'u ṭik ka blo gsal ba*). In *Tsongkhapa's Collected Works*, vol. 16 (*ma*), 869–903. Xining, China: Nationalities Press, 1998.

Tsongkhapa. *Essence of Eloquence* (*drang ba dang nges pa'i don rnam par phye ba'i bstan bcos legs bshad snying po*). In *Tsongkhapa's Collected Works*, vol. 14 (*pha*), 321–502. Xining, China: Nationalities Press, 2015 [2008].

Tsongkhapa. *Explanation of the Difficult Points of the Mind and Basic Consciousness* (*yid dang kun gzhi dka' ba'i gnas rgya cher 'grel pa*). Tibetan edition in English: *Ocean of Eloquence*. Translated by Gareth Sparem. Albany: State University of New York Press, 1993.

Tsongkhapa. *Notes on the "Anthology of Training"* (*rje rin po ches rwa sgreng du bslab btus rgyas par gsung dus 'jam dbyangs chos rjes zin bris mdzad pa*). In *Tsongkhapa's Collected Works*, vol. 14 (*pha*), 545–574. Xining, China: Nationalities Press, 2015 [2008].

Tsongkhapa. *Notes on the Wisdom Chapter* (*rgyal tshab chos rjes rje'i drung du gsan pa'i shes rab le'u'i zin bris*). In *Tsongkhapa's Collected Works,* vol. 14 (*pha*), 575–645. Xining, China: Nationalities Press, 2015 [2008].

Tsongkhapa. *Ocean of Reason* (*dbu ma rtsa ba'i tshig le'ur byas pa shes rab ces bya ba'i rnam bshad rigs pa'i rgya mtsho*). In *Tsongkhapa's Collected Works,* vol. 15 (*ba*), 3–311. Xining, China: Nationalities Press, 1998. In English: *Ocean of Reasoning*. Translated by Jay Garfield and Ngawang Samten. Oxford: Oxford University Press, 2016.

Tsongkhapa. *Thoroughly Illuminating the Viewpoint* (*dgongs pa rab gsal*). In *Tsongkhapa's Collected Works*, vol. 16 (*ma*), 443–751. Xining, China: Nationalities Press, 1998.

Tulku Thondup. *Masters of Meditation and Miracles.* Boston: Shambhala, 1999.

Tupten Kongchen Dorjé (*thub bstan kong chen rdo rje*). *Golden Mirror* (*dpe rgyun dkon pa'i bla ma 'ga'i rnam thar dang gnas ri ngo sprod mdor bsdus gser gyi me long*), 1–17. *sngags 'chang pad rdor gyi dpe tshogs* 6, 2008.

Waldron, William. *The Buddhist Unconscious: The ālaya-vijñāna in the context of Indian Buddhist Thought*. New York: RoutledgeCurzon, 2003.

Index

Abhidharma, 9–10, 86–88, 103, 107, 128–129, 151, 186
Abhidharmakośa. See *Treasury of Metaphysics*
Abhidharmasamuccaya. See *Compendium of Metaphysics*
Abhisamayālaṃkāra. See *Ornament of Manifest Realization*
absence. *See* emptiness; negation
accumulations, two, 17, 57, 119, 122, 158, 216, 221, 256–257, 266
adventitious stains, 121–123
afflictions, 41, 49, 79, 86–91, 96, 98, 129, 132, 134, 136, 139–141, 143–146, 148, 150–154, 156, 160–161, 165, 167, 178–179, 197, 202, 205–208, 215
aggregates, 15, 64, 76, 78, 81, 87–88, 90–91, 98, 101, 103, 105, 107, 128–130, 132–137, 149, 152, 156, 161–162, 164–165, 167–170, 177–179, 182, 189–190, 192–195, 198
Ajātaśatru Sūtra (*Ajātaśatrusūtra*), 250
Akṣayamati Sūtra (*Akṣayamatisūtra*), 30, 80
ālayavijñāna. *See* basic consciousness
analysis, 8, 10–12, 15, 17, 44–45, 59–60, 68–69, 75–76, 104–106, 112–116, 165–166, 168–169, 188–189, 192, 195–196, 200–202, 209–210, 225, 246–247, 249, 252
  See also ultimate analysis; conventional analysis
annihilationism, 60, 62–63, 76, 83, 144, 180–181, 213–214, 216, 218, 220–221, 223, 227, 248, 252
Anthology of Sūtras (*Sūtrasaṃuccaya*), 31, 34, 37–38, 102–103, 219, 250, 263
Anthology of Training (*Śikṣāsaṃuccaya*), 4, 34–35, 38–39, 46, 89, 118, 125, 159–161, 167, 179, 182, 198, 200–201, 204, 247–250, 254–255, 263
Arhat, 77, 88, 91, 94, 125, 127–129, 132, 136, 142, 145, 149, 153, 155, 158, 221, 225, 279n242
Āryadeva, 25, 31, 35, 64, 75, 142, 223
Asaṅga, 30–31, 96, 107, 143, 149
Aśvaghoṣa, 37
autonomous argument, 4, 32, 211, 214–215
Avalokitavrata, 223

basic consciousness (*ālayavijñāna*), 4, 11, 93–96, 102, 155–156, 169, 180–181, 214–215, 275n146
  refutation of, 105–108
basic nature (*chos nyid*, *dharmatā*), 48–49, 56, 69, 97–98, 120, 123, 141, 180
Bhāviveka, 31–33, 63, 101, 106–108, 138, 143, 157, 169, 211, 229, 238
  See also *Blaze of Reason; Essence of Madhyamaka*

denigration, 62, 66, 85, 99–100, 243, 252
Densely Arrayed (*Gaṇḍavyūha*), 43, 92, 96, 105, 255
dependent arising, 7, 16–17, 28–29, 61–63, 82, 85, 141, 151, 195, 216–220, 238–245
Descent to Laṅka Sūtra (*Laṅkāvatārasūtra*), 30, 84, 92, 96, 101–102, 105, 112, 239
Dharmadhātustotra. See *Praise to the Basic Field of Reality*
Dharmakīrti, 9, 149
See also Commentary on Epistemology
Dharmamitra, 31
Diamond Cutter Sūtra (*Vajracchedikāsūtra*), 133, 147, 250
Disciple (*nyan thos, śrāvaka*), 4, 14, 30, 42, 44, 60, 125–128, 132–133, 135, 137–142, 149, 154, 158, 206, 215
Dispelling Disputes (*Vigrahavyāvartanī*), 29, 31, 116–117, 217
Distinguishing the Middle and the Extremes (*Madhyāntavibhāga*), 16, 197, 202–203
Dzokchen (*rdzogs chen*) monastery, 2, 6

embodiment of buddhahood (*sku, kāya*), 57, 90, 122–124, 216, 250
Emanation Body (*sprul sku*), 124
Enjoyment Body (*klong sku*), 123, 141
Essential Body (*ngo bo nyid sku*), 123
Form Body (*gzugs sku*), 221, 257
Truth Body (*chos sku*), 90, 123, 221
emptiness, 7–8, 12–14, 17–18, 28–29, 42–44, 48–50, 54–61, 63, 65–66, 69–71, 80–87, 90, 98, 102–103, 106–107, 118–120, 125–137, 141–142, 145, 147–148, 150, 158–164, 180, 200, 206–207, 209, 212–214, 216–220, 239–240, 242, 244–245, 248–250, 252–257
See also selflessness; ultimate truth
entity of disintegration (*zhig pa'i dngos po*), 15–16, 183–186, 215
epistemology (*pramāṇa*). *See* source of knowledge
Essence of Madhyamaka (*Madhyamakahṛdaya*), 116, 140, 225, 227, 251
eternalism, 60, 62, 214, 218, 227, 252
existence on its own (*rang mtshan gyis grub pa*), 8–12, 16, 51–53, 61, 68, 73, 82–83, 86–87, 97, 100, 104–105, 107, 113–114, 116, 151, 163–166, 185, 211–215, 233–236
See also intrinsic existence; objective existence; true existence; ultimate existence

faith, 36–39, 203–204, 227, 254–255, 273n108
Form Body. *See under* embodiment of buddhahood
four applications of mindfulness, 160, 200
Four Hundred Verses (*Catuḥśataka*), 31–32, 37, 60, 77, 85, 103, 106, 117, 131, 150, 161, 167, 186, 214, 218–220, 237, 241, 250–251, 263
four noble truths, 44, 47, 77, 79, 86–87, 125, 128, 132–133, 141, 217–218, 273n103
Fundamental Verses of the Middle Way (*Mūlamadhyamakakārikā*), 15, 29, 31–32, 47, 57, 60, 62, 75, 83, 90, 116, 126, 130, 137, 139, 145, 176, 180, 183, 186, 189–190, 192–193, 195, 213–214, 216–218, 220, 225, 228, 232–235, 242, 245–246, 248, 250, 252, 255, 263

Gampopa, 2
Geluk (*dge lugs*), 1–3, 5, 13, 16
Gemang (*dge mang*) movement, 2